STABLE PEACE AMONG NATIONS

STABLE PEACE AMONG NATIONS

Edited by
Arie M. Kacowicz, Yaacov Bar-Siman-Tov,
Ole Elgström, and Magnus Jerneck

ROWMAN & LITTLEFIELD PUBLISHERS, INC.
Lanham • Boulder • New York • Oxford

ROWMAN & LITTLEFIELD PUBLISHERS, INC.

Published in the United States of America
by Rowman & Littlefield Publishers, Inc.
4720 Boston Way, Lanham, Maryland 20706
www.rowmanlittlefield.com

12 Hid's Copse Road
Cummor Hill, Oxford OX2 9JJ, England

British Library Cataloguing in Publication Information Available

Library of Congress Cataloging-in-Publication Data

Stable peace among nations / edited by Arie M. Kacowicz . . . [et al.].
     p.   cm.
     Includes bibliographical references and index.
     ISBN 0-7425-0179-5 (cloth : alk. paper). — ISBN 0-7425-0180-9 (pbk. : alk.
paper)
     1. Peace.   I. Kacowicz, Arie Marcelo.
     JZ5538.S78   2000
     327.1'72—dc21   00-028414

Printed in the United States of America

♾ ™The paper used in this publication meets the minimum requirements of
American National Standard for Information Sciences—Permanence of Paper
for Printed Library Materials, ANSI/NISO Z39.48–1992.

To our children

Contents

Figures and Tables

Figures

Tables

Foreword

I thought it would be appropriate in this foreword to recall the origins of my interest in the subject of stable peace and why I am pleased by the publication of this book. In 1992, when Shimon Shamir from Tel-Aviv University and I were fellows at the United States Institute of Peace, we discussed how best to characterize the state of peace that had emerged in Israeli-Egyptian relations. It was clear to both of us that some way of identifying different types of peace was needed to replace the simple distinction between war and peace.

Shamir's preferred typology at that time was a fourfold distinction among "adversarial peace," "restricted peace," "rapprochement," and "cooperative peace." Somewhat dissatisfied with this typology, I suggested as an alternative a threefold distinction among "precarious peace," "conditional peace," and "stable peace."[1]

Indeed over time a number of other typologies have been advanced. Clearly there is a need to bring together the different concepts and terms used to distinguish types of peace, to show the considerable extent to which they overlap, and to expose various ambiguities in their definitions. If a common, shared set of concepts can be developed, it will benefit research by providing a basis for a systematic and cumulative research on this important question. It has not been entirely clear when investigators were in agreement or disagreement in applying elements of their typologies to different empirical cases.

We are all indebted, therefore, to Arie Kacowicz in particular for his attempt to clarify and calibrate these various typologies, so that hopefully we can work together with a common standardized set of terms to characterize different types of peace, while focusing upon stable peace.

My own typology was influenced by important writings of scholars, in particular Karl Deutsch and Kenneth Boulding. Deutsch's concept of peace pointed in the right direction. His classic description of a "security community" emphasized that the peace it brought with it was based, among other things, on "the real assurance that the members of that community will not fight each other physically, but will settle their disputes in some other way" (Deutsch et al. 1957, 5). This identifies a core element of the definition of "stable peace." Moreover, his emphasis on the importance of developing a community remains of prime importance, though whether it is either a necessary or a sufficient condition for the emergence of stable peace in all situations needs to be subjected to empirical testing. However, I found Deutsch's concept of peace somewhat ambiguous and his various definitions of it inconsistent. Boulding's concept of stable peace was quite useful but in need of clarification and additional specification. He defined peace as a situation in which the probability of war is so small that it does not enter into the calculations of any of the people involved (Boulding 1978, 13). The full research program envisaged by Deutsch and his colleagues was never completed, though several books were published after his major publication.[2]

Balanced assessments of Deutsch's seminal contribution have been provided by a number of scholars, quite recently by Emanuel Adler and Michael Barnett (1998a). Perhaps the most systematic follow-up to Deutsch's book was the important study by Stephen R. Rock (1989). But I find inconsistency and some ambiguity in his treatment as well.

As Erik G. Yesson (1995, 5) reminds us, all these definitions evoke Immanuel Kant's insistence in his classic work *Perpetual Peace* that peace is not simply a "suspension of hostilities" but rather "an end to all hostilities," which means the nullification of "all existing reasons for a future war."

I would like to clarify my own threefold typology, which emphasizes the extent to which peace depends upon deterrent and compellent threats, as follows:

Precarious peace is a relationship of acute conflict between two states that may have already engaged in warfare in the past and/or have been and still are on the verge of major war. At least one state is dissatisfied with the status quo, and one or both see the use of military force as legitimate for either defending or changing the status quo. Peace, therefore, means little more than the temporary absence of armed conflict. Such a peace depends for its maintenance not merely on "general deterrence," a term introduced into the literature some years ago by Patrick Morgan, but may require frequent use of "immediate deterrence," that is, military alerts and deployments, issuance of deterrence threats in war-threatening crises. The Arab–Israeli relationship until recent times and the Indo-Pakistani relationship over many years are examples of "precarious peace."

Conditional peace describes a substantially less acute, less precarious conflict relationship. General deterrence plays the predominant role in maintaining peace except in quite infrequent crises or precrisis situations, in which one or both sides feel it necessary to resort to activities that provide immediate deterrence to avoid outbreak of war. The U.S.–Soviet relationship during the Cold War qualifies as an example of "conditional peace." During that era there were occasional but infrequent diplomatic crises over Berlin, Cuba, and the Middle East in which general deterrence was supplemented with immediate deterrence. Neither in precarious peace nor in conditional peace does either side rule out initiating military force as an instrument of policy, and deterrent and compellent threats of doing so do occur.

Stable peace is a relationship between two states in which neither side considers employing force, or even making a threat of force, in any dispute, even serious disputes, between them. Deterrence and compellence backed by threats of military force are simply excluded as instruments of policy. Two states that enjoy stable peace may continue to have serious disputes, but they share a firm understanding that such disputes must be dealt with by nonmilitary means. For example, in the Suez crisis of 1956, President Eisenhower made strong, credible threats of economic sanctions to pressure the British to withdraw their forces from the Suez Canal area.

This typology—and indeed others— is conceptual in the first instance. As in any typology, it can only be the starting point for attempting to characterize actual relationships between states and to undertake empirical research. Types should not be reified; they should not be imposed on historical cases in a mechanical, simplistic way that obscures relevant uncertainties and complexities. The test of a typology should be whether it facilitates empirical research and development of theory. A comprehensive research program on this fundamental aspect of international relations entails a number of questions and problems that I will now address.

One of these is the task of determining whether two states— whether or not they are democracies— enjoy a genuine stable peace. This may be difficult to discern for various reasons, and it is a matter of finding ways to distinguish between the existence of conditional peace and stable peace. The continued absence of war and war-threatening crises in a relationship, however significant in and of itself, is not sufficient to establish the existence of stable peace. Peace between two such states may not yet have been subjected to tough tests, such as disputes severe enough to stimulate one side or the other to consider or make use of immediate deterrence. In fact, if one sees beneath the surface of peace that the military on one or the other side is still preparing secret contingency plans of a serious kind for possible use of force, then one must question whether stable peace really exists. In such cases general deterrence may still play a role, though not a conspicuous one, in supporting what appears to be stable peace.

Moreover, while peace appears to be stable, leaders and publics on one or both sides may feel that it is not a sufficiently cordial relationship that includes all desired forms, activities, and institutions of a cooperative nature such as confidence-building measures, cooperation on nonsecurity issues, and dispute resolution mechanisms. Thus, Israeli scholars have felt it necessary to distinguish between "cold peace" and "warm peace" to call attention to the fact that Israel and Egypt have never managed to develop the kinds of interactions with each other that include the full repertoire of warm, friendly relations between neighbors. Can one say, nonetheless, that stable peace exists between Israel and Egypt? Has peace between them been subjected to tough tests? Does either side have contingency plans for possible use of force or for purposes of backing up immediate deterrence threats should they become necessary in a future crisis?

One may take note of the possibility, too, that while the dominant leadership on both sides, enjoying what appears to be stable peace, believes in and acts in accord with the requirements of stable peace, important elements of the elite or counterelites and of the public in general still regard the other side as posing a latent threat to its security. When this suspicion prevails, stable peace may be vulnerable. Such a state of affairs may characterize U.S.–Russian relations since the end of the Cold War. Certainly, leaders and elements of their publics have moved from the conditional peace that characterized U.S.–Soviet relations during the Cold War towards stable peace; but important elements of their political-military elite and of their publics evidently question whether general deterrence is no longer necessary and whether the possible need for resort to immediate deterrence in the future can be safely excluded.

A better example of stable peace is the relationship among most of the Western European countries embraced by the European Union and NATO, a development in the post–World War II era that engaged the interest of Karl Deutsch and his colleagues, and many others.

The research agenda should also include the study of the conditions under which and the processes by which states move from a relationship of precarious or conditional peace to one of stable peace. There may be many paths to stable peace: negotiated settlements; regime transitions (especially democratization); demographic changes; changes in military, economic, and transportation technologies; and social or normative changes. There are few studies of this kind as yet and many historical examples of such a development that should be studied and compared. A leading example, of course, is the already mentioned emergence of a security community in Western Europe. Other possible examples include Argentina and Brazil; South Africa and its neighbors after the end of apartheid; and the United States, Canada, and Mexico. Some of these historical instances are being studied by contributors to this volume.

Some years ago I asked Magnus Jerneck, then visiting Stanford University, whether Swedish or other Scandinavian scholars had studied the transition to stable peace in the relations among Scandinavian countries.

Jerneck, a political scientist at Lund University, checked with his colleagues in the history department at Lund. He was told that although the phenomenon was well known, no systematic studies of it existed. Accordingly, Jerneck and several of his colleagues formed an interdisciplinary research team that has stimulated much of the research reported in this volume.

Obviously, the interest in stable peace— its emergence, what it is based upon, how it can be recognized, and so on—overlaps with the democratic peace thesis that has received a great deal of attention and discussion, particularly in the United States. Much of this scholarly attention has focused on efforts to explain what it is about being a democratic polity that is the basis for the absence of war between two democratic states. Not enough attention has been given to the study of *historical transitions* in the relations between democratic states that have resulted in stable peace between them. It may matter, for example, whether one state in the dyad became a democracy through civil war, international war, revolution, occupation, or gradual political development.

In fact, much of the research regarding peace among democratic states does not distinguish clearly between conditional peace and stable peace. Distinguishing between these two types of democratic peace would be facilitated if more attention were given to historical studies of transitions to stable peace. An exemplary study of this is Stephen Rock's (2000) study of how the British employed a strategy of appeasement of the United States towards the end of the nineteenth century to remove the serious war-threatening disputes in their relations, thus paving the way from conditional to stable peace in their relationship.

The earlier Deutsch study and others have traced the development of stable peace among Western European countries. These other studies have focused on deliberate efforts after World War II to create the attitudes, policies, and structures for a new peaceful relationship between France and Germany, for example.[3] Such studies are important because they indicate that certain efforts and strategies can be adopted to bring into being a relationship of stable peace. Studies are needed of many other cases of transitions to stable peace. For example, considerable research is already available on the relations of the United States with Canada and Mexico, but it should be reviewed in order to identify and explain the critical turning points that led to what seems clearly to have become stable peace.

Broad generalizations about conditions and processes that have led to stable peace in different situations may be possible, but it would be well to act on the presumption that this process, as so many other phenomena in international relations, is subject to equifinality (referred to as "multiple causation" by some scholars). That is, similar outcomes (e.g., stable peace) can occur through different causal processes. Even when a common factor can be identified in many cases, the question remains whether that is a necessary or sufficient condition for the emergence of stable peace, and how much causal weight can be attributed to it.

What I have been suggesting is that it is best to regard the "democratic peace" phenomenon as a subset of the broader general phenomenon of stable peace. In this connection, I would like to raise the question whether stable peace is possible only and has occurred only between countries that are democracies. A more comprehensive research program would look for historical cases of stable peace between countries that are not democracies, or between states only one of which is a democracy. Some of the research on "zones of peace" by Arie Kacowicz moves in this direction. It is important to apply the distinction between conditional and stable peace also in such studies.

Finally, I believe it is important that a full research program should include efforts to judge whether lessons can be drawn from historical studies that may be of some relevance for efforts to move relations between adversarial states to stable peace or, at least, to something approximating it. Several years ago, when I was preparing a foreword to James Goodby's *Europe Undivided*, I was struck by the fact that he was addressing the desirability and feasibility of moving U.S.–Russian relations from conditional peace to stable peace. Following the publication of his book, the United States Institute of Peace has set up a working group to develop further Goodby's ideas. This study will examine several alternative future developments affecting the nature and scope of security in the Euro-Atlantic community. It will consider whether and how a democratic Russia can become a member of a Euro-Atlantic security community, all members of which enjoy stable peace. It is gratifying that the present book contains a chapter by Goodby describing this work.

In sum, there are ambiguities and inconsistencies in defining the concept of peace in research that addresses the possibility of stable peace or of democratic peace. In particular, it is important to clarify whether presumed instances of stable peace blur the important distinction between conditional and stable peace. These major conceptual issues needs to be addressed and clarified given their important implications for scholarship and policy.

Alexander L. George

Notes

1. For Shamir's typology, see Shamir 1992. My own typology is reported in the same issue (Goodby 1992). This foreword also draws on my presentation on the

Grawmeyer Panel at the annual International Studies Association meeting in Toronto in March 1997 and from my foreword in Goodby 1998.

2. See Lindgren 1959; Russett 1963; and Katzenstein 1976.

3. This literature is too extensive to cite here. See, e.g., Willis 1965. It includes, of course, the initiatives of Jean Monnet and others to bring about reconciliation between France and Germany and to create structures for cooperative economic development. Interestingly, it also includes the contribution of nongovernmental actors and organizations, such as Frank Buchman's moral rearmament movement.

Acknowledgments

In the first place, we want to express our gratitude to Alexander L. George from Stanford University for being an intellectual guide and source of inspiration in our quest to understand the conditions, dimensions, and prospects for success of stable peace among nations.

We gratefully acknowledge the valuable comments made by our collaborators in the research project "Stable Peace: The Case of Sweden." The project, which is multidisciplinary and involves the departments of political science and history at Lund University, is generously supported by a grant from the Bank of Sweden Tercentenary Foundation.

We also thank the Leonard Davis Institute for International Relations at the Hebrew University of Jerusalem, its former director Sasson Sofer, and its staff for hosting a binational seminar on Stable Peace in June 1996 in Jerusalem and for providing technical assistance in the final stages of the editing, especially by Ariela Abramovici. We also acknowledge the encouragement from the department of international relations at the Hebrew University of Jerusalem, as well as the help of Michal Simchoni in compiling the bibliography.

We would also like to express our gratitude to the participants in several conference panels on stable peace, including Tomas Niklasson, George Modelski, Clive Archer, Rex Li, and Magnus Norell at the Pan-European Conference in International Relations in Paris, September 1995; Mikael af Malmborg, Magnus Norell, Emanuel Adler, Shlomo Brom, Raymond Cohen, and Abraham Sella for their participation in the workshop in Jerusalem in June 1996; the ISA Conference in San Diego, April 1996; the Pan-European Conference in International Relations in Vienna, September 1998; at the ECPR Workshop in Mannheim, March 1999; and the CISS/ISA Conference in Paris, August 1999.

We want also to thank the eleven contributors to this volume for participating in a truly multinational effort to understand the dimensions, conditions, and prospects for success of stable peace among nations. Owing to their spirit of collaboration and voluntarism, this complex research project could become a reality. For making the research into a book, we have to thank the superb collaboration from Jennifer Knerr and her editorial staff at Rowman & Littlefield.

Finally, we dedicate this book to our families, especially to our children Itai, Ela, Keren, Yonathan, Ittai, Ludvig, Zackarias, Sebastian, and Josephine, with the hope that they will experience stable peace in the new millennium, not only in Scandinavia, but also in the Middle East.

The Editors, Jerusalem and Lund, December 1999

Introduction

Arie M. Kacowicz

This book is the result of multinational research that follows a series of international meetings, workshops, and conferences on stable peace convened in Paris in 1995, Jerusalem in 1996, Vienna in 1998, and Mannheim and Paris in 1999. These meetings involved scholars from Sweden, Israel, the United States, and Great Britain. Scholars at the University of Lund, Sweden, and their colleagues at the Hebrew University of Jerusalem, Israel, have become equally interested in the subject of stable peace in quite different political environments. For some of us in Israel, "stable peace" echoes tales of political (if not science) fiction and a teleological dream about a "new" Middle East ultimately following the path of the European Union, at best in a very distant future after the conclusion of formal peace agreements. Conversely, for some of our Swedish colleagues stable peace is a reality that can be taken for granted and studied historically as a long and evolving process, embedded in the long Scandinavian peace since the end of the Napoleonic wars. In both countries we share the same enthusiasm for learning about a subject that has been so far neglected.

While peace in general, like its opposite, war, has been the focus of numerous attempts of analysis and definition, the particular type called *stable peace* has been very little studied in international relations, with a few exceptions such as Kenneth Boulding (1978) and Alexander George (1992). Both view stable peace as one extreme on a scale depicting a series of conflictual and cooperative relations of varying severity. Stable peace can be defined as a situation or condition where "the probability of war is so small that it does not really enter into the calculations of the peoples involved" (Boulding 1978, 13). Stable peace is not, however, a utopian condition; there is no need for a total harmony of interests between or among the parties involved. The main point is that political and other conflicts that arise between or among states or other actors are consistently resolved

I

without resorting to military means. Thus, war and other types of violence or threats of war are no longer acceptable rational or legitimate means to settle domestic and international conflicts.

Stable peace may take place in dyadic as well as multilateral relations; furthermore, stable peace relations (for any given state) can also exist along with other types of relationships with other sets of states. The starting point for the study of stable peace in international relations should be the quality of the dyadic (bilateral) relationship, although our research focuses also upon relations among a group of states, within a subsystem or region. Stable peace can overlap with the emergence of a "pluralistic security community" (see Deutsch et al. 1957; and more recently Adler and Barnett 1998a). The major difference between these two is that while all pluralistic security communities assume a condition of stable peace, not every bilateral or multilateral situation of stable peace necessarily implies the formation of a common identity and "we-ness," as required in a security community. Therefore, stable peace is a larger phenomenon that encompasses, by definition, security communities. Similarly, although there is a close link between stable peace and democratic peace and the two may overlap, we contend in this volume that democratic peace is not a prerequisite for stable peace, nor are the two identical. Although democratic norms help to consolidate and preserve stable peace, they are not the only normative frameworks that determine peaceful relations among states, and stable peace may occur among nondemocratic states as well.

In the course of the book, we ask the following questions:

1. What is the nature of stable peace? What are its main features and aspects? How can we differentiate stable peace from other forms of peace (e.g., precarious, negative, on one extreme; or pluralistic security community on the other)? What are its major dimensions?

2. Why and how do stable peace relations emerge in the first place? How are warlike situations or fairly unstable and fragile peace conditions (such as negative peace and precarious peace) transformed into stable peace relations? Is stable peace usually preceded by precarious and conditional peace (negative peace), or is it possible to jump from warlike relations to stable peace relations without passing through other gradations or stages of peace?

3. What are the conditions for maintaining stable peace over time? Specifically, what are the necessary, sufficient, and favorable conditions for keeping and deepening stable peace in temporal, rather than cognitive, terms? How "stable" is stable peace? What constitutes stability over time?

4. In terms of policy implications, what are the lessons and patterns we can draw from historical and contemporary cases of stable peace at the regional level (e.g., Scandinavia, South America, and Western Europe)? Can we extrapolate from these historical lessons to assess the prospects for stable peace in other areas of the world, including the Middle East?

In this book, we aim to define in clear terms the complex concept and phenomenon of stable peace, as distinct from other types of peace. We are convinced that our project fills an academic lacuna in the subfield of peace studies regarding the lack of differentiation among diverging degrees of peace. This void is due to researchers' fixation on studying the causes of war and peace rather than examining the nuances, transitions, and further evolution of peace once a formal agreement concluding the state of war has been obtained.

Methodology and Content

To pursue the four research questions described above and test the validity of the importance attributed to stable peace, our study adopts the comparative historical method, similar to the "structured focused comparison" proposed by Alexander George (1979). We have selected a series of case studies of stable peace in the past and present, as well as some prospective cases. They range from easy cases (such as Scandinavia) through more difficult cases (such as in South America) all the way to very difficult or only potential cases (such as Israel and Egypt in the Middle East). The cases presented for comparison include:

- *The Scandinavian experience,* focusing upon the long Swedish experience and its security strategies towards its neighbors since 1814.

- *The South American case,* with special reference to the Southern Cone subregion and the relations between Argentina and Brazil and Argentina and Chile since 1979.

- *Israel and Egypt in the Middle East.* Since 1979 Israel and Egypt have maintained a bilateral relation of formal peace. The analysis of this case considers the prospects of moving or "upgrading" this bilateral relationship in the direction of stable peace.

- *Europe and the future of NATO.* Here the analysis considers whether and to what extent the acceptance of Eastern European nations into

NATO will bring about the extension of the Western European stable peace into Central and Eastern Europe. Paradoxically, there might be an inherent contradiction between expanding NATO to the East and strengthening a close and confident relationship between the United States and Russia, unless the ultimate goal is an undivided, democratic Europe that might incorporate democratic Russia.

- *German–Polish relations in* Mitteleuropa. This case study examines the evolution of German–Polish relations from a precarious to a conditional peace and finally, throughout the 1990s, to a stable peace.

In addition, the theoretical chapters refer to a series of historical and contemporary illustrations as additional case studies, including consolidated stable peace, failed attempts at stable peace, and other relations of peace:

- *The establishment of the European Communities (the European Coal and Steel Community among others) after World War II.* The specific reference is to the Schuman Plan and the evolution of stable peace relations between France and Germany in the aftermath of World War II, within the European Community.

- *The Baltic region.* With the dismemberment of the Soviet Union and the end of the Cold War, this is a prospective case of stable peace involving the Baltic republics, Sweden, Finland, and perhaps Russia.

- *Peaceful relations among the great powers, 1815–1854.* During the period of the European Concert from 1815 through 1854, the relations among Russia, Austria, Prussia, France, and Great Britain could be characterized as a stable peace (at least in its stabilization phase).

- *The ASEAN region.* ASEAN (Association of Southeast Asian Nations) is often considered a nascent pluralistic security community; its members have not been involved in a serious conflict since the 1963–1966 *Konfrontasi* between Indonesia and Malaysia.

Any examination of the diplomatic history and evolution of these case studies should be framed within a comparative method of structured, focused comparison, with the aim of drawing some practical lessons from these historical cases, whether successes or failures. We ask a series of questions that are relevant from both a theoretical and a policy point of view, including:

- What is the nature of stable peace?

- How does peace break out?

- How can peace be stabilized? How do we make it resilient over time?

- How is stable peace maintained and consolidated over time?

- What are the turning points on the way towards stable peace?

The book has two major parts, one theoretical/conceptual and the other empirical/policy oriented. Part 1 (Theory and Illustrations) includes chapters 1–9. Part 2 (Case Studies and Policy Implications) includes chapters 10–15.

In chapter 1 ("Stable Peace: A Conceptual Framework"), Yaacov Bar-Siman-Tov and I, from the Hebrew University of Jerusalem, define the conceptual parameters and the research borders of the subject. First, we review the literature on the causes of stable peace, including related research on democratic peace and pluralistic security communities. Second, we define the nature of stable peace, distinguishing it from other categories of peace. The bulk of the chapter focuses upon the development of a two-stage theoretical model of stable peace that might explain: (1) the transition from conflict resolution and initial categories of peace towards stable peace (*stabilization*); and (2) the maintenance and deepening of stable peace over time (*consolidation*). Rather than a single and parsimonious theory, we offer contingent generalizations and a clear taxonomy regarding the conditions for these stages.

In chapter 2 ("Domestic Political Sources of Stable Peace: The Great Powers, 1815–1854"), Joe Hagan, from West Virginia University, presents a theoretical framework linking stabilizing foreign policies to two domestic political factors: the orientation of a state's ruling leadership, and the strength and intensity of domestic oppositions. His basic assertion is that systemic stability is enhanced when key powers have ruling groups that, first, have relatively restrained and flexible orientations on foreign affairs and, second, are willing and able to insulate diplomacy from domestic political pressures. He bolsters his argument with a systematic survey of the relations between the great powers' ruling groups and their opponents during the Concert of Europe, 1815–1854.

In chapter 3 ("The International, Regional, and Domestic Sources of Regional Peace"), Benjamin Miller, from the Hebrew University of Jerusalem, investigates three sources of regional peace. Two of the sources are at the regional/domestic level: strong regional states and domestic liberalization. The third source is at the global or systemic level: great power involvement in the form of a great power concert or hegemonic stability.

Although only the first two sources lead to stable peace, the third contributes to stabilization and thus creates the opportunity for the evolution of stable peace. The three sources are deduced from the global-regional debate on the causes of regional war and peace. The two regional sources are also derived from the debate on democratization versus strengthening the state as the preferred approach for producing regional peace and security. Miller proposes a solution to both of these debates by differentiating among three levels of regional peace (cold, normal, and warm) and relating each of the three factors to a specific level of peace that it is expected to bring about.

In chapter 4 ("Pieces of Maximal Peace: Common Identities, Common Enemies"), John Owen, from the University of Virginia, offers five basic arguments about the relationship among stable peace, common identities, and common enemies. First, the relationship between maximal peace and common identity, to which several scholars in the stable peace program appeal, is necessary. Second, there is likewise a necessary relationship between a common identity and a common "other"; the former cannot exist without the latter. Third, in politics self and other are divided according to a vision of societal order. Fourth, a global maximal peace could only obtain when the same transnational enemy threatens all states, and such a situation would be inherently unstable. Finally, the development of a robust, stable peace among one group of states is likely to generate a group of enemy states. Thus, stable peace involves not only the elimination of violent conflict among certain actors but also the introduction of the possibility of such conflict with other actors.

In chapter 5 ("The Cognitive Dimension of Stable Peace"), Rikard Bengtsson, from Lund University, discusses the cognitive basis of stable peace. As in other chapters, stable peace is understood here as a relationship in which neither of the parties conceives of using military violence or threats thereof as a means for conflict management and resolution. Bengtsson argues that the cognitive phenomenon of trust is central to understanding stable peace. He explores in some detail the cognitive pair of trust and distrust and brings in the concept of confidence for the specific type of trust in relationships of stable peace; he then discusses reasons behind, and the effects of, different levels of trust. He illustrates his theoretical argument by relying on the contemporary experience of the Baltic Sea region.

In chapter 6 ("Stable Peace through Security Communities? Steps towards Theory-Building"), Raimo Väyrynen, from the University of Notre Dame, redefines and questions the concept of security community. Väyrynen juxtaposes the constructivist approach to international security studies with a more positivist approach that emphasizes the role of action and a material perspective, thus describing a complex interplay between subjective (or better, intersubjective) and objective elements of security.

In chapter 7 ("Birds of a Feather? On the Intersections of the Stable

Peace and Democratic Peace Research Programs"), Magnus Ericson, from Lund University, examines the relationship between the liberal/democratic peace research program (DP) and the research based on the concept of stable peace (SP). Ericson makes two important observations: First, while there are no necessary intersections between SP and DP, significant portions of DP theory purport to account for stable peace. Second, the strand of DP theory germane to the study of SP is constructivist, or at a minimum historically contingent, in its logic.

In chapter 8 ("The Economic Aspects of Stable Peace-Making"), Alfred Tovias, from the Hebrew University of Jerusalem, focuses upon the stabilization and consolidation of peace over time through economic means. According to Tovias, among the key factors allowing for stable peace is an economic one, defined as "irrevocable interdependence," in which the costs of discontinuing economic transactions between the parties (the "costs of dissociation") become prohibitive. Hence, war is not only unthinkable; it is also an irrational way to resolve conflicts or promote interests.

In chapter 9 ("Issue Treatment and Stable Peace: Experiences from Boundary Agreements"), Kjell-Åke Nordquist, from Uppsala University, brings together the concept of stable peace and the function of the boundary agreement as an instrument for establishing stable peaceful relations. Nordquist examines the way in which the agreement is constructed and how its construction relates to its durability. He also studies the political context within which such agreements have led to stable peaceful relations in the long term.

In chapter 10 ("From Adaptation to Foreign Policy Activism: Sweden as a Promoter of Peace?") Ole Elgström and Magnus Jerneck, from Lund University, assess the causes, consequences, and implications of the long Swedish peace since 1814, focusing upon the role of the Swedish statecraft. Through the examination of five cases of Swedish security policy, they aim to show when, to what degree, and under what circumstances peace-seeking activities might have made Sweden a producer of international peace, rather than just a consumer of peace offered by the great powers.

In chapter 11 ("Stable Peace in South America: The ABC Triangle, 1979–1999"), I examine the evolution and transformation of the long peace among Argentina, Brazil, and Chile towards stable peace. The chapter applies the two-stage model of stable peace to the Southern Cone of South America. Its initial stage of establishment (stabilization of relations after conflict resolution) aptly describes the bilateral relations between Argentina and Chile since their peace treaty of 1984. In contrast, the more advanced stage of consolidation of peaceful relations has characterized the Argentine–Brazilian relationship since 1990 and the traditional peaceful relations between Brazil and Chile since the end of the nineteenth century.

In chapter 12 ("Israel–Egypt Peace: Stable Peace?"), Yaacov Bar-Siman-Tov, from the Hebrew University of Jerusalem, questions whether the long and cold Israeli–Egyptian relations since 1979 could eventually evolve into a stable peace. Bar-Siman-Tov addresses these interrelated questions: (1) Is the Israeli–Egyptian peace stable (without being a case of stable peace)? (2) How can one explain the fact that the peace relations between the two states have never deteriorated to a danger of war or a threat of war? (3) What are the explanations for the emergence of "cold" peace? (4) What is the contribution of this peace to the stabilization of the Arab–Israeli conflict? (5) What are the paradoxes of comprehensive peace? and (6) What are the conditions and the prospects for stable peace between Israel and Egypt?

In chapter 13 ("Stable Peace in Europe"), James Goodby, associated with the Brookings Institute and the United States Institute of Peace, offers an academic, policy-oriented analysis of the crucial issue of establishing and consolidating stable peace in Europe. While stable peace has become consolidated in Western Europe and between those nations and the United States, the question remains how it can be extended throughout Central and Eastern Europe, to include Russia as well. Goodby suggests several strategies and policy recommendations to integrate Russia into an overall European architecture of stable peace.

In chapter 14 ("Stable Peace in *Mitteleuropa*: The German–Polish Hinge"), Adrian Hyde-Price, from the University of Birmingham, critically analyzes contemporary developments in relations between Germany and Poland, focusing on some of the key factors in the gradual emergence of stable peace between them. According to Hyde-Price, this evolution has been "overdetermined" by a number of developments, including political democratization, deepening economic and social interdependence, and the creation of institutionalized forms of bilateral and multilateral cooperation.

Finally, in chapter 15 ("Stable Peace: Conclusions and Extrapolations"), Magnus Jerneck and Ole Elgström provide an overall assessment and summary of this volume. They suggest lessons and patterns we can draw from these historical and contemporary cases of stable peace at the regional level, in order to extrapolate from them to other, less fortunate areas.

Notes

The author wishes to thank the other editors of this volume, Yaacov Bar-Siman-Tov, Ole Elgström, and Magnus Jerneck, for their comments and suggestions, and gratefully acknowledges the assistance provided by the Leonard Davis Institute for International Relations, Hebrew University of Jerusalem.

I

THEORY AND ILLUSTRATIONS

1

Stable Peace: A Conceptual Framework

Arie M. Kacowicz and Yaacov Bar-Siman-Tov

This chapter attempts to establish a road map and review some of the research avenues and findings on stable peace. It presents a short review of the literature, definitional issues, and a conceptual framework for the study of stable peace. We examine the distinctive nature, causes, conditions, dimensions, and prospects of stabilization and consolidation of stable peace.

Stable peace should be located along a continuum from the mere absence of war as a result of a balance of power or deterrence to conflict resolution and to the consolidation and expansion of pluralistic security communities. We identify stable peace as an ongoing and dynamic process, rather than as a single situation, which might take place in dyadic as well as multilateral (intraregional) relations. Furthermore, for any given state, stable peace relations can also exist along with other, less benign types of relations with other sets of states (Jerneck 1996, 2). In regional terms, stable peace is associated with concepts such as "security communities" (Deutsch et al. 1957; Adler and Barnett 1996, 1998a), and "security complex" (Buzan 1991), which have been used to describe the positive and peaceful security policy patterns that exist within a group of states. If peace prevails in a given geographical area over long periods of time, we might also refer to the existence of a "zone of peace" (Singer and Wildavsky 1993; Kacowicz 1995, 1998).

While we have developed some theoretical and empirical knowledge about conflict management and resolution, we do not know much about the conditions for maintaining and consolidating peace relations over time. Much of the existing knowledge refers to the Western European experience since 1945. This case may explain why peace is maintained among democratic, industrialized states, but the conditions for maintaining peace among regional states, some of them nondemocratic, have not been studied. The common assumption in the literature is that the level of peace may influence its emergence, maintenance, and consolidation. However, the literature concentrates more on differentiating between categories of peace than on discussing the conditions for stable peace after the resolution of a protracted conflict.

In this chapter we present a conceptual framework for the study of stable peace to elucidate its conditions and dimensions, in both theoretical and empirical terms. We suggest a two-stage model of conditions that might explain: (1) the transition from conflict resolution and initial categories of peace towards stable peace (*stabilization*); and (2) the maintenance and deepening of stable peace over time (*consolidation*). Rather than a single and parsimonious theory, we offer contingent generalizations regarding the conditions for these two stages. In our framework we address three clusters of questions:

1. *What is the nature of stable peace?* What are its main features and aspects? How can we differentiate stable peace from other types of peace, such as precarious, negative, or cold on one extreme; and warm or pluralistic security communities on the other? What is the relationship between stable peace at the dyadic and regional levels?

2. *Why and how do stable peace relations emerge in the first place?* How does the transition from conflict resolution to stable peace take place? How are warlike situations or fairly unstable and fragile peace conditions transformed into stable peace relations? Is stable peace usually preceded by other peace relations (such as negative or precarious peace), or is it possible to jump from warlike relations to stable peace relations without passing through other gradations of peace?

3. *What are the conditions for maintaining stable peace over time?* Specifically, what are the necessary, sufficient, and favorable conditions for maintaining and consolidating ("deepening") stable peace over the long term? What constitutes stability over time, as opposed to stabilization in the initial achievement of stable peace? How long is stable peace, and how is it consolidated, or further stabilized? (see Jerneck 1996, 3).

For the purposes of our study, stable peace is defined according to two basic dimensions: cognitive and temporal. The *cognitive dimension* implies that a relationship of stable peace in international relations exists when there is a joint understanding that war is unthinkable as an instrument for resolving conflicts between states. The *temporal dimension* refers to the longevity of stable peace. In this sense, we are interested in understanding both the initial cognitive conditions to get to stable peace (i.e., the subjective and intersubjective internalization and realization that war is out of the question) and how this stable peace becomes a long-lasting peace—how it is maintained, consolidated, perpetuated, and *institutionalized* over time. The three questions presented above set the agenda for our investigation of the empirical cases in the second part of the book. In the following pages we briefly discuss the existing literature on the causes of stable peace, present several definitions of stable peace and other categories of peace, and outline our theoretical framework on the conditions to obtain and consolidate stable peace.

State of the Art: What Do We Know about the Causes of Stable Peace?

The (Relative) Paucity of Studies about Stable Peace

Explanations of long periods of peace have usually been limited to an examination of the systemic long peace of the Cold War period (1945–1989) or, alternatively, of the peace between pairs of democracies that ultimately developed into a unique zone of democratic peace, such as that among the OECD (Organization for Economic Cooperation and Development) countries. In the latter case, peace among these industrialized democracies is overdetermined. There have been many reasons, ranging from economic development and prosperity through sharing of democratic norms and institutions, why those countries have remained at peace.

The question of how peace, once obtained, can be stabilized and maintained has been barely addressed in the literature, with the possible exception of the booming literature on the "democratic peace," a possible (but not sole) source of stable peace. The concept of stable peace has its philosophical antecedents in the work of Immanuel Kant, especially in his essay *Perpetual Peace* (1795). In 1957 Karl Deutsch and his associates published a seminal work on the required and favorable conditions for the development of pluralistic security communities among states that had kept peaceful relations among themselves. More recently, Stephen Rock has explored the historical process by which great powers may make a transition in their mutual relations from negative or precarious peace to stable peace (Rock 1989, 4). But Rock and Deutsch are two outstanding examples of a meager literature. The paucity of important research on the conditions of stable peace might be related to the inherent difficulties of identifying the particular variables that are significant in building up and maintaining the stability of peace in any international system or subsystem (see Boulding 1978, 63). Moreover, there seems to be a normative bias in peace research to focus on the earlier steps of conflict termination and resolution. Paradoxically, it seems much easier to study the causes and conditions of war than those of peace, although peace should be considered the normal situation (at least in statistical terms). Inter-state wars have become an aberration or deviation from the norm since 1945 (see Melko 1973; Gaddis 1986; 1991, 25; Holsti 1996). As with the study of deterrence, however, most of the research has focused on explaining the causes of failure rather than success, the anomaly rather than the norm, war instead of peace. When deterrence actually "works," we never know whether the reason has been deterrence or impotence, lack of motivation or resources to wage war, or both. Similarly, when peace is obtained and maintained, it is very difficult to discern the specific reasons why states have not turned to violence to settle their differences. Thus, we do not know with certainty whether peace has been an artifact or not.

Explanations of peace should be arranged according to levels of aggregation similar to those of the causes of war. At the systemic level, peace can be explained in terms of the evolving relationship between the great powers (see Hagan, chapter 2; Miller, chapter 3). For instance, a "long peace" between the United States and the Soviet Union characterized the international system from 1945 until the end of the Cold War and the demise of the Soviet Union. It has been explained by alternative and complementary causes, including the presence of nuclear weapons, the replacement of a multipolar with a bipolar configuration of power, and a roughly equal distribution of military power between the two superpowers (see Gaddis 1991, 27; Mearsheimer 1990, 11).

At the regional level, commonplace explanations of peace have focused almost exclusively upon advanced industrialized and democratic countries, the member-states of the OECD. For example, Bruce Russett and Harvey Starr adduce five causes of peace among these states: (1) a response to a common threat by an external (i.e., "systemic") enemy; (2) the construction of supranational institutions, such as the European Union; (3) the development of strong economic ties and links of social communication; (4) the achievement and continued expectation of substantial economic benefits to all the members of the region; and (5) the acceptance of the values and institutions associated with liberal democracy (Russett and Starr 1992, 376–98).

At the dyadic level, peace has been associated with geographical distance, asymmetrical distribution of power between the parties, alliance links and third-party threats, economic development and prosperity, institutional and transnational links, lack of militarization, political stability, and democratic regimes (see Bremer 1993, 233–35; Ember et al. 1992, 574–75). Among these alternative explanations, the recent literature on international relations has emphasized the democratic peace as the major theory of the causes of peace and war (Gleditsch 1993, 15).

Below the level of the state, explanations of peace have focused upon the role of leadership and personalities, in terms either of rational choice (Bueno de Mesquita and Lalman 1992) or of the ability of leaders to learn (Stein 1994).

To sum up, most of the academic research addresses the classical questions on the causes of war and the conditions for peace. However, it does not differentiate among different categories of peace nor cope with the related and important issue of how peace is preserved or even deepened once it is established.[1] To illustrate this point, we now turn to a brief examination of two research programs that directly address the subject of stable peace: the liberal/democratic peace and the study of pluralistic security communities.

Stable Peace and Liberal/Democratic Peace

The hypothesized relationship between democratic states is characterized by stable peace; that is, the absence of any expectations of military violence or threats thereof (see Ericson, chapter 7). The link between stable peace and liberal/democratic peace is quite evident at the cognitive, perceptual, and intersubjective levels. Democratic (or liberal or republican) dyads are peaceful because of the mutual expectations of nonviolence, due to the perception of a shared set of norms. This expectation is based on the parties' respective forms of domestic governance (i.e., democracy) and by their mutual recognition of this similarity. Expectations of nonviolence are at the heart of the liberal peace proposition, and these expectations have to be strong enough to avoid balancing behavior and the potential escalation of conflicts. In other words, it is not only war that is done away with, but also fear of war (Ericson 1996, 3; 1997; and chapter 7). Hence, democratic peace is analyzed as a possible mechanism to reach stable peace, though it is not the only known version.

According to John Owen (1994, 1997), a crucial foundation for stable peace among states is the similarity of their internal institutions. States with similar domestic regimes tend to identify with one another and thus to perceive similar interests. A state will try as far as it can to spread its own (domestic) institutions to other states, in order to harmonize their interests and policies with its own. To the degree that such a state succeeds in spreading its institutions, it will construct around it a zone of stable peace. Yet, here lies an embedded paradox: This zone of stable peace will never encompass the entire globe and bring about perpetual peace worldwide; similarity is by definition relative, not absolute, so that for states to be "like," they need "unlike" states against which to compare themselves. Therefore, stable peace must always be in pieces, usually overlapping with the expanding zones of democratic peace (see Owen, chapter 4).

The study of the transition from conflict resolution to stable peace has implications for broadening the research on the democratic peace thesis. Much of the research has focused upon efforts to explain how democracy brings peace. It would be desirable to examine as well the democratic states' historical transitions toward stable peace. Moreover, an examination of history and contemporary affairs might find cases of stable peace between countries that are not democracies (such as several of the ASEAN [Association of Southeast Asian Nations] members) or between states only one of which is a democracy (e.g., the relationship between the United States and Mexico until the 1980s). Hence, liberal/democratic peace should be reexamined as "only one sub-set of the broader generic phenomenon of stable peace" (George and Bennett 1997, 5–6).

In sum, stable peace and liberal/democratic peace might overlap, though they are far from being identical. Democratic peace can be a causal mechanism for the occurrence and further development of stable peace. Yet, stable peace is a *broader* phenomenon than liberal/democratic peace, in that the presence of democracies is a sufficient though not necessary condition for the emergence and maintenance of stable peace. It is clear that common democratic norms help to consolidate and preserve stable peace, though they are not the only normative frameworks that determine peaceful relations among states.

Stable Peace and Pluralistic Security Communities

The concept of pluralistic security communities can be kept separate from stable peace, despite their obvious overlapping in theoretical and empirical terms. They both belong to the same conceptual family; security communities can be considered as a most advanced version of stable peace.

For Emanuel Adler and Michael Barnett (1996, 1998a), pluralistic security communities are transnational regions composed of sovereign states whose people sustain dependable expectations of peaceful change. A common transnational identity ("we-feeling") includes both material dimensions and cognitive structures, which can be examined in constructivist terms.[2] The idea of security communities, originally introduced by Karl Deutsch in 1957 and recently refurbished from a constructivist perspective by Adler and Barnett, offers a dynamic and cognitive model of stable peace. The threshold of stable peace is foremost cognitive, and its process is characterized by fluctuations, not by equilibrium. According to Adler, democracy in itself is not a prerequisite for security communities; yet, a common cognitive structure, such as liberalism, is essential for their understanding and further development.

As with liberal/democratic peace, there is a clear overlap between the study of stable peace and the research on pluralistic security communities, whether from a constructivist or a more positivist approach. Again, the phenomenon of stable peace is broader and includes, by definition, the cognitive reality of security communities. The main difference between the two seems to be that stable peace does not require a common regional identity and a shared sense of "we-feeling." Security communities assume the preexistence of stable peace, while stable peace does not always imply a security community. After clarifying the links between stable peace and these related literatures, we can turn now to our first research question, regarding the definition(s) and taxonomy of stable peace.

What Is the Nature of Stable Peace?

In this section, we present several definitions of stable peace, while differentiating between it and other categories of peace. Moreover, we draw the distinction between stable peace at the dyadic and regional levels. While peace in general, like its opposite, war, has been the focus of numerous attempts at analysis and definition, stable peace has been very little studied, with a few exceptions such as Kenneth Boulding (1978), Alexander George (1992), Russett and Starr (1992), and the current work of some of the contributors to this volume.

Kenneth Boulding, the first contemporary scholar to present the idea of stable peace, defines it as "a situation in which the probability of war is so small that it does not really enter into the calculations of any of the people involved" (Boulding 1978, 13). Stable peace is then the "object of peace policy" and the "deliberate decision" of the related sides (Boulding 1978, xi). Similarly, Alexander George (1992) defines stable peace as a relationship between two parties in which neither side considers the use of military force or even the threat of it in any dispute between them. In other words, states that enjoy a relationship of stable peace may continue to have serious disputes and conflicts, though they accept that these should be managed and resolved only by peaceful means.[3] Russett and Starr define stable peace (among the OECD states) in the same way, as "the absence of preparation for war or the serious expectation of war with each other" (Russett and Starr 1992, 376). All these definitions conceive of stable peace in international relations as a situation, process, or kind of relationship involving two or more states characterized by the absence of a certain behavior or even its consideration—war, threats of war, and other violent means. Thus, the parties develop a common understanding and expectations regarding the continuation of their peaceful relations without resorting to the use of violence.

This definition of stable peace encompasses four major dimensions: (1) cognitive; (2) cultural and normative; (3) institutional; and (4) economic/functional. According to its *cognitive dimension*, stable peace exists when there is a joint perception and understanding that war is unthinkable as an instrument for resolving conflicts between (or among) states (see Bengtsson, chapter 5; and Ericson, chapter 7). The *normative dimension* emphasizes the development of a shared normative framework (of "peace norms," or a "Code of Peace") for the creation, development, and consolidation of stable peace according to international standards of peaceful behavior (see Jones 1991). The *institutional dimension* refers to the institutions and mechanisms necessary for cooperation and conflict management in the context of stable peace (see Hagan, chapter 2; Miller, chapter 3; and Nordquist, chapter 9). Finally, the *economic/functional dimension* focuses upon economic peacemaking as a way of stabilizing and deepening peace by establishing a common balance of prosperity rather than a balance of power or a balance of terror (see Boulding 1978; and Tovias, chapter 8).

It is important to point out that in terms of conflict, stable peace is far from utopian. Hence, there is no need for a total harmonization of policies and interests among (or between) the parties involved. In this sense, Boulding maintains that a relationship of stable peace "is not the same thing as having a common language, a common religion, a common culture, or even common interests" (Boulding 1978, 17). The main point remains that political and other conflicts that arise between (or among) states are consistently resolved without resorting to military means, or even threats of using them.

The degree of harmony of interests and cooperation between (or among) the parties may influence not only the nature and extension of peace but also the prospects of its maintenance. Thus, we should ask how different categories of peace might influence the maintenance and "deepening" of peace among (or between) the parties involved in the relationship.

Categories of Peace

Stable peace can be located on a continuum, as presented by Kenneth Boulding, Alexander George, Benjamin Miller, and Arie Kacowicz. Boulding's categories include "positive" and "negative" peace, as well as "unstable peace" and "stable peace." George's taxonomy refers to "precarious peace," "conditional peace," and "stable peace." Miller's continuum includes "cold peace," "normal peace," and "warm peace." Finally, Kacowicz's categories, in regional terms, include "negative peace," "stable peace," and "pluralistic security communities." These typologies are relevant in assessing the distinctive characteristics of stable peace, as opposed to other types of bilateral and regional peace.

The Categories of Kenneth Boulding: From War to Stable Peace, and from Negative to Positive Peace. What is peace? Probably the most significant quarrel in the field of peace studies relates to a proper definition of this term. A major debate, carried out by Johan Galtung and Kenneth Boulding since the 1960s, has been whether to define peace simply as the absence of war (in "negative" terms) or as a more encompassing concept, which includes also social and economic justice and some kind of world order that meets the needs and interests of the human population as a whole ("positive peace"). For instance, Johan Galtung juxtaposed the absence of war and "positive peace" by relating them to his notions of personal (physical) versus structural (socioeconomic) violence. The absence of personal violence constitutes mere negative peace, while the absence of structural violence means the achievement of positive peace. Hence, the concept of peace has both positive and negative connotations. For Boulding, *positive peace* is "a condition of good management, orderly resolution of conflict, harmony associated with mature relationships, gentleness, and love." In contrast, *negative peace* is defined as "the absence of turmoil, tension, conflict and war" (Boulding 1978, 3). Although Boulding does not mention how negative or positive peace is related to stable peace, it seems that stable peace is probably more than just the absence of war, although it is not necessarily positive peace in Galtung's terms.

Boulding (1978) traces four distinguishable patterns or alternating phases or conditions of the relationship between political entities, ranging from war to stable peace (3–13). After crossing the threshold of *unstable war*, Boulding distinguishes between *unstable peace* (where peace is the norm and "war is regarded as a breakdown of peace, which will be restored when the war is over") and *stable peace* ("a situation in which the probability of war is so small that it does not really enter into the calculations of any of the people involved") (12–13). The sources (i.e., causes) of the transition among these different phases relate to the "strains" and "strength" of the system, defined in cognitive and economic terms (31–66). Despite the brilliance of this insightful taxonomy, Boulding's conditions and causes remain underspecified.

The Categories of Alexander George: Precarious, Conditional, and Stable Peace. Alexander George refers to "the nature of the peace" instead of just "peace," and identifies different types of peace (George 1998, ix–xi). They include precarious peace, conditional peace, and stable peace.

- *Precarious peace* refers to an acute conflict relationship between two states when peace means little more than the temporary absence of war. Such a peace depends not merely on "general deterrence" but also on "immediate deterrence"—that is, timely use of threatening actions and warnings in war-threatening crises. For instance, the Arab–Israeli conflict, until recent times, could be characterized as a case of precarious peace (George and Bennett 1997, 3).

- *Conditional peace,* conversely, describes a less acute, less heated conflict relationship, one in which general deterrence plays the predominant and effective role in maintaining peace. The parties to the conflict do not often need to resort to immediate deterrence. Yet, neither in precarious nor in conditional peace does either party to the conflict rule out the use of force as an instrument of policy, so that deterrent and compellent threats occur occasionally. The U.S.–Soviet relationship during the Cold War can be depicted as a case of conditional peace (George and Bennett 1997, 3–4).

- *Stable peace,* in contrast to the two previous types of peace, is a relationship between two states (or among a group of states) in which any state considers it unthinkable to use military force, or even to threaten its use in any dispute involving them. The European Union is an excellent example of this type of relationship (George and Bennett 1997, 4).

While George notes the possibility of moving from precarious or conditional peace to stable peace, he does not explore the conditions under which two or more states move from one category of peace to another and whether there is a necessary sequence in this continuum.

The Categories of Benjamin Miller: Cold, Normal, and Warm Peace. A rather different categorization of peace is presented by Benjamin Miller (1997, 1998, and chapter 3), who speaks in terms of cold, normal, and warm peace:

- *Cold peace* refers to absence of war and of threats of force among the parties. While the underlying regional conflicts are being reduced or at least moderated, they are still far from fully resolved. Thus, there is a danger of returning to the use of force, so that war has not been excluded from the parties' strategic considerations and policy options. In this situation, formal peace agreements exist between (or among) the parties, but their relations are limited to the intergovernmental level, within the realm of security and political cooperation (Miller 1998, 4–5). This category might describe, for instance, the current peaceful relations between Israel and Egypt.

- *Normal peace* is a situation in which the likelihood of war is lower than in cold peace because most, if not all, of the conflictual issues have been resolved. The parties recognize each other's sovereignty, and there is a general agreement on such issues as boundaries, resource allocation, and refugee settlement. Normal peace is more resilient than cold peace and may be expected to endure changes in the international environment. Yet, war is still not ruled out as a policy instrument in case of a change of elites or the rise of revisionist parties (Miller 1998, 5). Normal peace lies between conditional peace and stable peace. The relations among most of the South American countries between 1883 and the 1980s might be a good example of normal peace (see Kacowicz 1998, 67–124).

- *Warm peace*, like stable peace, is a situation in which regional war is unthinkable in any scenario of international or regional change. Even if some issues are still disputed, the use of force is completely ruled out as an option for resolving conflicts. Hence, there is no planning for the use of force and no preparation of appropriate fighting capabilities. Instead, institutionalized nonviolent procedures for conflict resolution are preferred by both the governmental elites and the peoples of the region, leading to the formation of pluralistic security communities, as in Western Europe (see Miller 1998, 5–6).

In his typology, Miller pools together stable peace and pluralistic security communities. In his view, warm peace overlaps, though it is not necessarily synonymous with, stable peace. Warm peace will not always be stable, unless there is a compatibility of societal and normative values among the parties involved. In any case, in Miller's typology, warm peace characterizes stable peace more than normal and cold peace do.

The Categories of Arie Kacowicz: Negative Peace, Stable Peace, and Pluralistic Security Communities. In another categorization construed in regional terms, Kacowicz suggests that we can differentiate among three different gradations of zones of peace in an ascending order of quality from negative peace, through stable peace, up to the emergence of pluralistic security communities (Kacowicz 1995, 1998).

- A zone of *negative peace* (mere absence of war) is one in which peace is maintained only on an unstable basis and/or by negative means such as threats, deterrence, or a lack of will or capabilities to engage in violent conflict at a certain time. The possibility of war remains tangible and real. This category overlaps with George's precarious and conditional peace and with Miller's cold peace (and to a lesser degree, with his normal peace).

- A zone of *stable peace* (no expectations of violence) is one in which peace is maintained on a reciprocal and consensual basis. In this zone the probability of war is so small that it does not really enter into the calculations of any of the parties involved. This category is identical to those of Boulding and George and overlaps to a certain extent with Miller's warm peace (and to a lesser extent with his normal peace). Unlike negative peace, stable peace requires peaceful relations both within and among states. Thus, a zone of stable peace can be defined as a community or society of nation-states satisfied with the status quo, in which domestic and international conflicts might occur, though they are strictly kept within nonviolent limits.

- A *pluralistic security community* of nation-states, with stable expectations of peaceful change, is one in which member-states share common norms, values, and political institutions; sustain a common identity; and are deeply interdependent. The shared expectations of peaceful change are a function of common values, mutual responsiveness and trust, and the abandonment of war as a policy option to resolve conflicts. In this sense, pluralistic security communities represent an advanced form of stable peace.

According to this categorization, stable peace and pluralistic security communities greatly overlap. The former is a broader category of peace than the latter, since by definition every pluralistic security community assumes and implies stable peace, while not every zone of stable peace has to be a security community. The main distinction seems to be that a security community encompasses a higher sense of community and institutionalization through the sharing of a similar political system (such as democratic regimes), political institutions, and economic interdependence (see Kacowicz 1998, 10–11).

These typologies imply that there are some minimal or necessary conditions for the emergence and evolution of peaceful relations between the parties. Moreover, the maintenance and further consolidation of peace may deepen even more as we move from one category to another. All these typologies should be examined across four principal issue-areas: cognitive, temporal, spatial, and power relations. The *cognitive* issue-area refers to war as unthinkable; the *temporal*, to the time dimension and the length of the peaceful relationship; the *spatial*, to the geographic context (either bilateral/dyadic or regional); and the *power* to whether the relations among (or between) the parties are hierarchical or equalitarian. Before turning to the analysis of the necessary, sufficient, and favorable conditions for stable peace, we should clarify the geographical issue area by drawing the distinction between the dyadic and regional levels.

Dyadic Level versus Regional Level

Most of the scholars mentioned here discuss stable peace mainly at the regional level. For instance, Russett and Starr focus upon the member states of the OECD in the North Atlantic area. Similarly, Kacowicz addresses the regional level by considering zones of inter-state peace in South America, West Africa, and East Asia. The common assumption is that peace at the regional level may have a better prospect to be maintained when most, if not all, of the states of the region act together to stabilize and consolidate it through different levels of interaction, cooperation, and communication. In this sense, we should ask three questions: (1) Can a dyadic peace be stable? (2) What are the conditions for stable peace at the dyadic level? and (3) What is the relationship between dyadic and regional peace?

We argue that a dyadic peace is stable when the two parties agree to avoid war or threats of war in their mutual relationship and to use only peaceful diplomatic means to resolve any potential conflict between them. Moreover, if the parties share some characteristics such as democratic regimes, political stability, economic development, and prosperity and if their bilateral cooperation includes not only security issues but also extensive economic interaction, including institutional and transnational links, then their prospects for maintaining stable peace in the long run are similar to those of the regional or community level (see Kacowicz 1998, 33; Bremer 1993, 233–35; Ember et al. 1992, 574–75; and Gleditsch 1993, 15). The U.S.–Canadian relationship, or even the evolving relationship between Argentina and Brazil in the last decade, may fit this characterization of a dyadic stable peace.

Conversely, the relationship between a dyadic and a regional stable peace is complicated. Resolving and stabilizing a dyadic conflict in a region where there are other dyadic conflicts is necessary but not sufficient for stabilizing the region as a whole. It may encourage the resolution of other (dyadic) conflicts in the region, and/or its resolution may discourage other parties in the region from initiating violence. Yet, the lack of movement toward regional stable peace may endanger the maintenance of dyadic stable peace. This may happen when one or both parties to the dyadic stable peace are still involved in other regional conflicts, or when they have allies who are in conflict with the other party to the stable peace. This is probably the case of the existing peace relations between Egypt and Israel or between Jordan and Israel, when the Arab–Israeli conflict has not been yet comprehensively resolved. This case indicates the importance of the completion of dyadic peace as a necessary condition for reaching and consolidating a regional stable peace.

Why and How Do Stable Peace Relations Emerge?

Conflict resolution involves the reconciliation or elimination of fundamental differences and grievances underlying a given dispute. It occurs when the incompatibility between the preferences of the various parties to a conflict disappears, or when the sources of the conflict are removed. At the same time, conflict resolution does not necessarily prevent the development of a new conflict in the future that might derail the degree of peace obtained. Hence, we are interested in studying the process of transition from conflict resolution (through negative, precarious, conditional, and cold peace) towards stable peace. In other words, once formal (and sometimes informal) peace is obtained, we want to identify and trace the necessary, sufficient, and favorable conditions that stabilize peace in the short and middle terms.

In our conceptual framework we aim to differentiate, first of all, between *stabilization* and *consolidation* of stable peace. Stabilization is the initial stage in the transitional process toward establishing stable peace, coming immediately after the resolution of the conflict, and is a precondition for its further maintenance and consolidation. Stabilization of peace is limited to transcending conflict resolution and the minimal requirements for peacekeeping in the short and middle terms, when the parties are still confused about the major cognitive change in their relationship: ruling out war as a viable policy option to settle their differences. In this stage, the parties might prefer to limit their political and security cooperation to the minimal degree that is necessary for maintaining peace, without extending it to other domains. Hence, the parties might recognize the immediate political and security benefits from peace. Yet they will be reluctant to engage in economic cooperation or interdependence for which they are not yet ripe, and which they may perceive more as a potential threat to their sovereignty than as an opportunity for strengthening their mutual peace. At this initial stage, the parties usually limit their cooperation to security issues, through the formation of security regimes. The move from unilateralism (negative peace through balance of power or deterrence) towards bilateralism and multilateralism is a gradual and painstaking one.

Our study suggests that the stabilization of peace after the resolution of a protracted conflict implies a peculiar process of learning that we term "strategic" or "complex" learning. It is a new stage in the prolonged learning process that was needed for conflict reduction and resolution. Stabilization differs from the previous stages since it requires a redefinition or reevaluation of the parties' national interests, so that each party will perceive a mutual interest in establishing and maintaining the peace between them as the most important factor in assuring each other's security and even existence. In other words, each party learns that it is dependent upon the other to assure its security. This change in the perception of the national interest means that the parties regard war as an illegitimate instrument for attaining national objectives, so that they are careful not to pursue goals that are likely to trigger war. In sum, the parties redefine their national interests and develop a substantial commitment to the political settlement and to the new status quo. This type of learning is necessary for deepening and extending the initial trust between the parties, so that their nascent political and military cooperation will evolve and spill over into other domains over time.

The *necessary conditions* for the stabilization of peace are:

- *Stable political regimes.* The presence of stable political regimes that perceive the peace agreement as their greatest achievement might enhance their mutual trust and confidence in stabilizing and maintaining peace. This condition is suggested as an alternative to the presence of democratic dyads, in case not all parties are democratic.

- *Mutual satisfaction with the terms of the peace agreement and/or the existing status quo.* This means not only satisfaction with the territorial status quo but also with other terms of the agreement and/or the current situation, such as the distribution of other, nonterritorial benefits. Satisfaction will prevent, by definition, any ideas of revision of the territorial status quo or of the terms of the agreement, with the exception of those made by mutual consent. It is important to examine the issues involved in reaching agreement, focusing upon the terms of the settlement and their relevance for the maintenance and consolidation of peace afterwards (see Nordquist 1998 and chapter 9). This satisfaction should not be limited to the ruling political and military elites but should include economic and intellectual circles. Moreover, the notion of satisfaction is directly related to a subjective (and intersubjective) sense of fairness, justice, and reciprocity in reaching peace (see Franck 1990, 1995). Peaceful relations should fulfill the early expectations of peace, or at least there should not be a major discrepancy between those expectations and the evolving reality of peace.[4]

- *Predictability of behavior and problem-solving mechanisms.* These two conditions imply a high degree of certainty about the other party's intentions and behavior. In cognitive terms, there is a mutual recognition of the reality of stable peace, according to which neither side will consider the threat or use of military force to settle any potential conflict between them in the future. Moreover, differences of interpretation about key provisions of the agreement, as well as major unresolved issues and new problems that might emerge in the future, should be accommodated within the framework of the agreement(s) and should be resolved only by negotiations or other peaceful means.

- *Open communication channels; initial (mutual) trust and respect between the leaders.* There should be a certain degree of information exchange and a variety of communication channels, in order to secure a high degree of certainty and confidence, if not mutual trust (which develops later). An evolving trust and respect between the leaders should provide as well a formula that enables a better understanding and a working relationship between the parties. In this sense, it should be noticed that the degree of trust is both a source and a consequence of the stabilization process.

In addition to these necessary conditions, we can point out two additional, *favorable conditions* to obtain stable peace:

- *Third-party guarantees.* This condition implies that an external actor, usually a superpower or a great power, is taking responsibility in case of a potential violation of the agreement or different interpretation of its terms, especially within a regional framework of conflict resolution and peacemaking. The granting of third-party guarantees might become necessary in some particularly difficult cases, such as the involvement of the United States in the Middle Eastern conflict and its subsequent peace process.

- *Spillover effects and the provision of nonmilitary public goods.* Developing and expanding a peaceful relation should be perceived as beneficial not only by the political leadership but also by other military, economic, intellectual, and cultural elites. For instance, the parties mutually recognize that stabilizing peace is necessary for their further economic development and prosperity. Reaching stable peace should in fact provide public goods that are not limited to peace and security but include economic benefits, so that larger sectors of the population will enjoy the positive effects of peace. Hence, a spillover might affect both vertical and horizontal directions. In vertical terms, it implies a top-down increasing consensus regarding the legitimacy of stable peace, which is supposed to benefit the entire population in myriad areas, including welfare and development. In horizontal terms, that legitimacy is granted by the extension of the elites who benefit from peace.[5] It should be emphasized that while they are a favorable condition at this initial stage of stabilization, these spillover effects become necessary over the long term to maintain, consolidate, and deepen the stable peace.

These conditions refer mainly to the perceptions and attitudes of the parties regarding their initial development of peaceful relations, including their commitment and willingness to manage potential conflicts by peaceful means and according to new norms in which force or threats of force are excluded as legitimate means. Stabilization of peace aims to deepen the initial trust between the parties, mainly through confidence-building measures. This stage of building and establishing peace is characterized by a momentous cognitive and intersubjective change in the parties' mutual perceptions.

It is difficult to define the temporal outer limits of this stabilization stage; in other words, as we witness "enduring rivalries" in conflictive dyads, we might also envision the presence of "enduring stabilization" stages over long periods of time after the formal resolution of the conflict. Thus, the parties might prefer to remain at this transitional stage for several reasons (both domestic and international) without moving forward towards the consolidation of stable peace.

What Are the Conditions for Maintaining Stable Peace?

Over time, the parties may develop means and norms to guarantee and extend their peace that transcend mutual deterrence, compellence, and balance of power. The success of the stabilization phase may encourage them to strengthen their cooperation and to extend it into other domains. Political and security cooperation may gradually spill over to economic, cultural, and functional cooperation, which increases the benefits of maintaining peace. At this more advanced stage, we might trace the necessary, sufficient, and favorable conditions for maintaining and deepening stable peace—the phase of consolidation.

The literature explaining the conditions for the maintenance and consolidation of stable peace is still limited. Therefore, additional research and theoretical insights are needed. We mention here three studies that discuss some of these conditions: (1) Boulding's *Stable Peace* (1978); (2) a chapter by Bruce Russett and Harvey Starr in *World Politics* (1992); and (3) Kacowicz's *Zones of Peace in the Third World* (1998).

On the basis of the experience of the stable peace relations between the

United States and Canada and the United States and Mexico and within Scandinavia and Western Europe, Kenneth Boulding suggests the following conditions for the maintenance of stable peace:

- compatible self-images (Boulding 1978, 17);

- an increase in the strength of the system of relationship between (or among) the parties, in terms of a political learning process;

- the development of a community (Boulding 1978, 4);

- the removal of national boundaries from political agendas, except under mutual agreement (Boulding 1978, 109);

- a minimum amount of nonmilitary intervention by each nation in the internal affairs of other parties; and

- the development of an economic rather than a romantic, heroic attitude towards the national state (Boulding 1991, 108).

This is more of a descriptive laundry list than a set of causal variables. In more analytical terms, this list of conditions combines some commitments by the parties, such as accepting the territorial status quo and avoiding interference with each other's internal affairs, with some requirements for further interaction and cooperation, including the establishment of a political community. These latter conditions, however, are not explicit enough about the role of the learning process in consolidating stable peace.

Bruce Russett and Harvey Starr maintain that learning the causes of stable peace among the OECD countries "might have a key to promoting peace over a wider area, even the entire globe" (Russett and Starr 1992, 376). Specifically, Russett and Starr suggest the following hypotheses as conditions for the maintenance of stable peace:

1. *Cohesion in the face of outside threats.* Peace is a consequence of states coming together in response to a common threat by an external enemy—in this case, the former Soviet Union.

2. *Institution building.* Peace is a consequence of the construction of international institutions, especially supranational ones, that bind together several states.

3. *Economic ties and social communication.* Peace is a result of strong economic ties and links of social communication.

4. *Economic benefits.* Peace is the result of the achievement and contin-

ued expectation of substantial economic benefits to all the parties involved.

5. *Democratic practice and beliefs.* Peace is the result of the widespread acceptance in all the states involved of the values and institutions of constitutional democracy (Russett and Starr 1992, 376–98).

Russett and Starr admit that they do not make "a thorough, systematic test" of any of their hypotheses. Yet, they basically reject their first hypothesis, which is based upon a flawed realist analysis that ignores the theory and practice of integration, the positive aspects of interdependence, and the effects suggested in hypotheses 2 through 5 (Russett and Starr 1992, 398).

Hypotheses 2 and 3 are not as clearly rejected as the first one. Although institutions and community ties contribute to maintaining the OECD peace, it is evident that there was peace in the region even when institutional bonds were still insignificant. As for the two remaining hypotheses, they look to the authors "more persuasive." According to Russett and Starr, "both look plausible as applied to the OECD, and both also have a more general base of evidence from other times and places" (Russett and Starr 1992, 399).

On the basis of their analysis, it seems that certain *common characteristics* of the states involved are the most important conditions for the maintenance of their regional peace. They are democratic regime and values, a high level of economic development and prosperity, and a common cultural framework and normative consensus. At the same time, no less important is the *degree of states' interaction and cooperation*, which includes economic ties and interdependence, social communication, building of supranational institutions, integration, and transnational links that enable mutual economic benefits and continued expectations of joint economic rewards.

In addition, Russett and Starr suggest two conditions that complement the previous five:

6. *Leaders of vision* who are able to conceive and carry out the common plans to maintain the peace; and

7. *A learning process* that takes place simultaneously at the level of the governmental bureaucracies and the civil society, spilling over from the former to the latter.

Consideration of all these conditions seems reasonable enough, especially against the background of the OECD experience. However, it is not clear whether they are necessary, sufficient, or just favorable for the maintenance of stable peace, nor is it clear what the precise relationship between them is.

Kacowicz differentiates among three clusters of explanations that include nine conditions for the maintenance of regional peace in the international system. Those explanations are not mutually exclusive. The first cluster includes four realist and geopolitical conditions: (1) regional hegemony; (2) regional balance of power; (3) common threat by a third party; and (4) isolation, irrelevance, and impotence. The second cluster includes four liberal conditions: (1) regional democracy; (2) economic development and prosperity; (3) economic interdependence, integration, and transnational links; and (4) a normative consensus facilitated by a common cultural framework. Finally, the third cluster suggests a causal link between satisfaction with the territorial status quo and maintenance of regional peace. This satisfaction is evidenced by the upholding of the international borders of states in a given region (Kacowicz 1998, 34).

The first cluster, which is pertinent to understanding the maintenance of negative or precarious peace only, is irrelevant to the maintenance of stable peace in the long term. Conversely, the second cluster (liberal conditions), and the satisfaction with the status quo are much more important to the consolidation of stable peace.

Although *satisfaction with the status quo* refers basically to the territorial dimension, it also encompasses the economic, military, and diplomatic rules that govern a system, a subsystem, or even a given dyadic relationship at a certain point in time. Moreover, active satisfaction means a disposition not only to accept the existing order but also to uphold and defend it. This single condition constitutes an important building-block in the consolidation of stable peace, especially following the stage of stabilization after the resolution of a regional conflict in which border issues probably played a significant role.

Kacowicz suggests that a commitment to keep the territorial status quo and to maintain the regional order and peace can be measured both domestically and internationally in terms of norms of behavior and actual policy. The domestic sources of satisfaction with the territorial status quo are reflected not only through the declaratory and actual policies of the ruling elites but also through their legitimation by the opposition elites, interest groups, and the public in general. Political stability and legitimacy are most important, since they might influence the willingness to maintain stable peace, notwithstanding changes of government and even regime changes. For example, if territorial changes made in an agreement are not legitimized by opposition elites, their coming to power might lead to dissatisfaction with the status quo and encourage revision of the agreement. Internationally, satisfaction is expressed through compliance with international norms that support the territorial status quo across borders (see Kacowicz 1998, 50–59).

Similarly, Rikard Bengtsson (1996, 1998, and chapter 5) points to the centrality of *trust* as an essential condition for consolidating stable peace in the long term. Three common elements of trust are considered essential: (1) it reduces social and political complexity; (2) it involves expectations of future behavior; and (3) it implies that an actor (human or otherwise) accepts that his or her fate to some extent lies beyond his or her own control (Bengtsson 1996, 1). Thus, states involved in stable peace at the consolidation stage should trust each other and become interdependent, so that concerns about their security dilemma do not enter into their mutual relations over time. In sum, trust minimizes uncertainty and ambiguity among (or between) the parties; it contributes to the predictability of intentions and behavior; and it enhances and deepens the parties' sense of interdependence.[6]

As pointed out above, stable peace is characterized by the fact that the states involved take their national boundaries off their agendas, except by mutual agreement. Hence, international war becomes implausible, if not impossible (see Boulding 1990, 7). Moreover, the parties gradually develop a common normative framework for managing and resolving their international conflicts exclusively by peaceful means. Thus, two conditions seem necessary for the maintenance and consolidation of stable peace over the long run: *a general and continuous satisfaction with the status quo* established by the peace agreement; and *a common normative framework*, sometimes enhanced by shared characteristics of the actors, such as a common culture and identity. Moreover, we can postulate that the *presence of well-developed democratic regimes* within all the countries involved constitutes a sufficient, albeit not a necessary, condition for consolidating stable peace. In addition to these conditions, according to the liberal (economic) logic, economic prosperity, interdependence, and integration facilitate the consolidation and expansion of stable peace. Thus, spillover effects and nonmilitary public goods become essential ingredients in this advanced stage. The basic economic assumption here is that trading "goods" is better than trading "bads." Hence, the economics of peacemaking is supposed to maintain and keep the peace by establishing a balance of prosperity instead of a balance of power or a balance of terror (see Tovias, chapter 8). The realization of economic benefits is contingent upon the continuing cooperation between the parties through mutual trust and the institutionalization of their relations.

In theoretical and empirical terms, all these conditions may explain the maintenance of stable peace in regions such as Western Europe and Scandinavia, and in the bilateral relationships between the United States and

Canada, the United States and Mexico, and Argentina and Brazil. Yet, we ask two further questions to elucidate this stage of consolidation: (1) Are all the shared characteristics of the parties necessary and/or sufficient for maintaining stable peace? and (2) What is the relationship between these common characteristics and the nature of the actors' interaction and cooperation?

If common characteristics are necessary to consolidate stable peace, then stable peace by definition is limited to states that share them. From our analysis we conclude that (a) a shared normative framework is a necessary but not a sufficient condition for maintaining stable peace; and (b) the presence of democratic regimes is sufficient though not necessary for reaching and consolidating stable peace. Other common characteristics (such as level of economic prosperity and development, or political stability) are neither necessary nor sufficient but just "favorable" to consolidation and therefore should be complemented by the nature of the states' interaction. Yet, the empirical cases mentioned above indicate the importance and salience of these shared characteristics.

Even in the case of democratic dyads or a democratic zone of peace, it is the character of the states' interaction and their level of cooperation that ultimately shape the relationship of stable peace, as expressed through economic interdependence, integration, and transnational links. Hence, it seems that only the aggregation of common characteristics (e.g., shared norms and continued commitment to the status quo) *and* the type of interaction (e.g., establishing a relationship of interdependence at all levels, including transnational) guarantees the maintenance of stable peace in the long run.

In sum, the initial momentous cognitive change that established stable peace in the first place (i.e., ruling out war as an instrument of policy making), is internalized through the physical and institutional conditions that have evolved at the advanced stage of consolidation. At the cognitive level, the actors have, through complex learning, internalized their (successfully) completed peace process into domestic politics. At the institutional and physical levels, the parties have increased their cooperation in security and nonsecurity (i.e., economic, functional) areas. These processes together create and perpetuate a definitive change in the "cognitive maps" of the actors involved. In this new cognitive chart, the parties learn the significance of reconciliation and forgiveness, accepting the reality and legitimacy of "the other." Stable peace is now considered by the actors as a condition that not only ensures their security and stability but also brings about economic benefits, including prosperity and welfare. At this stage of consolidation, the cost of destabilizing peace is mutually perceived as prohibitive and intolerable.[7]

Conclusion

In this chapter, we have defined and clarified the concept of stable peace at the dyadic and regional levels and in cognitive and temporal terms. Stable peace is best understood as located near the end of a continuum from conflict termination and resolution all the way up to pluralistic security communities. In this sense, stable peace is recognized both as a cognitive reality that denies war as a policy option and as a continuous, long-lasting peace between nations, following the West European experience. From that particular historical experience we tend to derive also the necessary, sufficient, and favorable conditions for stable peace, which combine the common (shared) characteristics of the actors and their unique interaction and level of cooperation.

A relationship characterized by stable peace generally cannot be seen as resulting from a single predominant cause or condition; rather, it is a result of a number of interrelated factors. Consequently, we assume complex, multicausal explanations at different levels of analysis. In addition, it is possible to see different instances of stable peace arising from different causal processes (Jerneck and Elgström 1996, 7–8). In other words, a complex phenomenon such as stable peace implies equifinality, with several alternative causes and conditions leading to identical results.

Despite the recognition of equifinality, we should search for explanatory variables, trying to understand both the "peaceful" and the "stable" elements in the definition of stable peace. For this purpose, we have presented in this chapter a conceptual framework that addresses the two major questions surrounding this phenomenon: (1) Why and how do stable peace relations emerge in the first place (stabilization)? and (2) What are the conditions for maintaining stable peace over time (consolidation)?

The initial stage, stabilization, refers to the genesis of a relationship of stable peace. The parties involved have just reached a peace agreement and resolved their conflict or, without fighting a previous war, they have gradually "upgraded" their previous peaceful relations to a higher level. Yet, they differ in their characteristics, and their interaction and cooperation are still limited to the security and political domains. The immediate need is to stabilize their new peaceful relations. A successful stabilization may be considered a precondition for extending stable peace to include further economic cooperation and benefits to the parties. The necessary conditions that lead to the shift from conflict resolution towards stable peace include (a) the presence of stable political regimes; (b) mutual satisfaction with the terms of the peace agreement and/or the current status quo; (c) predictability of behavior and problem-solving mechanisms; (d) open communication channels, including an initial trust and respect between the leaders. In addition, we should mention two favorable conditions: (e) third-party guarantees; and (f) spillover effects and the provision of nonmilitary public goods, including economic development and prosperity. As noted above, even if all these conditions are fulfilled, the parties might prefer to remain at this stage for an indeterminate period of time.

The advanced stage, consolidation of stable peace, refers to peace maintenance over the middle and long term. If in the initial stage of stable peace we have focused mainly upon the cognitive dimension (i.e., ruling out war as a policy instrument), in this advanced stage we focus also upon the temporal dimension—how long and "stable" is stable peace? — as well as upon the institutional dimension—how is stable peace institutionalized through physical, political, and economic cooperation and integration? This is the stage of routinization of peace, where peace is basically taken for granted as the normal situation. The conditions that contribute to and guarantee this routine peace include a general and continuous satisfaction with the status quo established by the terms of the peace agreement or the general peaceful situation, and a common normative framework, sometimes enhanced by a common culture and identity. Only the aggregation of the parties' shared characteristics, along with the nature and quality of their interaction and cooperation (i.e., establishing a relationship of interdependence at multiple levels), guarantees the maintenance of stable peace in the long run.

Our conceptual framework partly overlaps with two important research programs that have become extremely popular in the discipline of international relations in the last two decades: the liberal/democratic peace and the renewed interest in pluralistic security communities, analyzed from a constructivist perspective. We acknowledge the contribution and relevance of those research programs, while we also point out the uniqueness of our own research agenda, which is broader and more encompassing.

As has been demonstrated in both deductive and empirical terms, liberal/democratic peace can be considered at best a subset of stable peace. Hence, stable peace does not necessarily imply democratic peace. Democratic regimes are not necessary for the establishment or even the consolidation of stable peace, though they might be sufficient for it, and they have a paramount impact upon the quality of preexisting peaceful relations. At the same time, stable peace can exist in the absence of democracy, as in the case of several ASEAN countries.

Similarly, the reality of pluralistic security communities represents another instance, or advanced stage, of stable peace. Yet, stable peace in itself is a broader phenomenon than the formation of security communities. Moreover, these communities can be studied from both constructivist and positivist epistemological standpoints (see Väyrynen, chapter 6).

Finally, the conceptual framework introduced in this chapter has to be applied to the empirical analysis of case studies of historical, current, and prospective stable peace at both the dyadic and the regional level. The following chapters address the stabilization of peaceful relations among the great powers in the nineteenth and twentieth centuries; the reality of stable peace in Scandinavia; the evolution of stable peace in the Southern Cone of South America since 1979; the long but not-stable-enough peace between Israel and Egypt since 1979; the promise of a new NATO in a new Europe promoting systemic stable peace; and the bilateral peaceful relations between Germany and Poland. Only the historical analysis of these several episodes across regions and time will allow us to draw some relevant policy lessons regarding the stabilization, consolidation, and comprehensiveness of stable peace.

Notes

We would like to acknowledge the comments of the participants in previous workshops on stable peace held in Paris (September 1995 and August 1999), Jerusalem (June 1996), and Vienna (September 1998) and the support of the Leonard Davis Institute for International Relations at the Hebrew University of Jerusalem, as well as the comments and suggestions of Alexander George, Orly Kacowicz, Galia Press-Natan, Yael Krispin, Magnus Ericson, Magnus Jerneck, and Ole Elgström.

1. An interesting exception is Rothstein (1999), who examines the issue of *reconciliation* after the signature of peace agreements.

2. See Raimo Väyrynen (chapter 6) for a critical review of the relationship between the concept of security communities and stable peace.

3. We should keep in mind that absence of violence should not be confused with absence of conflict. Thus, the achievement of peace does not necessarily imply the elimination of conflict.

4. There are cases of stabilization of peace relations that do not necessarily follow a formal peace treaty. Traditional enmity can be partly transformed, as witnessed by Swedish–Russian relations, without a previous war between the parties. U.S.–Soviet relations and relations among Latin American countries are other examples of stabilization of preexisting (negative) peaceful relations. We thank Magnus Ericson for his comments on this point.

5. We thank Yael Krispin for her comments on this point.

6. While trust explains how stable peace relations become consolidated and deepened, it can be argued that it is also part of the definition of stable peace (consolidated). This circularity can be explained if we refer to trust as the consequence of the previous stabilization stage and as a cause in the consolidation stage.

7. We do not argue here that stable peace is equivalent to perpetual peace. The process is not completely irreversible, so that it has not necessarily reached a point of no return. Consolidated stable peace can break down under enormous pressure, though this is very unusual. We thank Magnus Jerneck and Magnus Ericson for their comments on this point.

2

Domestic Political Sources of Stable Peace: The Great Powers, 1815–1854

Joe D. Hagan

This chapter examines one key aspect of the rise, persistence, and decay of stable peace: the role of domestic political conditions within the states at peace. Although most domestic political explanations in international relations theory center around the origins of war, recent years have seen important work on domestic explanations of stable peace in ways that go beyond simply the absence of war. The dominant strand of this literature is, of course, the democratic peace literature that documents the historical fact of no wars, diminished crises, and greater cooperation among democratic regimes. To a certain extent, stable peace research upon which this book builds has adopted the argument that democratic structures are an important factor in minimizing the threat of war. Some of this literature, though, looks directly at the beliefs and interests of ruling groups as well as patterns of oppositions to explain peace among a wider variety of states regardless of regime structure (e.g., Miller 1995; Goldmann 1988; Kacowicz 1995). But one key insight of that literature is that the democratic peace is not unique. Across historical periods (Miller 1995) and different regions (Kacowicz 1998), these sorts of studies identify stable peace that exists or has existed among a wider variety of states in a way that is politically entrenched but not limited to any particular type of regime, democratic or authoritarian.

This chapter looks exclusively at domestic political phenomena that underlie stable peace. Although domestic politics is but one condition of stable peace, this chapter seeks to move beyond the necessarily briefer treatments that explore domestic politics as a component of a larger theoretical framework. I begin with the idea that rulers with moderate beliefs about international politics are the pivotal domestic "prerequisite" to stable relations among states. In the first half of this chapter, I expand upon this insight by, first, elaborating upon the concept of moderation (including destabilizing effects of its extremes) and, second, considering how domestic politics may undercut the effective pursuit of moderate policies to sustain stable peace. In the second half of the chapter, I examine the interplay of these domestic factors during one key period of stable peace, that of the Concert of Europe, 1815–1854. My point is to show that this remarkable period of great power restraint and cooperation was characterized by well-established domestic political conditions that enabled moderate leaders to hold power and implement their policies in a reasonably flexible manner. Only in the 1850s did the domestic political bases collapse for stable peace, and the shift in domestic conditions in *all of the great powers* was key to establishing the more competitive and tenuous balance of power. This is purely an analysis of domestic conditions, though this survey highlights the deeper effects of leadership phenomena and domestic politics across both liberal and conservative states.

Leader Orientations, Domestic Politics, and Stable Peace

The framework upon which this analysis draws employs a "statist" approach in linking domestic political influences to foreign policy and, ultimately, to international system stability.[1] At its theoretical core is the group, or coalition, that occupies the "central decision making institutions and roles" in the political system, or what Krasner (1978, 12–13) defines as the state. The framework has a sequence of two components: who governs and under what constraints. The first dynamic concerns the ruling group's orientation to international affairs, that is, the leadership's core beliefs about their nation's position in the international system. The domestic prerequisite for stable peace is that the ruling groups in all of the key powers have a moderate orientation towards the international order. However, once in power, these ruling groups are not immune from further political pressure. The second dynamic linking domestic politics to foreign policy concerns the extent to which leaders face significant political opposition and the political strategies they employ to cope with it. Of particular concern here are domestic political pressures that undercut stable peace by pressuring the governments towards either hard-line policies or more rigid forms of extreme moderation.

Moderate Orientations and Stable Peace

The orientation of a state's leadership concerns the core beliefs and interests shared within this ruling group, that is, the national interest as defined by the ruling leadership. Like political psychology models of foreign policy (e.g., Holsti 1976; Jervis 1976; Lebow 1981; Rosati 1995), I begin with the assumption that the leader's belief systems have a strong imprint on how the state broadly orients itself towards the international political system. Following Vasquez (1993), I further assume that contending domestic political groups often hold alternative beliefs about the character of the international system and their nation's place in it and thus advocate alternative foreign policy strategies.2 For purposes of this analysis, I expand upon Vasquez's dichotomy between "moderates" and "hard-liners."3 Building on this distinction, these orientations are:

- *Hard-line orientation.* Leaders with this orientation advocate "a foreign policy that is adamant in not compromising its goals and who argue in favor of the efficacy and legitimacy of threats and force" (Vasquez 1993, 202). At the basis of this argument is the overall belief that the international system is inherently dangerous so that interaction with opposing powers is essentially a zero-sum game. Adversaries are thus viewed as having goals that threaten the security, well-being, and international status of one's own nation and its allies, while affecting a wide variety of substantive and regional issues. The severity and scope of these threats preclude the compromises and restraint inherent in cooperative foreign relations. Instead, confrontation—using political, economic, and military pressure—is the key to effective influence in foreign policy. Not only does military force provide the basis for deterring the aggression of adversaries, but also coercive diplomacy and the use of military force are key to containing adversaries and resolving disputes by forcing concessions.

- *Moderate orientation.* Leaders with this orientation advocate a "foreign policy that will avoid war through compromise and negotiation, and the creation of rules and norms for non-violent conflict resolution" (Vasquez 1993, 202). Thus, in contrast to militancy, this orientation is premised on a belief that international politics is not inherently dangerous in the sense that competition might require the use or threat of military force. Rather, although without assuming a harmony of interests, relationships among at least key powers are viewed as inherently non-zero-sum. In fact, these powers likely share certain common interests in maintaining the political, economic, and security structures within the system as a whole—including the prevention of conflicts that could undercut the established order. Those conflicts that do occur are perceived to be issue specific or situationally bound and are not considered to challenge the overall stability of great power relations. Thus, all powers have equally legitimate concerns and expect that disputes can be resolved cooperatively through mutual accommodation, self-restraint, and concerted actions.

For Vasquez (1993), a key piece of the "war puzzle" is the rise of hard-liners within the political systems in the major powers. This is a simple, yet powerful, argument. For example, a survey of leaders and oppositions in the European powers in the decades before World War I shows that rigidly hard-line political groups emerged in nearly all of the powers (except Britain) well before July 1914—in Germany between 1890 and 1897, in Russia and Austria by 1906, and in France by 1911.[4] Once in place, these states collectively created—at the systemic level—a "spiral of conflict" dominated by tightening alliances, growing dependence on the threat of force, and ultimately greater alarm about the domestic and international consequences of backing down in a crisis.

Similarly, a political explanation of stable peace can also be based upon Vasquez's logic. A minimum requirement of stable peace is that all of the key powers are controlled by political groups who are moderate with respect to their views of major power relations and, in effect, act without the expectation of war. This creates a system of interaction with entirely different dynamics, although still within the context of anarchy and without assuming a harmony of interest. Conflicts are contained in several respects. First, at least among the powerful actors, governments accept and adhere to the international status quo. Basic aspects of the balance of power are not called into question, including the political integrity of key actors (including buffer states) and the existence of those states. Second, the spiral of conflict is contained because governments do not define relations among the powers as competitive but instead recognize their shared interests and that cooperative relations may promote their security, political, and economic goals. Finally, governments perceive a need for joint action—in other words, a concert—as the key to resolving issues in international politics. Taken together, moderate powers not only have a consensus on key aspects of the system, but they also define their relationships in a way that minimizes the security dilemma typically inherent in international affairs.

All this is not to say that diplomacy among moderate powers is simple. Along with the fact that a hard-line regime may emerge in one of the states, there are several other subtler ways in which moderate governments can undercut stable peace if moderation is taken to certain extremes. One way is simply to withdraw from the system. Although this may result from a major foreign policy failure (such as defeat in war), it may also result from the rise to power of leaders who see international involvement as too costly, unnecessary, or immoral—that is, leaders who emphasize domestic reform or adhere to pacifism. Such withdrawal from international affairs undercuts stable peace by opening opportunities for the assertion of power by other actors and/or by provoking insecurities in other powers by dismantling reassuring security and trade commitments. A second form of extreme moderation is unilateral and forceful action in support of the international status quo. Not only may this action prevent reasonable adjustment to pressures (often domestically driven) in the international status quo, but also it may violate the sovereignty of other powers as nonsecurity aspects of the status quo are enforced with respect to economic and human rights concerns. For instance, protectionist actions undercut internationalist coalitions underlying support for the moderate trading order (Solingen 1998). Similarly, questions of human rights inevitably become matters of national sovereignty and thus provoke hostility not only from governing groups but also regarding the wider nationalist sentiment. In short, maintenance of a moderate international order requires foreign policies that are moderate but are implemented in pragmatic ways sensitive to systemic consequences. Like pragmatic diplomacy among hard-line powers, moderation invokes the "Goldilocks problem" in which a state must remain fully engaged but not too rigid in maintaining the system.

Domestic Politics and Moderate Foreign Relations

The other premise of this chapter is that moderate orientations are rooted in domestic politics. Moderate orientations are not simply strategic or tactical moves, nor are they tied to specific personalities. Rather, they are deeply entrenched within the domestic political system. Moderate beliefs (as well as hard-line ones) are a relatively permanent and shared characteristic of contending political groups, factions, or parties. Therefore, policy decisions reflect views that are relatively fixed across the ruling groups' tenure in power, and it may well be that these views have been in place long before a critical policy outcome; for example, the outbreak of war or the formulation of a peace settlement. But this is not to say that nothing is subject to change. The competition between moderate and hard-line policies is the outcome of deeper processes. Vasquez (1993) identifies one of these: learning from the experience of war. Added to this, from our political perspective, is the outcome of the competition between contending groups whose rise to power may be due to issues unrelated to international affairs, such as economic recession, legitimacy crises, and domestic political failure, all of which shift the support bases of rising and declining groups. In short, the rise—and fall—of moderate rulers is part of the larger domestic political process.

Once in power, though, groups adhering to moderate orientations are subject to domestic pressures that may lead them to distort moderate policies as depicted above, that is, by forcing withdrawal from international commitments or by creating pressures for unilateral or nationalistic actions to contain opposition. The magnitude of political pressures on foreign policy makers is a function of the strength and intensity of the oppositions. Domestic challenges to foreign policy can emerge from either of two political arenas reflective of the two ruling imperatives of building policy authority and retaining power (see Hagan 1993). Gauging opposition pressures requires information about, first, the extent to which authority within ruling institutions is fragmented among contending political groups and, second, the degree to which the ruling group faces organized opposition from other political groups in the wider arena.

At one level, the ability to pursue a moderate foreign policy is dependent on the fragmentation of authority across contending factions, parties, or institutions within the state structures. Ranging from the most cohesive to the most fragmented, three basic political configurations are:

1. an unusually cohesive leadership group dominated by a predominant leader who suppresses policy debate;

2. a pluralistic leadership group in which authority is lodged in a single institution controlled by a single political group; and

3. a polarized coalition of autonomous actors in which authority is shared across different parties or institutions.

Following Snyder (1991) and also Hagan, Hermann, and Hermann (forthcoming), the first and third leadership structures are more prone to aberrant decision making and thus are likely to distort foreign policy orientations. The last structure creates the severest sort of constraint, the ability of opposing groups to authoritatively block foreign policy initiatives. Thus, when faced by isolationist opposition, leaders are unlikely to sustain the commitments necessary to sustain stable peace. But when opposed by hard-liners, they are likely, at a minimum, to be pressured into unilateral actions that enhance the state's prestige and assert influence. This is not, however, to say that the politically optimum situation is the opposite extreme of a highly cohesive decision group. Such a decision-making body may also be prone to take rash disruptive actions—that is, it may become insensitive to systemic imperatives and be driven towards the more extreme forms of the moderate orientations. The optimum situation is, instead, the middle structure, in which a single group retains authority and there is open discussion of foreign policy alternatives. The interplay of these constraints likely tempers more extreme forms of moderation and enhances sensitivity to systemic imperatives, but not to the extent of enabling one side or the other to create authoritative deadlock.

Moderation in foreign policy is also jeopardized if the leadership perceives itself to be vulnerable to being overthrown by opposition groups in the wider polity and, in turn, resorts to using foreign policy to retain public support and deflect oppositions (Levy 1988, 1989). Such opposition can take a variety of forms, ranging from rising opposition parties in the legislature and other representative structures to noninstitutionalized protest movements that threaten the very stability of the government. The government's ability to deal with that opposition also depends on the intensity with which it is expressed. The intensity of this opposition ranges across three levels: (1) opposition limited to relatively specific policy issues; (2) challenges to the overall program of the state leaders and for control of state institutions; and (3) rejection of the basic legitimacy of regime structures and the position of the national political elite (i.e., antisystemic opposition). As with debates within a single decision structure, public debate over foreign policy by oppositions serves a beneficial purpose in moderating opposition positions. But when a strong opposition challenges the entire ruling group or even the regime itself, politics moves from policy issues to questions of domestic political stability. In these situations, debates over foreign policy are distorted by larger questions about the regime's future. Moderation and the avoidance of even its extremes are likely sacrificed in the quest to retain political office.

Knowledge of the fragmentation and vulnerability of the leadership is not, however, a sufficient foundation on which to link these domestic pressures to foreign policy. It is necessary to understand how and with what strategy they respond to opposition. There is, in other words, no single dynamic by which domestic politics influences war proneness. Instead, leaders can choose among three political strategies to deal with domestic opposition in the foreign policy process:

1. *Mobilization: logrolling and diversionary strategies.* In using this dynamic, leaders deal with opposition by using confrontational political strategies in which they try to maintain or enhance support for their regime and its policies through forceful and prestigious actions in international affairs—in effect, the nationalistic card.

2. *Accommodation and deadlock: bargaining and controversy avoidance.* Leaders in this scenario attempt to accommodate opposition by restraint in foreign policy, either through policy compromise with others in the government or by avoiding actions that the public is likely to perceive as controversial.

3. *Insulation: deflecting, suppressing, and overriding opposition.* While the other two scenarios indicate strong—though opposite—effects on foreign policy, the essence of this strategy is that leaders insulate foreign policy from policy pressures. This is done by deflecting domestic pressures by ignoring opposition challenges, suppressing opponents, or co-opting them with political favors or concessions on other policy issues.

Moderation in foreign policy is best served by insulating policy from nationalists and hard-liners who oppose self-restraint and cooperation with the other powers. Arguably, some bargaining and controversy avoidance might be helpful in generating options that enhance the government's recognition of systemic imperatives so long as key commitments are not undercut. In contrast, any form of the mobilizing strategy is likely to disrupt moderate relations. Logrolling by the regime, even among pro-moderate elements, is likely to reduce flexibility in moderate diplomacy. Meanwhile, any diversionary strategy will involve unilateral and assertive actions that, while impressing domestic audiences, will clearly raise questions about the acting government's restraint in world affairs.

In sum, two domestic political conditions undercut the ability of a moderate leadership to sustain the self-restraint and cooperation necessary to obtain and maintain stable peace. One is strong and intense opposition to the regime. The other is a highly fragmented regime, which is not likely to be able to resist the pressures to insulate the commitments and restraints of moderation necessary for cooperative relationships. Whatever the political strategy adopted by a leadership, either accommodation or mobilization, the effect will likely be dramatic—respectively, deadlock in which the state withdraws from key commitments or the assertion of the nation's power in a way that starkly questions its willingness to operate with concert-based diplomacy. Even in a milder form, playing the nationalistic card at any level is likely to undercut understandings that characterize stable peace. Stable peace, in other words, requires two features: first, relative domestic political stability; and, second, a clear aversion to playing the card of nationalism. Only then can the moderate orientation of all powers be implemented in a sustained manner.

The Domestic Political Roots of the Concert of Europe, 1815–1854

The defeat of Napoleon (for a second time) and the Congress of Vienna not only ended nearly twenty-five years of general war in Europe but also constructed the basis for stable peace among the great powers. Relations among the great powers were governed by a carefully crafted political equilibrium that was itself sustained by consensus and bounded by law and treaties (Schroeder 1994a).[5] European politics did not, in other words, degenerate into the balance of power politics that had dominated the eighteenth century among the same set of aristocratic powers. Thus, instead of reverting to zero-sum balance of power tactics, the Vienna Congress, first, created a settlement perceived by all great powers as fair and legitimate and, second, established norms by which traditional conflicts were resolved by consensus and collective action rather than by the unilateral use of military force. Domestic political factors were central to this restraint and cooperation, but not simply because these powers were ideologically similar.[6] What was really new was the change in the ruling elites' attitude towards the use of force against each other. Whereas eighteenth-century elites believed that war enhanced state power, nearly twenty-five years of war had taught them that "war *was* revolution" (Schroeder 1994a). These ruling groups now perceived a common interest in resolving international disputes through accommodation, because war would provoke revolutions at home. From a domestic political perspective, the key to stable peace was that all great power leaders were moderate in their orientation to international relations and, furthermore, were willing and able to contain domestic oppositions challenging their moderate policies.

This section's analysis surveys the domestic conditions between 1815 and the 1850s in each of the five great powers: Russia, Austria, Prussia, France, and Great Britain. Based on a larger survey of the domestic political histories of the great powers since 1815 (Hagan 1999), I examine three aspects of domestic politics in each great power:

1. the orientation of their ruling groups during this period, noting in particular when moderate leaders came to power;

2. the domestic political mechanisms that sustained moderate policies by enabling moderates to retain power and implement their policies without concessions to the opposition, calling for either hardline policies or extreme forms of moderation;

3. changes in ruling groups and domestic political conditions by the 1850s–1860s, at which time stable peace had collapsed with the Crimean War and the Wars of German Unification.

This is not another attempt to tell how domestic politics influenced great power diplomacy during these decades. My point is far more basic— namely, that domestic political conditions contain the competitive international relations (including the threat of war) that typically underlie great power relations.

Russia

Not unlike Stalinist Russia at the end of the Second World War, imperial Russia emerged from the Napoleonic Wars having turned back a foreign invader, liberated much of central Europe, and occupied the capital of the defeated empire. Yet, despite this military power and the domestic demands to insulate Russia from European commitments, the two autocratic czars during this period—Alexander I (1801–1825) and

Nicholas I (1825–1855)—were willing and politically able to engage Russia in cooperative postwar diplomacy.[7] For Alexander I this was not simply a restoration of the status quo. From the time of his ascension to power, Alexander's complex blend of autocratic, liberal, and increasingly mystical thinking led him to seek the role of arbiter among powers and take the lead in reconstructing a new system of European authority based on cooperation among legitimate autocratic governments. Nicholas I was also preoccupied with the threat of revolution, although he had a more "conservative and defensive view of the West than his brother" (Lincoln 1978, 109). Stressing the themes of "autocracy, orthodoxy, and nationality," Nicholas I remained committed to an active and cooperative foreign policy based on the shared legitimacy of monarchical regimes in Europe.

Active, cooperative foreign policy was facilitated by the czars' ability to insulate foreign policy from both conservative and liberal opposition, either of which could argue the merits of a more nationalistic and/or isolationist foreign policy. Alexander I, despite earlier sympathy to some constitutional authority, consistently repressed opposition at the center of authority, while Nicholas I abandoned any pretext of reform after coming to power in the midst of the liberal Decembrist uprising. But equally significant is that neither czar used foreign policy to mobilize support for the regime by manipulating nationalism at the cost of great power relations. Rather, both regarded the regime's legitimacy as tied to the survival of monarchical rule throughout Europe. In short, the otherwise controversial foreign policy of restraint and cooperation was facilitated by both czars' strategy of avoiding any reforms that would increase participation and repressing any opposition. However, this political stagnation ultimately proved the undoing of their foreign policy by the defeat in the Crimean War. Viewing the defeat as a result of Russia's failure to modernize, Czar Alexander II (1855–1881) introduced wide-ranging domestic reforms. Ironically, these reforms undercut Russia's commitment to the Concert of Europe. They required that Russia turn inward to deal with domestic affairs, while also loosening autocratic politics enough so that Alexander II found it difficult to insulate foreign policy from the rising demands of Slavic nationalists (see Geyer 1987).

Austria

Although diplomatically at the center of the Vienna settlement, the Austrian Empire was in a far weaker and more defensive position in 1815 than the other great powers (except for Prussia). This fact was recognized by the conservative Habsburg leadership under Francis I and Ferdinand II and by their chief diplomat, Metternich, who was in power for the next three decades.[8] Like other monarchies, Austria's identification with the other powers stemmed from the lesson that war created conditions for revolutions against the monarchical system. Although tied to Metternich's personal horror of revolution, this conservatism originated with Francis I's ascension to the throne in 1792 and his reversal of the enlightened reforms of Joseph II and return to the traditional aristocratic roots of Habsburg authority. Austria's postwar moderation (i.e., abandonment of its militant eighteenth-century diplomacy) was further defined by its repeated defeats by Napoleon's armies, the last of which removed those who sought to reform and mobilize Austrian nationalism and brought Metternich to power in 1809. Key to his diplomacy was achieving a political equilibrium that not only removed liberal threats to the Habsburg political order but also contained the threats to Austria posed by Russia and France. Although originally accommodating even Napoleon, the same logic underlay a moderate Austrian foreign policy *after* the war—that is, creation of a set of cooperative international norms and multilateral settlements that would protect Austrian interests. Hardly based on the idealism that informed Alexander I's postwar designs, Metternich's creative diplomacy was grounded in a pessimism—a "dissolution complex"—about the future of Austria domestically and internationally.

Metternich's accommodation with other powers also rested on domestic political realities within the Habsburg monarchy until the 1848 revolution, including constraints on *his* desire to use force to suppress liberal movements abroad. Most immediate was the fragmentation of governing authority, notably the power of the finance affairs minister, Kolowrat, who controlled domestic affairs and could restrict funding of the military and foreign interventions. In addition, Francis I's relaxation of centralizing reforms revived the influence of the local aristocracies and regional economic interests, thereby undercutting economic reforms at home and free-trade arrangements abroad. Finally, for at least three decades, Metternich was able to contain liberal and nationalist opposition throughout the empire. This policy created pressures that exploded with the 1848 revolutions that wracked not only Austria but also Hungary, Italy, and Germany. Although the Habsburgs suppressed the revolts (with Russian assistance), Metternich and other leaders were replaced by a new leadership under a new monarch, Franz Joseph, with a new chief minister, Schwarzenberg. This new leadership sought to revive the Austrian Empire by creating a presumably more efficient "neo-absolutist" system. Along with centralizing domestic reforms, this also involved the Austria's unilateral reassertion on the international scene, particularly in Germany. As with its humiliation of Prussia at Olmutz, the new leadership used hard-line diplomacy to prevent the decline of Austrian power in what they viewed as a competitive international system. This assertive diplomacy was also evident in Austrian threats towards Russia to intervene on the side of Britain and France in the Crimean War.

Prussia

Revolutionary France and Napoleon also had inflicted repeated military defeats on Prussia, and, like their Habsburg counterparts, the ruling Hohenzollern dynasty was alarmed by 1815 by its international weakness. Like Austria, Prussia did not revert to the realpolitik foreign policies of its eighteenth-century leaders such as Frederick the Great. After coming to power in 1797, Frederick William III continued a more relaxed absolutism, based on the support of the Junker aristocracy.[9] Although the severe defeats of 1806 led Frederick William III to tilt towards domestic reformers such as Stein and Hardenberg, the ideology and interests of the conservative monarchy shaped Prussia's position after the Napoleonic Wars. Liberal causes such as calls for a constitution and German nationalism were abandoned or curtailed, and Prussia reverted to a remarkably moderate—if not acquiescent—alignment with the other powers, especially with its Russian liberator. Furthermore, the Prussian monarchy identified with Metternich's fearful linkage of reform to instability (the reformers were gone from power by 1819) and deferred to Austria's leadership within the German Confederation. The domestic political basis for great power accommodation in Prussian foreign policy—and the avoidance of destabilizing war—changed little for the next four decades. Even after the shocks of the 1848 revolutions and Frederick William IV's temporary tilt towards liberal nationalism, Prussia quickly resumed deference to Austria and maintained a passive foreign policy until the end of the 1850s.

Yet decades of passivity in foreign affairs ultimately did not prevent political change. Not only did Hohenzollern diplomacy acquire substantial territory in 1815 (including the well-developed Rhineland) but also postwar politics allowed expansion of Prussian economic interests via the German Customs Union. The result was that by the 1850s Prussia was a substantially more powerful player, and this was recognized by modernizing factions in the monarchy. Led by Crown Prince William, these factions also favored reasserting Prussian power, particularly after the humiliation of Olmutz inflicted by Austria's Schwarzenberg during the 1848 revolutions. Major political changes were set into play in 1858 when Frederick William IV was declared incapacitated, and the future William I introduced subtle yet profound policy changes in modernizing Prussia's autocratic regime. First, he sought to restore the Prussian army, especially after its ineffectual mobilization during Austria's war in Italy in 1859. Second, the conservative William I agreed to adhere to the hitherto suspended constitution promulgated by Frederick William IV in the

1848 revolution. Yet, when elections were held, the relatively liberal parties gained control of the Reichstag, and a constitutional crisis ensued when the Reichstag refused funding for the military reforms. The crisis was contained by the appointment of Otto von Bismarck as chancellor; Bismarck broke the deadlock by emergency rule and then by military victories leading to German unification. This appealed to the nationalism of many liberals, but it marked a fundamental departure from the Vienna settlement by requiring a hard-line (albeit pragmatic) foreign policy driven by a ruling strategy that tied foreign policy closely to domestic political survival.

France

Although postwar France was widely assumed to be a revisionist power during this period, its remarkable feature was the moderation of its governments and their identification with the Congress system. Until the 1848 revolutions, French governments were controlled by monarchists who accepted the status quo and the imperatives of accommodation with the great powers.[10] This was especially true of the "moderate royalists" who accepted limited constitutional monarchy. The moderate royalist government of Louis XVIII identified squarely with the victorious great powers at the Congress of Vienna. Its highest priority internationally was to avoid an aggressive foreign policy that would provoke a great power invasion and, in turn, precipitate a domestic revolution. The ability of Louis XVIII to act with restraint, though, was compromised by the mounting opposition of the reactionary ultraroyalists, who increasingly dominated the government through the 1820s. Although they accepted the Congress system, they actually destabilized it by adopting the extremes of autocratic conservatism, such as suppression of domestic opposition, intervention against liberal change abroad, and eventually the use of foreign policy to gain prestige domestically. Yet the 1830 revolution soon ended ultraroyalist extremism and, after a brief outburst of republican nationalism, returned the moderate royalists to power in the "bourgeois monarchy" under King Louis Philippe and his parliamentary cabinets. Although relatively liberal on domestic affairs such as economic development, the new regime still resisted a nationalist foreign policy and adhered to a foreign policy of avoiding war and integrating France into the great power status quo.[11]

Unlike the revolution of 1830, the 1848 revolution transformed French politics, and the postwar moderation of French foreign policy ended with the election of the nationalistic and revisionist Louis Napoleon as the Second Republic's first president. At first, conservatives were able to restrain foreign policy ventures by controlling the legislatively based cabinet, but the coup d'état of 1851 (leading to the Second Empire) gave Napoleon III the political ability to restructure French foreign policy. To an extent, then, the reorientation of French foreign policy reflected Napoleon III's vague, opportunistic agenda challenging the Vienna settlement and promoting nationalistic change. Equally important, and in sharp contrast to the risk-averse ruling strategies of his predecessors, Napoleon III used foreign policy to mobilize public support for his fluid authoritarian regime. At first, this meant catering to conservative elements of French politics such as conservative Catholics. However, as the empire's base of support became more tenuous, Napoleon shifted to a riskier and more intensive use of foreign policy to appeal to the more liberal—and nationalistic—elements of the political spectrum. Reliance on this mobilizing ruling strategy, as much as his regime's revisionist foreign policy goals, ultimately trapped Napoleon III into war with Prussia and the destruction of the Second Empire.

Great Britain

What is striking about Great Britain, typically considered to be the image of liberal stability at home and pragmatism abroad, is that it was the *least* accepting of the postwar order established by the Vienna Congress.[12] Originally, the British cabinet was controlled by ultra Tories, who opposed further constitutional reform, had long suppressed dissent, and favored aristocratic interests. As one of the most reactionary governments in British history, it actually identified with autocratic regimes' fears of liberal change and revolution. Tory support for the Concert of Europe, as articulated by Foreign Minister Castleraegh at Vienna, actually dated back to the wartime diplomacy and postwar plans of Prime Minister William Pitt (the Younger). By the early 1820s, though, liberalizing trends in British politics began to undercut the moderation of British governments within the Congress system. The factional shift towards the liberal Tories by 1822 (with Canning as foreign minister) propelled Britain away from close cooperation with the other great powers. This not only involved withdrawing from regular conferences, but it also initiated what became a liberal political strategy: the use of foreign policy to mobilize public support at home by promoting human rights and liberal change abroad. This tendency was intensified by the liberalization of British politics with the First Reform Act and Whig party dominance throughout the 1830s, particularly under Foreign Secretary Palmerston, who held hard-line views of great power relations while manipulating liberal foreign policy themes to domestic audiences. Even when the now reformed Tories under Robert Peel returned (1841–1846) with a moderate foreign policy (under Lord Aberdeen), Britain's ability to cooperate with other powers (including liberal France) remained constrained by the vigorous public opposition by Palmerston and others promoting liberalism and British prestige.

By the mid-1840s, though, British politics became highly unstable. The Tory party collapsed over free trade, and the succeeding government was a fragile and fragmented coalition composed of defecting Peelites and a mix of liberal and conservative Whigs, including Palmerston as foreign secretary once more. With sharp divisions over domestic reform policies, strong pressures mounted for a liberal foreign policy as one of the few issues that could cement the coalition, something especially valuable for Palmerston's declining aristocratic wing of the party. While British foreign policy was constrained in earlier opposition to liberal France, the rise of the Russian threat in the Near East enabled Palmerston to blend his militant national security views with liberal themes on human rights. The Crimean War marked the culmination of these political pressures. Even though Palmerston was temporarily out of office, the British government during the crisis leading up to the Crimean War was hardly restrained and instead ignored Russian conciliation and escalated the confrontation to war. Victory in that war, though, did not enhance Britain's posture vis-à-vis the other great powers. Although Palmerston emerged more popular than ever, the war itself was unpopular and left much of British leadership and the public quite averse to any future interventions. That, along with the prolonged reform crisis leading to the Second Reform Act (1867), marked a sharp swing away from a politically driven, militant orientation to an excessive moderation premised on a withdrawal from continental commitments. Thus Palmerston and other hard-liners were hardly in a position to maintain the status quo at midcentury and, in particular, to resist the transformation of Europe under German hegemony.

By the late 1850s, then, the domestic political conditions for the Concert of Europe were eroding *in all of the great powers* and had entered into a spiral of decay that by 1870 transformed great power relations. The 1848 revolutions initiated this decay, especially in two of the five powers: the revisionist and nationalistic French Second Republic/Second Empire and Austria, where there was a neo-absolutist reassertion of imperial authority at home, within the German Confederation, and among the great powers. The Crimean War, although it involved mainly the two powers that did not experience revolutions in 1848, was an equally important disruption of the European Concert by domestic politics. Although originally an issue between a prestige-seeking France and a resistant Russia, the Crimean crisis was escalated repeatedly by Britain's weak Whig coalition, whose hard-line elements played upon public nationalism and liberalism. The outcome of the war hastened political decay further. Not only did the defeated Russia turn inward under the reformist Alexander II, but also the British government was constrained and soon dominated by moderate and antiwar elements within the emerging Liberal Party. These changes, then, set the context in which political changes in Prussia and decay in Austria could drive unification of Germany. In direct response to Austria's humiliation of Prussia by Schwarzenberg, William I asserted Prussian power within Europe and, in doing so, raised nationalism to mobilize domestic support for his conservative regime. Ultimately, there was little to deter Prussia from redrawing the map of Europe. In fact, by the mid-1860s, all of the other powers faced the culmination of extended political crises: Alexander I's liberal reforms in Russia, the *Ausgleich* creating Austro-Hungarian dual monarchy, party realignments and the Second Reform Act in Britain, and Napoleon III's liberalization of the Second Empire in France. The implications of these changes were not limited to permitting changes in the 1815 map of Europe. They also set into play new hard-line political dynamics—ones keyed to a competitive balance of power as well as to the appeal of nationalism.

Conclusion

This chapter has argued that domestic political conditions—essentially moderate rulers and political stability—must obtain in all key powers if stable peace is to be sustained at the systemic level. This is not an entirely new argument, and the contribution attempted here has been to delve more deeply into these political dynamics in a sequence of two analyses. The first explicated some of the problematic aspects of sustaining moderation, noting in particular extreme forms of moderation as well as domestic political pressures and leadership strategies that may result in foreign policies that undercut commitments and trust underlying stable peace. The second analysis examined domestic political conditions in each of the great powers during the Concert of Europe after 1815 until its collapse in the 1850s. Although this analysis did not attempt to trace the direct link between domestic politics and foreign policies, three sets of insights emerged from it.

First, at the creation of the Concert of Europe, the governments of all of the great powers were controlled by groups that had long adhered to moderate orientations recognizing the need for restraint in foreign affairs and the imperative of great power cooperation. This was true for both relatively liberal governments (Britain and France) and rigidly autocratic ones (Russia, Austria, and Prussia). It also held for weaker powers (Austria and Prussia), the flanking hegemons (Russia and Britain), and even for revisionist France. These moderate beliefs were well entrenched. In part, they reflected lessons learned from the horrors and defeats of the

French Revolutionary and Napoleonic Wars. But domestic components were critical here as well. Not only did governments view wars as precursors to domestic revolutions, but also the rise of moderate groups occurred well before 1815 and reflected a general reaction not only against liberal groups but also against nationalists seeking to modernize the monarchy.

Second, various domestic political mechanisms operated to preserve moderation in foreign policies throughout the life of the Concert of Europe. This partly had to do with political stability reflected by continuity in leadership and containment of revolutionary unrest. But other political factors were equally important. The extremes of moderation (e.g., antiliberal interventions) were avoided because of domestic constraints within monarchies (as in Austria) or by the removal of such leaders (e.g., the overthrow of the ultraroyalists in France). Similarly, hard-line leaders were also constrained, as evidenced in internal opposition to Palmerston's policies in earlier Whig governments and the quick removal of hard-liners in France (e.g., Thiers in France). But more striking about "revisionist" France is that moderate royalists (Louis XVIII and Louis Philippe) not only adhered to the Concert system but also consciously avoided the temptation to strengthen their regimes through playing the popular nationalistic card.

Third, the collapse of the stable peace involved the decay of these political conditions in *all* of the great powers by the 1850. Most of these changes were actually less dramatic and nonstructural. In only one case—France's Second Republic/Second Empire—did political change involve a revolution leading to a new regime with a new ruling group in power. Other cases involved more subtle leadership changes: the emergence of vulnerable coalitions in Britain, modernizing factions in the Prussian and Austrian monarchies, and the reformist government in Russia. Furthermore, some domestic political crises amplified hard-line tendencies and drove the aggressive policies of the most disruptive players. Note, for example, the decay of Whig rule in the midst of liberal and conservative realignment in Britain, the constitutional crises in Bismarck's Prussia, and ultimately the ambiguous patchwork of support in Napoleon III's ill-defined empire. Yet, other political crises also operated in the opposite direction, by forcing *withdrawal* from European affairs or by signaling political weakness and constraint. Indeed, by the critical 1860s, all powers but Germany had turned inward to cope with major reform crises and were either inviting targets (France and Austria) or were politically unable to intervene.

Taken together, the pervasive effects of domestic conditions—across countries and time—should be evident as a key element of the origins, persistence, and demise of the moderate orientations that underlay stable peace. Admittedly, international events and pressures drove these political dynamics of stable peace in Europe after 1815. Postwar moderation was learned mainly from the devastation of war (albeit with a strong domestic connection), while abandonment of Concert norms was in response to the hard-line policies of others—for example, William I's reassertion of Prussian power, Alexander II's withdrawal of Russia from a moderate foreign policy, and antiwar sentiment within the emerging Liberal Party in Britain. Yet, in other cases the shift to hard-line policies and the reinforcing domestic pressures were an outcome of prolonged domestic crises. Revolutions in Austria and France were obviously driven by political groups that no longer could be suppressed. The domestic realignments in Britain and Germany, which Palmerston and Bismarck sought to manage through coalition politics, were also essentially domestic. These political changes, as well as their deeper origins, point to the importance of the domestic sources of stable peace.

Notes

1. This analysis is part of a larger project on rulers and oppositions in the great powers from 1815 to the 1990s. While the analysis here concerns stable peace, this is not to dismiss periods of extended peace between 1870 and 1914 and 1945 and the present. Those periods do not qualify as stable peace because both were characterized by competitive great power relations with the threat of war and well-defined adversaries. I would point out, however, that the political bases of these periods of peace were different from that of the 1815–1854 Concert of Europe. Elsewhere I show that only during this period (with the possible exception of the post–Cold War era) did all great powers have relatively moderate, stable political systems. For a full overview of domestic political and great power relations, see Hagan 1999.

2. This idea lies at the heart of domestic political analyses of international conflict (Vasquez 1993; Levy 1983; Schweller 1994; and Kupchan 1995) and the "cultural" explanation of the democratic peace (e.g., Dixon 1994; Russett 1993; Wright 1942).

3. Vasquez (1993) is the clearest in conceptualizing contending positions and linking them to war proneness, but see also Snyder and Diesing (1977) on soft-liners and hard-liners. Useful U.S. foreign policy studies include those by Holsti and Rosenau (1984) on elite belief systems, Gaddis (1982) on alternative strategies of containment, and Yergin (1977) on the hard-line shift from the Yalta axioms to the Riga axioms in the origins of U.S. Cold War policies. Note that I have replaced Vasquez's term "accommodationalist" with the term "moderate."

4. The initial documentation of this can be found in Hagan 1999.

5. In addition to Schroeder's exhaustive study, I have drawn background material on the Concert of Europe from studies by Craig and George (1990); Bartlett (1996); Bridge and Bullen (1980); and Gildea (1987).

6. In effect, while in the past, domestic political unrest in another power was seen as simply weakening that power, after 1815, leaders perceived unrest as a transnational phenomenon that would spread across their own borders and threaten their own hold on power (see Bridge and Bullen 1980).

7. Judgments on Russian leaders and oppositions were based on, first, European political histories by Gilbert et al. (1971); Craig (1961); Droz (1967); Grenville (1976); and, second, Russian political histories found in Acton (1995); Riasanovkty (1984); Westwood (1993); Seton Watson (1967); Rogger (1983); Saunders (1992); and Lincoln (1978).

8. Judgments about Austrian leaders and oppositions are based on, first, the European surveys by Gilbert et al. (1971); Craig (1961); Droz (1967); Grenville (1976); and second, Austrian political histories in Jelavich (1987); Kann (1974); Sked (1989); Macartney (1968); May (1951); and Berenger (1997).

9. Sources used for identifying rulers and oppositions in Restoration Prussia and afterwards include, first, chapters in the European surveys by Gilbert et al. (1971); Craig (1961); Droz (1967); Grenville (1976); and second, Prussian political histories in Fulbrook (1990); Blackbourn (1997); Craig (1978); Holborn (1969); Ramm (1967); Carr (1991); Sheehan (1989); and Koch (1978).

10. Judgments about French rulers and oppositions are based on, first, the European surveys by Gilbert et al. (1971); Craig (1961); Droz (1967); Grenville (1976); and, second, on French political histories by Bury (1949); Furet (1992); Jardin and Tudesq (1973); Harvey (1968); Magraw (1986); Price (1993); Tombs (1996); and Wright (1995).

11. Also note that when republican elements went too far, as in the case of the Thiers government in the 1840 Near East crisis, the response from the monarch was clear-cut: immediate dismissal and the appointment of a more conservative government.

12. Judgments about British leaders and oppositions are based on, first, the European surveys by Gilbert et al. (1971); Craig (1961); Droz (1967); Grenville (1976); and, second, British political histories by Williams and Ramsden (1990); Speck (1993); Briggs (1959); McCord (1991); Evans (1906); Lee (1997); and Thomson (1950).

3

The International, Regional, and Domestic Sources of Regional Peace

Benjamin Miller

During a visit to Washington in the summer of 1996, former Israeli prime minister Benjamin Netanyahu declared to the U.S. Congress that democratization in the Middle East is a prerequisite for regional peace (*Haaretz*, July 11, 1996). Similarly, the head of the Israeli Nuclear Committee gave a talk in 1997 in which he suggested that Israel would be able to make nuclear concessions only following democratization in the Arab world (*Haaretz*, May 23, 1997, p. B5). Both were implicitly drawing on the democratic peace theory that claims that democracies do not go to war against each other, and therefore a community of democratic states ensures peace.[1] This theory has inspired the Clinton administration's policy of "enlargement," designed to expand the world's "community of market democracies" (Gowa 1995, 511 n. 1). President Clinton asserted that this strategy serves U.S. interests because "democracies rarely wage war on one another" (Gowa 1995, 511 n. 2).

Is promoting democratization indeed the best way to advance regional peace, particularly stable peace? Or is such peace more likely to be achieved through strengthening the regional states? Are the key factors for regional peace to be found in the global system? If so, what kinds of global forces are most conducive to the emergence of regional peace? This chapter will address these questions.

This chapter will investigate three sources of regional peace.[2] Two of the sources are at the regional/domestic level: strong regional states and domestic liberalization. The third source is at the global (systemic) level: great power involvement in the form of a great power concert or hegemonic stability. Although only the first two sources lead to consolidated stable peace, the third contributes to peace stabilization and thus creates the opportunity for the evolution of stable peace later on. The three sources are deduced from the global–regional debate on the causes of regional war and peace. The two regional sources are also derived from

55

the debate on democratization versus strengthening the state as the preferred approach for producing regional peace and security. I will propose a solution to both of these debates by differentiating among three levels of regional peace (cold, normal, and warm) and relating each of the three factors to a specific level of peace that it is expected to bring about. The proposed theoretical framework will integrate the regional and international perspectives on regional peace by establishing causal linkages between different causes of regional peace and the emergence of different levels of peace.

I will argue that the international mechanism can bring about only a relatively low level of peace (i.e., cold peace). This level of peace is not stable peace because the option of war is not ruled out, even though the likelihood of resort to force declines considerably for the near future. But cold peace can be conducive to a growing effectiveness of the regional/domestic-level sources of peacemaking, starting from the method of regional conflict resolution resulting in normal peace. Normal peace, in turn, is conducive to liberalization and therefore to the emergence of the highest degree of stable peace, warm peace. As I suggest elsewhere, three regions exemplify the three types of regional peace addressed here.[3] The peace between Israel and Egypt since 1979 is an example of cold peace. This cold peace was extended to the relations between Israel and the Palestinians and Jordan following the end of the Cold War, the U.S. victory over Iraq in the Gulf War (February 1991), and the convening of the Madrid conference in the aftermath of this war (October 1991). South America during most of the twentieth century is an example of a more stable type of regional peace, normal peace (Holsti 1996; Kacowicz 1998). A major illustration of the highest degree of stable peace, warm peace, is the evolution of the relations among the Western European states, most notably France and Germany, since the 1950s.

Theoretical Background: The International–Regional Debate

The question of the sources of regional peace is closely related to the debate on the relative influence of international/global versus regional/domestic factors on the evolution of regional conflict and cooperation.[4] The systemic or "outside–in" logic suggests that it is impossible to understand regional dynamics without focusing on the broader international context within which regional orders are embedded, taking into account the influence of external pressures and incentives working vis-à-vis the region. Indeed, in the modern interconnected world there can be no completely self-contained regions, immune from external pressures (Hurrell 1995a, 46–58).

Thus, the systemic/neorealist approach argues that the international environment shapes, constrains, and disposes the behavior of the regional actors (Waltz 1979). Because of the unequal distribution of capabilities in the international system and the dependence of small states on the great powers, small states have to adapt to the international environment created by the great powers and to the dominant type of interaction among them. Regional conflicts and their violent manifestations are caused by the political, economic, and cultural frictions fostered by the great powers.

According to this logic, the Cold War and its bipolarity have brought about numerous regional conflicts from the late 1940s to the mid-to-late 1980s. At the same time, international developments such as U.S.–Soviet cooperation under Gorbachev and later U.S. hegemony have determined regional patterns since the late 1980s.

Conversely, regional or "inside-out" perspectives suggest that regional states respond in the first place to local factors and developments because this is the most important environment that affects their security interests. According to this approach, the most immediate neighbors, rather than remote global powers, are the most critical actors in the foreign security agenda of small states. The regional environment creates the most direct external threats and opportunities for states (Wriggins 1992, 9). The regional argument is that regional dynamics have a high degree of autonomy from international developments (Doran 1992; Pervin 1997). To the extent that the global arena exercises influence, it is mediated by attributes of the region such as the degree of intensity of regional disputes and their characteristics (Buzan 1991, 214–15; Ayoob 1995). Thus, regional actors use great power assistance for their own goals that are unrelated to the global agenda. Regional dynamics are shaped by patterns of relations (notably, those of amity and enmity), the nature of the regional conflicts (ideological, territorial, nationalist, hegemonic, security dilemma), and by the domestic attributes of the local states (democratic or authoritarian, state–society relations, state-building, nation-building, regime stability, and elite security).[5] A group of neighboring states forms a "regional security system" by virtue of intense interaction among them.[6] These interrelationships are so consequential for the regional states that the behavior of any one of them is a necessary element in the calculation of the others. Such high security interdependence is frequently characterized by conflict (Buzan 1991, 193–94; Ayoob 1995, 57; Vasquez 1993). Analysts of regional security must concentrate on conflict patterns and processes unique to specific regions rather than assume that the causes of local conflicts can be attributed to the machinations of Cold War adversaries or ex-colonial powers or to the structure of the international system.

While this debate refers to international versus regional influences on regional peace in general terms, I will show that the regional/domestic perspective subsumes two different (and even competing) mechanisms for establishing and maintaining stable peace: liberalization and conflict resolution based on strengthening of the regional states. The debate with regard to these two regional/domestic-level mechanisms will be discussed in the following sections. From the global perspective one may deduce that the way to promote regional peace is through great power involvement in the region in the form of a concert of powers or the stabilizing hegemony of a single power. Thus, this study specifies three distinctive (although not mutually exclusive) roads to regional peace: great power engagement, strengthening the regional states, and democratization.

The Theoretical Framework: Differentiation of Outcome

One of the ways to compare the three mechanisms for regional peace is with regard to the degree or level of peace they bring about. For this purpose, I distinguish among three major ideal types or levels of peace: cold peace, normal peace, and warm peace. Cold peace is not stable because there is still a danger of resort to force. Warm peace is the most stable—the likelihood of war is the lowest. Normal peace is fairly stable, though somewhat less so than warm peace. The differences among these types of peace, and their degrees of stability, are summed up in table 3.1.

Cold peace refers to a situation of an absence of war and of threats of force among the regional states. The underlying issues of the regional conflict are in the process of being moderated and reduced but are still far from being fully resolved. Thus, the danger of a return to the use of force still looms in the background in case of changes in the international or regional environment. Regional wars may break out again owing to international changes in the global balance of power or the type and degree of great power regional involvement. In one or more of the regional states there exist significant revisionist groups hostile to the other states, and thus the potential coming to power of opposition groups in these states may also lead to a renewed resort to violence.[7]

There are formal agreements among the parties, but their relations are conducted mainly at the intergovernmental level, and there are strong limitations to transnational activity that involves nongovernmental players. There are still contingency plans (manifested in such factors as force structure, defense spending, training, types of weapons, fortifications, military doctrine, and planning) that take into account the possibility of war among the parties. Military force is not used in the current relations between the parties, even for signaling and show-of-force purposes. Rather, the focus is on using diplomatic means for conflict reduction, that is, a conscious attempt at further moderating the level of the conflict through crisis-prevention regimes and negotiations.[8] However, these fall

Table 3.1 The Ideal Types of Regional Peace

Indicator	Cold Peace	Stable Peace	
		Normal Peace	Warm Peace
Main issues in conflict	Mitigated but not fully resolved	Resolved	Resolved or transcended (rendered irrelevant)
Channels of communication*	Only inter-governmental	Mostly inter-governmental; beginning of development of transnational ties	Intergovernmental and highly developed transnational ties
Significant revisionist groups	Present	Possible	Absent
Contingency plans for war	Still present	Likely in case of rise to power of revisionist elites	Absent
Possibility of return to war	In case of international or domestic changes	In case of domestic changes	Unthinkable

*Although some may see channels of communication as independent variables, my analysis suggests that they are dependent variables, resulting from the three independent sources. Thus, e.g., in warm peace, both the possibility for transnational ties and their effectivenesss depend on the presence of liberal democracy in all the regional states.

short of full-blown reconciliation, and there is still a danger of the use of force in the longer run despite the formal diplomatic relations between the parties.

Normal peace is a situation in which the likelihood of war is lower than in cold peace because most, if not all, of the substantive issues in conflict have been resolved. More specifically, regional states recognize each other's sovereignty and there is an agreement on such issues as boundaries, resource allocation, and refugee settlement.

This level of peace is more resilient and stable than cold peace and may be expected to endure changes in the global environment. But war is still not completely out of the question in case of a change of elite or domestic regime in one of the key regional states; namely, the rise to power of revisionist elites. The relations among the states begin to develop beyond the intergovernmental level, but the major channels of communication and diplomacy are still at the inter-state level.

Warm peace is a situation in which regional war is unthinkable in any scenario of international or regional change. Even if some issues are still in dispute among the regional states, the use of force is completely out of the question as an option for addressing them. There is no planning for the use of force against each other and no preparation of appropriate capabilities for war fighting among them. Instead, institutionalized non-violent procedures to resolve conflicts are in place. These procedures are widely accepted by all the elites in all the regional states. None of the major political groups, in government or in opposition, that is likely to come to power in the foreseeable future in any of the relevant states is likely to return the relations to cold peace, let alone war. The regional states tend to form "a pluralistic security community." "They have come to agreement on at least this one point: that common social problems must and can be resolved by processes of 'peaceful change,'" that is, "the resolution of social problems, normally by institutionalized procedures, without resort to large-scale physical force."[9]

The relations among the regional parties include intensive transnational transactions alongside intensive intergovernmental and transgovernmental exchanges. The transnational relations take place in a multiplicity of areas and include completely open borders, a high degree of economic interdependence, a dense network of regional institutions, intensive people-to-people interactions, and tourism and widespread cultural exchange.[10]

Three Sources of Regional Peace

From the international/regional debate I will deduce three major sources of regional peace: two are regional/domestic, while the third is international (global, systemic). In order to go to war, regional states need both motivation and capabilities to do so. Moreover, it is the illegitimacy of the regional order that provides a motivation for war and therefore makes certain regions more war-prone than others.

There are two basic interrelated differences among the sources: whether they focus on capabilities or motivations of the regional states for war, and how the problem of regional legitimacy is addressed in each. First, let me introduce briefly the concept of regional legitimacy, which provides a coherent way to differentiate among the three sources. *Legitimacy* implies a belief in the validity or bindingness of an order (Milner 1993, 152). It has two components: normative and cognitive. The normative element refers to the *desirability* of the order and to a consensus that its moral value is consistent with the fundamental values of the participants. The cognitive component is the members' belief in the long-term endurance or *feasibility* of the existing order.[11] The legitimacy of the inter-state regional order includes: (1) acceptance of the legitimacy of the other regional states; (2) acceptance of their boundaries; and (3) agreement on their relative status, especially the identity of the regional hegemon, or leader.

Illegitimacy of the regional order is an underlying cause of regional wars, and to the extent that such regional illegitimacy is present, it makes certain regions more prone to wars than others. This is due both to the emergence of substantive issues of conflict (territories and boundaries) and to the enhancement of the security dilemma and power rivalries in the region under conditions of illegitimacy.[12] Thus, addressing the legitimacy issue may reduce the likelihood of war in a certain region.

The international source of peace (great power hegemony or concert) does not resolve the problem of regional illegitimacy. At best, it moderates the level of the conflict short of establishing regional legitimacy. The regional source of peace (conflict resolution) confronts the question of legitimacy directly and puts it at center stage. Finally, the domestic source (liberalization) transcends the issue of legitimacy by aiming at a radical change in the domestic character of the actors and their objectives.

One advantage of the international source of peace is that it can deal effectively with the *capabilities* of the regional actors to go to war. The regional balance of power depends heavily on external support, notably arms supply by great powers. As a result, great powers can constrain the regional ability to resort to force by imposing limitations on local military capabilities and by constructing an effective arms control regime. The regional/domestic approaches may address more effectively the *motivations* of the actors, either by changing those motivations directly related to the causes of regional wars (through regional conflict resolution) or by transcending the causes of such wars by transforming the domestic attributes of the regional actors themselves, as a result also radically changing their motivations regarding peace and war (through domestic liberalization).

Consequently, the big advantage of the regional/domestic sources is that they can establish and consolidate stable peace, whether normal or warm, whereas the international mechanism can at best bring about cold peace. Regional mechanisms are also less dependent on the continuing engagement of external powers in the region. Yet, the prerequisites for the success of the regional/domestic mechanisms are very demanding and sometimes extremely hard to reach. At the same time, to the extent that the conducive global conditions exist, they can be helpful in advancing peaceful regional settlements, even if only cold ones. These cold regional settlements may, in turn, lead to the success of the regional/domestic mechanisms for advancing stable regional peace.

The Normative Dimension of the Three Sources of Peace

The international source of peace is informed by norms related to the primacy and leadership of the great powers (the "great responsibles") in the international society. The great powers have special status, privileges, and "rights" to have a voice in the settlement of regional disputes, but they also have responsibilities for promoting international order, peace, and stability.

The norm of great power primacy differs markedly from the norms informing the regional source, which underline especially a respect for the sovereign equality of all states, irrespective of their size and capabilities.[13] Other major norms of the regional approach include a respect for the territorial integrity of other states and the sanctity of boundaries and nonintervention in the internal affairs of other regional states.[14] These norms point to the *regional* conflict resolution mechanism of peacemaking, which does not involve a special role for external powers.

In contrast to the regional norm of nonintervention, liberal norms are closely related to the *domestic* nature of the regional states. The liberal approach is based on democratic institutions and respect for human rights and civil liberties. Noninterference in domestic affairs applies only to fellow liberal states; there is a moral imperative to intervene in defense of human rights in illiberal states that infringe on the rights of their citizens.[15] Another normative difference between liberalism and the regional approach is that in liberalism the Wilsonian norm of national self-determination is superior to the norm of maintaining the territorial integrity of existing states, especially if these states are not liberal democracies.[16]

The International Sources of Peace

The international mechanism of great power regional involvement may be divided into two variants or modes, both of which are conducive to the advancement of cold regional peace: a great power concert and the hegemony of one power.[17] While there are important differences between these two modes, they are broadly similar in terms of their effects on regional peace, and therefore for the purposes of this chapter may be viewed as two variants of a single mechanism.

A concert refers to cooperation among a group of more or less equal great powers in resolving international conflicts, both among themselves and among third parties, and thereby making possible peaceful change.[18] Indeed, in a concert, in Hedley Bull's formulation, the great powers "join forces in promoting common policies throughout the international system as a whole" (Bull 1977, 225). To this end, the great powers hold regular discussions to define common objectives and determine how best to achieve them. The emphasis in a concert is on *multilateral* consultation, decision making, and action by the great powers with respect to the diplomatic agenda.

In principle, a concert should include all the great powers of the day. In contrast to this approach, which emphasizes cooperation among several powers, the hegemony proposition draws on the hegemonic-stability perspective.[19] This perspective, deriving from collective goods theory, suggests that the production of such common goods as peace and stability requires the presence of a single hegemon that is both able and willing to lead. The leader sees itself as a major long-term beneficiary of regional peace and is also able to shape and dominate the regional environment. For this purpose, the hegemon provides a flow of services and benefits to the small states that include diplomatic "good offices"and "honest brokerage," or mediation, as well as security guarantees, construction of arms control and crisis-prevention regimes, and deterrence and compellence of military aggressors. Leadership and mediation by a single broker should be more effective than that by several great powers, even if they concert their actions, because transaction and information costs are lower.[20] All in all, a single dominant country will be better able and more willing to provide these goods than a number of comparatively equal powers, which are more likely to compete among themselves for regional influence than cooperate to ameliorate regional disputes.

In either a hegemony or a concert, the hegemon or the great powers are likely to be *willing* to invest in regional conflict reduction and to effect a transition from a state of war to cold peace for two major reasons: the intrinsic importance of a region, and a shared threat. A distinction has to be made between different regions according to their standing in the great powers' balance of interests. Intrinsically important regions, whose value for the great powers stems from major material resources and also from geographic proximity to the powers, will draw great power involvement and attempts at stabilization.[21]

A major factor that enhances the willingness of the great powers to engage in promoting conflict reduction is the presence of a shared threat both to the great powers and to the status quo regional states on the part of an aggressive revisionist power or weaker regional states with divisive ideologies.[22] The presence of such a shared threat will motivate the powers to invest considerable resources in forming and leading a countervailing coalition, in deterrence and compellence of the aggressor, and also in a more general brokerage of disputes among the regional states.

As for the great power *ability* to stabilize the region, a hegemon or a great power concert is able to prevent local wars and to advance regional peace, albeit a cold one, in regions vital to the great power interests through four interrelated strategies:[23]

1. *Mediate and reduce* the level of the basic regional conflict and thus
   encourage or impose a cold peace. A hegemon or a concert can help
   the local states overcome the collective goods problem by being
   able and willing to pay disproportionate costs for achieving regional peace by providing valuable services as an honest broker. The
   great powers can serve as mediators able to employ powerful pressures and incentives that no other potential mediator can offer.[24]

2. *Guarantee* regional arrangements. The powers can guarantee a
   regional settlement and serve as final arbiters in case of disagreements among the parties about its interpretation. Concerns about
   the potential reactions of the powers will motivate the regional parties to adhere to the agreement and to follow its rules and procedures. Thus, the enforcement of the cold peace is more reliable
   under a concert or a hegemony.

3. *Reassure* local states and reduce their security dilemmas by the
   extension of security guarantees, preferably manifested in a regional deployment of their troops.[25] Peacekeeping forces of the great
   powers can separate the regional parties, minimize the prospects of
   clashes, and deter any offensive inclinations on their part. In the
   absence of trust among regional actors, the military presence of
   external powers helps to overcome the security dilemma and the
   mutual fears. Such a presence reassures the regional parties that the
   great powers will minimize the chances for blackmail, surprise
   attacks and preemptive strikes, hostile alliances, and arms races
   among the local parties by penalizing the violators of agreements
   and settlements (Waltz 1979, 70–71; Mearsheimer 1990).

4. *Deter* and contain potential aggressors and restrain aggressive
   local clients intent on wars of expansion by imposing diplomatic,
   economic, and, if necessary, military sanctions. Unlike a situation
   in which several great powers compete for regional influence, in a
   concert or hegemonic involvement the small states do not have a
   realignment option (Miller and Kagan 1997). As a result, the great
   powers need not worry about losing their clients. The client states,
   for their part, have less maneuvering room and are unable to
   escape the great power restraining pressure.

The main problem with the international mechanism for regional peace
is that it is unable by itself to proceed beyond cold peace. It is beyond the
capabilities of external powers to resolve problems of regional legitimacy
or induce domestic liberalization if the regional states themselves are

unwilling to undertake these tasks. Thus, a concert or a hegemony is unable by itself to resolve the underlying issues in conflict and to bring about stable peace in the region. The presence of revisionist regional states decreases the likelihood that normal or warm peace will emerge and that the threat of local war will be completely removed from the region's long-term agenda. Concerns about their own domestic legitimacy will lead authoritarian regimes to obstruct transnational relations among the regional states, preventing the development of warm peace.

Moreover, the cold peace is not expected to survive changes in the great power regional involvement. Thus, potential problems with the international mechanism include the powers' difficulty in sustaining domestic support for a long-term and costly regional engagement because of public demands to focus on internal affairs. Another danger is the collapse of the concert or the hegemony due to international rather than domestic factors. Changes in the global balance of power, due to a weakening of the hegemon's power or a rise in its competitors' capabilities, may lead to the loss of the hegemon's capacity to stabilize the region, because revisionist local states will be able to receive support from the hegemon's international competitors. The expectation of realist balance of power theory is, indeed, that any hegemony will be at best temporary because new great powers will rise or a counterhegemonic coalition will be formed. According to this theory, long-term hegemony is not feasible because of the effective functioning of the equilibrium mechanism that results in the recurrent formation of balances of power.[26] Balance of power theory also expects great powers to compete for influence in different regions rather than cooperate in joint peacemaking efforts.[27] As a result, a concert is also regarded by this theory as, at best, a short-term phenomenon that is likely to disintegrate into great power rivalry (Mearsheimer 1994/1995; Kagan 1997, 8). Another possibility is that in the absence of hegemonic leadership, the great powers may act as "free riders," that is, disengage from peacemaking efforts, rather than attempt to provide the collective good of regional peace.[28] As a result, cold regional peace is likely to collapse and even revert to war.

To sum up, while the great powers can be helpful in promoting regional conflict reduction, so long as they and not the local parties play the critical role in the peacemaking process, this process will amount to no more than a mitigation or moderation of the dispute, namely, a cold peace. It will fall short of a full-blown indigenous reconciliation among the local parties. Moreover, the durability of the cold peace depends on the strength and continued presence of the powers in the region. A collapse of the concert or the hegemon or their disengagement from the region may bring about a decline of the cold peace and a possible return to war.

Regional and Domestic Sources of Peace

Regional Conflict Resolution and State-Building Lead to Normal Peace. The regional and domestic sources suggest that rather than relying on external powers, the regional parties should focus on directly addressing the problems of regional legitimacy through negotiation and conflict resolution. More specifically, to advance regional legitimacy the parties should settle the substantive issues in dispute among them; for example, they should recognize all the other states in the region, agree on acceptable boundaries, resolve problems of refugees, and negotiate a fair division of scarce resources such as water. The resolution of all these issues should be informed by the major norms of the regional approach mentioned above.

Resolving the major problems of regional legitimacy will lessen the motivations of the regional states for going to war and thus will markedly reduce the likelihood of the outbreak of the major types of regional wars: security-dilemma wars, profit wars, and diversionary wars.[29] With regard to security-dilemma (or inadvertent) wars, in accordance with the logic of the conflict resolution mechanism, legitimacy of the regional order accounts for regional variations in the intensity of the security dilemma. When regional legitimacy is high, the intensity of the security dilemma is lower, and it is less likely that mutual fears of being attacked and preempted will dominate the relations among the regional states and potentially lead to war.

Problems of regional illegitimacy also provide substantive issues for wars of profit or expansion—namely, boundaries, territory, and struggle for hegemony. The resolution of such problems will directly reduce the likelihood of wars of profit. Diversionary wars, on the other hand, result from problems of domestic illegitimacy. According to the diversionary, or scapegoat, theory, these wars reflect an aggressive policy that arises out of domestic political weakness and insecurity of the ruling elites, who externalize domestic conflict and instability to strengthen their hold on power (Levy 1989; Lebow 1981; Snyder 1991). Thus, a resolution of regional legitimacy problems will not directly address this kind of war. Yet, diversionary wars are more likely under conditions of regional illegitimacy: it is much easier for an insecure elite in an unstable regime to initiate war in a region in which there is a low level of regional legitimacy, since such low legitimacy provides ready pretexts for war. Moreover, the enhancement of regional legitimacy will strengthen local states and increase their domestic stability by resolving destabilizing secessionist problems. Thus, mutual recognition and the acceptance of boundaries strengthen the regional states internally as well as externally, increasing the stability of their political regimes.

The relationship between stable and strong states and regional legitimacy is a complex one. While advancing regional legitimacy strengthens local states, its achievement is heavily dependent on the prior presence of stable regimes and strong states in the region. State strength, which is a separate concept from the realist notion of state power or capabilities, has three main dimensions: (1) the effectiveness of state institutions; (2) the level of identification of the citizens with the state; and (3) the firmness of the territorial identity of the state, namely, the extent of acceptance and permanence of its boundaries in the eyes of its neighbors and domestic groups. The latter two dimensions are interrelated and are the two most relevant for regional war or peace. A low level of citizen identification and a lack of firm territorial identity may result in attempts at secession and border changes that may spill over and involve a number of regional states, possibly resulting in war. Conversely, the stronger the states on these two dimensions, the greater the likelihood for normal peace.

To boost regional legitimacy, a mechanism of state building is necessary. Thus, the mechanism of conflict resolution may also be called the "statist" method, because it gives priority to strengthening the state and consolidating its power over separatist groups. This should be done by monopolizing the instruments of violence in the state's hands, namely, disarming the secessionist groups and maintaining the state's territorial integrity (Ayoob 1995, 182–84).

The state of normal peace is similar to what Buzan calls "a highly developed anarchy" (1984, 121). In such a situation "mutual recognition and respect among the units would be a major feature. Units would accord each other recognition as political equals, and boundaries amongst them would be fixed according to some set of common principles derived from factors such as race or nationality or geography. Ideological differences might be quite profound, but there would be agreement on political non-interference in each other's affairs" (121).

Conflict resolution will bring about a state of normal peace that will survive international changes in the global balance of power or in the type and degree of great power regional involvement. Yet, it cannot preclude a return to war if aggressive revisionist elites come to power in one or more of the key regional states, or if new substantive conflictual issues arise among the regional states.

The main problem with this approach is its feasibility in conflict-prone regions with deep-seated animosity among neighbors. Will neighbors with a long history of rivalry be able to overcome by themselves such a legacy of mutual fears and suspicion, and will they be able to agree on issues like boundaries, on which they have incompatible positions? The problem is especially difficult in regions populated by states that are considered illegitimate by some of their neighbors. Another major difficulty is the weakness and lack of firm territorial identity of many states, manifested in the presence of national/ethnic minorities that claim the right to exercise self-determination, establish their own states through secession, or be annexed to a contiguous state dominated by their ethnic kin (irredentism).[30] This tension is especially severe in some parts of the Third World and in the Balkans, owing to the artificially drawn postcolonial boundaries of the states and the arbitrary allocation of peoples and territory to states in these regions.[31] In some instances, postcolonial states are composed of distinct and sometimes hostile ethnic groups; in others, previously homogenous ethnic communities are divided between two or more states. Most regimes in Africa and the Middle East have faced major domestic legitimacy problems because they preside over artificial colonial constructs that are very vulnerable to internal challenges. Thus, most new Third World states have faced problems of either secession or irredentism soon after independence (Ayoob 1993; 1995, 34–35; Buzan 1991; Holsti 1996). This situation poses severe problems for conflict resolution mechanisms; as noted, achieving regional legitimacy is dependent on strong states, but in the absence of such legitimacy, it is difficult to achieve state building. In other words, state building is least feasible where it is most needed.

A related challenge to the conflict resolution mechanism is presented by powerful (although not domestically strong) revisionist states that claim to have historical/national/ethnic rights to control territories belonging to their neighbors. Domestic instability in these revisionist states produces additional incentives for externalizing internal conflicts and thus for the use of force against proximate states, which are not always able to deter such aggressors and defend themselves against them.

Another problem with the conflict resolution mechanism is that strengthening the regional states to advance regional legitimacy may be opposed to democratization. Although a democratic regime can be very helpful for strengthening the state in the long run, for the short run, democratization may further weaken a weak state and bring about its disintegration. For this reason, the conflict resolution/state building mechanisms give priority to consolidating state power over domestic groups at the expense of, and as a prerequisite for, democratization. Thus, liberalization and regional conflict resolution/state building constitute distinct and competing approaches to regional peace.

Domestic Liberalization Leads to Warm Regional Peace. Partly in response to the difficulties of the conflict resolution approach, the liberal approach argues that the best mechanism for achieving stable regional peace is not to focus on the substantive issues that are in conflict between the parties but to transcend them by following liberal prescriptions. In other words, the best way to reach peace is by liberalization—namely, democratization and a transition to free market and free trade—and by establishing effective regional institutions for collective security and arms control, regional economic integration, and cooperation in other issues of common concern, such as the environment. Another method for strengthening peace, according to this approach, is through advancing transnational contacts among nongovernmental groups and encouraging people-to-people ties through tourism and cultural exchange. Thus, this approach differs markedly from, and goes much beyond, the governmental, state-to-state character of the regional conflict resolution mechanism. Indeed, regional integration and transnational contacts might be seen by nonliberal, nationalist elites as posing a threat to their states' independence and autonomy, which is a mainstay of regional "normal" peace according to the conflict resolution/state building approach. In contrast to the focus of the conflict resolution/statist approach on noninterference in the domestic affairs of other states as a prerequisite for peace, the liberalization approach welcomes interference in the domestic affairs of nonliberal regional states to promote human rights, democratization, and transition to a market economy.

The cornerstone of the liberal approach is democratization, and all the other elements (free-market economies, regional institutions and integration, and transnational ties) only ensure warm peace once the regional states become liberal democracies. The great advantage of the liberal mechanism is manifested in the empirical record of the lack of fighting among liberal-democratic states.[32] Even if substantive conflict issues remain unresolved among liberal democracies, they do not resort to force. As a result, stable warm peace will be established in a region populated by liberal democracies. Indeed, the states in liberal-democratic Western Europe have established a warm peace among themselves in the post–World War II era.

The shortcoming of this approach is the demanding political and socioeconomic prerequisites for successful democratization (see Huntington 1991). For this mechanism to work, all the major regional states have to become stable liberal democracies. A major precondition for a stable democracy is the existence of a strong state, as defined above (Rothstein 1992; Ayoob 1995, 195). One of the obstacles to successful democratization and the emergence of a stable democracy is the presence of an intense ethnic conflict in divided societies (Diamond and Plattner 1994, xiv). Yet, these are precisely the places where the supposedly pacifying effects of democratization are most needed, not only because of domestic ethnic conflicts but also because of the close relations between such conflicts and regional conflicts due to the spread of ethnic groups across existing borders, especially in the Third World and the Balkans.

Another major problem with the liberalization mechanism is that, as noted, in the short term democratization may increase domestic instability and provide insecure elites with incentives to pursue the scapegoat strategy by initiating diversionary wars. Indeed, Mansfield and Snyder

(1996) show that at least until all the regional states become full-blown liberal democracies, the process of democratization itself may encourage the use of force and thus aggravate regional conflicts. Elites left over from the old regime compete for political power among themselves and with new democratic elites. One of the major strategies available to all these elites for gaining mass support is appealing to nationalist feelings. Once nationalism is aroused, leaders have a hard time controlling it in democratizing states, which tend to lack effective institutions. A nationalist public and belligerent pressure groups may push for a militant policy and restrict policy elites' freedom to maneuver. Especially bellicose are interest groups from the old regime that benefit from imperialism, military expansion, and war (Mansfield and Snyder 1996, 303, 315–31).

Democratization can increase citizens' identification with their state and thus strengthen regional states in the long run. However, in the short term democratization in fragmented societies, notably in Africa and some other parts of the Third World and the Balkans, may not solve social cleavages but may exacerbate existing ethnic problems (De Nevers 1993) and even embolden ethnic minorities to oppose openly their national boundaries and seek self-determination and secession.[33] One major route to democratization is federalism—decentralization of political power along territorial lines. In weak states, a loose federal system may reinforce separatist forces by guaranteeing them assets that they can employ for the secessionist cause, such as local police forces and government revenues (Holsti 1996, 184–85).

In other cases, democratization may weaken moderate/status quo regimes and elites that are the key to regional peace processes and make it more difficult for them to make concessions to longtime adversaries. Through an appeal to nationalist and religious emotions, a domestic opposition may use these concessions against the moderate elites and undermine their political base of support. Democratization may also bring to power radical forces that oppose regional reconciliation, such as fundamentalist Islamic forces in the Middle East.

Thus, democratization may bring about the disintegration of the regional states or the intensification of ethnic and regional conflicts or both, at least in the short term. If there is a stark choice between maintaining the state's territorial integrity and democratization, state elites are bound to prefer the former (Ayoob 1995, 182–84). At the same time, the historical record shows that in the absence of democratization, other liberal prescriptions such as economic interdependence, free trade, and regional institutions may not be sufficient by themselves to ensure regional peace (Mearsheimer 1990, 1994/1995).

Thus, the major challenge presented by the liberalization mechanism is finding how to dampen the short-term negative effects of democratization so as to arrive at stable liberal democracies and warm stable peace in the longer term. One possibility is to combine the liberalization mechanism with the international mechanism of great power involvement. The great power hegemon or a concert of powers may then prevent regional wars and maintain cold peace and thus allow the liberalization process to develop and ripen into warm peace. This was indeed the road to peace in post-1945 Western Europe.

Conclusion

To sum up, there is a trade-off between the regional and the international mechanisms for advancing regional peace. While the regional and domestic devices are more desirable than the international in that they are conducive to stable regional peace in the long term, they are less feasible, as problems of regional legitimacy are hard to resolve and liberalization depends on demanding prerequisites. In contrast, the international mechanism is more feasible, but it is unable by itself to go beyond cold peace and produce stable peace. Yet, as noted, the international method, when combined with liberalization, may fulfill an important role in achieving warm peace. The two regional and domestic mechanisms are also distinctive, and there are trade-offs and contradictions between them, notably with regard to strengthening or democratizing existing states and regimes and also with regard to the role of governments versus transnational actors in the peacemaking process. The conflict resolution/statist approach focuses on maintaining the traditional international norm of noninterference in the domestic affairs of other states, while the liberalization approach acknowledges the necessity to subordinate this norm to emerging transnational norms of democratization and human rights, which are seen as the most effective guarantees of a lasting peace (see Baker 1996, 563–71).

While the three levels of peace have been described as analytically distinct, they may also be regarded as successive stages in a regional peace process, with each stage conducive to the next. Thus, great power involvement (either in the form of concert or hegemony) is conducive to a cold regional peace, in which the substantive issues in conflict and the problems of regional legitimacy have been moderated or reduced but are still far from fully resolved. This progress may encourage the local elites to show the flexibility needed to proceed towards the resolution of the major legitimacy issues in conflict and thus the establishment of stable peace, first as normal peace. Normal peace is, in turn, conducive to a domestic liberalization of the regional states. As a recent study shows, democratization in Scandinavia and North America was preceded by the achievement of normal peace that quelled the rivalry among the states for regional hegemony

(Thompson 1996). International threats reinforce the power of antidemocratic forces in the domestic politics of states involved in a protracted conflict. In contrast, a moderation in the level of external threats reduces both the necessity and the pretext for the repression of democratic opposition (Gurr 1988). Such an environment is also conducive to a growing trust among the regional states, allowing for the establishment of regional institutions and the development of transnational relations and thus the evolution of stable warm peace.

Notes

The author would like to acknowledge the advice and comments on earlier drafts of Avi Kober, Avraham Sela, Uri Bialer, Elie Podeh, Norrin Ripsman, Gregory Gause III, Peter Katzenstein, Alfred Tovias, Joe Lepgold, Zeev Maoz, Galia Press Bar-Natan, Ram Erez, Boaz Atzili, Oded Lowenheim, Magnus Jerneck, Ole Elgström, Yaacov Bar-Siman-Tov, Arie M. Kacowicz, and especially Korina Kagan. The author is grateful for the generous financial assistance of Israel Science Foundation (founded by the Israel Academy of Sciences and Humanities), the Jaffe Center for Strategic Studies at Tel Aviv University, the Israel Foundation Trustees, and the Leonard Davis Institute for International Relations at the Hebrew University of Jerusalem.

1. For a recent comprehensive treatment, including evidence, explanations, refinement, and critiques of this theory, see the collection edited by Brown et al. (1996). For a recent critique, see Gowa 1995.

2. This chapter draws on a theory of regional war and peace presented in Miller 1999a; 1999b; 1999c; forthcoming.

3. For an empirical application to these three regions, see Miller 1998.

4. For a useful distinction between outside-in and inside-out approaches to regional orders, see Neumann 1994. On the international–regional debate, see Brecher 1963; Binder 1958; Russett 1967; Young 1968; Wriggins 1992; Väyrynen 1984, 1986; Doran 1992; Pervin 1997; Buzan 1991; Job 1992; Ayoob 1995; and Katzenstein 1996.

5. See Migdal 1988; Ayoob 1995; Barnett 1992; Job 1992; and David 1991.

6. See esp. the excellent discussion in Wriggins 1992, 3–13.

7. On revisionist versus status quo orientations of states' foreign policy, see Wolfers 1962; and Schweller 1994.

8. On crisis-prevention regimes, see George, Farley, and Dallin 1988; and Bar-Siman-Tov 1995, 34–39.

9. Deutsch et al. 1957, 5. See also Rock 1989; and Adler and Barnett 1998a.

10. On intergovernmental, transgovernmental, and transnational relations, see Keohane and Nye 1972; 1977.

11. This definition is cited in Miller 1995, 100. The classical analysis of legitimacy is Weber 1978, 212–16. The definition here draws on the discussions of foreign policy legitimacy in George 1980 (235) and of international legitimacy in Ikenberry and Kupchan 1990 (52–55). On legitimate order, see Kissinger 1964 and its critique in Hoffmann 1980, cited in Miller 1995, 275 n. 23. The extent of legitimacy of the regional order is related to the concept of satisfaction with the status quo, as developed by Kacowicz (1998).

12. For an analytical development of the causal linkages between regional illegitimacy and various paths to regional war, see Miller 1999a; forthcoming.

13. On the contrast between the norms of great power primacy and sovereign equality of states, see Klein 1974.

14. On the content of these norms in the context of the post-1945 Third World, see Jackson 1990; and Ayoob 1995, chap. 4.

15. See Doyle 1997, 388.

16. On self-determination in liberal thought, see Kegley 1995, 11; and Zacher and Matthew 1995, 115.

17. For more extended discussions of the relationship of a concert or hegemony and cold regional peace, see Miller 1999c, 1999d. On these two modes, as well as two other modes of great power regional involvement that are not conducive to promoting peace (competition and disengagement), see Miller and Kagan 1997. On the relationship between these two mechanisms and theoretical realist perspectives, see Miller 1996.

18. See Clark 1989, 121, 126–27. On a great power concert, see Jervis 1983; 1986; Kupchan and Kupchan 1991; and Miller 1994; 1995, chap. 4.

19. For overviews of this perspective and references to key works, see Nye 1990; Levy 1991; and Miller 1992, 1996.

20. On these types of costs, see Keohane 1984; and Oye 1986.

21. For the importance of different regions to the great powers, see Miller and Kagan 1997.

22. In contrast to a unifying ideology, a divisive ideology does not respect the autonomy and legitimacy of other like-minded states. Divisive ideologies include communism, hypernationalism, and fascism. Liberal democracy is the major example of a unifying ideology in the post-1945 era. See Walt 1987; and Rock 1989.

23. The ultimate expression of regional hegemonic order is what Buzan (1991, 198) calls "overlay."

24. On third-party conflict management, see Wallensteen 1991; and Dixon 1996.

25. On the concept of reassurance, see Stein 1991.

26. See Rosecrance 1986, 56–58; Layne 1993, 5–51; and Waltz 1979, chap. 6.

27. On the differences between the balance of power, concert, and hegemonic perspectives, see Miller 1992; 1996.

28. On the sources and effects of great power disengagement from regional conflicts, see Miller and Kagan 1997.

29. On these types of wars, see, e.g., Miller 1999a; forthcoming.

30. See, e.g., Diamond and Plattner 1994, xv. This reflects the tension between two contradictory principles of legitimacy or competing international norms: the territorial integrity of existing (especially postcolonial) states and the right of self-determination of ethnonational groups irrespective of current boundaries. The regional variant of the society-of-states perspective, which informs the conflict resolution strategy, gives priority to maintaining the territorial integrity of existing states over the right of self-determination.

31. See Ayoob 1995, 48; Buzan 1991; Jackson 1990; Job 1992; Kacowicz 1998; and Holsti 1996.

32. For explanations and critiques, see Russett 1993; Doyle 1997, part 2; and Brown, Lynn-Jones, and Miller 1996.

33. See Ayoob 1995, 182; Chipman 1993; Holsti 1996; and Kacowicz 1997, 16.

4

Pieces of Maximal Peace:
Common Identities, Common Enemies

John M. Owen IV

Only in a universal *association of states* . . . can . . . a true *condition of peace* come about. But if such a state made up of nations were to extend too far over vast regions, governing it and so too protecting each of its members would finally have to become impossible, while several such corporations would again bring on a state of war. So *perpetual peace*, the ultimate goal of the whole right of nations, is indeed an unachievable idea.
    —Immanuel Kant, *The Metaphysics of Morals* (1797)

Perpetual peace is often advocated as an ideal toward which humanity should strive. With that end in view, Kant proposed a league of monarchs to adjust differences between states. . . . But the state is an individual, and individuality essentially implies negation. Hence even if a number of states make themselves into a family, this group as an individual must engender an opposite and create an enemy.
    —G. W. F. Hegel, *Elements of the Philosophy of Right* (1821)

This allegedly nonpolitical and apparently even antipolitical system [the League of Nations] serves existing or newly emerging friend-and-enemy groupings and cannot escape the logic of the political.
    — Carl Schmitt, *The Concept of the Political* (1932)

The horrible wars of the twentieth century, and the possibility that the worst is yet to come, imposed a norm on most people whose countries participated in those wars. Whereas in 1914 many saw war as a good thing, it is now understood that war is bad and peace is good. This norm pervades most scholarship on international relations and is so powerful that it need never be stated. A corollary would seem to follow: if peace is good, then robust peace, perpetual peace, must be better. Especially in the nuclear age, it is assumed, we should all hope and work for a world in which the set of states among which war is unthinkable is as large as possible, to the point that it comprises the entire globe.

The assumption that the more robust the peace the better derives from the unstated premise that peace is an entirely positive phenomenon, one that involves the elimination, rather than the displacement, of violent conflict. In this chapter I make the uncomfortable argument that, insofar as "maximal peace" is constituted or caused by a common identity among the states it comprises, this premise is false. A common identity necessarily coexists with a common "other." Thus, when two states enter a relationship of maximal peace, they simultaneously enter a conflictual relationship with a common enemy. An enemy is not a state per se but rather a political ideology that is *transnational*, that is, one that has the potential of capturing more than one state. Maximal peace, in other words, understood as involving a common identity, *displaces rather than eliminates conflict*. Two conclusions follow. First, maximal peace entails costs as well as benefits and should not be pursued or expanded uncritically. Second, there can never be a global maximal peace.

In this chapter I argue the following. First, the relationship between maximal peace and common identity to which several scholars in the stable peace program appeal is a necessary one—that is, that a common identity should be seen either as part of the definition of maximal peace or as a necessary cause thereof. Second, there is likewise a necessary relationship between a common identity and a common other, namely, the former cannot exist without the latter. Third, in politics self and other are divided according to a vision of societal order. Thus a common *political* identity X requires a common "enemy" Y, that is, an entity that would negate one's vision of societal order. Neither X nor Y is a state or coalition of states per se but is rather a transnational ideological movement that can capture one or more states. Fourth, global maximal peace could only obtain when all states are threatened by the same viable transnational enemy, and such a situation would be unstable. Finally, the development of a robust peace among one group of states is likely to generate a group of enemy states. Robust peace involves not simply the elimination of violent conflict among certain actors but also the introduction of the possibility of such conflict with other actors.

Common Identities and Maximal Peace

For many researchers in the stable peace program, the highest form of peace (which I shall call maximal peace) is related to a common identity. The contributors to this volume conceive of peace among sovereign states as being of several types, falling along some sort of axis ranging from minimal ("precarious peace" for George, "cold peace" for Miller, "negative peace" for Kacowicz) to some maximal state ("stable peace" for

George, "warm peace" for Miller, and "pluralistic security communities" for Kacowicz). For each, this robust peace is defined at least in part as one in which the possibility of war is so remote that no state considers it in its interactions with the others. George stops at this minimal definition. Others, however, follow Deutsch et al. (1957) and Boulding (1978) in introducing other properties into robust peace. Kacowicz's pluralistic security communities comprise states with an "identifiable common identity." Miller's warm peace is stablest when the societal and normative values among the states are compatible; although Miller does not use the term, common identity is implied insofar as the two states understand that they hold a set of values in common. Elgström also implicates images of self and other in the quality of peace among states. Without excessive distortion, then, we can say that several researchers posit a relationship between robust peace and common identity, and that common identity has to do with values.

These scholars do not state explicitly whether the relationship between common identity and maximal peace is logical or contingent. That is, they do not assert that a common identity is part of the definition of maximal peace rather than a cause of it. Yet, as they present these concepts, it is difficult to imagine a common identity among states without maximal peace, or vice versa. Maximal peace must be more than the simple absence of war as a possibility in the thinking of statesmen, else Iceland and Mongolia would be in such a relationship; hence the appeal of most of these scholars to shared norms. At the same time, it is difficult to think of two states that perceive a common identity or shared norms at war or contemplating war; surely they would perceive divergent identities when they begin to consider using violence against one another. Only if it is conceivable that two states that share an identity would contemplate war against one another can a common identity be seen as unnecessary to maximal peace. The relationship is so close that the two would not seem to satisfy the "loose and separate events" condition required for cause and effect. In any case, the consensus would seem to be that the more robust the peace, the stronger the common identity.

Common Identity and a Common Other

If maximal peace does indeed require a common identity, then it becomes important to know what constitutes a common identity. "Identity" is a vague term, and nowhere more so than in the international relations literature. Identity as used here is a social concept, that is, one only has an identity in the presence of something that is other than oneself. The essential mechanism at work in identity formation is negation. A thing only gains a determinate identity in the presence of an opposite.[1] Therefore, a common identity requires, or coexists with, a common other.

Identity Formation

Spinoza's formula *determinatio est negatio* sums up how identities form. Hegel amplified the formula as follows. A thing comes into being only if it has qualities, such as "dark" or "northern." Something without qualities, something that cannot be described, lacks a determinate being. Qualities, however, are only known in contrast to other qualities (Taylor 1975, 232–39). There is no dark without light, no north without south. If an individual is to have an identity beyond merely "human being," in contrast to nonhuman beings (animals, plants, inanimate objects), he or she must also have qualities that distinguish him or her from other individuals. The inference is that personal identity is constituted by negation. Put another way, "identity" is from the Latin *idem*, or "same." No "same" is possible without a "different." Having a self requires having an other.[2] The implications of this negation thesis are enormous. We cannot treat identity in isolation but only as a set of qualities each of which has an opposite quality.

Social Identity

Obviously, persons identify with, as well as against, other persons; they expand the boundaries of "self" beyond their own persons. Two persons A and B will do this only in the presence of a third entity C that has a quality that contrasts with a quality that A and B share. If C is a dog, A and B identify with each other as human beings. If C is also a human being but A and B speak French and C does not, A and B will identify as Francophones. A and B will perceive nothing in common without some C that has at least one quality that A and B do not. Collective identities, in other words, form according to the same negation dialectic as individual identities. In industrial societies, to be on the political right means to hold roughly to a set of coherent views about the good society, but those views only come into being as negations of the views of the political left. It is literally true that if the right did not exist, the left would have to invent it. In fact, in trying to define themselves more precisely, right and left often do "invent" one another by exaggerating one another's extremism.

Three clarifications are necessary. First, identities do not reduce to one of two options. Persons have many qualities and thus multiple identities. A and B may identify against C in terms of language, but if A and C are European and B is North American, A and C will also identify with each other as Europeans. Thus identity is situational, although in politics one identity may come to dominate.

Second, the formation of a common identity does not necessarily entail altruism on the part of those who share that identity. In identifying with others, individuals do not have to agree to sacrifice their self-interests to those of the group. Rather, they see their interests as overlapping at least to some extent with those of the group. Whether they are right or wrong is a normative question.

Third, an individual who identifies with a group is not effacing his individual identity. That is, the individual does not necessarily come to believe that any conceivable gain to any member of the group is a gain to himself. Some types of gain may raise suspicions that others in the group have dubious intentions toward him. For example, a person who identifies herself as a citizen of a state may ordinarily believe her own utility is enhanced if national income rises by 2 percent in a year even if her own income is stagnant. She may change her mind if that experience is repeated over ten consecutive years. But simply because that possibility exists does not invalidate the assumption that that citizen normally identifies with her country.

Political Identities and Transnational Movements

Political Identities

Persons may identify with one another as Francophones, yet this common identity may have no political significance. How does a social identity become a political identity?

The answer turns on how politics is defined. Here I follow the common understanding of politics as having to do with governance, or how society is to be ordered. A Francophone identity takes on political significance when it becomes tied to societal order—for example, when Francophones begin to assert that they ought to have some role in governance *as Francophones*, or when non-Francophones assert the opposite. A political identity, then, contains a notion of legitimacy. It holds that a certain set of institutions, a certain ethnic group, a certain family, ought to govern or participate in governance.[3]

A political identity X is also, like any identity, relational: it only emerges in the presence of an opposite Y and is thus constituted by a struggle against that Y. Not only may no society be both republican and monarchical, but also republicanism and monarchism are defined as opposites. While the political identity X is threatened by Y, it simultaneously owes its existence to Y. That is, X intends to eliminate Y, but should Y disappear, X would follow. The same goes for Y vis-à-vis X; X and Y are mutually constitutive. In Greece in the fifth century B.C., "Greekness" and "barbarian-ness" were opposites. When the Persians tried to conquer Hellas and thereby eliminate Greekness, the latter became a political identity. As the Persian threat decreased, so did the political significance of Greekness. Those who wanted to prevent a war between Athens and Sparta tried to reanimate Greekness by reviving memories of the Persian enemy. They failed, but what is important here is that it was attempted at all: no political Persians, no political Greeks.[4]

The "elimination" of Y does not necessarily mean the killing or exile of individuals who identify as Y, but the elimination of their common "Y-ness." The Persians would have had to slay thousands of Greek soldiers, but their object was the elimination of Greek political independence, not of the people who at that moment called themselves Greeks. When identities X and Y are defined not only as mutually exclusive but also as permanent and unalterable, however, elimination can mean exile or even genocide. German National Socialism said that Jews by definition were not, and could never become, Germans; hence genocide (Mann 2000).

Yet, people have multiple political enemies and thus multiple, or at least multifaceted, political identities (Neumann 1996, 167). A liberal-democratic Westerner in the 1930s would tend to see both fascism and communism as an enemy; in fact, perplexity over which was the greater threat, and a wish that the two enemies would weaken each other, contributed to the West's indecision as to whether to tilt toward Germany or the Soviet Union. More fundamentally, one's nationality by definition is a political identity as well as is (in many countries) one's partisan affiliation, region, ethnicity, or religion. Why call one political identity more important than others?

The concern here is with common identities and enmities among sovereign states, so the only political identities of interest to us are those that become transnational. That does not imply that transnational political identity effaces national or other political identities. When the typical Russian, Pole, or Chinese became communist, he did not abandon his Russian, Polish, or Chinese identity (the assertions of socialist internationalism notwithstanding). Rather, he saw his national and transnational identities as complementary.

Liberals, who are normatively committed to tolerance, are no exception to the negation mechanism (Owen 1997, 29–30). Traditionally, liberals have attributed enmity to ignorance rather than to necessity. Tolerance has an opposite too—intolerance—and those who want a tolerant society necessarily define themselves in opposition to those who (they assert) do not. Those who allegedly do not favor a tolerant society are then intolerable to liberals: they must be converted or otherwise eliminated. For example, liberals typically consider a political party that favors replacing secular with religious law to be intolerant and intolerable; the political party replies in turn that liberal toleration is a sham. Similarly, liberals tend to believe that conflictual identities may be overcome by education. But Iver Neumann argues that this point is empirically problematic: "Normatively, it is an appealing thought that closer acquaintance makes for less othering, yet, it is simply an erroneous claim. Empirically, it is refuted by the work of a thousand anthropologists" (Neumann 1996, 166). In other words, liberalism does not replace politics. Rather, it constructs a new boundary between people and thereby new group identities: "tolerant" and "intolerant."

Negation in Political Science

The negation thesis is not new but haunts many classical treatises on international politics. Rousseau wrote that conflict inheres in the states system because each state "is forced to compare itself in order to know itself; it depends on its whole environment and has to take an interest in all that happens" (Rousseau 1991, 38). Hegel himself applied the thesis to international relations in his critique of Kant's "Perpetual Peace" (see second epigraph in this chapter).

Two twentieth-century realists, Carl Schmitt and Edward H. Carr, averred that collective or supranational identities may arise but that these may never become universal. Schmitt (1996) argued that the ultimate political act is to identify one's friends and enemies.[5] Politics was at bottom about setting or identifying boundaries. The League of Nations was for Schmitt not a universal, impartial league of peace but simply a superstate that created its own enemies, namely, those states dissatisfied with the status quo. Dissatisfied states were labeled "disturbers of the peace" rather than "enemies," but the League was in a state of war with them. The League was especially dangerous because in claiming to speak for humankind, it placed its enemies outside the bounds of humanity, thus implicitly justifying treating disturbers of the peace as inhuman.[6] Schmitt's contemporary Carr (1946) was famously critical of the League for a similar reason (its alleged utopianism), but he too thought that the post-1918 order pitted status quo against revisionist powers. Carr's solution to world order was a *Pax Anglo-saxonica*, a sort of Anglo-American hegemony.

More recently, Jonathan Mercer (1995) has applied ideas from the social psychology literature to international relations (IR) theory and concluded that constructivism does not provide a way to overcome the human need to divide ourselves into groups. A large number of experiments have confirmed that people divided into "minimal groups," or groups with no prior meaning, will favor their own group. Around these results, social psychologists have built social-identity theory and self-categorization theory, both of which posit that people need group identities. Although Mercer argues that two generic actors meeting in anarchical conditions will inevitably construct a norm of self-help, implying that collective identities cannot form, he acknowledges that France and Germany today have indeed moved to an "other-help" norm and that the European Union is building a supranational identity. His conclusion, however, is Hegel's: even if entities such as the European Union form, partially or wholly erasing the boundary between France and Germany, they necessarily build a boundary between themselves and the rest of the world.

Even the foundational texts of the stable peace literature are suffused with this negation dialectic. Boulding writes, "The only guarantees of peace are compatible self-images." Yet, self-images are at least to an extent produced by conflict: "Perhaps one reason for the biblical injunction to love our enemies is that they make us" (Boulding 1978, 17–18). Similarly, Deutsch et al. find that a necessary condition for the formation of security communities is "compatibility of the main values held by the political relevant strata of all participating units." These values are most effective when concretized into institutions, habits, and in general a "distinctive way of life." But "[t]o be distinctive, such a way of life has to include at least some major social or political values and institutions which are different from those which existed in the area during the recent past, or from those prevailing among important neighbors" (Deutsch et al. 1957, 46–48). Compatibility only emerges as the opposite of incompatibility.

Transnational Enemies

When two states have a common identity, they perceive some common quality. To say that two states have a common political identity is to say that they share a transnational vision of legitimate government and also that they share a transnational political enemy, the negation of their vision. Thus the important unit of analysis is not the state but transnational political norms.

Consider the change in the quality of relations among the Soviet Union, Great Britain, and the United States between 1942 and 1947. From 1942 until May 1945 these three states shared a common German enemy. Moscow, London, and Washington did not forget their political separateness, but a temporary collective identity formed as each found that it shared a crucial quality with the other: opposition to the Nazism that a hegemonic Germany was poised to impose upon their societies. Once Germany was defeated, the grand alliance began to fray, particularly between the Western powers and the Soviet Union. With the loss of the Nazi enemy, the differences between democracy and communism—differences that had hindered Anglo-Soviet cooperation in the 1930s—reappeared. At the same time, in spite of obvious differences in material interest, most states of Europe and North America coalesced according to type of internal regime.

The solidarity within the blocs cannot wholly be attributed to balance-of-power factors. The governments on each side felt threatened by the other's ideology as well as its weapons. In the late 1940s, the primary U.S. worry was not that a decimated Soviet Union would invade West Germany but that communist fifth columns directed from Moscow would subvert the regimes in demoralized West Germany, France, Italy, and elsewhere, moving these countries into the Soviet bloc (Leffler 1992, 496–97).[7] Throughout the Cold War, Moscow feared that any liberalization in Eastern Europe would lead its allies to defect from the Warsaw Pact. Thus, Khrushchev decided to invade Hungary in 1956 *before* Imre Nagy withdrew the country from the Soviet alliance.

Furthermore, as others have noted, balance-of-power theory would predict that some European states would switch alliances as the power balance between the superpowers varied. For example, when the United States opened up a vast "missile gap" between itself and the Soviet Union by the early 1960s, one or more NATO members should have defected to the Soviet side. Yet, no defections were ever attempted *except by states whose internal regime changed*. The closest to an exception was Yugoslavia, which after a late-1940s flirtation with the West settled on nonalignment. The Yugoslav and Chinese cases show that states of similar regimes do not always remain aligned, but these are exceptions to the rule.

From Transnational Enemies to Enemy States

If democracies and communist states were political enemies before they were threats to each other's physical security, and if the democracies and communist states thereby each held a supranational identity as democracies or communist states, how did they get that way? The process begins with two or more states in which there are parallel domestic political struggles. Such parallel struggles can lead to transnational identities and eventually the supranational identities that are the basis of maximal peace.

Subnational Identities. A supranational identity begins as a subnational identity, or group of individuals within a state who believe they have common interests. Every state contains individuals with conflicting ideas as to how best to organize common life. Like-minded individuals tend to coalesce into groups; equally important, groups tend to make individuals within them like-minded. The members of any such group, be it a political party, interest group, or some other collectivity, will perceive common political interests and will thus identify with one another to that extent.

Such groups typically also identify their own interests, and their group's interest, with the national interest; or, if they are revolutionaries or secessionists, with the interests of the nation-state they envisage. They do not perceive a tension between these interests: what is good for the group is good for the country and for themselves personally, at least in the long run. The national interest, then, is implicated in the question of domestic institutions. The members of a typical socialist party perceive personal, class, and national interests at stake in setting up socialist institutions.

Transnational Identities. For various reasons, such substate political groups often exist alongside like-minded groups in other states facing similar enemies. Like-minded groups may form spontaneously or in imitation, or a group in one state may create a counterpart in another state (cf. Starr 1991). Whatever the mechanism, groups in two states with similar internal goals for their states will then identify with each other and work for each other's success. The two will see themselves as part of the same group. In other words, a transnational identity will exist.[8] Thus if Venice and Florence are states and each has a Guelf and a Ghibelline faction, then Venetian and Florentine Guelfs will form a common identity, and so will Venetian and Florentine Ghibellines. Guelfs in one state will see the success of their fellow Guelfs in the other as implicating their own success; likewise for Ghibellines. Similarly, the Second International comprised the socialist parties of Germany, France, Great Britain, Russia, and several other states; each party perceived that its national interest lay in the progress of socialism in the other states and in general.[9] When the Soviet Union finally emerged, socialists in these other states sympathized with it.

Supranational Identities. Should the Guelfs gain control of Venice, the Florentine Guelfs will perceive that Venice is now an instrument of Guelfism. The Florentine Guelfs will perceive that the probability that they will gain control of Florence will rise with the successes of Venice; thus they will push their own state to be cooperative with Venice. Meanwhile, Venice will have an incentive to help the Guelfs gain power in Florence as well (Kaplan 1964, 106–21). Should Guelfs gain control of Florence, Venice and Florence will perceive a congruence of interests, in that each will see the successes of the other as furthering Guelfism in its own state. Venice and Florence will identity as Guelf states and enter a situation of maximal peace, whose basis is the existence of a common enemy, Ghibellinism.

Returning to Cold War bloc solidarity, Truman implemented the Marshall Plan to aid European recovery and offered Marshall aid to the Soviet Union and its satellites. But he knew that money was not enough to keep Western Europe in the American bloc. The regimes also had to be noncommunist. Stalin understood the same rule. He was not so foolish as only to make side payments to the governments of Eastern Europe or even to bully them with the Red Army troops stationed there. He was also compelled to ensure that dedicated communists took power in most states bordering the Soviet Union.[10] The regimes in Eastern Europe, North Korea, North Vietnam, and so forth shared a domestic, and transnational, enemy. Over the coming decades, Washington and Moscow were to expend vast amounts of blood and treasure trying to alter the internal institutions of states around the world. They knew that the identity of a state's regime mattered (Owen 1999).

In sum, one state may identify *with* another only in the presence of a third entity *against* which the two identify. Social construction can alter but not eliminate boundaries. Boundary shifts occur in two stages. First, substate identities become transnational when individuals in two or more states identify the same actual or potential domestic enemy (when Venetian and Florentine Guelfs form "Guelfism," and Venetian and Florentine Ghibellines form "Ghibellinism.") The system comprising Venice and Florence will then have a quality analogous to the "cross-cutting cleavages" with which students of comparative politics are familiar: one cleavage will be between Venice and Florence, the other, between Guelfism and Ghibellinism. Transnational identities become supranational when Guelfs gain power in both states and the two identify themselves as Guelf states.

The Enemy Must Be Real

It is fair to ask at this point why states with some common identity X could not have as their enemy some abstract Y that has captured no states or even persons. Fukuyama's end-of-history thesis (1991) implies that this is possible for liberal democracies now that all competitors to that regime have all been routed.[11] If so, the emergence of maximal peace among some states would not imply enmity with another entity: conflict would have been eliminated and not displaced, and in principle maximal peace could engulf the world. I consider two versions of this possibility here and argue that, on the basis of history, such a world is highly unlikely.

First, could states of type X (be they liberal democratic, socialist, Muslim, etc.) define themselves not against another transnational ideological movement but against some abstraction such as greed or environmental degradation or war itself? The first problem with this proposed solution is that states whose political enemy was greed or environmental degradation or war would have internal regimes rather different from any extant regimes. Liberal democracies are certainly not constituted by opposition to these evils. If they were, they would have to abandon certain aspects of liberal democracy (e.g., private property in the case of greed).

The second problem is that these evils are in practice no more abstract than are political ideologies. Enmity toward greed means enmity toward the greedy; enmity toward environmental degradation means enmity toward polluters; and enmity toward war means enmity toward those who would make war.[12]

Second, could X-states define themselves not against any regime that currently governs a state but against a hypothetically possible regime—for example a regime that existed in the past, such as Nazism? Only if Nazism existed in more than memory, as a concrete transnational threat to the liberal-democratic regimes. Enemies must be dangerous, and memories are not dangerous unless they activate actual persons. Thus, as noted above, the Hellenes' defeat of Persia was followed by enmity between democratic Athens and oligarchic Sparta. According to Thucydides, peace parties reminded their fellow Athenians and Spartans of their recently defeated Persian enemy, but since Persia was for the moment no real threat, it could not bestow a common Greek identity upon the Hellenes. Or consider the divisions between the eastern and western parts of the anti-German alliance toward the end of the Second World War, as Germany's defeat became apparent. As the common Nazi enemy receded, so did solidarity between the democratic British and Americans and the communist Soviets. After 1945 the memory of Nazism was not enough to overcome the real danger that communism and democracy posed to each other.

But what if Y existed as a serious transnational threat but not as the regime of any state? What if the whole world was made up of liberal-democratic states, at least some of which faced significant internal antidemocratic opposition? Here we arrive at the only hypothetical world in which all states might dwell in maximal peace: the transnational illiberal threat would provide the liberal states with a common identity, much as the transnational liberal threat provided the Holy Alliance with a common legitimist identity between 1815 and 1849. But such a situation would be precarious and probably short-lived. First, the X-states would of course attempt to eradicate Y and would have an overwhelming advantage by virtue of their control of every single state's coercive apparatus.[13] As argued above, eliminating Y would mean eliminating X, the basis of inter-state solidarity, and X-states would simply become states that would divide into new friend-and-enemy groupings. Second, Y could of course capture one or more states; those Y-states would then be enemies of the X-states, and maximal peace would again be particular rather than universal. In other words, maximal peace among all the world's states can only obtain when a transnational opponent to the regimes of those states is strong enough to threaten at least one of them but weak enough not to capture any of them.

What about a Liberal Peace?

Many will resist the thesis that states need a common enemy in order to have a common identity. The resistance will be based not only on a moral objection—is it really peace if it presupposes hostility?—but also on some compelling evidence: a liberal-democratic zone of peace, arguably comprising states with a common identity, has outlasted the death of the Soviet Union and the terminal illness of communism. Russett and Starr (1992, 398) agree with many in rejecting the hypothesis that a common external enemy is a condition necessary to stable peace. They argue that international institutions, economic ties and social communication, economic benefits, democratic practice and belief, or some combination thereof may provide a sufficient basis for stable peace.

Russett and Starr effectively critique state-centric realism. Realists' predictions in the early 1990s that challengers to U.S. hegemony would soon rise (Mearsheimer 1990) have thus far not come true. The unipolar moment is now ten years old and shows no sign of passing away (Lake 1999). It does indeed appear that no external enemy is necessary for maximal peace. Moreover, economic interdependence and international institutions doubtless do buttress the peaceful relations among the OECD (Organization for Economic Cooperation and Development) states. The gains that accrue to OECD states from one another's economic growth are real. Yet, interdependence is not necessarily a force for peace. Virtually all IR theorists acknowledge that state A's attitude toward state B's gains varies with A's assessment of the probability that B will use those gains against A. The disagreement is over the conditions under which such probability assessments will vary (Copeland 1995). I argue that they will vary with the degree of congruence of A's and B's internal regimes. The governments of states with antithetical systems of government, such as Japan and the United States in the 1930s, are likely to worry more about one another's gains; interdependence for such states may not be a force for peace. Governments of states with a common transnational ideological enemy, such as Japan and the United States in the 1950s, are likely to worry less; their interdependence is likely to be a force for peace.

In other words, because the enemy as defined in this chapter is not a state per se but a competing normative theory of how to organize common life in a polity that may capture one or more states, Russett and Starr's critique is beside the point. In fact, their own argument implies the existence of a common ideological enemy as a contributor to stable peace. In practice, three of Russett and Starr's four favored conditions for stable peace—international institutions, economic ties and social communication, and economic benefits—seem most successful among governments that share an ideological enemy. During the Cold War, when both superpowers constructed and underwrote economic integration within their blocs, each strongly preferred that every state in its bloc not have the other's regime type. Today, the most integrated bloc, the European Union, is ideologically homogeneous; more heterogeneous regimes such as the Association of South East Asian Nations (ASEAN) are less integrated.

The relationship between internal regime and integration leads us to Russett and Starr's final condition, common democratic practice and belief. As argued above, implicit in this condition is the existence of its opposite: undemocratic practice and belief. The common enemy is thus contained in this final condition. The OECD does not need the Soviet Union to hang together, but it does need the existence of a significant transnational antidemocratic enemy. Without it, there would be no *common* democratic practice and belief.

But are there such enemies today? It may be true that liberal democracy has proved itself the most adequate political system in history (Fukuyama 1991), but it is also manifestly clear that not everyone believes it to be true. The United States in particular is attempting to export liberal democracy to various countries by means of diplomatic pressure, economic aid, the promise of membership in international institutions, covert action, and even sometimes military force. (The United Nations, through its programs of civic education and election monitoring, is working toward the same goal.) To see which ideologies the liberal democracies consider their enemies, we need only observe which type(s) of regime the liberal states are attempting to extirpate. The regimes that America and its allies are trying to abolish are an inchoate lot, but they may be grouped under the label *identity politics*. These are regimes that reject liberalism's universalistic axioms that all persons are essentially the same, that their similarity consists in rationality, and that rationality necessarily leads individuals to desire personal autonomy, in particular through material productivity (Owen 1997, 32–37). Today's antiliberals believe instead in ethnic particularity, group autonomy, and in many cases religious fidelity (Juergensmeyer 1993; Huntington 1996b).

Ethnic and religious particularity is afoot within most liberal countries. In the United States, the so-called religious right and much of the secular left resist what they see as the moral pathologies of liberal individualism (while disagreeing on the particulars). Many on the right and left have also joined forces to support protectionism. In Latin America, the same hostility on the far left to global economic liberalism erupts into occasional violence. In places as diverse as Western Europe, India, Nigeria, Russia, and Canada, ethnic identities are resurgent. But antiliberalism is not limited to spectacular events and charismatic politicians. Mainstream politicians in democracies often find they must respond to constituencies threatened by liberalism, be they economic, political, or social.

These are many movements rather than one, and they tend to view one another with at least as much enmity as they do liberalism. The Ayatollah Khamenei, Hindu fundamentalists, and Patrick Buchanan would perceive little in common among themselves. But liberals tend to see them as essentially the same, and they exploit that alleged sameness to reproduce a strong liberal identity.[14]

That the governments of the OECD states have this domestic enemy in common contributes to their common identity. The French government's success against antiliberal policies and groups in France is good for liberal government in Germany, and vice versa. Thus, the governments of these states wish one another well. Were France to elect a National Front government that altered the institutions of the French republic in an antiliberal direction, France would fall under the suspicion of the liberal Western states. Other states would fear that Paris would support antiliberalism elsewhere. That does not mean that war would follow. But France would leave the Western community of maximal peace, just as Germany left it in 1933.

Although a test of this argument is beyond the scope of this chapter, the NATO war against Yugoslavia in 1999 illustrates the process by which liberal regimes and their illiberal opposites are coconstitutive. The Belgrade government throughout the 1990s labored to build a greater Serbia the old-fashioned way, by eliminating other ethnic groups from the territory it claims. Western governments and publics were appalled at the ethnic cleansing in which Serbs were engaging in Kosovo. Yet, many in the West, especially in the United States, opposed intervention in Kosovo because they did not see Yugoslavia as a threat to themselves. Clearly the Yugoslav state is no threat to the physical security of any NATO state, possibly excepting Greece. The statements of various leaders during the war make clear that the threat to the West is, rather, the existence of ethnic and religious nationalism, particularly in Europe.

Furthermore, the NATO–Yugoslav war helped solidify NATO by providing it with a common enemy. Statements of officials in many NATO countries implied that the chief reason for the war was to keep the alliance together. It is as if the NATO states know that it is in the interest of all for NATO to persist but that it needs an enemy to do so. In that sense, Slobodan Milosevic did liberal solidarity a favor by committing his atrocities. Should his regime be ousted, NATO will have a strong incentive to find new illiberal enemies, perhaps outside Europe.

Because antiliberalism is in such global disarray, liberalism is in an ideal situation: it faces enemies that hate one another but that it can portray to itself as a unified threat. History suggests, however, that at some point, new ideas will emerge that unify those who perceive they are losing under liberalism. What those ideas will be is impossible to say. But since contests over the best way to order society have not ended within countries, we have little reason to believe that conflict has ended among countries. Should people everywhere cease to care about common life, politics would disappear. Short of such a far-fetched situation, ideologies will always exist, and ideologues will always attempt to exploit the power of states to overcome their enemies.

Conclusion

Peace is certainly good, but maximal peace may not always be better. The common identities that constitute maximal peace among states form only in the presence of common enemies. These identities are based on competing visions of domestic order. The inference is that when two states form a common identity, their governments simultaneously develop a common enmity toward a transnational movement that would destroy their way of organizing social life. If that enemy has captured a third state, the two commonly identified states will not be in a state of maximal peace with that third state.

Thus when peace is deepened, conflict is conserved rather than eliminated. What changes with the arrival of maximal peace are the boundaries dividing blocs of states. This does not mean that we are destined always to be at war with states and movements who disagree with our ideologies: clearly, minimal peace is at least possible among enemy states (and the term "enemy" is usually prudently dropped at that point). The point is that maximal peace is not an unmixed blessing and should be pursued with great care. For example, if NATO is a zone of maximal peace, then its preservation and expansion could create new enemies. That may not be a bad thing—some actors and movements in world politics must be opposed—but NATO leaders must realize that this dynamic is at work.

I close with a theoretical comment. In recent years constructivism has entered IR theory as a challenge to rationalism's elision of identity. One conclusion of this chapter is that constructivism is right about the need to take identity into account, but probably not in the way that most constructivists have intended. Constructivists have included the existence of a common other as one basis for identity formation (Wendt 1994, 389; Risse-Kappen 1996, 366–67). But most constructivists are interested in other, nonconflictual mechanisms for identity formation. Constructivists are sometimes thought of as latter-day utopians because they ascribe priority to social over material forces (Mearsheimer 1994/1995, 39). In fairness, however, constructivists often stress the obvious point that social constructs are not always good and, moreover, that human beings cannot simply bring about world peace through an act of collective will (Wendt 1994, 393; Jepperson et al. 1996, 39). Constructivist writings do not assert that a single world political identity will eventually take shape, or is even likely. Indeed, like virtually all social scientists today, constructivists claim to be dysteleological, to reject the notion of a final cause pulling the human race toward itself. Still, the primary target of constructivism is usually realism, which is, among other things, the most pessimistic school of thought in IR (Owen 1998/99; cf. Carr 1946).[15] Arguing that we are not stuck with the Westphalian states system is not far from arguing that we are not stuck with wars and rumors of war. Since constructivists believe that norms have consequences and that practice can alter norms, it is doubtful that most constructivists want simply to argue out of arid, value-free intellectual interest that collective identities could form if social practices were of the right sort.

   If the approach of this chapter is that of constructivism, it is a pessimistic constructivism. It is not the pessimism of Machiavelli or Hobbes, who see actual or potential violence everywhere. It is certainly not the pessimism of today's neorealists who argue, against overwhelming evidence, that all states worry about all other states' relative gains virtually all the time. It is, rather, a pessimism that has become conventional wisdom at the end of this most barbarous of centuries. As Kant himself saw, we cannot eliminate boundaries but only shift them about and make them less provocative. Hence we cannot create a global security community. What we can do, and have done, is build pieces of stable peace and work to minimize violence among those pieces.

Notes

Earlier drafts of this chapter were presented at the Annual Meeting of the American Political Science Association, Boston, September 2, 1998; and the Pan-European Conference on International Relations, Vienna, September 17, 1998. The author thanks Yaacov Bar-Siman-Tov, Ole Elgström, Arie Kacowicz, Magnus Jerneck, Daniel Philpott, Randall Schweller, Joel Toppen, Alexander Wendt, and those in attendance at the Boston and Vienna sessions for comments. He also thanks Bradley Nelson for research assistance and the University of Virginia for financial support. Any errors are the author's sole responsibility.

   1.   There is much more to identity and identity formation than is outlined in this section. Entire subdisciplines are devoted to the question. Many if not most accounts of symbolic interactionists, social psychologists, sociologists, and anthropologists, however, do draw on the mechanism of negation outlined here. For a fine review of social identity literature and an application to international relations, see Mercer 1995.

   2.   Cf. Mead: "[F]unctional identities presuppose the unique and absolute differences between existent individual things. We hope this makes clear what we mean when we say that there is no identity without difference." Mead 1982, 197–98.

   3.   For a similar approach to world politics, see Skidmore 1997.

4. Thus Boulding 1978, 17–18: "To a distressing extent each party in a conflictual relationship is a creation of its enemies. In some degree Napoleon created Bismarck, Bismarck created Clemenceau, Clemenceau created Hitler, Hitler created the Pentagon, Stalin created the CIA. Perhaps one reason for the biblical injunction to love our enemies is that they make us."

5. Schmitt is generally recognized as one of the twentieth century's premier political theorists. He was also a Nazi, so the use of his ideas is morally problematic. As with his colleague Martin Heidegger, Schmitt's Nazism has not prevented scholars from searching his ideas for possible insights into politics. For a balanced treatment of Schmitt, see Bendersky 1983.

6. It is interesting to read a German intellectual's perception of the League as a powerful actor in 1932, given the League's subsequent (in)action and reputation for fecklessness.

7. For a contemporary British view, compare Ernest Bevin's 1948 memorandum to the cabinet, "The Threat to Western Civilization." Soviet domination of Eurasia would lead "either to the establishment of a World Dictatorship or (more likely) to the collapse of organized society over great stretches of the globe." Quoted in Latham 1997, 116.

9. It is true that the European socialist parties failed to prevent or even oppose war in 1914 (Waltz 1959, 128–37; Owen 1998/99, 166–67). But none of the states in question was socialist, and so the transnational movement had not captured any state.

10. Finland is an interesting exception to the rule.

11. But see Fukuyama's revision (1999), which speculates that technology is now able to alter human nature for the first time, thus raising the possibility that liberal democracy may not be the final form of government.

12. This last enmity is typically held by liberal states toward illiberal states; see Owen 1997.

13. It might also be argued that a peace that involved the violent elimination of a transnational movement would be a poor sort of peace. Nonetheless, inter-state peace is the concern of this volume.

14. For an exploration of the effects of antiliberal coalitions on world politics, see Solingen 1998.

15. Wendt (1994, 393) argues that realism is essentially materialism, not pessimism. But neoliberalism is also materialist; and such canonical realists as Thucydides, Machiavelli, and Rousseau are not materialists. What all writers in the realist tradition (cf. Doyle 1997) share is pessimism.

5

The Cognitive Dimension of Stable Peace

Rikard Bengtsson

Stable Peace, Trust, and Confidence

This chapter is devoted to a discussion of the cognitive basis of stable peace. I first explore in some detail the cognitive pair of trust and distrust and bring in the concept of confidence, after which I discuss reasons behind, and effects of, different levels of trust. To illustrate the central reasoning of the chapter, I use the experience of the Baltic Sea area.[1] The concluding section summarizes the main points and opens up a discussion of the political possibilities for increasing trust and attaining confidence.

Recalling the typology elaborated in the first chapter, I place stable peace at the end of a spectrum also covering precarious and conditional peace. Like Kenneth Boulding, I understand stable peace as "a situation in which the probability of war is so small that it does not really enter into the calculations of any of the people involved" (Boulding 1978, 12–13). This is paralleled by Alexander George's definition of stable peace as "a relationship between two nations in which not only the idea of going to war to settle conflicts but also the threat of military force has become unthinkable" (George 1992, 9). In this interpretation, stable peace can be coterminous with the notion of security community, defined by Karl Deutsch and his associates as a community in which "there is real assurance that the members of that community will not fight each other physically, but will settle their disputes in some other way" (Deutsch et al. 1957, 5).

We are faced with the task of discerning the distinguishing dimension among these peace stages (or, to put it another way, identifying the core trait of stable peace). The quotations above point toward a cognitive mechanism. Stable peace relationships and security communities rest on such a high level of mutual trust among the actors that military violence or threats thereof has become unthinkable as a means of conflict resolution, no matter the severity of the conflict. Hence, Deutsch and his collaborators argued that "mutual responsiveness" is of central importance: "We found that 'sense of community' was much more than simply verbal attachments to any number of similar or identical values. Rather, it was a matter of mutual sympathy and loyalties; of 'we-feeling,' trust, and consideration" (Deutsch 1957, 129). Along the same lines, Emanuel Adler and Michael Barnett maintain: "Members of a community of states might exhibit rivalry and other interactions associated with mixed-motive games, but what matters is that they have attained a level of mutual trust that eliminates reciprocal military threats or the use of violence as a means of statecraft" (Adler and Barnett 1996, 75). In the same vein, Alexander Wendt considers a security community a social structure "composed of shared knowledge in which states trust one another to resolve disputes without war" (Wendt 1995, 73). Relationships within the European Union may be given as an example in this context. No matter how serious the conflicts that arise among the member-states of the union, we expect these to be solved without resorting to military violence. Other frequently given examples are the relationship between the United States and Canada and the relations among the Nordic countries.

This emphasis on trust stands in stark contrast to conventional interpretations of international relations, which maintain that international anarchy is the defining character of the international system, resulting in unavoidable security struggles among states. Nicholas Rengger argues in this context: "On traditional accounts of world politics, trust is precisely the social virtue most obviously absent. Realist accounts of world politics throughout the twentieth century have always emphasized—though for differing reasons and to differing degrees—that world politics is, *par excellence*, the realm of the *lack* of trust; of suspicion, of fear, of no overall authority" (Rengger 1997, 469–70, emphasis in original). Similarly, Adler and Barnett note that most international relations scholars "elevate how anarchy makes trust highly elusive if not impossible" (Adler and Barnett 1998b, 46).

George's stage of precarious peace corresponds to this latter type of inter-state relations. As noted in chapter 1, such a peace is characterized by immediate deterrence and threats of military confrontation. Shimon Shamir, employing the term *adversarial peace*, characterizes such a relationship by "sharp ideological differences, intensive propaganda warfare, and mutual perceptions of grave threat and deep distrust, despite a formal peace" (Shamir 1992, 8–9). Alexander Gralnick, when discussing deterrence policy, explains: "Distrust is the basis of this philosophy [of deterrence policy], and trust is considered irrational since it is believed the adversary will nefariously exploit one's vulnerability. . . . All of this is based on the Hobbesian logic that there can be no trust among nations and that every 'window of vulnerability' must be securely barred" (Gralnick 1988, 176–77). Finally, Kjell Goldmann notes: "Trust, understanding, and the recognition of a mutual interest in avoiding confrontation may be overly difficult to attain between nations facing each other in a 'security struggle'" (Goldmann 1994, 146–47). Thus, it is evident that distrust is a central feature of precarious peace relationships. Although less intense, distrust between the parties is also characteristic of conditional peace. At the same time, however, elements of emerging trust may be found in relationships that have improved from precarious to conditional peace.

I suggest that we add to this typology a fourth category, *integrative peace,* in which the actors maintain a predominantly cooperative and positive relationship. The peace rests primarily, not on deterrence and competition in the security sphere, but rather on the identification of mutual interests, dependence, joint problem-solving, and norm-governed behavior. Such an integrative peace denotes a more positive peace than conditional peace but does not eliminate the security dilemma, as stable peace does. Although not as far-reaching as stable peace, integrative peace is characterized by trust rather than distrust.

We may summarize thus far that trust and distrust are relevant parameters when discussing international affairs. We also note that the kind of advanced trust envisaged in stable peace relationships is qualitatively different from that found in relationships of integrative peace. I suggest for the sake of conceptual clarity that we bring in the concept of *confidence.* This allows us to keep the commonsensical notion of trust as a central dimension of integrative peace relationships, while reserving confidence to denote the kind of trust found in stable peace. Such confidence rests on certainty as to others' intentions, resulting in an absence of reflection on alternative outcomes or lines of action.

Conceptual Exploration: Distrust, Trust, and Confidence

Trust and Distrust

Focusing upon the cognitive dimension of stable peace, it seems reasonable to take as a point of departure the frequent assumption in the social sciences that actors—humans, groups, states, or companies—face such a complex environment that decisions often have to be made under uncertainty. My understanding of uncertainty follows that of James Morrow, who argues that "uncertainty occurs when the probability of an outcome given an action is unknown or not meaningful" (Morrow 1997, 31). Similarly, Branden Johnson and Paul Slovic argue that uncertainty is seen as "a risk assessment presented in terms of a range of risk estimates, rather than a point estimate" (Johnson and Slovic 1995, 485). Uncertainty stems from imperfect information as to others' intentions and the consequences of alternative courses of action within an interdependent decision environment of strategic interaction. Thus, actors who need to make decisions in such a complex reality with imperfect information take risks when interacting with others to achieve whatever goal that has been formulated. In terms of rational choice analysis, actors are assumed to frame the problem in terms of probability and magnitude of an advantageous or desired outcome related to the probability and magnitude of an adverse outcome, that is, of being exploited. Needless to say, difficulties in estimating probabilities and magnitudes of different outcomes make such an exact calculation rather difficult; in short, uncertainty prevails.

The international environment is no exception. States are interdependent in various ways and do not always know the true intentions of other states. Robert Keohane argues that "uncertainty pervades world politics" (Keohane 1984, 257). Similarly, Charles Kegley and Gregory Raymond note: "Under even relatively stable conditions all members of the international community face great uncertainty" (Kegley and Raymond 1990, 246). This is very much the case within the security sphere, where actors are truly interdependent in terms of peace and war and are quite unlikely to know each other's true intentions. The notion of the security dilemma, so prevalent in realist analyses, reflects precisely this problem: interdependent action and unknown intentions. Depending on the assumptions states make about other states and the logic of the international system, they will be more or less inclined to engage in international cooperation or other arrangements involving risks.

Not only is it difficult to get correct information as to others' intentions, it is also often difficult to know the complete consequences of alternative courses of action, especially in the long term. Hence, we do not always know that the advantages we seek through taking a risk are greater than its potential disadvantages. Realists would argue that the natural thing to do given these circumstances would be to refrain from action, and this is often what happens, not least in international relations. There are many examples of potentially cooperative arrangements that were not engaged in because one or more of the parties simply did not dare. As Deborah Welch Larson argues: "States often fail to cooperate even when their preferences overlap, because policymakers draw incorrect inferences about the motives and intentions of others " (Larson 1997, 3–4). However, examples also abound of actors still engaging in interaction, despite not knowing the full consequences of different lines of action. To take part in an interaction under circumstances of uncertainty is, in our terminology, to show trust; to refrain from interaction signifies distrust.

Our discussion of uncertainty also points to the importance of reputation as a simplifying device for handling uncertainty. Jonathan Mercer views reputation as "a judgment of someone's character (or disposition) that is then used to predict or explain future behavior" (Mercer 1996, 6). A reputation for trustworthiness may, by simplifying reality, lead to increasing trust, whereas, a bad reputation may preclude certain interactions (see Larson 1997, 13–14; and Misztal 1996, 84).

There seem to be three common elements in the various but intertwined uses of the concepts of trust and distrust. First, both phenomena reduce social complexity; second, both involve expectations of future behavior; and third, the phenomena have to do with an actor's acceptance or rejection of the fact that his or her fate to some extent lies beyond his or her own control. Along these lines, Nicholas Rengger understands trust as "the exercise of discretionary power by some agent (individual or artificial) on behalf of another over matters that the trusting agent cares about" (Rengger 1997, 472). Annette Baier sees trust as the "accepted vulnerability to another's possible but not expected ill will (or lack of good will)" (Baier 1986, 235). Barnett and Adler note in this context that "trust always involves an element of risk because of the inability to monitor others' behavior or to have complete knowledge about other people's motivations because of the very contingency of social reality"(Barnett and Adler 1998, 414). This is also the view espoused by Larson, who argues that from a psychological standpoint, trust may be seen as "reliance on another at the risk of a bad outcome" (Larson 1997, 19).

These observations resemble those brought forward in the volume on trust edited by Diego Gambetta (1988), in which there is agreement around the following elements of a definition: "Trust (or, symmetrically, distrust) is a particular level of the subjective probability with which an agent assesses that another agent or group of agents will perform a particular action, both *before* he can monitor such action (or independently of his capacity ever to be able to monitor it), *and* in a context in which it affects *his own* action" (Gambetta 1988, 217, emphasis in original). In attempting a definition, then, I argue that *trust and distrust are an actor's cognitive responses to his expectations about the future behavior of a counterpart.* Thus, an actor demonstrates trust toward another actor if he voluntarily and without certainty as to the consequences accepts or increases his level of vulnerability vis-à-vis that other actor by allowing his future welfare to be dependent on behavior beyond his own control. Conversely, he demonstrates distrust if he refrains from accepting his vulnerability in a given situation.

The Nature and Logic of Confidence

In some corners of international relations certainty as to others' intentions seems to prevail. A relationship of stable peace implies that it does not enter into the minds of policymakers to solve conflicts by military means. Hence, no threats of military violence are perceived, no such risks are conceived, and the issue of betrayal or exploitation does not arise. The security dilemma, so prevalent in traditional interpretations of world politics, does not apply. In sum, confidence represents a situation in which an actor is certain as to the intentions of another actor.

Most of the literature dealing with these issues does not make any clear distinctions between the terms trust and confidence but uses them interchangeably. Bernard Barber notes: "Confidence, it would seem, has something to do with trust, but the relation between the two is not easy to establish" (Barber 1983, 87). One effort at differentiating the two is made by Niklas Luhmann, who proposes that trust involves a direct element of risk in the interaction with someone (or something), whereas confidence implies the absence of such a reflection on, or assessment of, risk. Luhmann explains: "The distinction between confidence and trust thus depends on perception and attribution. If you do not consider alternatives . . . you are in a situation of confidence. If you choose one action in preference to others in spite of the possibility of being disappointed by the actions of others, you define the situation as one of trust" (Luhmann 1988, 97). Barbara Misztal follows a similar line of reasoning: "Trust is a matter of individual determination and involves choosing between alternatives . . . while confidence is more [of a] habitual expectation" (Misztal 1996, 16). Both concepts rely on the counterpart's goodwill and involve the possibility of being disappointed. The important difference is whether one reflects on this vulnerability in being dependent on someone else's goodwill, which implicitly means also a consideration of alternatives (trust), or not (confidence). Gambetta argues: "Confidence . . . might be described as a kind of blind trust where, given the constraints of the situation, the relationships we engage in depend or seem to depend very little on our actions and decisions. In other words, confidence may also issue from wishful thinking and the reduction of cognitive dissonance; it would then be more akin to hope than to trust" (Gambetta 1988, 224). As this statement underscores, confidence does not in any way imply the impossibility of being disappointed. It is by no means a guarantee against exploitation; rather, one does not calculate the risk of being exploited.

In sum, confidence involves the same elements as trust: voluntary engagement; uncertainty of consequences; and acceptance of, or increase in, vulnerability. It follows from the principal difference between certainty and uncertainty that the dividing line between trust and confidence is that whereas trust involves an element of calculation, *confidence involves accepting or increasing one's own vulnerability without further reflection*. Confidence may thus be considered a positive end-point on a scale. In the words of Barnett and Adler, "The confidence that disputes will be settled without war, is unarguably the deepest expression of trust possible in the international arena" (Barnett and Adler 1998, 414). John Dunn argues in this context that the development from trust to confidence relaxes the strategic element involved in trust: "When it proves to have been strategically well conceived, trust as a modality of action may well generate its passive concomitant, convert a policy of trust into a condition of confidence" (Dunn 1988, 74–75).

Factors behind, and Effects of, Trust and Confidence

Factors behind Trust and Confidence

What can be said about factors behind different positions on the "trust scale"? I share Adler and Barnett's underlying assumption that multi-causality is at work; hence, no single factor provides the complete answer as to how to increase trust. In their discussion of achieving greater trust, they distinguish between precipitating conditions and factors conducive to the development of mutual trust and collective identity. By precipitating conditions are meant endogenous or exogenous factors according to which states "begin to orient themselves in each other's directions and desire to coordinate their relations" (Adler and Barnett 1998b, 37–38). Examples of such conditions include technological developments, external threats, and economic or environmental changes; the list is potentially open-ended. These factors, it is argued, do not primarily produce trust but lay the foundation for trust by moving states toward greater interaction. For instance, for the Baltic Sea region the end of the Cold War and of the superpower rivalry was such a change, allowing the states of the region to meet without the previous conflictual frame of reference. As Benjamin Miller argues in chapter 3, external changes determine the overall direction but not the exact composition of the relationship. Likewise, European integration and the enlargement of NATO and the European Union (EU) have forced or allowed the Baltic Sea states to rethink their security situation and meet each other under new circumstances, thus creating an *opening for* achieving greater trust.

As for factors directly conducive to the development of trust, Adler and Barnett highlight the structural factors of power and knowledge, as well as process factors such as transactions, international organizations, and social learning. Power is important, they argue, because "power can be a magnet; a community formed around a group of strong powers creates the expectations that weaker states that join the community will be able to enjoy the security and potentially other benefits that are associated with that community" (Adler and Barnett 1998b, 39–40). Hence, power is conducive to trust because of the positive images surrounding powerful states. The general move by the former Eastern bloc states to integrate with Western Europe may be interpreted in this way. In the Baltic Sea case, the power involved in the very orientation of the Nordic countries and Germany toward European integration has proved attractive to the other states of the Baltic Sea region.

Knowledge—or better, cognitive structures—highlights the importance of shared meanings and understanding for the enhancement of trust. Among other things, this encompasses the well-established notion of democratic peace. This idea rests on the empirical observation that democracies do not (or rarely) wage war against each other but settle conflicts by other means. Basically, there are two lines of thought as to why democracies tend not to fight each other: first, democratic norms and culture make war (especially against other democracies) unattractive; second, democratic structural constraints and limitations make impossible a decision to wage war (at least against other democracies).[2] Deutsch and his collaborators report similar findings with respect to security communities: "There had to be a compatibility of the main values held by the relevant strata of all the political units involved. . . . One of these values, clearly, is basic political ideology" (Deutsch et al. 1957, 123–24). Shared ideas, rather than liberalism, may be conducive to trust (Adler and Barnett 1996, 83; 1998b, 40–41). This structural factor of shared cognitive structure is also evident in the Baltic Sea region, where the states are either consolidated democracies or en route to consolidation, albeit with some uncertainty concerning developments in Russia.

When it comes to process factors, transactions between and among societies are thought to be important in breeding trust because increasing communication of various sorts decreases uncertainty and reduces risks of misperception, as well as highlighting the mutual dependence among states. In the longer term, common interests will replace conflicting ones. Goldmann notes: "Communication across borders is apt to make interests less incompatible in two ways, according to the theory of internationalism as interpreted here. One is to diminish misperception; the other is to increase empathy. . . . The peaceful exchange of goods and services is thought to create cooperative bonds between nations that are based not only on the deterrent effect of dependence but also on a growing communality of interest" (Goldmann 1994, 46, 48). Furthermore, from a different angle, Adler and Barnett argue that "a qualitative and quantitative growth of transactions reshapes collective experience and alters social facts" (Adler and Barnett 1998b, 41). Herein lies the frequently hypothesized connection among peace, cooperation, and trust/confidence.

Moreover, international organizations are thought to be conducive to the development of trust for a number of reasons. First, organizations

encourage trust by establishing behavioral norms, monitoring mechanisms, and sanctions to enforce those norms. Second, organizations may
alter the behavior of states by allowing them to rethink their policies and
preferences. As stated by Adler and Barnett, "Organizations, in this
important respect, are sites of socialization and learning" (Adler and Barnett 1998b, 43). Third, organizations may take on an autonomous role by
enhancing trust by facilitating a "commonness" of the involved states,
promoting some form of cultural homogeneity.

Finally, social learning has been defined as "an active process of redefinition and reinterpretation of reality—what people consider real, possible
and desirable—on the basis of new causal and normative knowledge"
(Adler and Barnett 1998b, 43). In this understanding, social learning goes
beyond learning as adaptation to a more effective way of conducting
affairs. Rather, it holds an element of redefining the situation on the basis
of new experiences and changes in beliefs. Social learning is brought about
by transactions and often occurs in institutionalized settings. Adler and
Barnett note that by "promoting the development of shared definitions of
security, proper domestic and international action, and regional boundaries, social learning encourages political actors to see each other as trustworthy. And it also leads people to identify with those who were once on
the other side of cognitive divides" (Adler and Barnett 1998b, 45).

It ought to be underscored that these process factors are mutually reinforcing. For instance, increasing levels of communication lead to the
establishment of international institutions, which in turn motivates social
learning. Social learning and the establishment of international institutions may then result in increased communication among societies. Adler
and Barnett argue: "In sum, we expect there to be a dynamic and positive
relationship between the transactions that occur between and among
states and their societies, the emergence of social institutions and organizations that are designed to lower transaction costs, and the possibility of
mutual trust" (Adler and Barnett 1996, 89).

This interrelated set of process factors is found to be at work in the
Baltic Sea area. Focusing here on intergovernmental regional cooperation,
in the aftermath of the profound changes in Eastern and Central Europe,
the Council of the Baltic Sea States (CBSS) was established in March 1992,
on Danish–German initiative. The members include the littoral states of
the Baltic Sea, Norway, Iceland, and the European Commission.[3.] The
underlying aim of establishing the CBSS was to provide a forum for closer contacts and cooperation among all states around the Baltic Sea, in
order to secure democratic and economic development and greater unity
among the member-states. After the first few years of general consultations, an action program was agreed on at the meeting of the foreign ministers in Kalmar, Sweden, in July 1996. Three main areas were brought

forward: increased people-to-people contacts and civic security, economic coordination and integration, and strengthened environmental protection. Working groups within each field were established, and continuous work now takes place in each of these fields.

In addition to the action program, the Swedish presidency of CBSS during 1995–96 also decided to hold a meeting of the heads of government of the Baltic Sea states. This summit, held at Visby, Sweden, in May 1996, added further political significance to the regional Baltic Sea cooperation. At Visby, the principles of the Kalmar action program were laid down and the importance of extended Baltic Sea cooperation underlined. Moreover, two concrete projects were initiated. First, a task force for combating organized crime was established. Second, the meeting called upon Swedish prime minister Göran Persson to coordinate cooperation among the heads of governments of the Baltic Sea states. For this reason, a special group—the Baltic Sea States Support Group—was established in the office of the Swedish prime minister to coordinate continued efforts of Baltic Sea cooperation, support the chairing country of the next summit, and work with the European Commission in implementing its Baltic Sea Region Initiative.

The follow-up to the Visby summit was held in Riga, Latvia, in January 1998. Much progress was noted in a number of areas. The task force on organized crime was deemed successful thus far, and it was decided to continue its work. Cooperation in a number of areas was agreed on, including civic security, culture, education, and work against child prostitution. Barriers to trade and other issues of economic cooperation and development will be dealt with through the European Commission, since these areas are integral parts of preparing for EU membership for a number of the member-states. Also in Riga, the heads of government decided to set up a permanent international secretariat for the continued coordination of Baltic Sea cooperation. The secretariat, located in Stockholm, replaced the support group and began its work in October 1998.

As this brief account illustrates, states decided to expand their cooperation by means of organizational developments, allowing for increasing dependence on the other states in the region instead of trying to decrease their vulnerability. These developments may be taken as indicators of increasing trust. This overview of organizational developments also highlights the increasing numbers of transactions among the states of the region; to be sure, most of these contacts go beyond intergovernmental cooperation and involve, for example, private enterprises, nongovernmental organizations, and individual citizens. As for social learning, although it is difficult to find independent evidence for this, judging from various declarations, it seems that policymakers share a common idea of the future of the Baltic Sea region. This is different from earlier periods, when competitive visions of the fate of the region persisted.

Related to these process factors are psychological mechanisms revolving around the notion of reciprocity. Keohane defines reciprocity as "exchanges of roughly equivalent values in which the actions of each party are contingent on the prior actions of the others in such a way that good is returned for good, and bad for bad" (Keohane 1986, 8; see also Keohane 1984,128–31). Such reciprocity is at the heart of various efforts— academic as well as practical—to find effective trust-enhancing or confidence-building measures through increased and deepened cooperation. Charles Osgood's strategy of GRIT (graduated reciprocation in tension reduction) is one such example (Osgood 1962).

Having gone through these factors and conditions, we are left with the question, How much is enough? How do we know the extent to which trust is increased through increasing volumes of interactions and further institutionalization of cooperation? More specifically, how do we differentiate between trust and confidence? While definitive answers are difficult to give, a number of criteria may be proposed as indicative of confidence as to the other actor's abstention from resolving conflict by violent means:

- Absence of military planning against the other actor(s) of the relationship

- Cooperation in areas of national security against internal and/or external security threats

- Unfortified borders; existing border checks directed at states other than the one in question.[4]

When employing these criteria to developments in the Baltic Sea region, we may conclude that the region as a whole has moved from being characterized by distrust during the Cold War to featuring a certain and increasing amount of trust at the present stage. We may not conclude that confidence is at hand, however. Whereas there is cooperation on national security matters in place, the criteria of absence of military planning toward each other and unfortified borders are not completely fulfilled. For example, not all border disagreements between Russia and the Baltic states are settled, and uncertainty as to Russian developments remains in the military planning of at least some of the other states of the region (Huldt 1997, 14; Klaar 1997, 25–28; Lejins and Ozolina 1997, 35–42; Vitkus 1997, 64–67, 74).

Effects of Distrust, Trust, and Confidence

Whereas the search for factors behind different levels of trust directly and indirectly has been an object of a considerable amount of research, less attention has been given to the implications of the outcomes of these different cognitive processes. In this section, we will consider the consequences of different levels of trust. There are two principal kinds of effects: those that are linked to the cognitive process in general and thus are not related to a particular level of trust or distrust, and those that follow from the particular level of trust or distrust.

As for the first category, two points are noted. First, as Robert Jervis and others have argued, cognitive phenomena often work as self-reinforcing mechanisms, so that, in our case, distrust creates more distrust, and trust creates yet more trust. Such cognitive spirals are likely to yield images of other actors as, for example, ally or friend, which, owing to the drive for cognitive consistency, are likely to be rather robust (see Jervis 1976, esp. chaps. 3–4; see also Larson 1997, 22–23). We should at this point, however, also note the obvious asymmetry between trust and distrust, in that an image of distrust may be difficult to change according to the logic above, whereas an image of trust may be instantaneously shattered (Larson 1997, 33).

Second, outcomes of trust and distrust affect the potency of decisions. As was noted earlier, one of the functions of cognitive processes resulting in trust or distrust is to reduce complexity, making decisions possible. In terms of the contents and implications of these decisions, we are now addressing consequences of particular levels of trust or distrust. Expected consequences of distrust would include increasing levels of suspicion, fear, and insecurity owing to the logic of spiraling. In the realm of political action, this becomes evident in abstentions from cooperative behavior and reciprocal reasoning, thus allowing uncertainty to dictate the outcome; and in attempts at decreasing dependence. Moreover, we would expect the potential, if not actual, use of deterrence or even force. As Larson has shown, mutual distrust may also result in what she labels "missed opportunities," that is, suboptimal outcomes that are due, not to fundamental differences of opinion, but to misunderstandings, misperceptions, suspicion, and lack of communication (Larson 1997).

Turning to trust, we would expect rather different consequences than if distrust prevailed. In general, trust would allow for increasing engagement in the interaction with other actors, which in turn may contribute to yet higher levels of trust. Moreover, we would expect diffuse reciprocity to follow, providing a foundation for more and different forms of interaction than would otherwise be the case.

In this context, we should also address the question of moving from high levels of trust into a state of confidence, thus advancing from uncertainty to certainty. This highlights the temporal dimension; in the same way that we would expect increasing trust generally to be an incremental process, we would also expect that time is of central importance for trust to develop into confidence, consolidating high levels of trust and eventually making it the default position. At the same time, given our cognitive perspective, this may be a question not of time but of substance—we should not rule out the possibility that a process ending in confidence is of rapid and unexpected character. The seeming automaticity of mutual confidence among current and new members as a result of expanding the European Union and NATO illustrates this point.

An interesting effect concerns the nature of security itself. From the perspective that security is what people make of it, the content of security is defined by policymakers who determine what policy areas or phenomena are granted special status, resources, and attention. With high levels of trust, or even a situation of confidence, a process of desecuritization occurs, in which fewer areas or phenomena need to be defined in security terms. Ole Wæver argues that Western Europe experienced such a process of desecuritization in the 1970s and 1980s; indeed, he argues that Western Europe as a security community or zone of stable peace is the very result of a process of desecuritization (Wæver 1998, 69, 80, 91). Elements of such desecuritization are emerging in the Baltic Sea area, where fewer issues than before are termed national security matters, and where cooperation rather than competition characterizes some of the remaining issues.

Conclusion

This chapter addresses the cognitive dimension of stable peace. As in other contributions to this volume, stable peace is understood here in terms of a relationship in which neither of the parties conceives of using military violence or threats thereof as means for conflict management and resolution. Such a peace represents something fundamentally different from conventional interpretations of world politics, in that, while there is not complete harmony of interests, certainty prevails as to other actors' nonviolent intentions, no matter the future conflicts of interests.

I have argued that the cognitive phenomenon of trust is central to understanding stable peace. To distinguish among different levels and instances of trust, the concept of confidence is employed for the specific type of trust found in stable peace. Trust and distrust both represent solutions to social complexity. Whereas distrust is said to prevail if an actor attempts to reduce his dependence on another actor for his future well-being, trust is characterized by an actor's accepting or increasing his current level of vulnerability, even when given an opportunity to decrease it. While trust may be the outcome of a deliberate political process, confidence represents the same outcome without any such process; that is, uncertainty and the need for deliberate risk-taking are no longer present. This does not exclude the possibility of betrayal; it merely means that the risk of betrayal has not even been considered. For these cognitive outcomes, the notion of reputation becomes important as a simplifying device.

Stable Peace in the Making? The Baltic Sea Area

The illustrations above show that stable peace is not at hand in the Baltic Sea area today. Whereas there is a certain, and increasing, level of trust among the states in the region, confidence as to others' intentions does not prevail, especially with respect to each state's relationship with Russia. Thus, the situation seems to be one of integrative, rather than stable, peace.

Baltic Sea developments permit a number of observations to be made. First, precipitating conditions for increasing trust in the Baltic Sea region are stipulated by the end of the Cold War and the twin expansions of the European Union and NATO. Second, the distribution of power has proved to be a structural factor directly conducive to the development of trust: some states are perceived as powerful because of their participation in European integration processes, and this has been important in bringing the states of the region into closer cooperation. In terms of shared cognitive structure, liberal democracy constitutes such a framework, since the states of the region are either consolidated democracies or on the way to consolidation, although a word of caution is needed in the case of Russia. Third, as for process factors for increasing trust, we note that a series of developments in transactions, institution-building, and social learning revolving around the work of the Council of Baltic Sea States has contributed to increasing levels of trust. Fourth, and partly in contrast to the prior points, the Baltic Sea case also illustrates the difficulty in distinguishing between precipitating and direct factors. In the Baltic Sea case, the end of the Cold War and subsequent developments on an all-European and transatlantic level represent precipitating factors, but they may also have had a direct bearing on the level of trust between the states of the region.

Confidence: Within Political Reach?

Given that increasing levels of trust and ultimately a state of confidence are politically desirable, the question remains whether it is possible to influence such a process by political means, or whether such developments lie beyond the reach of politics. Adler and Barnett's precipitating factors are primarily of a nonsecurity nature or are outside the relationship in question. Hence, they are beyond the reach of political efforts of most actors (although this was within the realm of the possible for the superpowers, to take but one example). Therefore it is unlikely that political efforts of the parties themselves can bring about such fundamental changes. Rather, and now turning to direct factors, political means may be used regarding the new situation that has risen. As for these direct factors, governments per se may not primarily engage in transactions among societies; instead, political mechanisms may be used to open societies toward each other, thus allowing other agents to take part in transactions and communication. Institution-building is a different matter. In such a process, political decision-makers have a central role in creating organizations that may foster the development or growth of trust on the political level. In the Baltic Sea area, this combination of creating possibilities for societal interaction and direct political institution-building has been attempted on a regional level. The exact mechanisms at work have yet to be revealed, however. At the same time, Wæver notes in the Scandinavian context that security communities or relationships of stable peace do not have to be founded on formal organizations or explicit security collaboration (Wæver 1998, 76).

The question of the political scope for developing and increasing trust may also be addressed by reviewing the extensive attempts at working with confidence-building measures. The European Cold War experiences most readily come to mind, although similar efforts are currently under way in other parts of the world as well. Even on the European continent itself such measures are of renewed interest, as in the Partnership for Peace framework. In the European Cold War experience, it is evident that incremental steps toward increasing vulnerability, combined with the use of verification measures, worked to foster trust. Conversely, these processes took place under a general layer of distrust, hence not in the neighborhood of stable peace. Research is needed to determine to what extent these experiences are transferable to situations where a substantial amount of trust is already present.

Notes

The author wishes to thank the editors and contributors of this volume for many fruitful comments and suggestions for improvement of this chapter, and for the friendly and cooperative atmosphere in which this book project has evolved. Moreover, he gratefully acknowledges the generous financial support by the Bank of Sweden Tercentenary Foundation, the Swedish Institute of International Affairs, and the Swedish Ministry for Foreign Affairs.

   1. The Baltic Sea area covers the littoral states of the Baltic Sea (Denmark, Estonia, Finland, Germany, Latvia, Lithuania, Poland, Russia, and Sweden), thus including former Cold War antagonists as well as major historical divides.
   2. For an introduction to the democratic peace literature, see Doyle 1983a, 1983b; Russett 1993; and Layne 1994. For an elaboration of the relationship between liberal peace and stable peace, see Ericson, chap. 7.

3. The Council of Baltic Sea States meets at the foreign-ministerial level once a year and in a group of senior civil servants about ten times per year. The presidency of the CBSS rotates among the member-states. For references on the empirical developments reviewed here, see <www.baltinfo.org>; Huldt 1997, 10; Möttölä 1998, 388–89; Sergounin 1998, 475–76; and Saudargas 1998, 5–6.

4. This is a shorter version of the list provided by Adler and Barnett. Since they distinguish between loosely and tightly coupled security communities, their list of indicators signaling a high degree of trust is necessarily more elaborated. See Adler and Barnett 1998b, 55–57.

6

Stable Peace through Security Communities? Steps towards Theory-Building

Raimo Väyrynen

The Research Puzzle

What makes security relations stable and, therefore, conducive to permanent peace? When and why is the peace in a region so stable that the outbreak of a major war is unlikely or perhaps even inconceivable? There are essentially two ways to answer these questions; either a given system must possess structural prerequisites of stability, or the social and cognitive conditions of stability must be embedded in the relations among the key actors.

The structural model has three variants. The focus on the imbalance of power, and especially the preponderance of the offensive capacity, assumes that the lack of balance fosters both offensive and defensive expansionism and undermines the political management of disputes. Thus, the offense–defense balance reinforces the foundations of peace. Conversely, the evolution of mutual, binding economic ties promotes stable peace, especially if the countries in the region are ruled by liberal–internationalist coalitions that have mutual interests in free trade and economic growth (Solingen 1998, 64–71). Finally, collective security can mitigate mutual military competition and, ultimately, eliminate international anarchy. Stable peace can be achieved by the mutual commitment to defend each other against any aggression.

All these approaches to stable peace have their merits, and one may even doubt whether a robust theory of stable peace can be constructed without them. They all suffer, however, from the neglect of a societal perspective; the actors do not react only to objective external conditions, they also draw upon intangible resources such as knowledge, trust, and predictability. Trust may be ephemeral, but it can be institutionalized to build social order. In fact, a stable society largely works through institutions that also define who is included and who is excluded—for example, who can and cannot be trusted (Williams 1997, 291–94).

Trust and predictability as aspects of stable peace are considered in societal theories of security, such as those of security communities. By its very nature, these theories pay major attention to the definition and construction of social reality and the ways in which it shapes the relevant actors and the relations among them. Therefore, it can be called a societal approach to stable peace.

The materialist and societal approaches to security do not need to be opposed, but they can be complementary, as the structure can be internalized. Thus, for instance, an offense–defense balance or free trade can build up confidence and predictability. The reverse relationship works differently, though, as perceptions and expectations alone cannot alter material realities. Yet, it can be argued that trust, predictability, and other social variables are key ingredients of the stable peace because they ultimately define the choices made by actors in various material contexts. For instance, the impact of the offense–defense balance on policy outcomes depends critically on the nature of information and degree of confidence between the actors.

The distinction between materialist and societal thinking goes to the very heart of security studies. The materialist approach sees security as a result of the specific configuration of observable factors—for example, the distribution of economic and military power or the nature of political systems. The societal approach is not oblivious of these structural factors, but it puts more emphasis on the political participation and social transformations and, in that sense, the social construction of security.

The primacy of the "external" reality in materialist models leads to the view that security has to be maintained by the threat of, and resort to, enforcement actions, while the "internal" nature of reality in societal models stresses more the relevance of mutual norms and their self-enforcement. What guarantees that a security arrangement is durable and credible? Is the restraint due to deterrence the main source of security, or are there other, internalized guarantees of stable peace hinging on predictability and trust?

Deterrence obviously contributes to predictability, but it does not, per se, create trust. The existence of trust requires at least some identification with the other because without such association actors would be self-contained and devoid of any common basis. Identity can thus become a positive, although inadequate, factor of peace; too much identification and trust without appropriate safeguards can lead to a moral hazard. This discussion harks back to the basic nature of international relations; the societal approach is accepted by those who see anarchy permitting not only self-help, stressed by the materialists, but also other-help, in which purely egoistic interests are transcended.

This chapter explores the possibility that a security community, both as an institution and as a societal practice, can contribute significantly to stable peace and become almost synonymous with it. The conventional research on military alliances and other security organizations has paid hardly any attention to security communities, despite the fact that the concept has existed for at least half a century. It has, therefore, remained largely unintegrated with the "mainstream" theories of international relations.

The realist, material definition of security completely neglects the role of perceptions, identities, and even structural societal factors. The realist approach purports to be rational, but often a major gap remains between the structural logic and its decisional consequences, as decisions simply cannot be derived from structures alone. The constructivist approach suffers from a similar problem; the impact of identities on decision-making is, as a rule, poorly defined. The focus on identities alone hardly makes it possible to predict specific choices made by the actors. To put the matter otherwise, neither balancing of power nor common bonds of identity are adequate in accounting for security decisions.

For constructivists, the balance of power is not "real," but a particular speech act, a way to talk about inter-state relations. In political discourse, governments divide other governments into friends and foes and define relations with them in power-political terms. Constructivists argue that the focus on "objective" military capabilities and threats reflects the victory of positivist and instrumentalist thinking. It transforms social facts, such as military capabilities, into "objects of knowledge, control and management" (Williams 1998, 215). For them peace and war are constructed meanings and social practices, not analytical concepts or properties of social systems (see Buzan, Wæver,and de Wilde 1998, 24).

The materialists or the rationalists, on the one hand, do not usually focus on norms, but if they do, the premise is that the norms work primarily through the manipulation of the incentives of actors and thus constrain their behavior. The constraints are due either to the internalization of cost-benefit calculations or to the existence of an external enforcement mechanism to produce compliance with the relevant norms.

Constructivists, on the other hand, claim that norms are shared understandings that constitute actor identities and interests. They agree with the rationalists that norms create incentives and opportunity costs but suggest that their influence goes deeper. The existence and influence of norms mean that the agents and the environment interact; international relations are therefore socially contingent. The rationalist and constructivist approaches are often considered mutually exclusive, although some argue that they can be synthesized (Checkel 1997). At a minimum, they can be considered complementary; for instance, constructivism and game theory are said to share some common assumptions (Jepperson, Wendt, and Katzenstein 1996, 39).

The objective understanding of security appears to be close to the rationalist paradigm, while constructivism stresses the subjective or intersubjective aspects of security. It has been rightly pointed out that it is neither politically nor analytically helpful to define security entirely in objectivist–rationalist terms. Taken to extremes, such an approach leads to the situation in which concepts such as security are fetched from outside politics and are supposed to have universal validity (Buzan, Wæver, and de Wilde 1998, 29–31). However, this does not mean that security should be defined entirely in intersubjective terms. There is always a complex interplay between subjective and objective elements of security.

In this chapter I make an effort to specify the material–societal relationship as a step towards the development of a theory of security communities. The material and societal elements of security meet in the concept of trust that has intersubjective and institutional foundations, but which at the same time can be linked with essential factors, such as economic interdependence and military confidence. In fact, the existence of a durable security community requires both objective and subjective elements of security that together constitute a necessary precondition for such a community.

Defining the Security Community

The notion of "security" in the concept of security community is problematic. It can be interpreted in more or less demanding senses. In the more demanding sense, security means peace, and a security community is thus a peace community. Following this line of thinking, Karl Deutsch and others point out that a pluralistic security community requires that "the keeping of the peace among the participating units [is] the main political goal overshadowing all others" (Deutsch et al. 1957, 31). For this reason, as for instance Ole Wæver notes, the pluralistic security community is a "non-war community" (Wæver 1998, 71; see also Adler and Barnett 1998b, 34–35).

Technically, the concept of security community has two elements: security and community. In defining security, I adopt the Deutschian perspective as to the definition of stable peace primarily in terms of the absence of physical violence. There are, surely, also nonmilitary threats to security, but their inclusion in the definition of the security community would mean that even if stable peace prevails in a region that is plagued, for instance, by an economic crisis or environmental degradation, it cannot be called a security community. The adoption of the broad definition of security would unduly raise the threshold of the security community by bringing in secondary, nonmilitary concerns.

For this reason, I define security in a rather restrictive manner as a *low past, present, and future probability of using serious coercive force between or within nations*. Coercion can be both military and economic in nature as both types can inflict major damage and pain on the targeted people. Peace is broken, and the security community unrealized in the region, if people are subjected to physical destruction and suffering. In other words, peace and security mean, ultimately, freedom from coercion and its threats.

Compared with more radical uses of the concept, my definition is rather conventional. It considers only serious coercive military and economic threats to the existence and freedom of relevant individual or collective actors. Empirically, the degree of security in a system can be assessed through the frequency and intensity of the (unilateral) use of military or economic force. If, in addition, there is also a broad subjective and intersubjective consensus in a region that the probability of military and economic coercion is low, then it can be said to be secure.

The rationalist paradigm considers, as a rule, only external threats to security, although there has been a recent trend towards applying the concept to internal conflicts as well. In particular, there has been an effort to transfer the model of security dilemma from inter-state to interethnic or intersocietal relations (Posen 1993; Snyder and Jervis 1999; Roe 1999). However, it is true, as Robert Mandel (1994, 21–23) suggests, that internal threats, however serious, need a different "conceptual toolkit" than the analysis of external threats to security.

One possible solution, in particular in the periphery, is to equate security with the state-building process, as a "subaltern realist" (Ayoob 1997) has suggested. Then, the establishment of public order through state-making would become the defining aspect of security. This approach does not yet solve the problem of how safe public spaces within nations are linked with secure and peaceful inter-state relations. This problem can be addressed by the following simple typology that divides both inter-state and intersocietal relations into secure and insecure types, in which security is defined by the amount and intensity of physical violence and coercion (see table 6.1).

Type 1 meets both requirements of a security community, while types 3 and 4 clearly violate them. From the standpoint of the definition of the security community, type 2 is most problematic; can we speak of a security community if civil wars rage within countries? My answer tends to be in the negative, although it may make sense to distinguish between a comprehensive security community (when both inter-state and intersocietal peace prevail) and the inter-state security community (type 2).

Table 6.1 Inter-State and Intersocietal Types of Security

	INTERSOCIETAL RELATIONS	
	Secure	Insecure
INTER-STATE RELATIONS		
Secure	1. Peaceful international and national society	2. Nationally contained civil wars
Insecure	3. Coherent states fighting international wars	4. "State of nature": international and national anarchy

According to Ayoob (1997, 135–37), a comprehensive security community can be best achieved when "territorial satiation, societal cohesion, and political stability" prevail within states, as is the case in most industrialized countries. The absence of these internal traits—that is, effective statehood—often leads also to inter-state violence. Thus, the inter-state security dilemma is due less to the uncertainty of the state actors about the defensive versus offensive intentions by the others than to the prevalence of malign and predatory motives of the governments trying to stabilize their internal and external position.

Trust and Community

The concept of community can be defined in both constructivist and rationalist terms. A constructivist definition would probably state that "community" refers to a human collectivity that is constituted by shared norms and understandings among its members. Owing to common values, identities, and goals, they feel solidarity with each other. Communities can even be "virtual," linked by communication media, but usually they are attached to a particular locale.[1] The glue holding the communities together is the collective identity formation and, more specifically, shared values, identities, and meanings. Collective identity establishes patterns of diffuse reciprocity manifested in mutual responsiveness among the members of the community (Deutsch et al. 1957, 129–33; Adler and Barnett 1998b, 30–33, 47–48; see also Williams 1998).

The rationalist approach would build the definition of community on the concept of interest. The members of a community try to control resources that are of value to them. As no member can usually obtain control over all relevant resources, he engages in transactions with other members. The aim is to make sure that his access to resources improves or that the remaining resources are not used against him. Transactions that trade resources and interests in a regulated framework create a social system and perhaps even a community.

The next question is whether it is possible to bring values, rules, and interests together in a definition of community. How are these phenomena related to each other? One way of trying to integrate them is to rely on the concept of trust, which is one way to deal with the problem of risk in decision-making. In the rationalist framework, the placing of trust is a wager in which the outcome is not guaranteed. However, once trust is placed, there are incentives to convert the asymmetric relationship into one of symmetric trust (Coleman 1990, 98–99, 177–80). Over time, relationships of mutual confidence may develop into "a culture of trust" that becomes a contextual property shaping actors' behavior (Kegley and Raymond 1990, 258–60).

In a more abstract vein, it may be argued that a trusting relationship shapes identities, reinforces norms, and helps to overcome diverging interests of the members. Conversely, common identities and norm compliance obviously contribute to increasing trust and help to resolve interest conflicts. The existence of a community presupposes that its members have reasons to trust the other members to comply with the common norms and behave in an expected way.

As mentioned above, in international relations trust is a contextual property and has an important function, to "underwrite the capacity of a system to function peacefully and to bond its members in agreements" (Kegley and Raymond 1990, 248). Common identity means cognitive proximity and, together with trust, facilitates cooperation in spite of uncertainties. In fact, "trust and identity are reciprocal and reinforcing" and help to create a security community (Adler and Barnett 1998b, 45–48).

The insertion of the concept of trust in the definition of community seems to take it back into the constructivist court.[2] The situation is more complicated than that, though. Trust is not only shaped by common identities and cultural values, but its placing usually involves also a proper calculation of potential risks. We do not only trust because of a certain measure of common identity, but we also try to obtain safeguards against cheating by the other side. In the rationalist account, the placement of trust is based on the maximization of the expected utility under risk. The notion of expected utility contains, in and of itself, the idea that the trustworthiness of the other actor is limited, so that potential risks are involved at least until the relationship becomes more fully institutionalized (Coleman 1990, 97–108).

However, in addition to the utility calculations, trust is also based on experience, loyalty, and bonding; that is, there is an ideational and historical element in it. Trust is a combination of past experience and hope for the future. Various safeguards against the betrayal of trust and the exploitation of underlying vulnerabilities strengthen the relationship but may, as signals of suspicions, undermine confidence. The focus on safeguards tends to place more emphasis on the role of norms and their enforcement than on shared values and meanings in defining trust.

Combining material and subjective elements of security, we can define a security community as a collective arrangement whose members have reasons to trust that the use of military and economic coercion in their mutual relations is unlikely. Trust, as the key element of the security community, can be further divided into predictability and assurance. Predictability emanating from trust gives rise to expectations of consistent behavior, while assurances (or safeguards) reduce the probability of deviant action and its damage.

The definition adopted above should be compared with the pioneering work of Karl W. Deutsch and his associates, which still provides the best point of departure for further studies on security communities. In pluralistic security communities, as opposed to amalgamated ones, the units retain their sovereignty but develop a sense of community and institutions that are able to create long-term, dependable expectations of peaceful change. This means that conflicts are expected to be resolved without resorting to large-scale physical force (Deutsch et al. 1957, 5–7).

Deutsch's definition of security does not explicitly use the concept of trust, although it surfaces in a couple of places in his analysis. He thinks, for example, that trustworthiness improves the mutual predictability of behavior, especially if it is grounded in deeper feelings of commonality than mere familiarity. Trust also contributes to mutual responsiveness, although the latter is more contingent on the density of communications (Deutsch et al. 1957, 56–58, 129–30). In sum, Deutsch seems to consider trust mostly as a precondition for better predictability of the actors' behavior and, thus, as an aspect of expectations rather than as a synonym or a dimension of security.

Adler and Barnett (1998b, 38) are more specific about the role of trust in the security community. For them mutual trust and collective identity are necessary conditions of dependable expectations of peaceful change and, thus, of the security community. They also draw attention to structures (power and knowledge) and processes (transactions, organizations, and social learning) that are conducive to the development of mutual trust and collective identity. Peaceful change is the critical concept also in their theory of security community.

A key element of my own definition of mutual trust is that the serious use of coercion is unlikely. It is consistent with Deutsch's idea that trust is primarily connected with the predictability of behavior. Predictability is, in turn, closely linked with expectations about the peaceful nature of change, which are at the heart of the security community. The other aspect of trust is assurance that expectations are, indeed, dependable. There should be a "real assurance," as Deutsch says, that trust and predictability do not break down and that war ensues.

Ole Wæver (1995b, 218–19) suggests that a security community can experience "security rivalries" (as is the case in the Franco-German relationship within the European Union [EU]). This stance follows logically from his view that in the EU, the state model still dominates and national identities differ; as a result, the West European security community is not yet full-fledged. Wæver himself rejects the community approach to European security in favor of a concert-based system because it considers the power element, while the security-community theory does not specify the mechanisms by which war is ruled out (Wæver 1995b, 214–15, 226–30).

It goes without saying that members of the security community can have mutual political disagreements and even rivalries. However, it should also be clear that if states threaten each other militarily, they do not belong to the same security community. This murky area concerns "security dilemmas" and "security rivalries." If they are defined, as they should be, as a potential condition for using military force, then most dilemmas and rivalries are incompatible with the idea of the security community. The issue is obviously complicated by the fact that "dilemma" and "rivalry" refer to different types of security problems; the former concerns primarily the collective-action problem, while the latter refers to more direct inter-state confrontations.

The opposite problem is revealed, on the one hand, in the criticism that the concept of security community is redundant with the concept of peace. To be empirically meaningful, research in the field should be able to identify cases in which community members' dependable expectations of peace have broken down and coercion has ensued. On the other hand, there may be security orders that witnessed the absence of war between members, without the existence of any community between them. Does this mean, for instance, that a hegemonic or balance-of-power system cannot be a security community? Obviously, such a system can be a nonwar community, but not necessarily a peace community

If the emphasis is only on the (inter)subjective aspects of community, identities and bonding, then expectations and predictability are pushed to the background. As a result, "shared identity . . . is a necessary condition for a pluralistic security community" (Adler 1997a, 263). Such an emphasis on identity means that the strategic aspects of behavior in the security community are downgraded. It is assumed that actors are endogenously shaped by, and react to, norms and identities that constitute them. They are expected to draw upon common identities as resources rather than calculate instrumentally whether their expectations about future cooperation are dependable and assurances real enough to warrant reliance on the other states.

Conversely, the proponents of rational choice focus on a strategic setting in which actors decide among different options on the basis of their preferences, beliefs, and available information (Lake and Powell 1999). In this regard, a key difference between constructivism and rationalism appears to be that the latter stresses more the uncertainty and instability of a given situation in which the use of force is often a ready option. Constructivism is biased toward a self-fulfilling prophecy in which common identities and the expectation of peace reinforce each other and make the use of force unlikely.

Internal Wars and Security

In previous studies, security communities have been defined primarily in the context of inter-state relations, while intra-state conditions, even civil wars, have been largely excluded. Thus, Arie Kacowicz (1994, 1998) considers South America and West Africa incipient or potential security communities, even though many of their members have been suffering from internal turmoil and violence. For instance, the breakdown of public order in Liberia and Sierra Leone and the multiple cross-border links between their devastating civil wars, or the links between Nigeria's internal political situation and its military actions in West Africa, make one wonder whether a security community can exist in such a region.

Kacowicz contends that members of coherent security communities are usually democracies that are, for a number of reasons, better at keeping peace; they tend to be economically developed and mature states in which domestic institutional constraints limit the resort to military force. Liberal democracies are also likely to accept the territorial status quo and the international normative order; hence, they do not try to impose changes on the environment by the force of weapons. Yet, if the region in which inter-state wars have been absent comprises mostly nondemocratic states, the zone tends to be one of negative peace (Kacowicz 1995, 1998).

This seems to suggest that nondemocracies shun positive cooperation and are at best able to avoid wars in their mutual relations. Provided that the security community is defined as a nonwar community, this solution does not yet make the theory redundant with the theory of democratic peace, since nondemocratic countries can live in stable peace with each other. Karl Deutsch largely agrees with this conclusion in observing that a consensus on "main values" would be sufficient to create a pluralistic security community. Differences in political and economic values need not undermine such a community provided that its members do not "develop a militant missionary attitude" (Deutsch et al. 1957, 123–25).

Similarly, Adler and Barnett (1998b, 40–41) conclude that liberalism promotes a civil society with transnational ties and, in that way, a security community, but they also seem to acknowledge that there are other paths to such a community. Security communities have a territorial dimension, but their "cognitive space" can also be shared by noncontiguous actors if their identity ties are strong enough (Adler 1997a, 250–55).

The key conclusion seems to be that countries governed by democratic, liberal–internationalist coalitions usually have cooperative and peaceful relations with one another, while statist–nationalist coalitions are more prone to external and internal conflicts (Solingen 1998). However, non-democracies are not destined to external aggression or internal war; they too can live in peace and be members of a security community. However, the probability of external war and internal instability is higher in their case than for liberal democracies whose security communities are, therefore, more mature.

Common sense suggests that a region can be a security community only if its members are also internally at peace and face only a low probability of civil war. Thus, the absence of inter-state war is not a sufficient condition for the existence of a security community. In addition, its members must be internally in peace, at least to such an extent that domestic instability does not spill over to other countries of the region. In other words, the existence of a security community presupposes that security externalities created by countries of a particular region are predominantly positive in nature (see table 6.1). The spread of negative security externalities across borders is inconsistent with the idea of the security community (see Lake 1997, 48–57).

Negative cross-border externalities may not lead to inter-state wars or internal wars in other countries, but they often destabilize the entire region and stymie expectations of peaceful change. Therefore, a region in which states are internally violent and unstable can hardly be meaningfully called a security community. For example, it is unwarranted to consider West Africa a zone of peace, even in the negative sense of the peace concept. Its devastating civil wars have produced so many refugees, so much arms trafficking and smuggling, and other "externalities" that the region will need a long time to build a stable political and economic environment.

In summary, the existence of a pluralistic security community should require a low probability of violence in both the external and the internal relations of its member-states. Thus, peace and security have both an extra- and an intra-state dimension that are conceptually distinct but must empirically co-exist if a region is to be regarded as a security community.

Obviously, political and economic liberalism is a strong candidate to account for the emergence of robust security communities, for the very simple reason that it is both internally and externally peaceful. The connection is not, however, one-to-one, as there are (semi-)democratic countries that have suffered from large-scale violence (e.g., Colombia, India, Sri Lanka, and even the United Kingdom). In general, it has been observed that all efficient governments, and not just the democratic ones, are able to avert internal violence (Benson and Kugler 1998). This casts doubt on the argument that liberal democracy and its commitment to external peace can alone define the existence of a mature security community. Internal peace must also be one of its defining characteristics, especially if internal instability threatens to have negative security externalities.

The Constructivist Challenge

The general Deutschian emphasis on communication networks leading to trust, social learning, and institution building as paths to security communities has been recently adopted by constructivist scholars (Adler and Barnett 1996, 63–72; Adler and Barnett 1998b; esp. Adler 1997b). They see the creation of security communities as the formation of "cognitive regions" whose borders are defined by the intensity of shared understandings and common identities.

Identity is the key element of a cognitive region; shared self-definitions create internalized norms that allow people from different countries to know each other better and thus respond more effectively to the concerns of the others. Social learning, especially if coupled with positive functional processes, contributes in a critical manner to the emergence of security communities and the norms upholding them. States as social actors tend to behave according to the international norms that the shared values and identities have constituted (Adler 1997a, 264-65; Adler and Barnett 1998b, 44-45).

The critical argument in the constructivist approach is that changes in state identity affect the national security interests or policies of states. In that way the configurations of state identities also affect security communities and other international security arrangements. Thus, a military alliance or other security coalition reflects, in the first place, the difference or commonality of its members' values and identities (Jepperson, Wendt, and Katzenstein 1996, 60–63).

The constructivist approach to international security studies has some obvious merits. It suggests that norms, as collective expectations, recognize and validate particular identities of actors and thus "constitute" them. International normative expectations shape domestic interests and policies, and thus the identities of the national actors. Yet, the choices made by national actors affect international structures. The effort to explicitly bridge the domestic and international systems is perhaps the main merit of the constructivist approach.

The constructivist approach assumes that security communities are, as a rule, built by states, especially liberal ones, that share similar identities. Methodologically, the focus on common identities and norms created by social interaction makes them endogenous to the state and leads, as noted above, to overemphasis on the harmony of social relations (Mercer 1995, 233–36). Moreover, the constructivist interpretation can fall into the trap of tautology; common identities help to establish a security community whose existence—that is, the absence of war—proves that the participants share common identities. To put it another way, we are in trouble if the common identity is considered a necessary precondition for the emergence of a security community, while its existence is regarded as an indicator of shared identity and meanings.

To some authors, security as a socially constructed concept has meaning only in a given discursive and structural context that cannot be generalized. In other words, an issue becomes a security problem when it has been named as such, or "securitized." In this reasoning, insecurity is a situation in which a threat has been identified by a "securitizing actor," but no successful response has been taken to eliminate or manage it (Wæver 1995a, 54–57; Buzan, Wæver, and de Wilde 1998, 40–42).

The constructivist approach to security makes sense to the extent that an issue is hardly a security problem unless it has been defined as such by the actors and/or referents. If the problem is widely perceived as a threat, a shared understanding may emerge and lead to common action. Constructivism is inadequate, however, in dealing with responses to security threats. For instance, the constructivist framework of security studies developed by Buzan, Wæver, and de Wilde (1998) has hardly a word to say about the instruments by which the security threats can be dealt with. Obviously, they think that the choice of instruments depends on which issues are securitized and how it happens, but this does not help much. In general, the constructivist approach to security seems to be unable to theorize about the role of military power and its use.

The tautological trap is also lurking in the language of "constitutive processes," which are "a set of processes whereby the specific identities of the acting units in a system are built up or altered" (Jepperson, Wendt, and Katzenstein 1996, 66). If the pluralistic security community is defined in terms of a dependable expectation of peaceful change, this expectation creates a norm that is supposed to define the identity and interests of the participating states. The result is a methodological loop that cannot fail.

Emanuel Adler seems to avoid this pitfall by suggesting that security communities "rest on shared practical knowledge of the peaceful resolution of conflicts." He points out that the practice of peaceful conflict resolution is more widespread among liberal states that have well-developed civic cultures. Therefore, because of their capacity for conflict resolution, liberal cognitive regions either already are, or are likely to become, security communities, because such capacity reduces the risk and expectation of war (Adler 1997, 257–59; see also Adler and Barnett 1996, 76–77; 1998b, 33–34).

Here the tautological trap is partly avoided, as the intervening capacity of conflict resolution decides whether a common identity can be converted into a security community. However, if this capacity is considered solely as an attribute of liberal states, one falls into the trap of being redundant with democratic peace. The possibility should also be allowed that nondemocratic states could avoid mutual conflicts because they, either separately or together, have adequate conflict resolution capabilities as well. Whether this is the case or not is an empirical and not a definitional issue.

Two Hard Cases

This section discusses briefly two "hard" cases to show that the relationship between identity and security community is not as simple as sometimes suggested. In so doing, I intend to challenge some of the recent constructivist scholarship. These hard case studies are based on the hypotheses that (a) a common identity and shared understandings may have other motivations than peace- and community-building; (b) progress towards a security community can be released by external changes rather than by the redefinition of identities; and (c) what looks like an identity and security community may not be one. The two cases examined in this section are the Association of South East Asian Nations (ASEAN) and the Baltic countries.

ASEAN

ASEAN is often considered at least a nascent pluralistic security community; its members have a common identity that stresses restraint, non-confrontation, and consultation. Moreover, the members of ASEAN, especially its original core, have not been involved in a serious conflict since the 1963–66 *Konfrontasi* between Indonesia and Malaysia. This is quite remarkable, especially in view of the tumultuous postindependence period in the 1950s and 1960s. By stressing the evolution of their common identity, norms, and the general "ASEAN Way" of solidarity, the association has been seen as moving towards a pluralistic security community.

It is not difficult to find counterarguments to the assumption that ASEAN is a security community. Its member-states, especially Malaysia, continue to have territorial disputes with other members, though most of them are not very serious. They have also been converting their economic resources into large-scale arms acquisitions that have tipped the balance in favor of offensive weapons. However, these weapons are seldom targeted specifically at other members of ASEAN; they are more a type of insurance against the uncertainties of the post–Cold War era and a potential instrument for the territorial disputes in the South China Sea and the rise of China (Collins 1999, 99–106).

These counterarguments do not necessarily make much of a dent, however, since the advocates of ASEAN as a community of common identity and security acknowledge that it is as yet far from perfecting these features (Acharya 1998, 214–18). On the positive side, it has been stressed that ASEAN's conflict resolution capacity has withstood the test of practice and proved to be able to avoid violent conflicts and keep peace in the region (Caballero-Anthony 1998).

Without denying the gradual rise of the ASEAN Way, one has to place it in a larger historical and political context. The institutionalization of ASEAN has been mostly spurred by external challenges. The declaration on a Zone of Peace, Freedom, and Neutrality (ZOPFAN) was adopted in 1971 as a response to regional uncertainties in the aftermath of Nixon's opening to China. The Treaty of Amity and Cooperation (TAC) of 1976 was intended to create a new code of regional conduct after the collapse of South Vietnam. Finally, the establishment of the ASEAN Regional Forum (ARF) in 1995 was motivated by the need to provide a new, broader multilateral forum to deal with the uncertainties of the post-Cold War world.

The ASEAN model puts a heavy premium on the national sovereignty of the member-states and the security autonomy of the region as a whole. These twin principles are manifested in the emphasis on noninterference in internal affairs and keeping extraregional powers at arm's length. These general principles of national sovereignty and regional autonomy have served important common interests, such as regime security and the containment of opposition (Leifer 1996, 11–16; Khong 1997, 326–37; and Narine 1998, 196–204).[3]

Consultations, solidarity, and restrained behavior are not necessarily indications of a common identity, at least not a positive one. Rather, they reflect the commitment of the ASEAN leaders not to interfere in, or even comment on, the internal affairs of other states. This has permitted the leaders to continue their nondemocratic rule at home, undisturbed by the political pressures of the neighboring states. In reality, "solidarity" has meant the mutual acceptance of the primacy of regime security in the region. Thus, while common identity may exist, it is used as a means to other, more sinister objectives than to promote peace; it can be an excuse for the domestic policies pursued rather than a constitutive factor. For instance, ASEAN's central role in the international response to Vietnam's invasion of Cambodia not only propped up its own unity and international profile but also legitimated its members' internal practices (Narine 1998, 204–8).

In summary, while a measure of common identity has emerged in ASEAN, the lack of democratic traditions and practices has failed to make it a "liberal cognitive region" leading to a pluralistic security community. Regional consensus on procedures to promote sovereignty and regime safety obviously creates common, though partial, identities among the national elites. Such an elite consensus should not, however, be confused with widespread popular identities that are needed to create a pluralistic security community.

Recently, the essence of the ASEAN Way has been challenged by several new developments. Its enlargement to include Vietnam, Cambodia, Laos, and Burma is based on the rationale of countering the spread of Chinese influence and also of expanding the ASEAN Way and the regional security system to the Asian continent. The enlargement has, however, created entirely new problems. The increasing political and ethnic diversity of the member-states and their historical divergences reduce further any regional identity that may have existed in the original ASEAN.

Moreover, human rights violations and political instability in Burma and Cambodia, together with the extraregional pressures and intraregional promises to deal with these problems, are challenging some key principles of the ASEAN Way. This concerns in particular the almost absolute respect for national sovereignty and noninterference in the internal affairs of member-states. In the new situation the debate has already started within ASEAN on the possible use of "constructive intervention" and "flexible engagement" to reform the political systems of Burma and Cambodia (Collins 1999, 106–13; Henderson 1999, 24–26, 33–40, 48–55).

Cooperation in the ASEAN framework may have progressed far enough that the risk of inter-state warfare in the region has disappeared for good (Caballero-Anthony 1998). If this is the case, the ASEAN Way has shown one possible route to a security community. But this does not mean that Southeast Asia is yet a secure region. Internal violence continues within many of its member-states, and economic and environmental crises are creating new transnational security threats, including migration and irregular economic activities. Moreover, ASEAN has turned out to be incapable of responding in any meaningful way to the regional financial crisis and the Indonesian political transition it prompted (Henderson 1999, 40–48). Thus, even if ASEAN would formally qualify as a nascent security community, the dated methods and limited impact of its inter-governmental cooperation show that such a community is inadequate to deliver more comprehensive peace and security.

The Baltic Sea Region

During the Cold War, the Baltic Sea region was a security complex in which two military alliances and neutral countries met each other. However, the Soviet Union was much more strongly present in the Baltic system than the United States, while Germany's policy was restrained. Moscow considered the Baltic Sea mare nostrum, and, having occupied the three Baltic countries in 1940, it did not give them a chance for political self-realization. Yet, these countries, especially Estonia, retained much of their North European identity but were unable to express it during the Cold War.

Once the Soviet constraint had been lifted, the Baltic countries started a frantic search for membership in NATO and the European Union. However, the Western powers have been reluctant to make a security commitment to the Baltic region because of the fear of unintended or even perverse consequences of such a move for themselves. Therefore, no robust regional security organization has been set up to cover the entire Baltic Sea region. It remains a network of cooperative security ties that does not involve robust institutions or firm commitments (Knudsen 1999; and Väyrynen 1999, 204–7).

It can also be argued that the common identity of the Estonians, Latvians, and Lithuanians is largely due to their common aversion to being subjugated to Russia. From this follows their common interest to seek a counterbalance to Russia in NATO and the European Union. Empirical research indicates that the Baltic people identify primarily with Germany, the Nordic countries, and to a somewhat lesser degree with the United States, rather than with each other. They also seem ready to defect from mutual cooperation if an opportunity opens up to promote unilaterally their own interests.

Thus, the Baltic identity has been, at least in part, defined to meet Western expectations and, at the same time, distinguish itself from Russia and its sphere of influence rather than to create a Baltic community from inside. The Baltic security goals are pursued primarily through economic, political, and military integration with NATO and the European Union. In other words, the definition of the Baltic identity seems more to reflect these interests than to drive policy in its own right (Möttölä 1998; Väyrynen 1998, 1999).

A puzzle for the constructivist theory is that the common identity of the Balts, and perhaps identities in general, seem to have only a secondary place in the search for security. In other words, identities facilitate and justify, rather than constitute and define, security. Surely, the constitution of the Baltic identity is consistent with the orientation of the practical politics of security and integration by Estonia, Latvia, and Lithuania. However, rather than identity defining interests, the process seems to be reversed. The Baltic countries' primary interest is in the acquisition of positive security guarantees ("safeguards") from NATO against Russia and, for political and material reasons, full membership in the European Union. They refer to a common Baltic identity when it is useful to do so, but seldom independently of these goals.

In what sense do the Baltic countries form a security community? Despite some territorial and economic disputes, Estonia, Latvia, and Lithuania are not expected to become involved in war with each other. To the contrary, they have set up various common military institutions to improve training and interoperability (with NATO) of their limited forces. Neither is there the slightest fear of war with any of the Western powers. In that sense, the Baltic countries are a part of the extensive Euro-Atlantic security community. On the other hand, the expectation of a military conflict with Russia is excluded neither from the governmental policies nor the popular imagination. With Russia, one can think, at best, of a security regime embedded in the institutions and actions of the OSCE (Organization for Security and Cooperation in Europe). This hints at the need to explore the role of external actors in the emergence of security communities.

External Actors

Security communities are defined by a set of mutual expectations among their members about the peaceful character of social change. This approach tends to focus on the inside of the security community and pay less attention to its relations with the external environment. However, in real life, the outside environment has an impact on the security community, and the community can, in turn, influence that environment. The focus on the inside can possibly be defended by saying that everything is endogenous, that is, that identities, values, and meanings are social and, therefore, structured independently of state boundaries. Thus, in "cognitive regions" the external and the internal have a different meaning than in "territorial regions" where the focus on the external is more appropriate.

Deutsch and his associates consider only briefly an external military threat as a cause for the establishment of a security community. They are ambivalent about the effects of an external threat. The positive effects are, at best, transitory, and the outside pressure may even prevent or slow down the process of community-building (Deutsch et al. 1957, 156–57). Their point of departure seems to be that the security community has to be built from within, autonomously of the external environment.

In ASEAN, China and Vietnam have been perceived as the main threats, but this perception has changed over time and has not been shared equally by all members. Yet, the fear of external destabilization of the national "resilience" has been a major motivation to exclude the outside powers from the region and promote its internal, elite-driven cooperation. Obviously, these motives cannot be easily separated from domestic concerns, but it is equally clear that external factors cannot be neglected in explaining the development of the ASEAN Way. Yet, the members of ASEAN have seldom been able to formulate a joint policy towards extraregional problems. Most recently, they have been split by the East Timor crisis (Chongkittavorn 1999).

In the Baltic region, the impact of external actors has been even stronger than in Southeast Asia. The potential threat of Russia has no doubt pushed the Baltic countries to closer cooperation with each other and NATO than would have been the case in its absence. They have been able to formulate a rather consistent policy towards NATO and, with differing national nuances, towards Russia. The Baltic countries and the West form a security community, but it is more shaped by norms, values, and expectations than by common institutions and defense commitments. This reflects the Western effort to accommodate Russia rather than challenge it, at least in the regions that were previously parts of the Soviet Union. Therefore, the security community between the Baltic countries and the West is a "loosely-coupled" rather than a "tightly-coupled" organization of mutual aid (Adler and Barnett 1998b, 30).

Thus, Russia as an external actor has been able to stymie, or at least slow down, the efforts of the Baltic countries to join NATO. This means that we face an interesting discrepancy here. In the constructivist sense of values and identities, there seems to be a mutual security community between the Baltic countries and the West. However, in the Realpolitik sense, a security arrangement against external threats does not exist, because NATO has been unwilling to extend security guarantees to Baltic countries. In other words, a security community does not necessarily contain commitments to defend the country against external risks; the community of identity is not the same thing as the community of protection. Neither does the security community necessarily assure joint policies by its members towards external actors or issues.

These observations suggest that the focus of the constructivist analysis on identities and values may underestimate the role of action in international security relations. After all, the peaceful settlement of disputes and safeguards against the use of physical force can only result from political action. Such action is also needed to convince the nonmembers of security communities that their interests are taken into account in the process. Otherwise, they may turn against the community project and damage it by their reactions.

Conclusion

If stable peace is defined by the lack of anticipation of major violence between or within states involved, then it necessarily comes close to the concept of security community. In fact, stable peace is a key characteristic of a security community. It has been suggested, though, that there are differences between them in the methods by which peace is maintained. Stable peace is due to reciprocal and consensual cooperation that has decided, for instance, to keep territorial disputes off the political agenda, while peace in a security community is internalized by common identities, values, and norms and is thus more institutionalized (Kacowicz 1998, 10–11).

This distinction would justify the observation that security communities are "value communities" and produce stable peace by sharing identities and meanings. Yet, stable peace in a broader sense can also be achieved by other means, such as the balance or the concert of power. This distinction is not trivial and deserves further discussion.

This chapter started with a discussion of two models of security that were dubbed material (or rational) and societal (or constructivist). It was noted that the former regards security as a result of the configuration of external factors, while the latter sees it as endogenously constructed.

The theorists of security community clearly support the constructivist approach that leads to an emphasis on common identities and values as a necessary condition for creating secure peace. This approach has also tended to consider liberal values and policies as essential features of a security community. Recently, its supporters have expanded the model in two different directions. First, the possibility has been allowed, although somewhat vaguely, that common values other than the liberal ones can provide a basis for the security community. Empirical evidence indicates, though, that the opportunities opened by this extension are quite limited. Second, the security-community theorists have paid attention to material factors, such as transactions and technology, that can augment institutions and knowledge as bases of the security community. However, in the empirical work, only limited attention has been paid to the material conditions of security communities (Adler and Barnett 1998a, 1998b).

The stable-peace theorists have adopted a broader range of methodological approaches but have not excluded the cognitive models informing the security-community theories. In fact, they often trace stable peace to such cognitive processes as trust and learning, though more from the perspective of political processes than identity formation. Stable-peace theorists often ground their explanation in various versions of the democratic-peace theory; in that respect there are links with cognitive liberalism. In fact, it seems that stable-peace theorists have underspecified their explanatory models by not going more boldly beyond the liberal–democratic framework of analysis to which the security-community theorists are, to a large extent, confined.

This study adopted trust as the key concept in defining a security community. It can even be considered a common denominator of the security-community and stable-peace theories. Trust is obviously generated by the strengthening of norms and institutions, social learning, and the construction of common identities. The case studies of ASEAN and the Baltic region indicate that their member-states have enough confidence that war between them is unlikely, so that they might qualify as potential security communities. However, the same cases hint that this trust cannot be generalized beyond the narrow focus on war avoidance. There is only limited mutual trust that effective and positive common positions can be formulated with respect to nonmilitary regional and many extraregional problems as well.

The sharing of values, norms, and identities is clearly conducive to the formation of security (i.e., nonwar) communities and can help to interpret their emergence. However, norms and identities are not sufficient to account for the (in)capacity to deal effectively with broader political and economic issues. The constructivist approach also has difficulties in addressing adequately the problem of responses to security threats, as well as the problem of action in general. Obviously, other theories are needed to account for the political, military, and economic dynamics that contribute to stable peace in the regional and global contexts. Security community remains an important, perhaps the most central, aspect of stable peace, but it is unable to account for it in its entirety.

Notes

I am particularly grateful to Emanuel Adler for detailed comments on an earlier version of this paper. It is not his fault that I did not agree with all his suggestions, although with many I did.

1. It is interesting that the most comprehensive reader on the constructivist approaches to security does not contain any systematic discussion of either community or security community. See Katzenstein 1996.

2. Again, it is interesting that the subject index of Katzenstein 1996 does not even contain the concept of trust. Adler's earlier work (1997a, 254–55) mentions it only briefly.

3. In the first two decades of ASEAN's existence, its member-states cooperated in repressing the ethnic and ideological uprisings to such an extent that one can speak of coordinated counterinsurgency and state terrorism that purported to prop up regional and domestic stability. See Väyrynen 1988, 175–85.

7

Birds of a Feather? On the Intersections of Stable Peace and Democratic Research Programs

Magnus Ericson

This chapter concerns the relationship between the liberal–democratic peace (DP) research program and research based on the concept of stable peace (SP). The connection is broad and not limited to the term peace. DP and SP share a common opposition to basic assumptions associated with the dominant realist perspectives on international relations. The concept of stable peace challenges the realist notion of an inescapable security dilemma, and the DP proposition challenges the realist neglect of ideas as well as the neorealist supposition that all units (states) are similar in all respects but power. Unlike neorealism, liberalism leaves the door open for unit-level differentiation in that it discriminates between different types of states and assigns some behavioral significance to this difference.[1] The possibility of unit-level variety and change also allows for transformation in the patterns of interactions.

Both SP and DP represent an idealist tradition within international relations in that they imply the possibility of fundamental change and progress. At the same time, neither represents a utopian vision. Nor do they deal with subject matters removed from security traditionally defined in relation to the age-old issue of military violence. While they provide images of inter-state relations that are quite different from the static and glum realist conceptions, they nevertheless maintain a state-centric focus and accept anarchy as both real and relevant. Rather than rejecting the relevance of the realist subject matter, they speak to it from a different perspective.

In light of the fact that scholarly debates concerning the contemporary peace among great powers have tended to assume a connection between SP and DP, the relation between the two has been curiously underexplored. Singer and Wildavsky speak of "zones of peace and democracy" characterized not by the absence of conflict but by the fact that "no one will believe that [conflict] can lead to war" (Singer and Wildavsky 1993, 3). Russett and Starr likewise refer to a "zone of peace" (roughly encompassing the OECD countries) within which there has been no war for fifty years, "nor much expectation of or preparation for war" (Russett and Starr 1992, 375, 374). While the idea that DP and SP presently coexist as an empirical phenomenon thus has its proponents, little has been done in terms of explicitly disentangling the concepts analytically and tracing their developments historically. In a way, this chapter aims at contributing to such an undertaking.

Apart from the short introduction and an equally brief conclusion, this chapter is divided into three parts. In the first section I define stable peace and outline one of its potential and most common research tracks (of which DP is the most thoroughly investigated subcategory). In the second part, I recap and frame the main variants of DP theory in terms of their causal logic and explanatory aims. In conjunction with this I also identify the conceptual overlap between this body of research and stable peace. In the course of my discussion, I stress two important observations. First, while there are no necessary intersections between SP and DP (that is, you may logically have one without the other), there are significant portions of DP theory that purport to account for stable peace. To some extent the inverse relationship—that the study of SP has developed in association with, and depended on, liberal theory—is also true. Second, the strand of DP theory germane to the study of SP is constructivist, or at a minimum historically contingent, in its logic.

In the third section I argue that development and refinement of DP theory may benefit significantly from employing the concept of stable peace in conjunction with other qualified definitions of peace. Differentiated notions of peace allow researchers to discriminate better among various cases. Research can then yield more precise judgments of what the role of democracy has been, and may be, concerning inter-state relations in different historical settings. More detailed case studies are therefore probably needed, as these permit a positive use of the concept.[2] To illustrate the benefits of such an approach, I relate insights gained from research on the Norwegian–Swedish relationship in the early twentieth century.

Stable Peace and Its Potential Causes

The Concept of Stable Peace

Over two centuries ago, Immanuel Kant outlined his hopes for a world characterized not by war but by a *perpetual peace*. This peace would mean not only the cessation of "active hostilities" but also the removal of the threat of future wars. Anything less would not be a true state of peace but only a truce (Kant 1991, 98). The term *security community* was, in a similar vein, coined by Karl Deutsch and his collaborators in 1957 (Deutsch et al. 1957). To Deutsch and his colleagues, a security community is an area or rather "a group of people" within which there is no expectation of either violence or the threat of violence as a means for solving conflicts. A pluralistic security community (encompassing two or more states) consequently represents a form of *international peace* of a certain quality. It designates not merely the absence of war but *the absence of any fear of military violence* stemming from any of the states in the community. Later on, Kenneth Boulding defined *stable peace* as a situation where the involved states share and expect a nonviolent self-image, so that "the probability of war is so small that it does not really enter into the calculations of any of the people involved" (Boulding 1978, 13). To him SP was only one of four possible conditions—the others being stable war, unstable war, and unstable peace—one of which at any given time characterizes *expectations* concerning international relations (Boulding 1978, 10–17). More recently, Alexander George has offered yet another suggestion on how to differentiate forms of international peace from each other (George 1992).

Kant, Deutsch, Boulding, and George clearly sound a common note. There is one type of inter-state relationship that is qualitatively different from merely the absence of war yet relevant to a traditional focus on inter-state relations from the perspective of military violence. However, to define peace in terms of community, or to describe it as perpetual, would invite unnecessary associations. On one hand, Deutsch's community concept relates explicitly to a process of integration, thus involving it with a notion of its cause. Kant's use of the term perpetual, on the other hand, suggests a temporal dimension that is not necessary and only ascertainable after the fact. Following Boulding and George, therefore, I define stable peace as characterized by the expectations that neither military violence nor threats thereof will be employed in the mutual relations between specific states. If a peace is stable, war is unthinkable. Stable peace has no *necessary* relation to duration, nor must it be understood as the result of specific causes. It is also the end point in a typology of expectations of military violence in inter-state relations. At the extreme end, war is already at hand. At the second step there is no war, but the threat of imminent war is still felt. Following Alexander George, we may term this precarious peace. At the next stage—conditional peace—the threat of imminent war is no longer present, but the fear of future threats (should certain conditions change) remains. The final category is stable peace.

A Liberal Approach to Stable Peace: The Nature of States

Research centered on stable peace and related concepts may deal with the hypothesized *effects* of stable peace in terms of integration, trade, and international cooperation in general. Investigations may also concern favorable conditions for the *establishment* of stable peace or involve the search for causes of variations up or down the typology across dyadic (or multilateral sets of) inter-state relations in history. Thus, stable peace becomes one of the possible values that the dependent variable may assume, while no necessary assumptions guide the selection of the independent variables. Typically but not surprisingly, such attempts are grounded in liberal theory.

In terms of international politics, much of liberalism maintains a focus on the state. Unlike realist views, however, the prevailing liberal view of the units is not Weberian but pluralistic. This has two consequences. First, the notion of a pluralist state assigns a causal role for the composition and relative weight of different domestic interests in explaining the state's collective external behavior. Second, the organization of the domestic political process may form the basis for a more general differentiation among states. Unlike realism, moreover, there is a normative strand within liberal theory that stresses individual rights and the positive value of peace. When these insights are combined, liberals predict that polities that are liberal in their organization (democratic and free) will seek liberal aims in their foreign relations (such as peace). Liberal organization of the state is also assumed to include economic freedoms, which in turn favor types of reproduction generally dependent on peace (trade and commerce), thus diminishing the utility of territorial conquest (Rosecrance 1986).

Logically, variables representing causes may be sought on a variety of levels and combined in a number of ways. One type of variable could refer to systemic structures, another type might be used to infer potential causes from the process of interaction itself (assuming learning), and so on. The type of units (states) involved in the relationship that is to be studied *is* an obvious category of potential independent variables. Indeed, as long as SP applies unevenly across time and space, a scheme categorizing states according to internal characteristics is useful to a general theoretical approach. One possible way of differentiating between states pertains to their domestic political organization as it is manifested in their formal institutions and legitimizing ideology. Distinctions in this manner may draw on the mode of reproduction (trading states and territorial states), cohesion and degree of consensus (strong states and weak states), or popular rule (democracies and autocracies). Such distinctions, wedded to ideas that one particular form of polity contributes to a propensity for peace, are well represented in contemporary international relations theory.

The Legacy of Kant. The notion that changed unit-level characteristics and associated behavior would put an end to war and the threat of war was advanced by Kant, whose idea of a perpetual peace, as noted, resembles stable peace. Key to Kant's argument, and to liberal theory in general, are the benefits of freedom. To Kant the application of reason to effect a perpetual peace depended on the existence of free individuals. This required the transformation of the states in the international system from the despotism of his day to the republics of an imagined future. The establishment of republican constitutions in every state would constrain the rulers (and the people) from going to war, as they themselves would bear the costs of doing so. Kant also believed that republicanism was the only system of governance that accorded with "the concept of right" and could withstand the threat of despotism and violence, which he abhorred. Republicanism is thus the first of Kant's definitive articles of a perpetual peace, but to this he added two more. All states must form a federation of peoples securing every state's rights; and finally, all states must abide by a worldwide agreement on "hospitality"—an international law mandating something like free travel and communication (Kant 1991, 100–108; and Gallie 1978).

International peace and harmony, then, will result from just and representative national governments, which will tend to establish some sort of international federation with open international borders, which among other things will make trade easier. These features are also part and parcel of contemporary theories on peace presented next.

Trading States, Strong States, and Democracies. One of the best-known attempts to explain peace through unit-level differentiation is Richard Rosecrance's notion of trading states and military states (Rosecrance 1986). He suggests that how states are organized affects the rationality of different strategies of reproduction, linking a dependence on trade with peace. It is not just the structure of government that matters but, fundamentally, that this leads to or reflects different relative cost/utility values for war (Rosecrance 1986, 38). Behind this connection lie various processes stemming from changes in environmental factors (such as technology) and favoring trade over war as a means of maximizing utility in a competitive world. Historically, the trading option has been chosen by states that no longer had the power or stomach for political military adventures and that could not hope to overturn the existing balance of power. Thus, for an increasing number of states war has become an outdated and cost-inefficient alternative (Rosecrance 1986, 24).

Another attempt to account for variations in peace and war by referring to the structure of states is advanced by Kalevi Holsti (1991). He describes how war itself and the issues fought over in wars have changed over the last several hundred years. Variation is mainly conceptualized diachronically and first and foremost concerns contextual issues rather than explicitly the units themselves. Accepting *consequential* differences across time introduces a dynamic that tends to translate also into synchronic variation. Holsti notes that *purposes* change over time and differ between units. These changes reflect a "fundamental social transformation" that takes place not only internationally but also "within societies." Purposes, according to Holsti, matter just as much as influence and power, and they are subject to variation (Holsti 1991, 330). Holsti (1996) follows up on these preliminary conclusions and attempts to construct theoretically grounded hypotheses dealing with the present and the near future. His view is that variations across time and in specific histories have combined to produce contemporary units that differ widely. Most important, legitimacy is conferred according to rules that differ across time and space. This harks back to the discussion of purpose in his previous book. Holsti borrows from Buzan the idea that states consist not only of institutions and a physical base (territory and population) but also of an idea. The state has a purpose, which must be expressed in terms of a legitimizing principle, or notion of community (Holsti 1996, 98; and Buzan 1991, 69 ff).

Statehood and notions of a legitimate community do not always coincide perfectly but appear in different combinations (Holsti 1996, 17, 41). Given his purpose—to understand why war breaks out in some places but not in others—Holsti settles for a dichotomous differentiation: states are either weak or strong (Holsti 1996, 82–83). The core of his argument is that strong states do not wage war on one another and are peaceful internally as well. The opposite is true for weak states. The strong state is characterized by high horizontal and vertical legitimacy—that is, there is a basic agreement both on who belongs to the polity and on the rules determining who gets to govern it. Rule is based on consensus. The division of public and private realms is clear, the state is internally sovereign, and the military is under effective civilian control. Finally, "strong states have a fixed and permanent international personality, defined most basically in their territorial dimension" (Holsti 1996, 94–95). If strong states coexist in an international society of institutions and procedures for cooperation and problem-solving, stable peace becomes a clear possibility (Holsti 1996, 141–49).

What then are the differences between these attempts and the DP proposition? Rosecrance and Holsti conceptualize this differentiation mainly in absolute terms. Holsti focuses on agreement on the rules of peaceful change—a community within units making peace possible between them—and Rosecrance invokes the importance of relative cost. As we shall see, the DP proposition also presupposes the importance of cost, as it implies the importance of inside and outside legitimacy advanced by Holsti. In addition, the notion of identity is brought into the analysis. With respect to explaining stable peace, moreover, the DP proposition is clearer in its logic. Rosecrance describes a condition approximating stable peace in a "trading world," and Holsti proposes this possibility explicitly in reference to strong states. It is unclear, though, exactly how this condition is brought about. The DP proposition fares better by including the concept of a shared democratic identity. Both Holsti and Rosecrance actually invoke the positive value of unit-level democracy, but in essence they make the argument that it is not democracy per se that accounts for the crucial differences in behavioral patterns. Finally, the DP proposition is by far the most thoroughly researched one resting on the notion of unit-level differentiation.

The Liberal Democratic Peace

DP as a Robust Probabilistic Generalization

The democratic peace (or liberal peace) proposition as a political ideal, then, is of old lineage. Over the last decade and a half, its social scientific status has been enhanced dramatically by several empirical findings suggesting that democratic states do not fight one another.[3] There have also been attempts to show that this thesis holds even if other explanations are controlled for, or when hegemonic positions are at stake, and that it is not a purely Western phenomenon but in some sense has universal validity (Crawford 1994; Ember, Ember, and Russett 1992; Schweller 1992; Maoz and Russett 1992). The strict version of the DP proposition is that democracies have never fought each other (and never will) and that what we have may be something as rare as a social scientific law (Levy 1994). Normally, however, the proposition is merely framed as an unusually robust probabilistic generalization (Elman 1997a; Ray 1995; and Maoz 1997).[4]

The Role of Formal Domestic Institutions. The theoretical explanation for democratic or liberal peace is sometimes presented as having two main analytically separate components—domestic institutional structure and prevailing norms—but sometimes these are combined under the general heading of liberalism. It is in any case possible to identify in the literature a number of hypothesized causes. First, the way states are formally organized is believed to influence their propensity to go to war. In fact, in large-*n* studies, the democracy/autocracy dichotomy is usually operationalized by reference to such structures and regulations. Democracies have, through their representative systems and general political freedoms, established checks on the use of violence in both domestic and international relations. This makes it hard for elites to oppose the general interests of the state. In autocracies, however, elites may simply follow their own narrow interests and ignore the interests of the people, because their insulated position shields them from the costs associated with war.[5]

It is important to note that a preference for peace on the part of "the people" is implicit in the structural argument. This can be attributed to a number of underlying conditions. As we noted earlier, a common liberal view is that for "trading states," territorial expansion through coercive violence is not highly valued because making war is expensive and offers few gains. The accumulation of wealth is dependent on peace, not conquest (Rosecrance 1986). Peace may also be valued because the *loss* as well as the *taking* of human lives associated with war is itself viewed as a cost, regardless of economic consequences (MacMillan 1998).

The Role of Norms. The second main component of the explanation for the democratic peace makes explicit the ideational dimension. Democracy is associated with a system of norms that a priori identifies violence as a cost and designates war as a last resort, an always unfortunate thing, and an especially *illegitimate* means of conflict resolution when applied to relations among liberal (free) or democratically governed states. Such countries are expected to behave prudently and to have just causes for their grievances (see Owen 1994, 89).

The so-called normative argument hence indicates that liberal values may in some instances lead to war to liberate subjugated peoples, or that liberalism more generally may inspire crusading in the defense of freedom (Doyle 1983a, 1983b). This part of the argument draws on the dyadic level of analysis and is employed to account for the apparent separate peace among democracies. In this way of slicing the theoretical accounts, the (mostly) structural explanation is monadic, while the (mostly) normative is primarily dyadic.

Monadic and Dyadic Explanations. This categorization of structure and norms as monadic and dyadic is by no means necessary. Russett outlines two possible explanations for the separate peace among democracies that both stress the dyadic level (Russett 1993, 35–42). According to the structural institutional model, peace results from mutual perceptions of constrained leadership that minimize fears of surprise attack, making room for "international processes of conflict resolution to operate." Alternatively, in the cultural normative model, peace results from mutual perceptions of mutual adherence to a shared set of norms of peaceful conflict resolution. Conversely, John MacMillan attacks precisely the idea of exclusiveness embodied by the concept of a separate peace. To him, it misrepresents the liberal legacy—respect for individual political rights, democracy, and an aversion to violence—and understates its record as a consistent counterhegemonic force that exerts a *general* pacifistic influence. His argument is normative but does not refer to the dyadic level of analysis (MacMillan 1998; and Ericson 1998). The idea that liberal norms have a general pacifistic influence has other supporters as well (Rummel 1983).

Regardless of whether the focus is on monadic or dyadic effects, both the normative and the structural components need to be present in some degree for the liberal democratic peace to obtain. Democratic structures need to be in place for the democratic norms to have an effect. The substantive content of these norms is also important. MacMillan describes liberalism as pacifistic, while Owen and Doyle in effect argue that this pacificism is contingent on the absence of a just cause. We might surmise that MacMillan's focus is narrower than Doyle and Owen's, and that the latters' categories of "liberals" encompass not only those MacMillan speaks of but also other (potentially more aggressive) groups that he does not discuss. MacMillan's main concern is the ideology itself, not the actions taken by people embedded in a political process and faced with conflicting concerns. His description brings up a few instances where liberals acted against the dictum of pacifistic liberalism because they were pressured to do so.[6] To sum up, the mainstream argument in effect supposes the presence of democratic structures and a normative view of war as something of a last resort that needs strong justification.

DP as Separate from SP. This is what Miriam F. Elman defines as the mainstream proposition of democratic peace: a probabilistic generalization of the unlikelihood that democracies go to war with one another (Elman 1997a). Her reading of the arguments supporting the proposition is that they are theories "of foreign policy with specific predictions about motives that actors should reveal in crisis decision making" (Elman 1997a, 47). Stable peace, of course, is not a theory and does not specifically focus on foreign policy but is, rather, a concept defining the nature of inter-state relations. DP *does* make a prediction about inter-state relations in terms of a separate peace. This peace is unqualified, however.

In conclusion, to the extent that DP is about the nonoccurrence of certain events—that is, to the extent it is used to account for why war did not break out during a particular crisis, explaining this nonevent as a foreign policy outcome—it does not really intersect with the stable peace research program. Nor is the more unusual version of monadic peacefulness—no matter the alleged strength of pacifistic behavior resulting from liberal norms—about stable peace, since it does not explain the quality of relations but only the intentions or aims of foreign policy.

Democratic Peace as Stable Peace

A Conditional Generalization. As noted, most of the studies on democratic peace have focused on the nonoccurrence of wars. Judging from some of the theoretical explanations offered by its proponents, the thesis on democratic peace is not limited to the absence of war (what Kant would call a "truce") but in some cases suggests that relations between democracies approximate stable peace. Both Owen and Russett postulate that there exists an identity—that of being a democratic or liberal state—that exerts influence on the actors *prior* to any rational calculation.

Interestingly, Owen ostensibly argues against the conclusion that true liberal dyads would necessarily enjoy a relationship of stable peace. In his own words: " I answer skeptics who assert that if there really were a liberal peace then liberal states would never threaten to use force against one another. I show how in many cases their domestic institutions may fully constrain the leader of liberal states only when war is at issue and public attention is engaged" (Owen 1997, 6).

Owen in effect says that he does not endorse SP as a *test* of liberal peace. It is, however, important to note that he is not talking about countries that have previous knowledge and opinions about one another—states with a "set" status as liberal. It is reasonable to expect that, given historical developments and the general contextual variation across time and space, the ability for countries to be identified (and to identify each other) as liberal democracies also varies. I claim that Owen's reasoning can logically be interpreted to support the argument that DP explains SP. States that view each other as democratic (that are known to each other and have a set status) and that do not experience any dramatic domestic battles over such an interpretation will most likely enjoy a relationship of stable peace.

In other words, in Owen and Russett's scheme, the mutual identification as democratic is the key mechanism facilitating peace, rather than actual constraints on ability to act that may become evident only *after* threats have been made. Russett is clearer than Owen on this point, as he quite explicitly identifies his "cultural normative" explanation as predicting stable peace between democratic states (Russett 1993, 42). This is a DP proposition with a slightly different focus in its causal logic and an altogether different dependent variable from the more usual one. First, it rests on a normative argument. War is wrong or evil, not because a cost–benefit analysis given particular contextual circumstances yields that result, but in and of itself. Second, it is a dyadic explanation, wedded to the notion of a separate peace. It is not an explanation that can be made from the perspective of a single unit. Even if there were—and there might be—

units who would forswear all inter-state violence and stick to that promise, they would depend on the existence of like-minded units for stable peace to develop.

Table 7.1 is a summary of the discussion so far. If we for a moment imagine that the various arguments could be analytically separated, the combination of rationalistic (structural) arguments versus normative ones and the monadic- and dyadic-level explanations yields a two-by-two matrix. I would claim that the different combinations can logically be interpreted as assuming each other both vertically and horizontally.

At the upper left, we have nothing but the democratic structure and can consequently say very little about outcomes. If we had added that all democracies are trading states, we might be able to say that they probably would fight fewer wars than otherwise. Crucially, however, this structure itself indicates that the collective as a whole—the people rather than elites—is responsible for decisions to go to war. If we move down to the lower left, this structure is combined with a pacifistic ethos, explaining why democracies would be generally pacifistic. If we move horizontally to the upper-right quadrant, the ethos is once again absent but information about the constitution of potential enemies is added. The dyadic structural explanation is still based on a rationality calculation, but since neither state, all other things being equal, will be inclined to start a war, a separate peace among democracies is a possible outcome. If we move down to the lower-right quadrant, finally we have all the ingredients necessary. Rationalistic calculations in both states are possible because of structural organization, and both share the liberal democratic ethos and identity. The result then is stable peace.

In sum, explaining stable peace in terms of liberal democracy necessitates that dyads are peaceful because of the mutual *expectation* of nonviolence due to the perception of a shared set of norms. This expectation is predicated by the parties' respective forms of domestic governance and by their *mutual recognition* of this. It is hence not enough to value the other state's choice of constitution: *expectations of nonviolence* are at the heart of the proposition, and these expectations have to be strong to avoid balancing behavior, and the potential escalation of conflicts, even to the point of war.

Constructivism and the Role of Ideas in Democratic Peace. This strand of liberal theory, drawing on a notion of ideas and common international identities as causal forces, is somewhat akin to constructivist reasoning. Emanuel Adler, for instance, identifies the study of this particular construction (the shared identity of democracies invested with social meaning making war impossible) as a prime research object (Adler 1997b). Alexander Wendt argues that social structures consist of "shared knowl-

Table 7.1 Variants of the Democratic Peace Proposition

	Monadic	Dyadic
Structural	Cost-Benefit *(democracies are disinclined to start expensive wars)*	Cost-Benefit *(separate peace among democracies)*
Normative	Pacifism *(democracies are overall pacifistic)*	Identity *(separate stable peace among democracies)*

edge, material resources, and practices" (Wendt 1995, 73). Structures are "reproduced or transformed by practice" and are thus not objective entities (Wendt 1994, 389). Identities, for instance, may change or expand not only as the result of domestic convergence or dependency but also through interaction. If all goes well, a social structure of distrust, centered around the perception of a security dilemma, may be replaced by a security community, a social structure "composed of shared knowledge in which states trust one another to resolve disputes without war" (Wendt 1995, 73). Similarly, Thomas Risse has argued specifically for a social constructivist interpretation of the democratic peace in terms of a "rule learned through the process of interaction" (Risse-Kappen 1995a, 503). Risse does not support this view with any independent empirical data, but he has elsewhere described a process of changing identities as a result of close cooperation among the NATO member-states during the Cold War. This analysis, focusing on the "role of norms and communicative action," does not concern the establishment of the democratic peace per se, however, but is about its strengthening and reproduction (Risse-Kappen 1995b).

The arguments framed by Wendt and Risse perhaps help clarify the difference in the conceptions of DP as a probabilistic generalization about the nonoccurrence of war and DP as a theory of stable peace. John Owen himself, moreover, suggests that a possible avenue for further developing the liberal approach would be to apply the "ideational framework of Alexander Wendt and others" (Owen 1994, 123). Even Bruce Russett, who has also espoused views that fall into the categories of liberal universalism that constructivists criticize, flirts with this approach. Statements such as "images may be founded to a large extent on myth as well as on reality" at least leave the door open to a constructivist interpretation (Russett 1993, 31). As we shall see, the supposition of constant or contextually independent effects of DP cannot be sustained if the concept of SP is employed. Whether constructivist or not, therefore, the DP proposition as a theory of stable peace must be construed so as to be open to the influence of historical developments.

The Value of SP to DP Research

The previous sections have established the conceptual overlap between SP and DP and have identified DP as a possible explanation for stable peace. In this part of the chapter, I shall argue that the explicit employment of stable peace may be of great practical value to DP research. The foremost function of SP in this regard is as a tool that enables us to disaggregate the DP proposition (see Cohen 1994).

Let us for a moment return to the variety of DP arguments identified previously. Some explanations required very little of a state for it to qualify as a democracy. Others brought notions of identity into the equation. Expectations of behavior or quality of relations also differed, ranging from mere reluctance to go to war to predicting intrademocratic relations of stable peace. For the sake of simplicity, we said that these explanations might be arranged on a scale, where successive levels of causation are added. If we invoke the normative-dyadic explanation, we in effect argue that the domestic structural model will apply as well. The opposite relation—that is, that if the domestic structural explanation applies, so will the normative dyadic—cannot be assumed, however.

This raises two points of concern. First, if the dependent variable is defined only as absence of war—as is the case in much or most of the DP literature—we cannot say anything about the validity of explanations that invoke shared identities. Second, if the selection of cases is based on very wide and inclusive definitions of liberal democracy, so as to increase the number of cases and thus the statistical significance of the results, we may obscure the different levels of explanation. Instead, we might offer a package of liberal democratic effects that are assumed to obtain across history but most likely do not. In consequence, if we want to learn something specifically about the normative-dyadic explanation, not only must we carefully operationalize the dependent variable (SP) to distinguish it from other types of effects, but we must also carefully identify when and where the independent variable—a liberal democratic self-image—obtains.

An obvious objection to the above is that it overstates the autonomy of the respective levels of explanation. While they can be analytically separated, and we theoretically can imagine empirical cases that would allow the application of some but not all of them, the different explanations all stem from the same source and will, in reality, appear in conjunction. Liberal democracy—defined in general terms as freedom of speech and organization, in combination with sufficient suffrage—does in fact include a democratic self-image, whether this is formally expressed or not. In other words, states that, to a reasonable degree, *are* liberal democratic *know* that they are and expect peaceful behavior from their democratic counterparts. This is indicated by the behavior of states so identified. This section is devoted, in part, to refuting such an assertion.

A Foray into History

Consulting historical data from the perspective of SP can illuminate the relevance of DP in two ways. First, by assuming that the DP package actually implies stable peace as a probabilistic generalization, it becomes possible to falsify the generalization without coming up with any actual wars. This has been done, even without explicit reference to SP. This application of the concept, moreover, is easy in the sense that all you have to do is to uncover proof of the absence of SP. It is, in other words, a negative test, congenial to quantitative methods. Employing SP in a positive manner, drawing on the dyadic normative version of DP and the apparent relative abundance of empirical cases, requires a different research methodology, namely, that of the more detailed case study. It too can be of value and can actually strengthen the claims of the relevance of the DP proposition.

Stable Peace as a Negative Test. SP as a negative test obviously rests on the assumption that the implied effects of democratic dyads in fact include SP. If they do, one can show that while there may be reasons to believe in the general existence of democratic peace at least after World War II, there is reason to be highly skeptical about it in the period leading up to, at a minimum, World War I. The objections raised by Christopher Layne concerning the alleged influence of democracy are particularly instructive (Layne 1994). Layne focuses on *near misses*, showing that it was not democracy but traditional power concerns that prevented war from breaking out in four cases of conflict between democratic states from 1861 to 1923. Layne is engaging in process-tracing to uncover the mechanism, not just the outcome, of these conflicts. However, these findings may be disputed to the extent that others may find more support for liberal restraint in each of his cases than his samples uncover (Owen 1994, 110). What Layne *does* show, however, is that the peaceful outcomes of the confrontations he studied were not certain beforehand. *Stable* peace was therefore not at hand.

This impression is further strengthened by Henry Farber and Joanne Gowa's study of militarized inter-state disputes (MIDs)—a category of behavior that is broader than war and also includes overt, nonaccidental, government-sanctioned military threats. Farber and Gowa show that prior to World War I, the probability of democratic dyads' engaging in MIDs was actually higher than it was for other types of dyads. The democratic peace is only evident after World War II, when, they argue, it may just as well be explained in a traditional realist manner as the result of converging interests and external threats (Farber and Gowa 1995).

Stable Peace as a Positive Test. If the use of SP as a negative test perhaps cannot be appealed to as a means of invalidating the DP proposition in its entirety, it is certainly an indication that a package claim will not hold. The extension of DP to include SP will not fit a probabilistic (universalistic) pattern. It may, however, still work as a conditional and constructivist theory. Such an aim is not far-fetched. Stable peace has been said to be prevalent in "the West" (Singer and Wildavsky 1993), or among "strong states" (Holsti 1996), or even more commonly among democracies (Russett 1993). When these terms are translated to concrete examples of actual states, the overlap is significant. The dominance of democracies obtains also among the empirical illustrations of the SP theorists themselves. Deutsch and his colleagues mention a number of pluralistic security communities in their study—United States–Canada, United States–Great Britain, United States–Mexico, Norway–Sweden, Sweden–Denmark, Denmark–Norway, Great Britain–Netherlands, Great Britain–Norway, Great Britain–Denmark, and Great Britain–Sweden. In Adler and Barnett's edited book on security communities, Western Europe (Wæver 1998), the United States and Canada (Shore 1998), and the United States and Mexico (Gonzalez and Haggard 1998) are discussed as well. Finally, Boulding mentions the United States and Canada and the United States and Great Britain as cases of stable peace (Boulding 1978, 16–17). He also brings up the United States and Mexico, Scandinavia, and Western Europe as a whole (Boulding 1978, 45–46). SP may have a variety of causes and exist independently of DP. Democracy appears at this time, however, as a plausible contributing cause in a number of cases. To further investigate its role in the historical construction of SP, though, more detailed case studies based on carefully operationalized concepts are needed.

The Scandinavian Experience

We shall conclude our discussion with a brief illustration of the positive value of SP to DP research. While the Scandinavian case as such is typical DP-research, the normal unqualified dependent variable and the blanket assumption of democracy as offering a package of effects severely limit the ability to learn something from this experience.

After the Norwegian–Swedish union was dissolved without bloodshed in 1905, the two countries established cordial relations that in time grew into what has been identified as an early example of a security community. Some scholars have even dated the establishment of a Scandinavian security community to around 1907, the year Norwegian integrity was officially guaranteed by the great powers of the day (Deutsch et al. 1957, 35, 65; Lindgren 1959). In the democratic-peace literature, moreover, the Scandinavian countries are commonly referred to as democratic or liberal from some time during the latter 1800s onwards.[7] The restraint shown by both sides during the delicate process of divorce and the subsequent rapprochement seem to indicate that irresponsible elements were restrained and that a politically influential popular opinion recognized that peace was in everybody's best interests and trusted their counterparts to feel the same way. Norway and Sweden, then, appear to be a shining example of the workings of the democratic peace. The path to Scandinavian stable peace, though, was in fact far from automatic and entailed the construction of a democratic identity invested with social meaning making war a nonoption.

On the basis of military staff preparations and scenarios, as well as public statements and actions, the Norwegian–Swedish relationship between 1905 and 1935 can be described as follows (Ericson 2000).[8] Throughout the crisis of 1905, the relationship can be best described as precarious. Between 1906 and 1918 both sides experienced the peace as conditional. Tensions were not uniformly high, but (Norwegian) fears and (Swedish) military preparations for military offensives resurfaced intermittently. The 1920s was a period of ostensibly very good relations but included a lingering fear on the part of the Norwegians concerning Swedish behavior during a potential international crisis. From the early 1930s on, however, these fears dissipated, cooperation (also in terms of communication between the military staffs of both countries) intensified, and the relationship became one of stable peace.

What, then, was the influence of democracy upon the evolution towards stable peace? The shifts in Swedish preparations coincide with governmental turnovers between liberals and conservatives (1911, 1914, and 1917). Tensions were reduced during liberal governments and heightened during conservative ones. The end of World War I and the coincidental (and significant) Swedish constitutional reforms of 1918/1921 greatly improved relations, and neither side prepared any new aggressive plans after 1917. Moreover, in the postwar period, references to democracy as an important indication of probable behavior appeared in Swedish general staff reports. However, Norwegian sources continued to refer quite explicitly to the possibility that a great power conflict involving Germany against Great Britain and Russia might pit the two Scandinavian countries against each other. Democracy by itself was at this point insufficient to engender SP. By the early 1930s, though, the on-again, off-again German–Russian cooperation, the defeat of Wilhelmine Germany, and its eventual replacement by the distinctly undemocratic Nazis at a time when Sweden had become distinctly democratic had quenched the fear that the two Scandinavian states would end up on opposite sides in a war. The semiauthoritarian Wilhelmine welfare state had been a somewhat credible source of identification for a less than fully democratized Sweden. It could be appealed to for leadership and viewed as a source of protection against the Russian threat. When this alternative ceased to exist and the options were totalitarian Nazis or liberal democracies, the choice was obvious. Democracy had become more relevant by its clear contrast to an unacceptable alternative. Once the perception had been removed that differing allegiances could develop in a crisis, the relationship could progress from a conditional to a stable peace.

Conclusion

Over two hundred years ago Immanuel Kant connected the vision of perpetual peace to the conversion of despotism to republicanism. Today, the much heralded discovery of a democratic (liberal) peace rests in part on the assumption that states share identities that allow them to divine the true, nonmalevolent intentions behind each other's actions prior to any particular reckoning of motives or rational cost–benefit calculation. Like Kant's perpetual peace, these hypothesized relationships between contemporary democratic states are not subject to the anarchy-induced military security dilemma and are hence qualitatively exceptions to traditional assumptions about inter-state relations. Inasmuch as this is true, democratic peace is not merely an extraordinary string of instances where war failed to break out; it is also a stable peace.

In spite of the occasional remarks by its proponents that the democratic peace *is* indeed a stable peace, this issue has been underplayed by the otherwise fairly exhaustive debates between critics and proponents of the democratic-peace hypothesis. This neglect has allowed the democratic peace to assume a universalistic and ahistorical character, whose mettle is continuously being tested by, mainly, quantitative studies focusing on the occurrence or nonoccurrence of wars rather than on the quality of peace between or among the states in question. The general lack of attention to the question of a democratic security community may reflect the fact that most of the hypothesis's detractors are neorealists. These critics wish neither to entertain the possibility of the existence of such communities nor to indulge themselves in reasoning based on the idea that fundamental change can occur across time. The idea of democratic peace as stable peace, coupled with the empirical data that it *does* exist, indicate that the development of democratic peace is not automatic but requires some sort of learning. It also suggests that it is historically specific. In other words, what democracy is and what it means to be democratic are human constructs that have to be understood in terms of their historical context. Such a perspective does not mean that the democratic peace hypothesis is of no value, but it should lessen the utopian slant with which it has been associated and point to the importance of not formulating a general theory based on contemporary snapshots of history. The future may, after all, be quite different.

Finally, the connection between DP and SP is more than circumstantial or fleeting and is not reducible to the fact that DP in its normative-dyadic version indicates the potential for SP. Boulding made a reverse connection between these two subjects by invoking traditional liberal arguments when he discussed the democratic selection of leaders and democratic checks on their behavior, as well as the role of a positive national ethos, as prominent forces for stable peace (Boulding 1978, 53). Deutsch, likewise, was firmly rooted in a liberal tradition, although he put a greater emphasis on transactions and integration than on domestic institutions in his attempt to account for the growth of security communities (Deutsch et al 1957). What is more, Kant, Deutsch, and Boulding all brought up identity in presenting their arguments and even in defining their concepts. Kant spoke of a confederation of republican states united by their cosmopolitan ideal. Deutsch talked of "we-feeling," and Boulding focused on compatible self-images.

Clearly, while not dependent on one another, DP research and SP research exhibit a number of theoretical affinities. The Scandinavian experience nicely illustrates some of the benefits—for both SP and DP—of making explicit use of their theoretical overlap in empirical studies. First, the DP package of effects is disaggregated. Over a period of thirty years, a democratic dyad exhibits precarious peace, conditional peace, and finally stable peace. Second, the role of democratic structures, democratic norms, and a democratic identity are all shown to matter, not just in preventing war, but also in moving from one type of peace to another. Third, the case illustrates that the achievement of a shared identity and SP are not automatically deducible from unit characteristics in isolation from contextual pressures but are a contingent development. To better assess the historical cases of SP, more case studies are needed. Existing typologies may need further refinement, and issues of operationalization need further attention. However, the use of explicit theories and hypotheses in structuring case studies is crucial. At present, I believe the DP proposition offers a plausible and relevant avenue for such structuring.

Notes

The author is grateful to the editors, both for their patience and for their hard work. Their professional yet relaxed approach has made being a contributor to this volume a pleasure. The author also wishes to thank the Bank of Sweden Tercentenary Foundation, the Swedish Institute of International Affairs, and the Swedish Ministry for Foreign Affairs for their substantial and important financial support. For an expanded version of the arguments presented in this chapter, see Ericson 2000.

1. Unit-level functional differentiation refers to the existence of actors in the international system that command different types of resources and have different kinds of ambitions concerning reproduction and function (trading companies, mercenary companies, territorial states, and theocratic empires are possible candidates). Structural differentiation concerns different modes of internal organization by units that may be functionally alike, such as the territorial state. Waltz (1979) discusses functional differentiation only and concludes that the efficiency imperative will produce, and has produced, like units. He does not discuss structural differentiation, but the term is used by Buzan and Little (1996).

2. The need for case studies to develop DP theory beyond its probabilistic version has been noted elsewhere. See Elman 1997b, 881–83.

3. Immanuel Kant is often credited with formulating in 1795 the proposition that liberal (or republican or democratic) states do not fight one another (Kant 1991). Among its main current proponents is Michael W. Doyle, who in his original study explicitly based his reasoning on Kant. Doyle also supplemented it with a quantitative study on wars and types of governments, covering the period 1816–1980, using the data collected by Melvin Small and David Singer in the Correlations of War Project (Doyle 1983a, 1983b). Doyle and others have been unable to find one single instance where two liberal states went to war during the period in question. Doyle defines "liberal regimes" in terms of states where the citizens possess juridical rights and that allow private property and a market economy; where (male) suffrage is above 30 percent and female suffrage is granted within a generation of being "demanded by an extensive female suffrage movement"; and where the elected body (the legislative branch) has "an effective role in public policy and [is] formally and competitively (either inter- or intra-party) elected" (Doyle 1986, 1164).

4. According to Doyle, it has to be probabilistic because if the democratic peace or the liberal thesis "is anything like normal science," there will be exceptions to the rule (Russett et al. 1995, 182). Russett's categorizations thus differ slightly from Doyle's (states do not, for instance, have to be market economies to qualify as democracies), and James Ray's definitions of war and democracy are also different, yet all support the thesis (Russett 1993, 11–16; Ray 1995; and Maoz 1997).

5. This, taken by itself, suggests that democracies ought to be more pacific generally (and not just towards other democracies), which is a much harder proposition to defend than that of a separate peace between democracies. Among the main writers in the field Rummel (1983) is the one who most emphatically defends this proposition. Doyle, Russett, and many others focus primarily on the separate peace between democracies.

6. MacMillan argues that the German Social Democrats opposed war in 1914 but

voted for the defense funds because they feared consequences of marginalization in the domestic political arena (MacMillan 1998, 215 ff).

7. Doyle counts Sweden as democratic from 1864 on and Norway as democratic from 1905, the year of its independence (Doyle 1983a, 210).

8. The passages on Sweden and Norway draw on a previous study by the author, using archive material, diaries, and memoirs, as well as secondary historical sources. To list them all here would be redundant, and instead I refer to the original study as the source. The bulk of the material referred to in this chapter consists of Swedish and Norwegian general staff documents kept by the Krigsarkiv in Stockholm and the Riksarkiv in Oslo, respectively. The original study (Ericson 2000) of course contains detailed references to the particular documents.

8

The Economic Aspects of Stable Peace-Making

Alfred Tovias

Some Early Thoughts about the Schuman Approach

The point of departure of this chapter is Robert Schuman's assertion that "peace is not solely the absence of war but the achievement of common objectives and peaceful tasks undertaken together." Was he thinking already in terms of stable peace? In any case, Schuman's approach was different from George Marshall's perspective as presented at Harvard University on June 5, 1947, not only because their aims were different, but also because of the different nature of the methods proposed to cope with the declared aims. The Marshall Plan was part of a grand strategy to contain the Soviet menace and stressed financial inflows from third countries for the reconstruction of war-torn economies and the reignition of economic intercourse among Western European countries. Conversely, the most important objective for Schuman in proposing in 1950 the creation of a European Coal and Steel Community (ECSC) was to contribute to peace consolidation and maintenance between France and Germany.

The Schuman approach stressed regional self-reliance and therefore regional self-respect. It was thus much more ambitious and demanding than Marshall's approach. The principal difference between Schuman's approach and other cooperative attempts after World War II was that Schuman did not believe in variable geometry. Neither did his approach rely on the proliferation of institutions for purely functional and techno-cratic considerations (an idea defended already in 1944 by Mitrany). "Community" member countries, including former enemies, were expected to cooperate among themselves rather than with nonmember countries. It was to be cooperation "for better or for worse," independent of the subject matter, although within the scope delimited by the constitutional treaties and in the context of the institutional framework established by the latter. In that respect, Schuman believed that a structure was needed to create political, economic, and social synergy among former belligerents in Europe. Such a structure would create a bond among them and would encourage everybody to treat problems from a European viewpoint. Whereas the Anglo-Saxon concept of functionalism had a purely opportunistic flavor, Schuman's concept of "community" was akin to marriage. Not by coincidence, Schuman was a devout Catholic and a Christian Democrat, as were many of the early Europeanists after 1945 (Adenauer and De Gasperi, to name just two). But there was a common denominator to all post-1945 approaches, namely their pragmatic, non-doctrinal Europeanism. Concrete steps were needed to build trust, while too much obsession with grand design could lead to failure. However, the Treaty of Paris giving birth to the ECSC did not contemplate the legal possibility for members to withdraw from membership. The legal bond created among members was to be permanent, with no possibility of opt-outs or divorce. It was in fact a Catholic marriage.

The Conceptual Framework: Comparing Notes with Other Contributors to the Debate

My chapter is related to the quest by Kacowicz and Bar-Siman-Tov for conditions for maintaining peace over time. I am interested here in the stabilization and perpetuation of peace over time by economic means. Following Boulding (1978, 13), I am inclined to adopt his definition of stable peace "as a situation in which the probability of war is so small that it does not really enter into the calculations of any of the people involved." A thesis of this chapter is that among the key factors allowing for stable peace is an economic one, to be defined later as "irrevocable interdependence." In order to have it, there is no need for a common language, religion, or culture among former belligerents. It is not that war is unthinkable but rather that it is an irrational way to solve conflicts or promote interests. As we will see, former enemies are deterred from resuming war because of the huge economic costs of dissociating again among themselves. This works because people and their leaders have a business-oriented attitude, not one based on principles. That people are not "romantic" or "heroic" but "materialistic," and their attitudes are businesslike, is an explicit assumption I share with Boulding. In what follows, I assume that the resumption of hostilities or violence between two former enemy states leads to a decrease in the interdependence levels attained and that this is what nobody wants, not the hostilities themselves. This assumption might not hold in the short run. For instance, we might have for short periods, as actually happened in the European Community (EC) between France and Spain, navy boats of one of the countries chasing and even bombing ships of the other for allegedly fishing in its territorial waters. Thus, stable peace in my view does not rule out entirely the use of military force, at least occasionally, as distinct from war.

Stable peace by irrevocable interdependence does not require that the parties have the same political regime or share values, apart from a common belief in the market system. This conforms perfectly to the notion defended by Kacowicz and Bar-Siman-Tov. It requires less from the members of the scheme than "pluralistic security communities." In Miller's terminology (chapter 3), a state of irrevocable interdependence lies, conceptually speaking, somewhere in the space between normal and warm peace.

Borrowing from the hierarchical distinction made by Boulding whereby the integrative system is above the exchange system, which itself is above the threat system, Arad, Hirsch, and I proposed to stabilize peace by devising a structure that allows movement from the threat system to the exchange system (Arad, Hirsch, and Tovias 1983, 4). We recognized that moving to the integrative system after the end of a war is a step too steep to climb in the short and medium run. The latter would imply attaining the so-called "we-feeling" among former enemies that calls for a change of perceptions, which in turn implies a change in culture and in ideology. It might also imply a change in the behavior of each citizen and not only of the leaders or the establishment. For instance, in order to get "real" Europeans, you must get people who not only think like Europeans but also speak different European languages. That in turn is easier to conceive if Germans marry French and give birth to Franco-German children. All this takes time. Arad, Hirsch, and I were much more modest in claiming that in order to have stable peace it is necessary "only" to substitute an exchange system for a threat system. We based this idea on the simple observation that it is in the economic realm that it is easiest to start to build stable peace, economic relations being the least affected by emotional and ideological factors.

We coined the concept of "balance of prosperity," as opposed to the "balance of terror" familiar to all international relations scholars. The former occurs when the benefits of bilateral cooperation are substantial and the realization of these benefits is conditional upon the continued cooperation of former enemies. Following Schuman's approach, we posited that fleshing out peace required a previous and conscious political decision to develop what we called "vested interests in peace" (VIP), which would be mainly developed by economic interaction between former enemies. To prevent war and maintain peace, a balance of prosperity, rather than a balance of terror or a balance of power, has to be established.

In terms of Russett and Starr's conditions for peace maintenance (Russett and Starr, 1992), it is a combination of conditions four (economic benefits) and two (institution building), as well as three (economic ties and social communication). There is neither need for the first condition (cohesion in the face of outside threats) nor the fifth (democratic regimes).

We follow the principle whereby people with empty stomachs tend to be more frustrated and therefore more aggressive. Accordingly, we should clearly distinguish between aiming at economic prosperity and well-being in former belligerent countries as a factor tending to diminish tension between them, and aiming at economic prosperity through *cooperation* with the former enemy. In the first case, the aim can be attained by many means; for example, cutting defense expenditures, asking for economic assistance from third parties, or asking for reparations from the former enemy. All this is compatible with Miller's cold peace and has nothing to do with stable peace, because the latter requires positive interaction between former enemies. Therefore, in the opinion of this author, one cannot really say that there is stable peace between Iceland and New Zealand, since there are almost no contacts between their people.

The Link between Peace, Economic Development, and Economic Cooperation

Peace is necessary for economic development and prosperity, not the other way around. But once there is economic prosperity, many private agents would visibly lose their recently gained prosperity if there were a disruption brought about by renewed hostilities. This follows a liberal logic, where economic prosperity is contingent on interdependence and integration, which in turn facilitate the establishment of stable peace.

The kind of economic benefits we are talking about here are contingent on continuing cooperation. Mutual trust might be sufficient to maintain and enhance these economic benefits, but otherwise institutional or rule-based arrangements with in-built stabilizing power can do the trick, should mutual trust be momentarily lacking (e.g., by reliance on backup instruments such as dispute settlement mechanisms).[1]

In such a setting the main cause to explain why peace is maintained is the type of interaction among former enemies—in our case irrevocable interdependence—rather than the common characteristics of the different actors. The paradox with economic cooperation is that it helps to build trust, but you need to trust the other party in order to engage in economic cooperation in the first place. Cooperation is then a voluntary exercise and it should not be imposed. Therefore, we must assume inevitably that there is sufficient political will among the leaders of the former enemy countries to try consciously to bind the hands of their successors by maximizing vested interests in peace and thus the objective costs of dissociation.

Costs of Dissociation and Irrevocable Interdependence

The costs of dissociation are the costs of discontinuing economic transactions in which the parties had engaged beforehand. Costs of dissociation are a function of the gains from trade but are larger than the latter, since resources have been invested to conduct the transactions themselves that cannot be entirely recovered in case of disruption. Costs of dissociation are higher the fewer the alternatives to the loss of the former enemy as a supplier or as a client.

Will the fear of these costs prevent the establishing of a balance of prosperity between former enemies? No, if both are assured that each of them will incur those costs if the other decides to sever relations and if both agree about the relationship between these costs. The costs must not be identical or symmetrical in absolute terms for each of the former enemies. Much depends on the economic size of the latter, but not everything. The important thing is that both perceive themselves as interdependent.

Does this bilateral interdependence prevent the resumption of war and guarantee the maintenance of peace? No, unless the costs of dissociation for both partners become unbearable and exorbitant; only in that case do we reach a state of what can be called irrevocable interdependence. In fact, irrevocable interdependence is the equivalent of mutual assured destruction in the balance of terror system. From a purely rational viewpoint, the latter has the advantage for each of the partners of not requiring the cooperation of the other partners. The disadvantage, of course, is the element of uncertainty, which is not present in the balance of prosperity system proposed here, since it is possible to determine mutually the level of transactions and to calculate in advance with certainty the costs of dissociation for both partners.

If the leaders of former enemy states wish to enhance peace, they might have to give incentives to private agents to move towards irrevocable interdependence whenever the normal interplay of market forces does not lead to that ultimate stage. These incentives might take the form of subsidies, tariff preferences, insurance schemes, dispute settlement mechanisms, and so on. The leaders of both countries might, as well, have to follow on a daily basis the transactions being decided upon by private agents and give their approval to them. Thus, they might be able to discard those transactions that are destabilizing or that might move former enemies from a situation of normal interdependence to a situation of dependence of one of them upon the other. In other words, we must maximize the cost of dissociation for both partners and try to prevent those costs from tilting too far in favor of one party at the expense of the other. Although the economic welfare of both former enemies grows thanks to spontaneous economic cooperation, it does not grow equally or symmetrically. We know of no economic theory concluding that international trade will benefit all partners equally. But this is more or less what leaders should strive for to maintain stable peace and minimize friction and rivalry. They want to have a balanced interdependence. It might not, however, be enough to reach a balance of prosperity based on irrevocable interdependence.

To make sufficient if not irrevocable interdependence a reality, leaders must enlist in the case of market economies the private sector in the endeavor. They must promote if not maximize vested interests in peace. Political support for such a policy is a function of the increase in economic welfare as a result of the implementation of that policy. Domestically, new economic transactions raise the welfare of some groups at the expense of others. But from a political economy perspective not every group has the same political clout. When calculating net economic welfare within each country, which in turn affects VIP, we must take this into consideration. To try to convince every economic agent of the usefulness of a given transaction might be paralyzing unless compensation is offered to those losing out. This seems unrealistic if the compensation is to be paid by the former enemy and even by those economic agents winning out domestically. This is why it might be better to discard altogether transactions that hurt domestic groups that are politically articulate in any of the former enemy countries.

All the obstacles linked to distributional issues reduce the suitability of advanced forms of economic integration. They equally raise doubts as to the feasibility of any integration formulas leading to Vinerian trade creation, replacing inefficient producers in one partner country by efficient ones in another one.[2] Such options may be viable from the economic standpoint, but would be much less so for the local politician in the inefficient producer's country. For that reason I follow Arad, Hirsch, and Tovias (1983) in recognizing the supremacy of political considerations over economic ones in the evaluation of potential economic arrangements. Economic integration agreements can be instrumental in fostering peace, but they can also be detrimental in increasing economic rivalry. Competition may even lead to political rifts, which must be avoided, especially in sensitive situations such as building peace between former enemy countries in the quest for stable peace.

Furthermore, it is important to avoid the illusion that economic integration per se will solve endemic economic and demographic problems of former enemy countries. Any economic arrangement should be regarded as auxiliary to economic restructuring and growth efforts undertaken by individual countries.

The Advantage of Being Neighbors

The establishment of formal peace leads almost automatically to the elimination of formal boycotts and the establishment of most-favored nation
(MFN) relations.[3] This leads to reverse trade diversion, which can only
improve welfare. Reverse trade diversion occurs because the discrimina-
tion against the former enemy made when war started, which led to trade
diversion, is finally eliminated. Trading (again) with your former enemy
is more significant than trading with any other country in the international system, because normally that enemy is your neighbor, or might be
located between you and other important trading partners or between
you and the only sea in your neighborhood. So it is logical that on a random basis part of your foreign trade will be with your former enemy. But
you will trade with it more than that because by doing so you will economize on transfer costs, which include transportation and communication
costs and the excess of export over domestic marketing costs. You can
economize in inventories and storage facilities as well. You might only
need to use one mode of transport, not several. You might economize in
representation costs, since you can serve that market on an arms-length
basis. It is also likely that many economic agents in your country know
the neighbor's language, customs, and culture. There are several possibilities here. Either they are the same as in your country, or the members of
your civil society remember them from before the war, or many of these
members originate from that country to begin with.

Therefore, imports and exports will not only be diverted away from
third countries, but they will also be expanded beyond diversion because
of all that has been said above. Arad, Hirsch, and Tovias (1983) called
these forms of trade *export diversion, import expansion,* and *export expansion.*
There are two other categories of transactions that are frequently neglected. They concern sectors where decreasing costs (i.e., increasing returns to
scale) prevail. In that case local production of the good or service might
have taken place in spite of potential overseas competition because transfer costs isolated the country de facto. There were no exports or imports
of the good or service. The opening for business of the borders with the
former enemy enlarges the local market by adding a secondary market,
thus decreasing costs. This can be called *export creation;* that is, a nontrad-
ed good or service becomes tradable. A second category is constituted by
goods or services, which were wholly imported from overseas because
the size of the local market was not enough to justify local production.
The addition of the neighboring market changes the picture, so that production for the regional market might be justified now on an economic
basis. This can be called *output creation.* New trade flows can also emerge
on the basis of access across the new open border to inputs that are not

available locally. By combining these new inputs with the local ones, the country can become competitive internationally for the final goods issued from these inputs.

To manufacture and market new products it will be necessary to make up-front investments in manufacturing, distribution, and servicing facilities. The viability of these investments will depend on continued access to markets and/or sources of supply located in the territories of former enemy countries. This is why for this type of transaction, the institutional framework of relations between former enemies is so important.

The opening of geographic borders for business is important in another respect: It might lead to the establishment of regional offices for the distribution of third-country goods and services or for the purchase of local goods and services. Commuting and supervision time is shortened for third-country economic agents. Thus, regional spillover effects may be even more important than new direct trade between former enemies.

What Are Normal Economic Relations?

It is clear that trade relations across formerly closed borders (resulting from war, tension, etc.) could create a high degree of (reverse) trade diversion, thereby contributing to the welfare of all producers. The reason for this phenomenon is that before entering trade relations, neighboring countries were procuring goods and services outside the region at high prices. Normalization of trade relations can only increase welfare, never decrease it. By dropping trade boycotts and mutually granting MFN status, intra-area exports and imports would replace extra-area ones, just as they have in post–Cold War Europe, where renewed trade channels have been established across the former Iron Curtain. Other welfare-enhancing factors are newly created exports and output creations resulting from proximity and economies of scale, as mentioned above. Industries can reduce production costs in the long run by using inputs imported from former enemy countries and exploiting complementarities with them.

But is this enough, given the existence of psychological barriers to trade among former enemies, or should political leaders artificially promote trade relations as an overcompensation for invisible barriers, such as lack of trust? What is normal trade, if it happens that among the former enemy countries one or all of them had signed preferential trade agreements with third countries before the advent of peace? Should normalization be confined in that case to General Agreement on Tariffs and Trade (World Trade Organization)—type relations, based on MFN treatment? In some cases, as in the Middle East, it is also difficult to get a notion of what "normalization" of economic relations implies. Nobody has a clear idea what "normal" means, since before the war some states might not have existed or might have been occupied by an outside power.

The relative importance of getting "normal" (MFN) market access in the former enemy country compared to "preferred" market access depends on the MFN level of tariffs applied by the latter. For Syria, for example, it will be by far more important to get MFN treatment from Israel than to go all the way to industrial free trade. On the other hand, for Israel, normalization might not mean much, since Syria is still a fairly closed country as far as trade and investment is concerned.

More generally, what sort of discriminatory trading arrangements in favor of former enemy countries should one look for? Global agreements such as free-trade areas (FTAs) are suitable to partner countries whose economic structures are relatively similar and diversified. A more suitable integration formula among complementary economies might be sectoral integration, following the ECSC example in post–World War II Europe. Concluding sectoral FTAs in sectors where the former enemies concerned are competitive, although in different segments of the same production process, might be the optimal solution.

Can Normalization Lead to Irrevocable Interdependence?

Does normalization ensure stable peace? Does integration? The answers to these questions depend in fact on the trade potential between former enemies and therefore on their relative economic structures. In principle, neoclassic trade theory expects that there will more trade between distant countries (a priori less likely to be enemies) than closer or neighboring countries. It has been only after 1945, and even more so in the 1980s, with the emergence of large-scale production of heterogeneous products, that economists have discovered the importance of long-run economies of scale and economic geography. Thus, the importance of the regional econ-omy led to the development of the "new trade" theory. It is obvious that bad political relations are more of an obstacle to the fulfilling of potential economic intercourse predicted by the "new trade" theory based on intra-industry trade, joint ventures, foreign direct investment, and close collab-oration than predicted by neoclassical trade theory.

What happens if there is no objective economic potential between for-mer belligerents? To begin with, we must be sure to gauge that potential correctly. In many cases, empirical analysis is deficient, because it is based on economic data describing the interaction between each of the former enemies and third countries. These studies calculate the trade that could be diverted away from third countries towards the former enemy. This leads to a huge underestimation of the potential, as we explained above.

Even so, even if we take new trade into account, it could be that the potential would still be small in relative terms (e.g., 10 percent of the total external trade). Not only that, but what if technological advances such as the Internet constantly diminish more than proportionately the costs of communicating or transacting over long distances, when compared to short distances? It is then perfectly reasonable to think that attaining a state of irrevocable interdependence with neighbors will be increasingly difficult. It also follows that what might be considered irrevocable interdependence today between France and Germany will become revocable interdependence with time because of the increasing availability for France of equally profitable transacting alternatives with more distant countries.

Underlying all the strategies explored in this chapter is the assumption that relative economic size matters. As important as direct trade relations are from a political viewpoint, if the main objective of policy-makers after the establishment of peace is to achieve a rapid improvement in the economic situation of their countries, they should perhaps focus on deepening their institutional trade relations with their main trading partners. This might not be, even in the best of cases, their former enemies. For instance, one apparently new minor agricultural concession by the EC within the framework of the Israel–EC FTA agreement, such as higher quotas on avocados and citrus fruit, may create more jobs in Israel than across-the-board preferential tariff reductions on industrial imports by Syria,which has a gross national product less than 0.25 percent of the EC's. Clearly the underlying economic structure of the former belligerent can tell us if a state of irrevocable interdependence is attainable or not. A good example of where that was by far *not* the case was the European Free Trade Area.

Enhancing Factors

The Importance of Initial Conditions

In assessing the likelihood of attaining irrevocable interdependence, we must consider the framework of economic relations each of the former enemies lives in at the time peace sets in. One alternative is to build structures from scratch, as in the nearly tabula rasa reality that characterized much of post–World War II Europe. Another is to build a superstructure on top of the existing one, such as in the present Middle East, with Israel having plenty of FTA agreements with non-Arab countries and the latter having recently concluded wide-ranging agreements with the European Union under the Euro-Mediterranean Partnership. This is a priori much more complicated. It might imply in some cases that the former enemies will first consider relinquishing existing institutional links with countries not of the region or with former allies.

Discriminatory Trading Arrangements

Eliminating tariff and nontariff barriers among former belligerents, whether across all sectors or partially, is the most obvious way to move in the direction of irrevocable interdependence. The static and dynamic effects of regional trade liberalization might by themselves be enough to reach irrevocable interdependence. This in fact was the bet made by Monnet and Schuman when they proposed the creation of the ECSC to consolidate peace between France and Germany. Jan Tinbergen, winner of the first Nobel Prize in economics, spoke of negative integration when referring to those formulae. It is hard to conceive a political situation in which former enemies would agree voluntarily on common trade and competition policies just after the conclusion of a peace agreement. Even Schuman and Monnet understood that "positive economic integration" was feasible only after trust had been built by less ambitious cooperation schemes. Not only that, but to consider a common trade policy, the level of economic development of the former enemies, as well as their geostrategic economic interests, should be similar. Former enemies rarely fulfill both conditions, an exception being France and Germany in the 1950s.

The Role of Institutions

This was a factor also taken into account by Schuman. Trade and investment between former belligerents can be promoted by the creation of suitable institutional arrangements. Such arrangements are needed to codify formal procedures so as to ensure stability in the relationships between former enemy countries and increase the level of business security. Partners in bilateral and multilateral business ventures make significant investments in production, distribution, and service facilities, as well as long-term supply and purchase commitments. Suitable institutional arrangements (such as dispute settlement mechanisms) must reduce the risk to the bare minimum, a condition that will also facilitate foreign investment and the establishment of international joint ventures. The establishment of institutions solidifies the political element of the arrangement, since these institutions become permanent fora for discussion between partner countries. The status of these institutions can vary according to the level of authority they have to make binding decisions in the name of the contracting parties, the level of government agencies they represent, and the frequency of their common action. These institutions can range from purely technical committees to regular, periodic meetings at a ministerial level.

Elimination of Natural Barriers

Natural barriers between former enemies can also impede irrevocable interdependence. These cannot be easily changed, but leaders wishing to stabilize and maintain peace will not only explore the possibility of signing different kinds of discriminatory trade agreements (such as FTAs), but will also push forward projects such as construction of bridges, tunnels, roads, and railroad tracks that can mitigate if not eliminate these barriers.

Absence of Vested Interests in War

As there are vested interests in peace, there might also be, after the formal conclusion of peace, vested interests in war. If there is a military-industrial complex, it might heavily counteract moves taken by leaders to maximize VIP. Obviously the less extensive the vested interests in war, the easier it will be to achieve irrevocable interdependence. These vested interests are a function not only of the size attained by the professional army and the defense industries, but also of the degree to which army personnel can be easily recycled in the civilian sector, the possibilities for reconversion of the defense industries, the amount of dual-use technologies, and so on. The less professionalized the army and the more it is based on reserve personnel, the smaller will be the vested interests in war.

The Example of the ECSC

The Schuman Plan has been compared to the foreign policies of medieval princedoms, where dynastic marriages were encouraged between royal families to consolidate links. The royal couple became a sort of hostage to both sides, and both states had some interest in keeping the peace.

Schuman's method has been called "pacifusion": pooling coal and steel resources to prevent the reemergence of an autonomous military-industrial complex in former enemy countries. In fact, the newly created Federal Republic of Germany did not have an army yet in 1950. Therefore, accepting the Schuman Plan implied renouncing control of a future arms supply industry based on coal and steel inputs. The aim was to make not only war but also the preparation for war impossible among the (Western) European states.

Institutions such as the High Authority of the ECSC were to play an important role. At the first suspicious sign the authority could inspect and prevent any hidden rearmament using coal and steel products. Interestingly, Schuman also considered other forms of structural interdependence, such as interlocking the electricity grids.

But "pacifusion" required a permanent strategic commitment by the leaders, the first step being reconciliation and only then the search for European (common) solutions to outstanding problems. The theory was that reconciliation would come about by former enemies not only learning to live together (side by side), but also to work together for their common and mutual benefit. There was no talk of sharing a common destiny. Only empirical research can tell if attitudes were really changed by the mechanism of working together proposed by Schuman or rather by something else (e.g., youth exchanges, tourism, and denazification programs).

The ECSC experiment evolved under favorable conditions. For instance, natural barriers after the war were almost nonexistent. Monnet in his speeches could always stress that an absurd delineation of political borders in a region rich in iron and coal had been consolidated throughout history. These borders not only created friction and rivalry but also a misallocation of resources. He could easily assert, referring to the regions bordering France, Germany, Belgium, and Luxembourg, that the aim was "to reconstruct this natural basin whose unity has been mutilated and whose development has been limited."[4]

Moreover, the ECSC treaty stopped short of adopting a common trade policy, although it stipulated a common regime for investment, competition, adjustment, and research. This led some scholars to regard the 1951 Paris Treaty establishing the ECSC as aiming at more ambitious and elaborate institutional structures than the 1957 Rome Treaty, reflecting the more interventionist era of postwar reconstruction. But in fact, the ECSC was an "FTA plus," as everybody recognizes now.

This notwithstanding, the establishment of the ECSC really represented a conscious effort to use economic intercourse as an instrument to secure peace; other, more advanced forms of integration did not seem feasible at the time. Thus, the ECSC demonstrates quite clearly that economic transactions can play an important role in stabilizing peace between former enemies.

The Limits of the Method Proposed

Boulding already recognized in reference to stable peace that "the web of economic interdependence is undoubtedly a significant variable both structurally and dynamically though it is very complex and it is not always easy to see which way it will go" (Boulding 1978, 63). He mentions the classical economists as being naive in thinking that trade would bring peace simply because it would produce mutual dependency. He also saw that the breaking off of trade and investment relations was one of the costs of war and that the higher the costs of war, the greater the strength of the peaceful system established.

Was Boulding right in being so skeptical? In any case, neither he nor other researchers made a conscious effort to justify this skepticism. This chapter is an effort to identify the reasons for the skepticism and the circumstances under which the strategy of irrevocable interdependence might succeed.

To begin with, the underlying economic structures of the former belligerents might not be conducive to the establishment of a balance of prosperity, because basically, even in the case of peaceful relations, they would transact mainly with third countries, not between themselves.[5] Clearly what might be a factor favoring the establishment of this balance is proximity. It so happens that most wars are based on territorial disputes and therefore involve neighbors. Proximity is a factor favoring trade and investment, all other things being equal. Peace can extend the range of the tradable sector simply by allowing for the opening of borders. Peace can also allow for the development of common infrastructures (joint power generation, transport, and communication facilities) and the establishment of regional offices by third-country purchasing and marketing agents.

Assuming now that striking a balance of prosperity is not a problem from a technical and economic viewpoint, the second problem is that it might a priori be less credible than establishing a balance of terror. The challenge for leaders is to propose ways to make the one as credible as the other. A balance of terror has the advantage that it is established by sequential unilateral decisions. Not so a balance of prosperity, which is based on transacting, and as we know, "It takes two to tango." Thus, there must be a framework or some institutions for the preservation of the rules of the game, possibly a dispute settlement mechanism. This degree of sophistication is frequently difficult to envisage among former belligerents, given the lingering lack of trust and the high level of animosity between at least part of the populations involved.

There is another problem with the balance of prosperity. Many economic transactions can have destabilizing effects and therefore be counterproductive. Former enemies might put an inordinate focus on the relative instead of the absolute value of mutual gains. In other words, they are very touchy about the *distribution of gains*, not only about their absolute size.

Donald Puchala (1970), not someone to be suspected of anti-EC sentiment, wrote in an article reviewing French-German relations after the war
that economic intercourse created conditions within which both governments could work towards cooperation at other levels. He argued, however, that the creation of the ECSC added an "endurance factor to political relations between governments and helped to overcome political
strain, by increasing the level of mutual confidence. Yet economic cooperation was a supportive factor at most."

As shown in this chapter, the ECSC was established under auspicious
conditions. What about the Israeli-Arab post-conflict setting? To quote
Hirsch, economic integration, as conceived by Schuman and Monnet,
could, in the very different circumstances of the Middle East, have quite
undesirable consequences.

Notes

1. See the contribution of Bengtsson in this book (chap. 5) for a discussion of the
concept of trust.

2. Jacob Viner (1950) distinguished between the trade creation and trade diversion
effects of creating a customs union. Vinerian trade creation takes place when domestic
high-cost sources are replaced by low-cost imports from the partner in the customs
union.

3. MFN treatment requires granting a new partner, including a former enemy
country and/or a country previously boycotted, the same treatment previously granted to a third party.

4. From a speech by Jean Monnet on August 10, 1952, in Monnet 1955, 85.

5. Another, rather odd, possibility is that one or both former enemies have huge
economies not dependent on foreign trade for their well-being. Even the United States
does not conform nowadays to this definition.

9

Issue Treatment and Stable Peace: Experiences from Boundary Agreements

Kjell-Åke Nordquist

Stable peace has remained a vision throughout centuries of the modern state's existence. With a few exceptions, such as the often mentioned cases of Switzerland and Sweden, most countries have not lived without war for a period of, say, a century. In the minds of many people—and leaders—such a situation was abnormal; war had to be counted upon as a recurrent evil. The end of the Cold War has challenged this attitude. Deterrence and capacity for mutual assured destruction lost their immediate political relevance, and different dimensions of the realist perspective, along with new approaches to international relations, became relevant. Problems that few scholars were exploring during the Cold War are now increasingly in focus, owing in part to their relevance for the development of Grotian and liberal principles of inter-state relations.

The end of the Cold War removed some major obstacles to a substantial treatment of the stable peace idea and created a new basis for research. One obvious development is that the number of peace agreements increased significantly after the end of the Cold War. It is then relevant to ask whether these agreements should be lasting or not.[1]

While the end of the Cold War represented a major structural change on the global level, a fundamental feature of the territorial state is still the same: its territorial boundaries. As long as one's own boundaries do not change, stable boundaries are to be preferred. They mean stable identity for any territorially based social order. Boundary agreements, then, are instruments by which states regulate their territorial identity. If any inter-state agreement is to be stable, boundary agreements should be stable as well. They form the outer limits of the state's influence as well as its responsibility. Thus, in the history of boundary agreements, there is a lot of introductory rhetoric about a "final solution," "settling definitively," and establishing a "*paix perpetuelle*" between the parties.

The idea of stable peace, on the one hand, and the function of the boundary agreement as an instrument for establishing stable peaceful relations, on the other, are here brought together into an inquiry about the conditions for establishing and maintaining stable peace. These questions concern the way the agreement is constructed, how its construction relates to its durability, and the political context within which durable agreements are becoming examples of long-term stable, peaceful relations.

Theoretical Approach and Material

Boundary agreements concluded since the mid-1900s and followed up to the end of the twentieth century form the empirical basis for this study. The theoretical framework is developed in chapter 1 by Kacowicz and Bar-Siman-Tov and will not be repeated here in detail. In this chapter, the distinction between stabilization and institutionalization of stable peace is used as a point of departure for analyzing stable boundary agreements and their fate, especially in the institutionalization phase. Basically, two questions are asked: Under what conditions are boundary agreements durable? And under what conditions do durable boundary agreements become institutionalized?

Security Community and the Democratic Peace

During the twentieth century stable peaceful inter-state relations became the norm in some regions—not only in the North Atlantic area but also, for example, between Australia and New Zealand—even in times of a regional, or even global, war. Karl Deutsch and his colleagues described these relationships in their 1957 study, terming them a "pluralistic security community." A security community, according to Deutsch, is characterized by common values, mutual expectations, economic growth, administrative capacity, and broad areas of societal communication and relations, among other things.[2]

The examination of some characteristics of a security community has been revived in international relations research in the last decade, particularly with respect to the democratic peace proposition. This proposition is an important contribution to the theoretical problem of stable relations, since it identifies a particular sphere of peaceful inter-state relations. Its contribution to discussions of stable peace is not without limitations, however. Democratic peace, for instance, does not include the relationship between states with different types of regimes or between authoritarian dyads. Such relations remain unexplained. In addition, the theoretical support for the democratic peace needs further development. For our purpose, it is sufficient to relate the findings in this chapter to some version of the democratic peace proposition. This chapter is concerned with the conditions for stable peaceful international relations, irrespective of regime type.

Holsti on War Issues

Several authors have remarked on the paucity of research on issue treatment and conflict resolution with respect to stable inter-state relations. Holsti's 1991 study seems to be very relevant for our purpose. A major study on the issues and the structure of major peace agreements, it deals both with characteristics on the system level and with issues in major wars throughout the same period. Holsti's point of departure is that scholars have neglected three problems in this context: the role of issues generating international conflict; the "meaning of war," that is, the attitudes of decision-makers towards the use of force; and the link between peace settlements and war. Unfortunately, Holsti does not follow up the issue aspect on the systemic level.

Holsti examines major multilateral peace settlements in the period 1648–1989. He constructs, as "arbitrary judgements" (Holsti 1991, 337) an eight-point list of "probably necessary [but not sufficient] conditions" for peace. The list includes: (1) governance (states should "be prepared to act jointly" to respond to major "transgressions of rules"); (2) legitimacy ("The peace settlement that establishes both the results of the war and the foundations for the post-war order should not create the breeding ground for a new war to overturn the results of the previous conflict."); (3) assimilation (of previous warring actors); (4) a deterrent system in support of a settlement (a coalition of victors "that is committed to the settlement"); (5) conflict resolution mechanisms; (6) a consensus on war as a system problem; (7) procedures for peaceful change; and (8) an anticipation of future issues (Holsti, 1991, 337 ff.).

Holsti finds that no major peace agreement meets more than five of the eight prerequisites. He concludes that to create stable international relations, major peace settlements must anticipate issues and devise means to cope with them. Holsti's analysis shows that so far no major settlement has been able to do so.

Holsti's conditions for an international order do not require an armed conflict in order to be relevant. In fact, most of them deal with the regulation of the issues that created the war ended by the settlement. Instead, the eight points are system oriented. Thus, although his accounts include issues that generated wars in previous periods, he does not develop this aspect in the final analysis. An interpretation from reading Holsti is, then, that issues are regulated or resolved on a system level rather than in bilateral or multilateral agreements. To the extent that an agreement is important for its own durability, then, it is because of its system-creating effects rather than its treatment of incompatibilities or adaptation to its surroundings. Thus, Holsti's study does not examine the influence of an agreement's treatment of issues.

Analysis of Boundary Agreements

The following sections examine boundary agreements made after conflicts that were active in the period between 1942 and 1979 (see table 9.1). The agreements were concluded in the period 1942–1984, so in most cases the agreements have been in force for a few decades.[3] A boundary conflict is defined as a conflict over the definition, delimitation, or demarcation of a boundary line. Thus, conflicts over the formation of a new state, for instance, are not included, nor are territorial changes after armed conflict. Up to 1991, fifteen agreements related to boundary conflicts active in the period 1942–1979. Since 1991 a few new agreements have been made after the failure of a previous agreement; for example, the nondurable 1942 agreement between Ecuador and Peru was replaced in October 1998 by a new comprehensive agreement. These fifteen agreements are relevant to the first of the two questions, dealing with conditions for durability. The durable agreements among these fifteen constitute the material for the second question, concerning the transition from stabilization to institutionalization, leading to stable peace. A durable agreement is defined as an operative political document that has been in force at least fifteen years and has survived at least one change of government.

The first fifteen years is the period of stabilization. The subsequent institutionalization can take different forms and have different qualities.

The Stabilization Phase: What Makes Boundary Agreements Durable?

Although Holsti´s study does not deal with boundary agreements per se, he makes one observation that is particularly relevant to territorial questions, which we will use as a point of departure. Holsti writes: "Closely related to the problem of peaceful change is the peace-maker's ability to anticipate the kinds of issues that will generate international conflict in the future. The territorial settlements, institutions, and system norms should include provisions for identifying, monitoring and handling not just the problems that created the previous war but future conflicts as well" (Holsti 1991, 339). It is the anticipatory component of agreements that will be analyzed here. It highlights the tension between an agreement maker's tendency to focus on the problems causing conflict and the

Table 9.1 Length and Durability of Boundary Agreements after Inter-State Conflicts Active between 1942 and 1979

Period	Parties	Length (Years)	Durable?
1961–1998	China, Nepal	37	Yes
1963–1998	Mali, Mauritania	35	Yes
1970–1998	Algeria, Tunisia	28	Yes
1972–1998	Algeria, Morocco	26	Yes
1973–1998	Argentina, Uruguay	35	Yes
1984–2000	Argentina, Chile 2	16	Yes
1970–1998	Ethiopia, Kenya 2	28	Yes
1960–1998	Burma, China 2	38	Yes
1942–1953	Ecuador, Peru 2	11	No
1975–1980	Iran, Iraq 2	5	No
	Previous Agreements		
1881–1896	Argentina, Chile 1	15	No
1947–1955	Ethiopia, Kenya 1	8	No
1941–*	Burma, China 1		No
1829–1832	Ecuador, Peru 1	3	No
1937–*	Iran, Iraq 1		No

*Period not counted because of intervention of World War II (1939–1945).

ability to foresee potential problems.

The approach dealing with potential future issues is here called "adaptation." If an agreement goes beyond its immediate purpose of locating the boundary line and takes into account one or more geographic or social features directly affected by the boundary, it is adapted to its environment. Such an adaptation is positively connected to the agreement's durability:

	Durable	Not durable
Adapted	8	2
Not adapted	0	5

We have previously argued that a durable agreement is likely to support stable peace. Adaptation, then, seems to be an effective approach for boundary negotiations in establishing stable peaceful relations. Thus, it increases the likelihood of stable peace.

Types of Adaptation and Durability

Two types of adjustments have been identified (see table 9.2; for a more detailed analysis, see the appendix to this chapter): *exchange,* where a party gets a new resource in exchange for a loss of another; and *partition/sharing,* where the parties either split or share a specific resource.

Sharing includes a continuation of relations with regard to the resource, while exchange is dissociative and interruptive. While the two nondurable adapted cases both involve partition, the lack of durability cannot be related to the approach taken. The failures were due to the independence processes, in one case of Burma and in the other, Kenya. It seems more likely that the type of adaptation is not as important to durability as the existence of adaptation as such.

The Poststabilization Process:
Four Types of Institutionalization

The stabilization phase included the first fifteen years; agreements that passed this limit were called durable. We will now deal with the *poststabilization* period, leading up to the situation as of today. Institutionalization, the phase in which peace is maintained and deepened over time, includes

Table 9.2 Types of Adaptation and Durability of Agreement

Adaptation	Durable	Not durable
Partition/sharing	Algeria–Morocco	Burma–China 1
	Algeria–Tunisia	Ethiopia–Kenya 1
	Argentina–Uruguay	
	China–Nepal	
	Ethiopia–Kenya 2	
Exchange	Argentina–Chile 2	
	Mali–Mauritania	
	Burma–China 2	
None		Iran–Iraq 1
		Iran–Iraq 2
		Ecuador–Peru 1
		Ecuador–Peru 2
		Argentina–Chile 1

Table 9.3 Type of Institutionalization Process and Boundary Agreements
Involved

Nonreproducing		Reproducing	
Pseudo	Nominal	Indirect	Direct
China–Nepal	Burma–China 2	Argentina–Chile	Argentina–Uruguay
	Algeria–Morocco	Algeria–Tunisia	
	Mali–Mauritania		
	Ethiopia–Kenya 2		

both a quantitative dimension—the number of years—and a qualitative
dimension, which includes norms, mutual respect, nonmilitary ways of
dealing with conflictual issues, and similar social forms. In the following
pages, eight long-term boundary agreements are analyzed with respect to
their role in the parties' bilateral and regional relations. These cases show
that there is no straight line between the age of an agreement and its
degree of institutionalization. Instead, agreements experience very different types of bilateral and regional developments (see table 9.3).

Nonreproducing processes do not go beyond their formal basis; that is,
they remain within the limits set by the agreement. Even if the long-term
existence of the agreement gives the appearance of institutionalization,
this is a pseudo or nominal form of institutionalization. Reproducing
processes, in contrast, grow beyond their foundations in the boundary
agreement and develop into norms and practices that work towards stable peaceful relations in mutually reinforcing ways.

Pseudo Institutionalization: Regional and Strategic Issues Prevail

In this category, the boundary agreement is in force in a political context
where one or more strategic issues dominate the relations between the parties. A typical case in point is the China–Nepal boundary. Here, the strategic conflict between India and China and the sensitive relations between
Nepal and both of these major powers override the boundary agreement,
when it is functional at all. Thus, the institutionalization of the boundary
peace between Nepal and China may be as much a function of Sino-Indi-
an relations as of the qualities of the agreement. Both parties to the agreement are playing the regional strategic game. Although the boundary
agreement seems to solve some sensitive issues, then, it is wrong to
assume that an institutionalized stable peace has been established by the
long period of agreement-based peaceful relations between China and
Nepal since 1961.

Nominal Institutionalization: No Sign of Integration

In some cases, there is no significant change in the boundary situation over a long period of time during which an agreement is in force. This situation adds years to the statistics, but does it contribute to the evolution of an institutionalized peaceful relationship?

The relationship between Burma and China is a case in point. China's policy toward Burma was the same as its policy toward Nepal: "equality" in boundary treatment with its small neighbors. As a matter of ideology and foreign policy, China vowed that, even as a major regional and global power, it would never be party to what it viewed as unfair and unequal treaties such as those forced on it by Russia and Great Britain in the 1800s and early 1900s.[4] There was thus an ideological basis for peaceful boundary relations between China and Burma in the first decades of their relationship. At the other end of the period of the agreement, we find the 1988 takeover of the Burmese SLORC (the State Law and Order Restoration Council), which introduced an authoritarian military regime, leading to increasing international isolation.[5] In short, the boundary with China has been settled in a seemingly acceptable way. It was adapted, which is positive according to the analysis in the previous section, and there have been no major regional (or international) developments drawing attention away from possible bilateral boundary problems during the period. Instead, the status quo has been maintained—that is, the situation has been kept within the span of variation that is not unusual in that part of the world. No substantial changes of relevant political structures have taken place while the boundary agreement has been in force.

The Algeria–Morocco, Mali–Mauritania, and Ethiopia–Kenya boundary agreements have similar histories. In all three cases, one of the parties was at some part of the period involved in an armed conflict (the Western Sahara conflict for Morocco and Mauritania, and the Somali conflict for Ethiopia, which also affected Kenya). These conflicts have drawn attention away from functioning boundary relationships, but they have not led to any substantial institutionalization in terms of cooperation on the political, economic, or other level that concerns bilateral boundary relations.

Indirect Institutionalization: Nonboundary Developments

In some cases, issues unrelated to boundaries or border areas arise while a boundary agreement is in force. In the case of Argentina and Chile, specific remaining boundary disputes not covered by the agreement have been resolved, the latest one in 1999. These minor issues have not threatened the development of improved relations or trade and regional cooperation after the two countries' democratization (Argentina in 1983, Chile in 1989). In addition, the countries have held joint military exercises in the Beagle Channel area (see chapter 11). The development of Mercosur is probably the most substantial and visible example of the Southern Cone integration process. Argentina and Chile are significant parties to this process, and their boundary relations have steadily improved, in large part because of their democratization and the regional normative development taking shape in the 1990s through economic, environmental, and political cooperation. But because some boundary issues remain in the region—for example, between Argentina and Uruguay—the boundary situation as a whole cannot be categorized as stable.

Direct Institutionalization: New Mechanisms and Norms for Boundary Problems

Direct institutionalization occurs when boundary issues regulated in an agreement are dealt with within structures other than the agreement. When states integrate their mechanisms for dealing with particular issues and cooperate on a variety of other issues (some of which may be boundary related), new institutional mechanisms are established that take over the agreement's role as a normative and institutional basis for peaceful, stable relations. These mechanisms become the proper platforms for dealing with boundary and border issues. Such a situation is found in the case of Argentina and Uruguay, where a gradual development of bilateral as well as regional relations (Mercosur, for example) has taken place, while the boundary—and those issues related to the boundary agreement—has been minimally addressed. In this way, the boundary agreement has been institutionalized directly, through the development of nonboundary relations. In the Argentina–Uruguay case, this development stems from the time of the agreement signing (1973) with the Argentine–Uruguayan Economic Cooperation Agreement (CAUCE) in the 1970s, a series of trade agreements in the 1980s, and the Treaty of Asunción in 1991 paving the way for the Mercosur process in the rest of the 1990s. The boundary agreement has thus been institutionalized through regional and bilateral cooperation and emerging integration.

Within the Organization for Security and Cooperation in Europe (OSCE), the borders of the signing states were formally recognized in the Helsinki Agreement of 1975, and any change of their location should require mutual acceptance by all parties. In practice, as the European Union (EU) has become a reality, the relativization and reduction of European boundaries has gained momentum. For instance, the Schengen Agreement has led to a gradual elimination of passport control within the EU. Also, regional and border area development programs aim at diminishing the dissociative character of boundaries. Of course, the end of the Cold War and the fall of the Berlin Wall were necessary for this development outside the traditional Western European area. The EU specifically demands that countries applying for membership sort out boundary issues before serious membership negotiations can take place, thus encouraging a practice that some countries have applied bilaterally, namely, sorting out practical problems of boundary demarcation before any political agreement involving the boundary is made. In other cases, political leaders have met first, set out rules and principles for the demarcation, and hoped that everything would go smoothly on the ground. This has not always happened. The 1942 Ecuador–Peru agreement is perhaps the best-known example of how such a strategy has failed (at least until 1998).

Conclusion

This chapter has addressed two questions: (1) Under what conditions are boundary agreements durable? and (2) Under what conditions are durable boundary agreements institutionalized? Durable agreements were defined as lasting for fifteen years, and the first, or stabilization, phase of establishing stable peace was considered to equal this period. Agreements that lasted longer made up the group from which observations on institutionalization could be made.

As the variable for testing durability, we applied Holsti's observation (1991) that the ability to anticipate future problems is a major feature of effective peace agreements. This ability is here called adaptation. Boundary agreements that had adapted their provisions to geographic or social conditions in the disputed areas were significantly more durable than agreements without such adaptation. These agreements go beyond the problem of locating the boundary line and adopt provisions that establish a boundary regime that makes cross-boundary contacts smoother than they otherwise might have been. Thus, adapted agreements contribute to the stabilization of peaceful boundary relations between states.

For the institutionalization phase, four different types of institutionalization were inductively identified: pseudo, nominal, indirect, and direct institutionalization. Only the last two categories include substantial institutionalizing mechanisms, such as regional cooperation or bilateral mechanisms to deal with issues addressed by the boundary agreement. Agreements within the pseudo and nominal categories have lasted for a long time, and for that reason they may well be de facto stable and institutionalized. However, these agreements have been in place within a political context in which the boundary issues have been set aside for other, more pressing issues, making it difficult to assess the degree of institutionalization.

We can thus conclude, first, that even if an agreement seems durable, we cannot assume the durability is due to the agreement's inherent qualities. Second, and more interesting, if we want to further the durability of a particular agreement, it is probably more efficient to develop contextual conditions, such as the norms and practices within which the agreement functions, than to try to renegotiate or otherwise raise issues that have been dealt with by the agreement. This direct form of institutionalization can effectively handle issues that arise because of a changing environment—issues that even the best of agreements have difficulty foreseeing at the time of signing. Open, constructive adherence to an agreement, combined with a conscious and direct institutionalization process, can thus make the agreement an important building block in stable peaceful relations between states.

Appendix

Table 9.4 Geographical Conditions and Types of Adaptation in Boundary Agreements

| | Geographical Condition/Adaptation? | | | |
	Natural Resources	National Identity	Minority Relation	Type of Adaptation
Algeria–Tunisia	Oil/yes			Sharing
Algeria–Morocco	Iron ore, Tindouf/yes	Greater Morocco/no	Berber peoples/no	Partition/sharing
Argentina–Chile 2	Oil/yes			Exchange
Argentina–Uruguay	Subsoil resources/yes			Partition/sharing
Burma–China 1	Minerals/yes		Hill peoples/no	Partition/sharing
Burma–China 2	Minerals/no	Union integrity/yes		Partition/sharing
China–Nepal		Mt. Everest peak/yes		Partition/sharing
Ecuador–Peru 1		Historic rights/no	Indian population/no	

continued

Table 9.4—*continued*

	Geographical Condition/Adaptation?			
	Natural Resources	National Identity	Minority Relation	Type of Adaptation
Ecuador–Peru 2	Amazon River/no	Historic rights/no	Indian population/ no	
Ethiopia– Kenya 1	Water and grazing/yes		Galla people/ yes	Partition/ sharing
Ethiopia– Kenya 2	Water and grazing/yes		Galla people/ yes	Partition/ sharing
Iran–Iraq 1	Oil/no	Arabistan/ no	Ethnic links/ no	
Iran–Iraq 2	Oil/no	Arabistan/ no	Ethnic links/ no	
Mali– Mauritania	Water (wells)/yes	Historical relation/yes	Nomadic tribes/no	Exchange

Note: Argentina–Chile 1 is not included because no relevant geographical conditions could be identified.

Notes

1. Nineteen agreements have been concluded since 1989 in the sixty-seven major armed conflicts between 1989 and 1997. The number of major armed conflicts per year has steadily decreased over this period, from thirty-three in 1989 to twenty-five in 1997. (Wallensteen and Sollenberg 1998).
2. See Deutsch et al. 1957.
3. For a full case description, see Nordquist 1992.
4. Chinese boundary disputes today include disputes with India and Tajikistan. Also, bilateral negotiations are under way with Russia to resolve disputed sections of the boundary; with North Korea, a short section of the boundary is undefined. There are disputes over the Spratly Islands, a complicated issue involving Malaysia, the Philippines, Taiwan, Vietnam, and possibly Brunei; with Vietnam over the Gulf of Tonkin; and over the Paracel Islands occupied by China but claimed by Vietnam and Taiwan. Finally, China holds claims on the Japan-administered Senkaku-shoto, which is also claimed by Taiwan (Senkaku Islands/Diaoyu Tai).
5. In 1993, the Chinese minister for foreign affairs visited Burma, the first high-level political visit between the two countries since 1988.

II

CASE STUDIES AND POLICY IMPLICATIONS

———————

10

From Adaptation to Foreign Policy Activism: Sweden as a Promoter of Peace?

Ole Elgström and Magnus Jerneck

Sweden has not been at war since 1814. According to most observers, the long Swedish peace has not been caused by Swedish foreign policy measures alone. Because Sweden is a so-called nonessential power (Mouritzen 1996), one could even argue that its uniquely long peace is either a result of great power politics or just sheer luck. Minor powers are often drawn into an unwanted war, either by an invasion or by being pressured to join an alliance. Sweden was not occupied by the Germans during World War II, a situation that would be regarded by some observers as an instance of luck.

Although the peace of small states in some situations is an expression of external political dominance, one should not totally neglect the importance of foreign policy strategies carried out by the minor powers themselves. Even though the structure of the international system is assumed to constrain the ability of most countries to fully control their own destiny, there is often a certain, albeit limited, opportunity to choose different foreign policy paths. Given a specific international configuration, different strategies may produce different outcomes in terms of war and peace.

Our initial assumption is that Swedish statecraft has had at least *some* leverage on the processes leading to this privileged position of a lasting peace, directly or indirectly. Thus, our research aim is to show when, to what degree, and under what circumstances peace-seeking activities might have made Sweden a *producer* of international peace, however marginal, rather than just a *consumer* of peace offered by the great powers.

Since the early nineteenth century, Sweden has adhered to a variety of foreign policy doctrines, even though nonalignment and neutrality have been their common traits. These orientations do not a priori imply isolation or political remoteness; nonalignment and neutrality can be either active or passive. In short, modern Swedish history illuminates the tension between small-state strategies of political adaptation, primarily reflecting various levels of susceptibility to external pressures, and attempts to embark upon avenues of deliberate small-state activism on the international scene.[1]

By comparing five cases of Swedish foreign policy, covering a period from the early 1800s to the present day, we hope to achieve two things: first, to identify patterns of *adaptation* and *activism* in the conduct of Swedish security strategies; and, second, to draw some tentative conclusions about the *causal relationship* between these foreign policy measures and the durable Swedish peace. Two of our five cases deal with nineteenth-century strategies (the 1820s, and the 1850s and 1860s), whereas the other three are about twentieth-century foreign policy (the 1920s, the 1960s and 1970s, and the 1990s). In comparing these cases, we should be aware that they, to some extent, are related to each other. Thus, instances of continuity in foreign policy may be understood in terms of path dependency.

Even though peace has prevailed, its character has shifted throughout the time period in question, from a more fragile to a more consolidated peace with the outside world. To characterize these situations of peace, we follow a conceptualization introduced by George, Boulding, and others.[2] The most volatile situation, on a scale depicting a range of conflicting and cooperative relations, is called *precarious peace*. Typical for relations of precarious peace is fear of, or plans for, imminent war. A less tense form, *conditional peace*, exists when there are no imminent fears of war "but a general lack of confidence in the other party's military intentions in the somewhat longer run, or the perception that war or threats of war are possible given certain conditions" (Ericson 2000, 68). Hence, the security dilemma is still in operation.

The highest form of peace is *stable peace*. This is a stage in which the parties totally exclude the possibility of solving conflicts by using military force. In a state of stable peace, the security dilemma has been abolished. It is a situation where "the probability of war is so small that it does not really enter into the calculations of any of the people involved" (Boulding 1978, 13). George and others stress that stable peace relations rarely (or never) require a total harmony of interests among the involved parties. The main point is that political and other conflicts that arise among states are consistently solved by means other than military ones. This does not entail the abolition of all coercive behavior between states, as long as war or the threat of war is perceived as being outside the realm of expected behavior.

Even stable peace relations may exhibit varying degrees of permanence. Thus stable peace itself is hardly an unalterable state, even if it by definition would be a rather robust one, with a measure of resilience. Eras of peace, even if long-lasting, do not necessarily imply stability, as defined here, or an increasing degree of stability. It is obvious that the long Swedish peace, sometimes part of a larger European zone of peace, was not always equivalent to stable peace.

Five Cases of Swedish Security Policy, 1814–1999

We know that Sweden was not involved in any war during this period. This does not mean that plans never existed for getting the country into war. At least in some situations in the nineteenth century, war-aiming strategies were considered. Learning from the Swedish experience, it is obvious that a state may strive for war and nevertheless get peace. However, our focus is primarily on the various peace strategies and their outcomes.

To lay the groundwork for a study of the interplay among structural constraints, strategies, and peace, the historical data in the five cases are ordered in relation to three analytical subheadings: context, identity and roles, and activism or adaptation. *Context* is the shorthand label for the international environment. It refers not only to a spatial demarcation but also to the significant political configurations including great powers as well as international organizations. The category of *identity and roles* refers to the political attributes of Sweden, in terms of self-image and international aspirations. Systemic factors and national identity, and the interplay between them, are important to help us understand not only Swedish foreign policy changes but also the Swedish capacity to fulfill the country's goals, in terms of war or peace. The third category, *activism or adaptation* denotes the different strategic measures applied to pursue various foreign policy goals. Being a key variable in the analysis, it requires some further elaboration.

An activist state tries to safeguard its autonomy by increasing its international influence capability. Acting deliberately in the international arena instead of hiding, an activist state is eager to take a lot of initiatives (Elgström 1982, 38). Using a parallel terminology, such a state is unsatisfied just being responsive to the activities of others. If a country acts regularly and with certain energy, it may become recognized as an activist member of the international community of states. Having acquired such a status, it may be perceived as being driven by the desire not only to participate but also to take a prominent part in world affairs. However, activism is more than behavioral intensity. It is as much a matter of taking an offensive, outward-going stance as opposed to a more defensive attitude in world politics.

Activism is driven by the ambition to change the international order. The means may be aggressive and war-prone, or more peaceful. In the

Swedish case, however, activism, understood as revisionism and territorial conquest, has been, with a few exceptions, of relatively little importance. Adaptation, in contrast, is taken to mean status quo–oriented strategies such as hiding or appeasement or adjusting to current power distributions.

The distinction between activism and other forms of foreign policy behavior is analytically qualified in a typology of policy strategies, originally presented by Kjell Goldmann (1978).[3] Instead of two behavioral options, the typology identifies four strategic paths.

As is shown in figure 10.1, the classification is built upon two dichotomies. The first is the activist dimension, making a distinction between policies of *change* and policies of *adjustment*. A policy of change occurs when an actor tries to alter the international system. A policy of adjustment takes place when an actor accepts the basic structural qualities of the international environment and wishes to accommodate or adapt to the demands raised by external actors. The second distinction is made between *positive* and *negative* policies: positive policy aims at diminishing the motives of other actors to initiate conflict behavior, negative policy aims at increasing the costs to other actors of initiating a conflict.

There are several examples of positive, or *nonconfrontation*, strategies (I and III). Among strategies of type I, disarmament policies may be mentioned, as well as confidence-building measures, mediation, and policies to strengthen global mechanisms for conflict resolution and distribution of scarce resources.[4] Various modes of positive adjustment strategies, type III, exist. *Adaptive acquiescence* (Mouritzen 1988, 1993, 1994) to great power wishes is a well-known phenomenon in the repertoire of weak-state strategies; sometimes this is labeled appeasement or concession policy (Petersen 1989, 183). Concessions are usually given to actors that are seen as a direct threat. Bandwagoning may thus be interpreted as a type III strategy.[5] Another adaptive policy is positive reassurance. By sometimes employing reassurance strategies or even concessions alternately to different great powers, smaller powers try to maintain good relations with them all. When doing so, they might act in accordance with a principle of *symmetrical benevolence*. Such behavior could also be labeled "balancing policies," that is, strategic means "by which the small state attempts to maximize the freedom of maneuver which might exist in the power balance between the big powers, for instance through *temporary* alliances, shift of alignment, etc." (Kelstrup 1993, 141). Sometimes this foreign policy behavior takes the shape of a "pendulum" movement (see Elgström and Jerneck 1997).

Negative policies that *raise the stakes* for an adversary initiating a conflict (II and IV) are numerous. Type II strategies try to make war more costly by changing or reshaping central features of the international structure. To this

POLICY AIMS (STRATEGY TYPE I)		
	Positive	Negative
ACTIVIST DIMENSION (STRATEGY TYPE 2)		
Change	I	II
Adjustment	III	IV

Figure 10.1 Security Strategies

category belong efforts to strengthen international norms against aggressive behavior or attempts to form collective security arrangements. The strategies belonging to category IV are archetypal for international politics, departing from a realist outlook based on the notion of anarchy and self-help. Strategies of deterrence, unilateral or multilateral, are central here.

An activist policy is to be found in category I or II; a policy of adaptation belongs to category III or IV. In the following five cases, Swedish security strategies and their outcomes are discussed and analyzed.

Case 1: The 1820s—Balancing within the Concert of Europe

Context. The first decades after the Napoleonic Wars were the heydays of the Concert of Europe.[6] Even though the system with regular great power consultations gradually came to an end in the 1820s, peace and concord lasted for another few decades. With the Congress of Vienna (1814) and the two peace treaties of Paris (1814 and 1815), a new European security system was created. Behind the novel international order stood the four victorious great powers—Great Britain, Russia, Austria, and Prussia—but soon also defeated France. The Concert was a great power condominium, controlled and managed by the five great powers. A clear distinction was made between these great powers and "powers of second rank," such as Sweden. Regionally, Sweden's security policy choices were directed towards Russia and Great Britain.

Identity and Roles. Sweden's position as a great power was long gone in the 1820s. It had lost Finland to Russia in the war of 1808–09. Although Sweden was allowed to form a union with Norway, formerly a Danish possession, as a reward for its participation in the Napoleonic Wars, it was clear to everyone that Sweden was now a power of second rank.

Even though this can be regarded as the starting point of a so-called consolidation phase in Swedish politics, with the aim of safeguarding the result of the Napoleonic Wars (Elgström and Jerneck 1997), the great power identity lived on. Sweden's aspiration was to participate in great power deliberations, especially when the fate of the Baltic area was concerned. The Swedish monarch, Karl XIV Johan, dreamed about playing an active role in European politics and complained bitterly when he was not permitted to do so. Realizing the limits of Swedish power, the king started to present Sweden as being the strongest of the powers of second rank and to act as a spokesperson for this group of states.

The early years of the post-Napoleonic era were thus a period of search for a new security identity. Neutrality was not yet part of the Swedish credo. It was not until 1834, in the face of an acute crisis between Russia and Britain, that neutrality was introduced, and then as a basically ad hoc solution, not as a principled policy.

Activism or Adaptation? During this period Sweden pursued a policy of adaptation. King Karl Johan anxiously tried to balance between Great Britain and Russia in order to be able to stay out of any war between the two major regional powers. The configuration of the great powers was, however, consistently deemed to induce constraint and cautious balancing, at some times favoring Russia, at other times Britain. In this sense, his policy was peace oriented.

King Karl Johan´s attempts to play a more significant and active role in shaping European policy largely failed. The great power concert did not encourage small-state ambitions of this kind. In some cases, Sweden was actually forced to rescind activist decisions in response to reactions from its neighbor, Russia. Elements of appeasement thus infiltrated Swedish policy but were generally countered by overtures toward the balancing great power.

Consumer or Producer of Peace? The foreign policy intention expressed in this case may be described as one of establishing peace, primarily by means of balancing and nonconfrontation strategies (alternative III in figure 10.1). The actual outcome in terms of existing peace relations between Sweden and its two counterparts or adversaries, however, differed somewhat from the pronounced Swedish preferences. With Russia, which Sweden regarded with great mistrust over the years, the period was mainly one of precarious peace relations, sometimes approximating a situation of conditional peace; military threats and possible hostilities were never totally ruled out. With Britain, the situation was different. The existing zone of peace was actually rather stable as far as Swedish–British relations were concerned. Even if war between them could not be ruled out in case of great power conflict, the ordinary level of tension was quite low. The intensity of contacts as well as the cultural affinity indicated that the peace relations were at least conditional or even semistable.

As a consequence, Swedish peace expectations were limited; there was never any peace activism based on principles. War was in no way excluded as an instrument of foreign policy, in the appropriate situation. In George's terminology, the expectations never went further than conditional peace. The conclusion that Sweden lived in a zone of peace during the years of the European Concert (1814–1848) (see Kacowicz 1995) may be correct on a general level; however, unilateral declarations of neutrality indicated that Sweden still felt that war was a distinct possibility.

The interesting question in this respect is whether Sweden was able to contribute to the existing peace of Europe. Within the confines of the Concert, the great powers shared the objective of a stable, nonrevolutionary environment and decided to cooperate to reach this goal. The system was decidedly status quo–oriented, and conflicts were never allowed to expand into a general war. The major powers tried to maintain a rough balance of power to prevent conflict escalation and the rise of a new hegemon (see Hagan, chapter 2).

The Concert of Europe signified that small states were excluded from the governance of Europe. All major decisions were made by the dominant powers. A certain freedom of movement was left for powers of second rank as long as the equilibrium of power remained and in the absence of a great power crisis. However, the Swedish imprint on this security architecture was marginal, to say the least.

Case 2: The 1850s and 1860s—Cautious Neutrality
Follows Plans for Military Intervention

Context. The Congress of Vienna system had begun to erode by the middle of the nineteenth century. The Crimean War was the first instance where the major powers failed to exercise restraint and abstain from armed conflict against each other. After the war, unilateral action to change existing borders was reintroduced as a weapon in the arsenal of the great powers. The strong wave of national liberation and unification that swept over the continent was unforeseen and created tensions among the dominant powers.

The balance-of-power principle continued to exert normative influence but was in reality subject to severe strain, as illustrated by the aftermath of the Crimean War. In the following decades, considerable uncertainty reigned as regards the actual distribution of power. The Prussian victories over Austria (1866) and France (1871) changed the balance and made united Germany the leading continental power.

Identity and Roles. Sweden's great power aspirations, which had surfaced during the Crimean War, were virtually gone towards the end of the period. Instead, an incipient small-state identity, closely linked to neutrality, can be observed. Neutrality became a principled Swedish policy orientation at this time and was increasingly associated with a number of positive values, such as peace and prosperity. It was also increasingly institutionalized and treated as a natural, uncontested Swedish approach. The small-state identity was reinforced by an awareness of the country's extreme military weakness.

Politically, Sweden was identified as a liberal monarchy. Liberal forces had exerted considerable influence on Swedish foreign policy since the 1840s. The Swedish democratization process led to parliamentary reform in 1866. The elected representatives showed little interest in strengthening the Swedish defense and even less in supporting military adventures. Externally, a strong stance was taken not only against despotism (as, for example, in Russia) but also against republican forms of government (as in France after Napoleon III).

Activism or Adaptation? Perceived changes in the balance of power, nourished by lingering great power ambitions, resulted in plans for military activism during the 1850s and early 1860s, especially during the Crimean War. This war was seen, at least in royal circles, as an opportunity for a final showdown with Sweden's archenemy, Russia. In this respect, ambitions of system change were at work. However, before Sweden could enter the war, a peace treaty was concluded between the Western alliance and Russia. When the royal hopes for military honor turned out to be just a pipe dream, Swedish revanchism and great power ambitions quickly faded away.

Towards the end of the 1860s, neutrality became highly adaptation oriented, with strong traits of passivism. Thus, a low diplomatic profile was recommended to avoid being drawn into great power conflicts.

Consumer or Producer of Peace? During this second period, when the situation was balanced between peace and war, the war option was occasionally regarded as an alternative, at least among some segments of the Swedish elite. The means used were mostly negative and confrontational, corresponding primarily to alternative IV in figure 10.1. To the extent that the Swedish government had the ambition of safeguarding peace, the expectations as to the assumed outcome in principle went no further than that of precarious peace, especially with Russia.

Gradually, however, a more robust peace became an increasingly prominent objective. The long peace of Sweden acquired a value per se. Sweden turned to a principled policy of neutrality. There was in Sweden a widespread attitude that "war is unthinkable," in the sense that armed conflict with a great power was no longer seen as an alternative. Sweden's great power aspirations gradually retreated over the decades, and after 1872 they had more or less vanished. When they disappeared, aspirations of stable peace relations gained strength. At the same time, Sweden continued to live in an environment mainly characterized by conditional peace with all its neighbors. There were still no signs of Sweden as an active promoter of peace. Thus, in the 1850s and 1860s it mainly remained a consumer of peace rather than a producer of peace.

Case 3: The 1920s—War Prevention and Idealism

Context. The victorious powers of World War I, led by Woodrow Wilson, drew the contours of the new postwar international order based on democracy, stable peace, prosperity, and self-determination.[7] With the establishment of the League of Nations, balance of power as a deterrent of war was replaced by the principle of collective security. As a primary alternative to multilateral military operations, economic sanctions were introduced as a means of securing peace on a grander scale.

The fairly narrow geographical confines of nineteenth-century European politics were expanded to areas outside the borders of the European continent. The United States became a prominent player, whereas the defeated powers were reduced to second-rank states or less. France and Britain both mattered politically after World War I. As the leading democratic state, however, the United States exercised a very strong normative power, resulting in a democratic crusade in Europe and elsewhere.

Identity and Roles. The Swedish self-image of a neutral, nonaligned country was fully developed in the 1920s. As a member of the League of Nations (1920), however, it had to compromise its policy of neutrality by accepting the idea of collective security. Generally speaking, Sweden soon accepted the status of a responsible member of the emerging international community of democratic states.

Parallel to its international involvement, Sweden became a full-fledged democratic state. In the 1920s, the seeds of the later quite famous Swedish model were sown. A modern, peaceful society, it internalized the idea of playing the role of a forerunner in politics.

Activism or Adaptation? During the latter part of the nineteenth century, Sweden accommodated to international realities, deemphasizing its wish to play an important political role on the international scene. For more than half a century, Swedish neutrality was essentially passive. However, the 1920s marked a clear change in orientation and outlook. Guided by ideas of idealism, Sweden ventured to participate in the reform of the old international system, applying techniques used in democratic systems of governance (the domestic analogy).

Sweden embarked upon a path of war prevention, advocating the use of multilateral diplomacy and mediation in combination with international law enforcement and arbitration. As opposed to previous periods when it kept a low diplomatic profile, the 1920s were a period of extrovert ambitions and far-reaching hopes for a better world. However, the shortcomings of collective security in the 1930s, the impotence of the League of Nations, and the growing threat of Fascism and Nazism gradually turned Swedish activism into a more pessimistic mode.

Consumer or Producer of Peace? In the aftermath of World War I, Sweden lived in a secure zone of peace. Its former belligerent neighbors, the Soviet Union and Germany, had lost their great power status owing to the verdicts of the Versailles Congress. Great Britain, France, and the United States, the victors of the war, posed no threat to Sweden. The long-term expectation of existing peace relations between Sweden and its environment went much further than mere conditional peace. From a normative point of view, stable peace was the only possible option.

Swedish peace activism was strong and based upon principles. The foreign policy intention was to consolidate peace, primarily by reshaping the international power structure. The behavior corresponded to alternatives I and II in figure 10.1.

The League of Nations functioned initially as a prominent political forum, not least for "nonessential" states like Sweden, although U.S. reluctance to join the organization put a damper on its capacity to act with necessary force. Within the confines of its statutes and Wilson's Fourteen Points, Sweden shared the objective of making the League of Nations the guardian of the new international order. To Sweden, the League was *the* instrument for maintaining security and stability.

The existing international system was status quo–oriented, to the extent that future wars based on territorial revision of any kind were absolutely ruled out as an option. The new order created a relatively stable policy environment for smaller European states. Considerable room to maneuver was left for powers of second rank as long as they adhered to the basic ideas of peace maintenance and justice. To Sweden, this meant that it had access to an important norm-creating arena outside its national territory.

However, the 1920s must be seen as a case of easy stable peace, made possible by Anglo-American dominance in combination with the defeat—and humiliation—of previous great powers in Europe. As a consequence, the Swedish security environment during the 1920s was extremely safe, leaving room for a whole range of experimental approaches in foreign policy. As long as the normative soil was fertile, idealist Swedish activism was one of several contributing factors to peace. However, its basic idea did not stand the real test, as its core strategies were not able to contain the ambitions of German and Italian aggressions.

Case 4: The 1960s and 1970s—The Era of Active Foreign Policy

Context. The superpower competition between the United States and the Soviet Union—the Cold War—dominated European security policy.[8] The international environment was permeated with strong elements of multilateralism. Alongside global trade negotiations and a large number of global conferences, demands from the less-developed countries (LDCs) for a "New International Economic Order" were voiced.

The Nordic balance—the intricate interplay between Danish, Norwegian, and Icelandic membership in NATO and Finnish and Swedish neutrality—stabilized the East–West frontier in northern Europe and turned the Baltic area into a region of détente.[9]

Identities and Roles. From the 1970s on, Sweden played the role of a representative and a model for small states. This involved an active defense of the rights of weak nations against power abuse from the superpowers. Taking on this task, Sweden referred both to its long tradition as a peaceful country and to its policy of nonalignment and claimed that these characteristics made it particularly well suited for global activism.

Swedish neutrality, still very much a part of Swedish identity, was no longer seen as a restriction on proactive behavior. Membership in military alliances—and in the European Economic Community—was out of the question, but neutrality was not perceived to create obstacles for active norm creation or international criticism. On the contrary, Sweden saw it as a moral duty to promote détente, peace, human rights, and human welfare. The role as a promoter of global solidarity, with a massive foreign aid program as a main element, partly rested on Sweden's domestic, social-democracy-inspired solidarity tradition. The national ideal of a welfare society was transferred to the global arena (cf. Lödén 1999).

The norms of democracy are mirrored in the value placed on international public opinion. It was believed that honest criticism could also influence the behavior of powerful democratic states (Jerneck 1983). Yet, although democracy was an objective of Swedish foreign assistance, very few demands were made at this time on recipient countries. Political conditionality was a concept still unheard of.

Activism or Adaptation? The Swedish endorsement of international law and international organization (including a major role in many UN peacekeeping operations since 1965) was strongly supported during this period by an active foreign policy. It was characterized by an emphasis on unorthodox instruments of foreign policy and a large number of Swedish policy initiatives (Elgström 1982; Jerneck 1983; Bjereld 1995; Lödén 1999). Sweden openly and sharply criticized the superpowers for their interventions in smaller states (e.g., the United States in Vietnam and the Soviet Union in Afghanistan) and nondemocratic states for their abuses of human rights. Initiatives were taken to speed up disarmament processes, and proposals were put forward to abolish nuclear weapons.

In its search for global solidarity, Sweden initiated a large foreign aid program, primarily directed to poor nations with "progressive"—but not necessarily democratic—governments. Sweden supported the demands for a New International Economic Order. In international bargaining fora, Sweden tried to act as a mediator between the LDCs and the larger, rich nations.

Sweden based its policy of neutrality on a comparatively strong military defense, meant to deter any potential enemy from violating Sweden's sovereignty. Thus, unconventional global policies were combined with more traditional security policy in Sweden's immediate surroundings. Even though the Baltic was a fairly safe area, the superpower rivalry, and especially the threat from the Soviet Union, underlined the importance of a strong military deterrent.[10] Whereas the unconventional activist policy in more distant places was largely influenced by idealist thinking and small-power righteousness (Elgström 1982; Jerneck 1983; Lödén 1999), the core of Swedish security policy versus its eastern neighbors was basically realist, and as such an expression of considered necessities. In the political rhetoric, though, strong military capability was seen as the prerequisite for a credible policy of neutrality.

Consumer or Producer of Peace? The bipolar balance of power, built on mutual nuclear deterrence, created a relatively stable policy environment for smaller European states, although the "long peace" of the Cold War was chiefly conditional, if not precarious. Superpower détente, which characterized most of the 1970s, gave smaller states a chance to act more freely than had been possible during periods of more tense great power rivalry.

The environmental conditions were thus fairly permissive in terms of security policies. They created a window of opportunity for Sweden, in which it could help sustain international peace through a proactive foreign policy (strategies I and II in figure 10.1). Was Sweden, however, successful as a promoter of peace? The gradual change in the international power structure, leaving room for various forms of "soft power" (see Nye 1990), opened up avenues of small-state influence, primarily through open criticism and the promotion of ideas. The importance of norms and democratic values within the confines of an international society further underlined the importance of such new power resources. Backed by deliberate aid policies, Sweden tried to exercise moral or normative power in various parts of the world. Even though Sweden could not in any radical way transform the European security architecture, based on superpower dominance, material interests, and spheres of influence, it did contribute, albeit marginally, to the international discussion on how to create a durable system of peace on the global level. In short, Sweden gained an international influence that reached politically and geographically beyond its formal status as a minor power in the periphery of northern Europe.

Case 5: The 1990s—Shifting Paradigms

Context. The post–Cold War era has turned Russia into a second-rank power, leaving the United States as the only remaining superpower.[11] The U.S. dominance, almost total in military affairs, is to some extent contested when it comes to economic performance and leadership. The European Union (EU) plays a predominant role in the broader European region.

Ideologically speaking, democracy, the rule of law, and the free-market economy have almost outmatched alternative ways of social organization. Regarding norms, the sovereignty principle is compromised, both in practice and at the ideational level. Even though territorial integrity is still thought to be a cornerstone of international cooperation, global trade, regional processes of integration, and universal ideas of human rights have clearly shown that the principle is under siege.

Geographically speaking, security concerns have expanded beyond the borders of individual countries. The serious conflicts in parts of the former Soviet Union and the Balkans have, however, put more focus on the problem of expanding the OECD community of peace and creating stable peace throughout the European continent without antagonizing Russia (see Goodby, chapter 13).

Identity and Roles. Even though security has a global scope, Swedish security concerns have in a way been narrowed to a European perspective. Still advocating the importance of the United Nations, Sweden has gradually become a fairly enthusiastic member of the collective foreign policy arrangement developed within the European Union, as well as within the frames of NATO-defined cooperation (such as Partnership for Peace).

Although Sweden is formally a nonaligned country, neutrality as a policy option has in practice been ruled out. As a member of the EU and several other organizations, the country's international loyalties have changed character. A traditional small-state attitude that minor powers are morally superior in world politics is still a prominent feature of Swedish foreign policy doctrine. Yet, Sweden is trying to reorient itself, moving from a position of nonalignment and high moral standards, at least in rhetoric, to a less ideological stance, featuring more foreign policy realism. This new policy line is, for instance, expressed in open support for military intervention in the Yugoslavian crisis and also in the endorsement of the EU Common Foreign and Security Policy (see Strömvik 1999).

As part of a larger democratic community, Sweden supports the idea of safeguarding democratic values throughout the world, including human rights. The introduction of political conditionality in foreign aid is one aspect where Sweden has abandoned its previous skepticism to conform to Western aid practice.

Activism or Adaptation? In comparison to Swedish activism in the 1960s and 1970s, the present direction and content of Swedish foreign policy constitutes a paradigmatic shift. Traditional neutrality is gone and has been replaced by an intensified cooperation in security affairs. Processes of internationalization that narrow down traditional state autonomy nowadays permeate Swedish activism.

A radical disarmament of Swedish military forces during the 1990s has made Sweden redirect its doctrine of war prevention. Crisis management, preventive diplomacy, and peacekeeping operations in former combat areas have to a large extent replaced traditional military defense of the national territory. Together with Finland, Sweden argued in favor of incorporating the Petersberg tasks in the Amsterdam Treaty.

Parallel to this development, Sweden is anxious to keep its position as a trustworthy member of the United Nations. Hence, it continues to exercise verbal politics as a means of influencing normative standards. Yet, it seems fair to say that Sweden has more and more chosen a path of political adaptation rather than one of a full-fledged activism. Instead of being critical of great power behavior, Sweden now acts as a strong supporter of NATO and EU policies.

Consumer or Producer of Peace? While still adhering to the principles of stable peace, the strategic repertoire to achieve these goals has been expanding, leading to a greater complexity in available policy options. In the terminology of figure 10.1, alternative IV is of reduced importance, whereas certain tendencies towards adjustment policies (III) go hand-in-hand with activist modes of behavior such as disarmament proposals, confidence-building measures, economic sanctions, and foreign aid (I and II). The element of adjustment is not of a traditional kind; it is, rather, a matter of accommodating Swedish foreign policy to a new moral standard, encompassed by the majority of the well-developed democratic states. A rather telling example is the Swedish endorsement of the NATO-led campaign in Kosovo during the spring of 1999. Just a few years ago, such a policy stance would have been impossible.

By joining the "club," Sweden has left its traditional attitude of spectator and antiestablishment critic partly behind.[12] In doing so, it has probably increased its potential to have a say in security affairs of relevance for Sweden. Furthermore, the principle of (small-state) adjustment cohabits quite well with the principle of change, because the major Western powers are now cooperating in order to advance general principles of human dignity in world affairs.

One should not forget, however, that the traditional instruments of foreign policy are still valuable. To the extent that soft power is privileged in certain instances of international policymaking, principled ideas and moral standards can still make some imprint on world affairs, including peace. The new moral order in world politics fits very well into this interpretation of power. To the extent that Sweden can contribute to the definition of the European zone of peace, it can be depicted as a producer of peace. Yet, changes in the international scene clearly demonstrate that small countries like Sweden have limited possibilities to decide their own destiny.

Swedish Peacemaking Capacity

In this final section, we wish to address two problems raised in the introduction. First, we would like to summarize how strategies of activism and adaptation have been applied during the five time periods considered above. Second, we would like to make a few further observations as to whether the chosen policies have had any impact upon the durable peace of Sweden.

Changing Security Strategies

We have demonstrated how a small, nonaligned, and nonessential state like Sweden has used a variety of foreign policy strategies from the early 1800s to the advent of the new millennium. These snapshots of Swedish foreign policy indicate that there has been a gradual shift of orientation, from an adaptive stance in the nineteenth century to a much more active Swedish foreign policy posture throughout the twentieth century. In Goldmann's terms, Sweden has gone from adjustment to change-oriented strategies (from strategies III and IV to I and II).

The Swedish basic foreign policy doctrines of the nineteenth century contained elements of both activism and adaptation, even though balancing, quiescence, and adaptive acquiescence dominated the picture. As we have seen, Swedish policymakers actively tried to keep a balanced position between the country's great neighbors by being friendly to all of them and by keeping out of all forms of armed conflicts between and among them. We have elsewhere labeled this phenomenon a pendulum policy (Elgström and Jerneck 1997). Sweden also, especially in the late nineteenth century, consciously tried to avoid drawing too much attention to its policies by implementing a strategy of quiescence, or hiding (see Schroeder 1994b, 117). But at times Sweden had to appease imminent threats to its security. In the 1820s Sweden had to withdraw already announced policy initiatives when faced with strong Russian reactions. In connection with the Polish rebellion of 1863, Sweden had to rely on deferential verbal tactics and positive reassurances to the Russian court to mitigate the negative impact of earlier activism.

To prevent being drawn into a great power war, Sweden has mostly relied upon unilateral declarations of neutrality. The time-bound, expedient ad hoc neutrality of the early 1800s was gradually replaced by a principled policy of neutrality from the late 1860s onwards. Strong traits of passivism permeated this new doctrine. Not until the 1920s did a change occur, turning neutrality into a policy of outspoken activism.

Swedish twentieth-century activism is much more offensive and complex than that practiced during the preceding century. The strategies of the 1920s marked a new era in Swedish foreign policy, as the idea was fully established that small-state strategies should be applied to strengthen international norms against great power interventionism. The foreign policy means of multilateral diplomacy, arbitration, and international disarmament proposals were supplemented in the 1960s and 1970s with Third World aid and open criticism. Both in this latter period and in the 1990s, moral persuasion became a major instrument of Swedish foreign policy. Even though the roots were to some extent laid down in the previous century, the normative core elements of this modern form of active neutrality were more fully developed during the first decade after World War I.

Sweden not only changed its strategic deliberations but also rearranged its priorities as to the establishment of peace. Its foreign policy intentions as regards peace and war were rather stable during the major part of the nineteenth century; peace was to be preserved, but not in all circumstances. Under the right conditions (certain victory!), participation in war was clearly a conceivable strategy. Whereas peace was a secondary goal in the first decades of the nineteenth century, primarily tied to Sweden's striving for consolidation, it became during the middle of the 1800s even *less* important as a goal in itself.

As the fruits of the long peace became increasingly visible, peace as an overall value in itself gained strength, however. From the early 1870s onwards, peace became a top priority, even though the existing zone of peace in Europe in the years 1871–1914 (Kacowicz 1995) could not automatically be pictured as one of stability and robustness, especially as far as Russo-Swedish relations were concerned. On the verge of the twentieth century, the constraints against resorting to arms had become formidable. In terms of our peace typology, Swedish aspirations moved from conditional to stable peace, a standpoint that has been a crucial part of Swedish foreign policy ever since.

What factors have had an impact on the choice of strategic paths and the reformulation of political goals? The images of, and expectations concerning, the surrounding actors—states as well as organizations—were obviously important. It is clear that Sweden was more or less doomed to be a small power, unable to play any significant role in European developments, unless it redirected its foreign policy. Furthermore, major changes in international power distribution worked as a strong impetus for reconsideration of strategies and orientations. Outbursts of Swedish policy activism can thus be interpreted as deliberate attempts to increase Swedish autonomy in a fluid international context. Thus, the ending of great power wars is proposed to be a major indicator of change in small-state policy. Swedish policy reconstructions after the Napoleonic Wars, the Franco-German war (1871–1872,) and the two world wars are excellent examples, as is the reorientation after the Cold War.

It is also important to remember that resource scarcity and defective war-waging capacity have been essential factors in determining which strategy to choose in most of the cases under scrutiny. Sweden's disastrous lack of military preparedness in the 1850s deterred several high military commanders, a group that could otherwise have been considered likely to support military involvement, from advising such enterprises. Even though the measures are a result of a strategic choice, they certainly reflect the fact that Sweden had to reconcile its power ambitions with changing material conditions, nationally as well as internationally. Thus, on the one hand, one can argue that Swedish disarmament policies in the aftermath of World War I and the Cold War followed the logic of crude economic reasoning.

On the other hand, one can follow an opposite path, saying that military capability gradually became a *function* of a principled peace policy rather than the other way around. In the 1920s, unilateral Swedish disarmament was the advocated policy to attain peace; in the period following World War II, armed neutrality based upon a strong military defense was the preferred option, whereas in the 1990s a radical policy of disarmament once again came into fashion. Both policy stances clearly illustrate that the use of military means can always be regarded as subordinate to the realization of the overall peace objective of Swedish foreign policy.

Irrespective of whether the reorientation of Swedish security strategies has been driven by a logic of economic scarcity, it seems definitely to be the case that military spending *and* a pronounced policy of neutrality reflect changing geopolitical conditions. In the 1920s and in the post–Cold War era, periods both characterized by a situation of relative détente, Swedish neutrality faded out and was replaced by the principle of collective security. As compared to the period after World War II, the paradigmatic shifts of the 1990s point in a direction of a more rule-adhering Swedish foreign policy, explicitly supporting the idea of collective security arrangements. An argument for neutral Sweden to sign the UN Charter in 1946 was that the principle of collective security would never be put to a serious test in the United Nations because of great power veto and thus would never come into real conflict with the Swedish interpretation of neutrality.

The cognitive patterns and self-images among the top decision-makers were also very important for the changing attitude toward the role of military means in Swedish foreign policy. When the traditional great power image definitely gave way to a small-state identity, the conditions for conscious peace strategies were considerably improved. The change definitely ruled out territorial conquest as a strategic pathway of state reproduction (see Hall 1999; Ericson 2000) and paved the way for ideas of national self-determination and the creation of a new international role.

In terms of national attributes, popular opinions seem to have had a strong impact on royal decision-making even before the advent of modern democracy. In general, the hypothesis that decreasing ruler autonomy results in higher possibilities for peace-promoting strategies (Kiser, Drass, and Brustein 1995) seems to be confirmed in the Swedish case. Growing pluralism increases the chances that opponents of military adventurism will be given the opportunity to be heard. Furthermore, the idea that democracies should not fight each other gained a strong foothold in Swedish foreign policy discourse of the early twentieth century. The definite breakthrough of democracy in the 1920s finally institutionalized the doctrine of stable peace as the overall foreign policy guideline (Ericson 2000). The democratic identity has also inspired the active promotion of democratic values as part of Sweden´s policy of global norm propagation.

Structure and Strategy: Systemic Constraints,
Peace, and Actor Autonomy

In our empirical cases we have shown how a small and nonessential power like Sweden has reflected upon its identity and international environment while choosing foreign policy strategies in relation to peace. What was, however, the relationship between the security policies pursued and the Sweden's actual status as a country at peace? What was Sweden's real peacemaking capacity?

Whether Sweden through its behavior really made any substantial contributions to the establishment of peace is difficult to corroborate empirically. This is due partly to the enormous complexity of the matter, partly to the problem of counterfactuals. Still, such an analysis is possible in more principled terms. We would like to reflect here upon the question whether or not it was possible for Sweden to carry out its political intentions.

Did Sweden ever possess the real capacity to make an independent contribution to its long peace, or was the peaceful outcome a result of chance or favorable external conditions? In times when relevant great powers were in a stable balance of power (the 1820s, the 1960s and 1970s), the possibility for Swedish activism increased. During the nineteenth century, however, Sweden never engaged in system-changing behavior (with the exception of its war-oriented efforts during the Crimean crisis), and it was discouraged by the dominant powers from doing so. To the extent that Sweden had some leverage on the processes leading to a lasting peace, it was by means of adaptation or hiding. Sweden was primarily a consumer of peace and did not contribute to any systemic developments towards stabilization of peace.

The 1920s were, like the 1990s, a period of system transformation. Sweden´s geopolitical position was excellent and permitted a strategy of multilateral peace activism. The fact that the international environment still relied more on power than on principles, as shown by the rise of the Fascist powers, changed this beneficial situation. The attempts—including Sweden's—to create a rule of law in international affairs had failed. The country´s success in staying out of World War II depended probably more on luck than on purposive Swedish peace strategies.[13]

In the Cold War era, another period of permissive great power balance, the impact of Swedish activism has been highly contested. In Europe, Sweden had little chance to influence the superpower relations directly or in the short run. Its attempts to encourage arms reductions and détente were often ineffectual. Still, its neutrality may have contributed to making the Nordic area a zone of nonfriction. Sweden may also have helped create a normative environment conducive to peace. Its normative efforts were global and not limited to the Nordic region. Sweden played a not insignificant role as norm entrepreneur (Finnemore 1996), and the norms of peace and solidarity it propagated may have gradually infiltrated international society.

The same can be said about the 1990s. The environment is now more conducive to the use of soft power, including moral persuasion. Peace and democracy are consensual values, at least rhetorically. The use of military force is strongly discouraged. In this environment, purposeful actions to spread specific values may be successful, either in a regional context (the EU) or globally. So although it can hardly be claimed that Sweden played any significant role in bringing about the European zone of peace, this environment is a fertile ground for its attempts at influence.

The empirical summary of the five cases gives rise to a few general observations based upon the notion that the international environment at times is more permissive to small-state attempts to exercise international power. Changes in power configurations may lead to a more fluid situation, creating windows of opportunity. The passage of time might be a strong factor in changing the fundamentals of the international system, leading to a redefinition of political power. Such a transformation of basic power structures may either inhibit or improve small-state capacity to act successfully.

In addition, a state's capacity to change the rules of the game in a favorable direction is in itself a considerable advantage. It is quite clear that Swedish peace strategies during most of the twentieth century have had the purpose of either reshaping the system or consolidating the gains of an international society built upon norms rather than pure anarchy. Even though Sweden may not have been successful in creating peace in specific instances, it may have been successful in contributing to the structures that either prevent war from breaking out or stable peace from breaking down by supporting mechanisms of path-dependency and lock-in. Such behavior is more likely to be rewarding in the late twentieth century, with its system of democratic peace, than in the nineteenth-century context of systems of balance of power or concert built around autocratic states. If that is the case, Swedish influence as a peace producer has been indirect rather than direct.

Notes

We gratefully acknowledge the valuable comments made by our collaborators in the research project "Stable Peace: The Case of Sweden." The multidisciplinary project, which involves the departments of political science and history at Lund University, is generously supported by a grant from the Bank of Sweden Tercentenary Foundation

1. For further discussion of this conceptualization, see Elgström and Jerneck 1997; and Elgström forthcoming.

2. See George 1992 and the foreword to this volume. See also Boulding 1978; Kacowicz 1995; Bengtsson (chap. 5); and, last but not least, Kacowicz and Bar-Siman-Tov (chap. 1).

3. Goldmann´s typology has also been used in a study of Swedish foreign policy change during the postwar period (1950–1975). See Lödén 1999.

4. Mediation in international conflicts is a good example of high-level activism. See Stenelo 1972 and Bjereld 1995.

5. See Walt 1985. As pointed out by Schweller (1994), bandwagoning can be employed for profit, in deliberate attempts to gain advantages by joining apparently winning coalitions.

6. The accounts of cases 1 and 2 are based on Elgström and Jerneck 1997 and Elgström, forthcoming. For more references, see these works.

7. For sources on the case of the 1920s, see, e.g., Ericson 2000; Norman 1990; Wahlbäck 1990; and Möller 1990.

8. See Elgström 1982; and Jerneck 1983, 1990. See also Bjereld 1995; Nilson 1991; and Dahl 1999.

9. For an overview of some of the academic debate on the Nordic balance , see Noreen 1983.

10. In fact, Sweden had had a very close yet informal relationship with NATO since the early 1950s.

11. For sources concerning the 1990s case, see, e.g., Sundelius 1995; Gustavsson 1998; and Dahl 1999.

12. This was, however, not he case with the monetary cooperation in the EU. When the EMU started January 1, 1999, Sweden was not a member. See Calmfors et al. 1997.

13. The situation was quite complex, however. Germany was heavily dependent on Swedish iron ore for production of weaponry. Since Sweden traded with Germany throughout the war, an occupation of Swedish territory would have been counterproductive from a German point of view.

11

Stable Peace in South America: The ABC Triangle, 1979–1999

Arie M. Kacowicz

In this chapter, I assess the evolution of the long peace among Argentina, Brazil, and Chile towards stable peace and the possible emergence of an incipient pluralistic security community between Argentina and Brazil. In theoretical terms, I compare and contrast the two-stage model of stable peace, as developed in chapter 1. Its initial stage of establishment (stabilization of relations after conflict resolution) aptly describes the bilateral relations between Argentina and Chile since their peace treaty of 1984. In contrast, the more advanced stage of consolidation of peaceful relations has characterized the Argentine–Brazilian relationship since 1990 and the traditional peaceful relations between Brazil and Chile since the end of the nineteenth century. In empirical terms, I examine the bilateral cooperation between Argentina and Brazil in economic and security issues since 1979; the resolution of the pending territorial disputes between Argentina and Chile in the 1980s and 1990s; and the trilateral security cooperation among Argentina, Chile, and Brazil. Finally, I draw some theoretical and policy-oriented conclusions from this rather encouraging regional story.

Since the end of the Pacific War among Bolivia, Chile, and Peru in 1883, the South American region has been considered a zone of negative peace, with the exception of two international wars: the 1932–1935 Chaco War between Bolivia and Paraguay, and the war between Ecuador and Peru in 1941. A number of long-standing territorial disputes eventually escalated into international crises, such as the tug-of-war between Argentina and Chile over their Patagonian border in 1902 and again in 1978 over the Beagle Channel Islands. Yet, the vast majority of border disputes in South America have been resolved peacefully, leading to some cession or exchange of territories.

Until the 1980s South America was a zone of negative peace only. However, with the spread of democracy, the Southern Cone of South America has been moving in the direction of stable peace and perhaps even an incipient pluralistic security community among the member-states (and peoples) of Mercosur (Argentina, Brazil, Paraguay, and Uruguay). The return to democracy in Argentina (1983), Brazil (1985), and Chile (1989) has clearly improved the quality of the peace among these three countries and the level of rapprochement between Argentina and Brazil since 1985 and Argentina and Chile since 1990. The link between stable peace and liberal/democratic peace is quite evident at the cognitive, perceptual, and intersubjective levels. At the same time, the transition to democracy does not necessarily automatically imply peaceful, nonmilitary solutions to international conflicts or a tendency for civilian regimes to reduce the level of military expenditures and arms production (see Acuña and Smith 1995). Moreover, the movement towards stable peace between Argentina and Brazil started in 1979, when the two countries still had military regimes. Similarly, the 1984 peace treaty between Argentina and Chile settling the Beagle Channel dispute was obtained when a newly democratic government in Argentina (Raúl Alfonsín's) still confronted the military dictatorship of General Augusto Pinochet in Chile.

Stable peace of differing degrees now characterizes the relationships among the three major countries of the Southern Cone of South America: Argentina, Brazil, and Chile ("the ABC triangle"). While Brazilian–Chilean relations can be considered an "easy case" of stable peace, and the Argentine–Brazilian dyad is a "fairly easy" case, Argentine–Chilean relations are more difficult to categorize as consolidated stable peace. Yet, the improved relations among the ABC countries have also affected Bolivia, Uruguay, and Paraguay. In the relationships among Argentina, Brazil, Paraguay, Uruguay, and even Chile, the outbreak of an international war has become unlikely, if not impossible. Moreover, with the resolution of pending territorial disputes between Argentina and Chile and the end of the enduring rivalry between Argentina and Brazil, all of the countries of this subregion have become satisfied with the territorial status quo, with the exception of Bolivia's demands for an outlet to the sea.

Within the ABC triangle, Brazil and Chile have sustained a relationship of stable peace since the end of the nineteenth century, partly motivated by the perception of a common enemy or threat (the Argentine Republic) and partly by the fact that they do not share a common border. Traditionally, the Brazilian–Argentine rivalry (which lasted until 1979) overlapped and interpenetrated the Chilean–Argentine rivalry (until 1984), so that the intensity and outcomes in one were strongly influenced by the developments in the other (see Resende-Santos 1998, 6–7; Hurrell 1995b, 256; Muñoz 1986, 156, 160). Yet, there is no symmetry in the dyads that compose this triangle of peace, as there was no symmetry in the level of conflictive relations of those dyads before stable peace. Argentina and Brazil have moved along the continuum from negative peace through the stage of stabilization (1979–1990) towards consolidation of stable peace (1991–1999), up to the point of forming (perhaps) a loose pluralistic security community. The transition towards stable peace in the Argentine–Chilean relationship has been more difficult and less smooth, moving from providentially avoiding a war in 1979 towards conflict resolution in 1984. Since then, the two countries have experienced a steady improvement of their economic and security relations up to the June 1999 resolution of their last territorial dispute over the Hielos Continentales on their southern border. In economic terms, both Argentina and Chile and Argentina and Brazil (though not necessarily the three countries together) have made substantial progress toward economic integration. In security terms, however, the extraordinary bilateral nuclear confidence-building process that has developed between Argentina and Brazil has no parallel in the entire region (see Leventhal and Tanzer 1992, 1–8; Redick, Carasales, and Wiebel 1995, 107–23). In this context, some authors have argued that a loosely coupled, if still imperfect, pluralistic security community can be identified within Mercosur, built around the cognitive and material changes that have taken place in the core relationship between Brazil and Argentina. This might be a bounded community, with Chile's position remaining ambiguous and with the rest of South America at peace but still beset by a range of traditional and new security challenges (see Hurrell 1998, 260; Olmos 1986; Kacowicz 1994; 1998, 118–21; Oelsner 1998). In any case, whether the ABC triangle (or at least the Argentine–Brazilian dyad) has become a pluralistic security community remains an open question.

Manifestations of Stable Peace in the ABC Triangle

Argentina and Brazil: Security Cooperation and Economic Integration

Among the South American international disputes of the twentieth century, the Argentine–Brazilian rivalry was the longest and most deeply rooted and the one most influenced by geopolitical doctrines (Child 1985, 99–100). It had important reverberations in the domestic and international politics of the region as a whole and a direct impact upon the three buffer states of the Southern Cone—Uruguay, Paraguay, and Bolivia—in particular. From the second half of the nineteenth century to the late 1970s, the relationship between the region's two major powers was a complex mixture of conflict and cooperation, as a function of disagreements about their territorial borders and their competing hegemonic ambitions in South America. In the bloody Chaco War of 1932–1935 Argentina and Brazil supported opposing sides. From the early 1920s and especially after

World War II, the two countries were often immersed in an arms race that included the development of nuclear technology. Moreover, they adopted diametrically opposed positions regarding the role of the United States in the region and have engaged in a fierce competition over resources such as Paraguayan hydroelectric energy and Bolivian oil and gas. The possibility of an armed conflict (a "hypothesis of conflict") remained a very tangible element in the military planning of the two countries until the early 1980s. The Argentines regarded Brazil as an expansionary military, economic, and demographic power that threatened areas to its south, west, and southwest. Conversely, the Brazilians regarded their smaller neighbor with suspicion and uneasiness, fearing the kind of volatility and aggressiveness that Argentina demonstrated in its invasion of the Falklands/ Malvinas in April 1982 (see Guglialmelli 1979; Selcher 1985, 101–18). At the same time, the Argentine–Brazilian rivalry never escalated into militarized crises such as those between Argentina and Chile; moreover, their enduring rivalry, unlike that between Peru and Ecuador, did not include opposing claims to a disputed territory.

A turning point in their relations occurred in 1979, when their respective military regimes came to a resolution of the hydroelectric conflict over Paraguay and the use of the Paraná River waters (the building of the Itaipú dam). This led to a gradual rapprochement that included economic and military cooperation, especially in the nuclear area. After democratization took place in both countries, they launched a bilateral integration program (ABEIP) in 1986, which epitomized the upgrading of their bilateral relations in the direction of establishing stable peace. This was followed by the historical Argentine–Brazilian Declaration on Common Nuclear Policy at Foz do Iguaçú (November 28, 1990), which established a binational cooperative organization of nuclear cooperation (the Brazilian–Argentine Agency for the Accounting and Control of Nuclear Materials, ABCC). This bilateral nuclear-nonproliferation regime, coupled with increased economic integration at the bilateral and regional levels, has consolidated stable peace between the two countries. In the mid- and late 1990s, a large number of military exchanges and mutual visits between the two armies, as well as strategic symposia and common maneuvers, have become commonplace. As Thomas A. O'Keefe, president of Mercosur Consulting Group, cogently summarized, "The whole hypothesis of war between Argentina and Brazil has been junked. ... I don't think that anyone in the Argentine military or in the Brazilian military still sees the other as a potential threat" (quoted in Brooke 1994).

Against the backdrop of a long tradition of rivalry and competition, the dramatic changes that have characterized the Brazilian–Argentine relationship since 1979 are remarkable. We can identify two major phases in this transition towards stable peace. The initial stage of stabilization or understanding took place between 1979 and 1990. The second stage, consolidation, followed the integration agreements of 1986 and especially the establishment of a nuclear bilateral regime in 1990–1991 and the launching of the regional integration project, Mercosur, in March 1991. What is particularly puzzling is the fact that the initial stage of stable peace was established when the two countries still had authoritarian military regimes. Less surprising, though, is that consolidation of stable peace was possible ten years later, within and between more or less well established democratic regimes.

Establishing Stable Peace: From the Resolution of the Itaipú Dispute (1979) to the Launching of Bilateral Economic Integration (1986–1990). In the late 1970s Brazil initiated a policy of "Latin-Americanization" towards its Spanish-speaking neighbors, including the creation of the Amazon Pact for joint development of the Amazon Basin, to increase its own economic growth and development. Domestically, the ascendancy of moderate military officers in Brazil and the launching of liberalization contributed to a general climate of openness towards its neighbors. From the Argentine standpoint, the military junta became quite aware of its power inferiority vis-à-vis Brazil in economic and conventional military terms—excluding, perhaps, the specific area of nuclear development, in which Brazil was finally catching up to Argentina's lead, making an escalating nuclear arms race a real possibility. Moreover, the mounting tensions with Britain over the South Atlantic Falklands/Malvinas issue and the deteriorating relations with Chile following the 1977 arbitration award that gave it the Beagle Channel Islands prompted the Argentines to seek an accommodation with Brazil against the prospect of an imminent war with Chile (see Hurrell 1998, 235–38; Resende-Santos 1998, 7–22; Segre 1990). These converging motivations led the two countries to resolve in October 1979 a thirteen-year dispute over the hydropower generation of energy along the Paraná River in the tripartite border among Argentina, Paraguay, and Brazil. In 1980 Argentina and Brazil further expanded (and improved) their relations by exchanging presidential visits and a package of ten agreements, including joint arms production and nuclear cooperation, covering joint research and the transfer of some nuclear materials. Given the historic competition between the two countries and the regional supremacy and prestige attached to nuclear development, the bilateral nuclear rapprochement reached in 1980 was a watershed (Barletta 1997). It was partly prompted by the growing difficulties both parties experienced in gaining access to nuclear supplies and technology amid mounting economic difficulties and foreign debt crises throughout the 1980s (Hirst and Bocco 1992, 216–20; Marzo, Biaggio, and Raffo 1994, 30; Stanley 1992, 201–3).

With the return of democracy to Argentina (1983) and Brazil (1985), nuclear cooperation between the two countries further expanded, as the core of a larger, ambitious program of economic integration. On November 30, 1985, Presidents Alfonsín (Argentina) and Sarney (Brazil) met at Foz do Iguaçú to inaugurate a program that took a concrete form on July 31, 1986, with the signing of the Argentine–Brazilian Integration Act and the Integration and Cooperation Program (ABEIP), together with twelve protocols for cooperation in various areas, including nuclear energy. The ABEIP represented a breakthrough in Argentine–Brazilian relations, after a century-long struggle for subparamountcy in South America. Its significance was primarily political, not economic: setting aside decades of rivalries and competition in order to create the basis for a long-term cooperation. In 1985–1990, nuclear cooperation peaked, as part of a larger effort to bring about economic integration in the region. The new civilian governments initiated nuclear confidence-building bilateral measures that altered well-entrenched perceptions of rivalry in both countries. As a result, a full-fledged regime of cooperation emerged in the nuclear area, aimed at promoting technological development and strengthening mutual trust and transparency, while assuring the international community that neither country intended to develop or produce nuclear weapons. Both governments sought through these initiatives to improve bilateral relations, and thereby to promote democratic consolidation and economic integration.

One has to look at this bilateral nuclear cooperation as a step toward broader integration in both political and economic terms. The convergence of national interests between Brazil and Argentina in 1985–1990 led to their integration in the economic sphere, first at the bilateral level (1986–1989) and later through the incorporation of the two smaller buffer states of Paraguay and Uruguay within Mercosur (since 1991). Owing to the macroeconomic crises that affected both countries in the mid- and late 1980s, the economic results of this integration process were meager, even insignificant. Thus, paradoxically, nuclear and military cooperation became the most successful sector of the bilateral integration program and the ultimate guarantor of economic integration in better times to come.

Consolidation of Stable Peace: From Upgrading Nuclear Cooperation (1990–1991) towards a Pluralistic Security Community. Building on a history of nuclear cooperation that had been formalized since 1980, the presidents of Brazil and Argentina, Fernando Collor de Mello and Carlos Menem, on November 28, 1990, adopted the Argentine–Brazilian Declaration on Common Nuclear Policy at Foz do Iguaçú. The declaration formalized and institutionalized the evolving nuclear regime between the two countries, marking a significant departure from their former approach to nuclear nonproliferation. Besides reconfirming the determination to use nuclear energy exclusively for peaceful purposes, the declaration approved a common accounting and control system to apply to all nuclear activities of both countries (SCCC) and to verify that nuclear materials in all nuclear activities of both parties were used exclusively for peaceful purposes. Moreover, the declaration called for negotiations with the International Atomic Energy Agency for the conclusion of a safeguards agreement based on the SCCC, ultimately signed at Guadalajara, Mexico, on July 18, 1991 (see Stanley 1992, 192–95; Redick 1995, 341–59; Pande 1993, 431–33; Goldemberg and Feiveson 1994, 10–14).

The consolidation of stable peace between Argentina and Brazil in the 1990s was based upon two intertwined pillars: nuclear and security cooperation, and economic integration. The relaunching of economic integration (this time, more successfully) has to be understood against the end of the Cold War, the move towards market liberalism worldwide, and the trends of the "new regionalism." This was epitomized by the creation of Mercosur, including the "core" of Argentina and Brazil and the smaller buffer states, Uruguay and Paraguay. Its establishment in March 1991 has been by far the most important and promising scheme of regional integration in the whole of Latin America. From a starting point of low economic interdependence, inter-state relations among Mercosur members entered a new phase in the mid-1990s as the associative process, moving from a free trade area towards a customs union and an embryonic common market, expanded and strengthened. Hence, there is a genuine dynamics of interdependence between (and among) the economies of the region, so that the focus of diplomacy has moved from political cooperation to economic integration. In terms of the logic of consolidated stable peace, as economic interdependence has grown, the possibilities of military conflicts have decreased. Economic interdependence and integration are supposed to cover myriad areas, including space activities, nuclear cooperation, joint development of waterways (the River Plate basin), roads and bridges linking the two countries, and energy integration (see Hirst 1999, 35–47; Peña 1995, 113–22).

While nuclear cooperation in the 1980s paved the way for economic integration in the 1990s, the salience of economic integration has facilitated, in turn, the deepening of security cooperation among the armed forces of Mercosur, especially those of Argentina and Brazil. As a logical outcome of regional integration, confidence-building measures (CBMs) involving the land, sea, and air military forces of Argentina, Brazil, and Uruguay have taken place. In September 1996, Brazil and Argentina conducted their first joint army maneuvers since 1865, when Brazil, Argentina, and Uruguay joined forces as the Triple Alliance in a war against Paraguay. In 1997 Brazil and Argentina also signed a memorandum of understanding regarding measures of mutual security. This marks a significant level of change in the two countries' relations, given that not long ago their military strategies considered the possibility of direct confrontation between them. It should be emphasized, though, that the aim of current military cooperation is not an institutionalized defense mechanism or a pluralistic security community. Rather, the goal is to increase confidence and transparency, adopting the idea of a no-war zone in the Southern Cone and the final scrapping of conflictive postures (see CARI 1993, 27–33).

Argentina–Chile: Resolution of Territorial Disputes and Economic Cooperation

In contrast to the Argentine–Brazilian traditional quest for prestige and influence, Argentina and Chile confronted the problems of one of the longest land frontiers in the world and a history of territorial disputes and militarized crises, leading to occasional armed clashes that always stopped just short of war. Throughout the nineteenth century, both Chile and Argentina claimed the southern Patagonia region. After concluding a boundary agreement in 1881, they resolved most of their territorial differences, although the conflict over the Beagle Channel lingered until 1984.

The long Beagle Channel dispute revolved about the issue of how and where to define the dividing line between the South Atlantic (Argentina's sphere of influence) and the South Pacific (Chile's sphere). The dispute turned into a serious international crisis in 1978, following Argentina's rejection of a British arbitration award giving three Beagle Channel Islands to Chile in 1977. Argentina's military government adopted a hardline policy that included military preparations and serious threats of war. In December 1978 war was narrowly avoided, perhaps providentially, by a severe South Atlantic storm that prevented a naval confrontation between the two countries and by a last-minute papal diplomatic intervention. After intense negotiations that lasted for more than five years, Argentina and Chile finally signed the Treaty of Peace and Friendship on November 29, 1984, which had previously been endorsed by a vast majority of Argentine citizens in a referendum. In the treaty, Chile's sovereignty over the Beagle Channel Islands was recognized, though there was an explicit limitation about projecting its sovereignty beyond a surrounding twelve-mile-wide zone.

The 1984 treaty signaled an important improvement in bilateral relations, away from negative peace towards stable peace. It represented a watershed in the relations of Chile and Argentina, which at least three times in their long history had come to the verge of war. The 1984 settlement allowed common developmental and economic concerns to come to the fore, replacing previous divisive national security and geopolitical matters. Since October 1984, the bilateral links between the two countries at different levels have noticeably intensified. Both countries have worked hard and promptly to make up for lost time in physical and economic integration and energy cooperation.

Argentine–Chilean relations further strengthened after Chile's return to democracy in 1989. In 1990, both countries signed an agreement of economic integration (Acuerdo de Complementación Económica) that included the construction of a gas pipeline from Neuquén, Argentina, to Santiago, Chile. In 1991, Chile and Argentina settled twenty-two minor boundary disputes by negotiations and tripled their bilateral trade. Chilean investments in Argentina have jumped from about $100 million in 1989 to $2 billion in 1994 and to $5.5 billion in 1996 (see Brooke 1994; Palomar 1996). As in the Argentine–Brazilian case, stable peace has become an enduring reality across the Andes, in spite of two lingering territorial disputes. The Laguna del Desierto dispute was submitted to arbitration, the award this time favoring Argentina. The last dispute, over two thousand square kilometers of glaciers in Hielos Continentales, was finally resolved in a bilateral agreement of December 1998, ratified by the congresses of both countries on June 2, 1999 (see CARI 1995; La Nación on Line, June 2, 1999). Since August 1988, Chile and Argentina have held joint naval exercises in the Beagle Channel area. Although the Argentine military has probably reached an easier understanding with its Brazilian colleagues than with its Chilean counterparts, Chilean officers have participated as observers since 1992 in the military meetings and exchanges of the four Mercosur countries. Moreover, together with Argentina and Brazil, Chile contributed to the reform of the Tlatelolco treaty on the prohibition of nuclear weapons in the region, becoming a signatory in January 1994. It also ratified the Mendoza Agreement of 1991 banning other weapons of mass destruction. Finally, in June 1996 Chile signed an association agreement with Mercosur, though shying away from full membership.

Argentina and Chile signed a memorandum of understanding on mutual security in November 1995, within the framework of the Organization of American States' meeting to promote CBMs. The two countries created a permanent committee on security to deepen their security cooperation. Among the declared goals were (1) to strengthen the channels of communication in the area of defense; (2) to expedite information about military maneuvers; and (3) to promote academic activities that will foster cooperation on matters of security (see Diamint 1998). To further foster the rapprochement between the two countries, their defense ministers declared on July 18, 1997, that they would ask the International Monetary Fund and the World Bank to help work out standard accounting procedures for defense spending in the whole region. That would make it possible to compare budgets in a realistic way, reducing the misinformation and suspicion that favor hawks and arms dealers and harm rational defense planning. In this context, it should be noted that some residual mutual mistrust and suspicion linger between the two countries, at least at the military if not the political level. Hence, the consolidation of stable peace might take some time and effort. This was evident, for instance, in the seven years or so that it took legislators in both countries to ratify the treaties by which the two governments were so eager to settle their last territorial dispute over the Hielos Continentales.

The historical record shows convincingly that the relations between Argentina and Chile have moved steadily away from conflict towards stable peace. However, it is less obvious whether Argentina and Chile have already consolidated their stable peace and moved in the direction of a pluralistic security community, as in the case of Argentina and Brazil. Mistrust and suspicion linger, especially from the standpoint of the Chilean military, whose procurement and planning are still focused upon the traditional roles of power projection and the protection of its borders vis-à-vis Peru, Bolivia, and Argentina (see Hurrell 1998, 257–58; *La Nación on Line*, May 6, 1997).

Security Cooperation in the ABC Triangle, 1991–1999

In historical terms, the security cooperation institutionalized among the ABC powers in the 1990s following their transition to stable peace can be regarded as an improved version of their experience before World War II. Under an umbrella of regional stable peace, the three countries have adopted a policy of autonomy towards growth and development, prioritizing economic development and integration at the expense of old-fashioned and outdated narrow military considerations. In this context we should understand a series of joint initiatives taken in the realm of security cooperation and coordination, arms control, and the fostering of regional CBMs in the Southern Cone of South America in the 1990s.

Probably the most important measure on consensual security cooperation adopted by the ABC triangle has been their decision to join the Tlatelolco regional regime of nuclear nonproliferation. On February 14, 1992, Presidents Collor de Mello (Brazil) and Menem (Argentina) proposed a series of amendments designed to facilitate Argentine and Brazilian accession to the Treaty for the Prohibition of Nuclear Weapons in Latin America (Treaty of Tlatelolco). Both nations had chosen to remain outside the treaty, which had been ratified by all other Latin American nations with the exception of Chile and Cuba. The proposed amendments were adopted by the Tlatelolco parties in August 1992 and subsequently ratified by Chile and Argentina, which became full parties to the regional regime on January 18, 1994. Brazil ratified the Treaty of Tlatelolco on May 30, 1994 (see Carasales 1996, 325–35).

In addition to nuclear nonproliferation, another highlight of security cooperation and arms control has been the Joint Declaration on the Complete Prohibition of Chemical and Biological Weapons, signed at Mendoza, Argentina, on September 5, 1991. The agreement was initially signed by Argentina, Brazil, and Chile and later by Bolivia, Ecuador, Paraguay, and Uruguay. Except for Bolivia, all signatories of the Mendoza Agreement have ratified the chemical weapons convention as well.

Conditions for Establishing and Consolidating Stable Peace in the ABC Triangle

Why and how did stable peace relations emerge in the first place in the case of the ABC triangle of South America? How did they evolve and consolidate over time? To answer these questions, we have first to differentiate between the two stages of stable peace (stabilization and consolidation) and, second, to specify the different conditions in each case. In empirical terms, it should be emphasized that while Argentine–Brazilian relations have already reached the stage of consolidation, and even approached the possibility of a pluralistic security community, Argentine–Chilean relations lag behind, somewhere between the establishment and the consolidation of stable peace.

Conditions for the Establishment of Stable Peace

In this section, I assess the causal mechanisms that facilitated the stabilization of relations and the movement beyond mere conflict resolution towards establishing stable peace. In the cases of Argentina and Brazil and Argentina and Chile, the relevant conditions were (a) stable political regimes; (b) mutual satisfaction with the peace agreements and predictability of behavior; and (c) open communication channels and problem-solving mechanisms. Third-party guarantees have not been relevant in the context of the ABC triangle.

Democratization and Stable Political Regimes. The condition of stable political regimes is linked to the return of democracy to the region, which has positively affected the prospects for stable peace. Although the movement towards stable peace was initiated in 1979 by military authoritarian regimes in the case of Argentina and Brazil, and while Chile was still an authoritarian regime in 1984, the spread of democracy throughout the Southern Cone constitutes a sufficient, albeit not a necessary, condition for establishing stable peace.

By the late 1970s and early 1980s, a widespread process of democratization swept away the military governments in the entire region, with the exceptions of Paraguay and Chile (which were not democratized until 1989). The security dilemma was partially resolved through the democratization process, leading to a quantitative and qualitative improvement of bilateral relations, especially between Argentina and Brazil and between Argentina and Chile. The return of civilian regimes signified a clear retreat from the pernicious geopolitical bases of foreign policy; instead, regional cooperation and integration were now favored. In the Southern Cone the initial Argentine–Brazilian rapprochement of 1979–1980 was enlarged after both countries returned to democracy in 1983 and 1985, leading to bilateral economic integration (since 1986) and later to the establishment of Mercosur in 1991. Moreover, the return to civilian rule in Argentina was a crucial factor in ending the long dispute with Chile over the Beagle Channel in 1984.

In the case of *Argentine–Brazilian relations,* the decision to forgo the production of nuclear weapons was closely linked to the return of democratic rule in both countries after decades of military governments. Democratization provided a crucial impetus to the ongoing nuclear rapprochement and to the evolution of their relationship into the nonproliferation regime. Presidential leadership and strong foreign ministry support were key to overcoming the resistance of some sectors among the military regarding the transparency of the nuclear regime. A related factor was the civilian leadership's desire to restrain and control some of their armed forces by incorporating the national nuclear programs into a bilateral civilian accounting and control regime. Similarly, on the economic front, it seems that only the establishment of well-entrenched stable democratic political regimes, after the initial transition of the mid-1980s, could guarantee the implementation of a comprehensive policy of economic integration and cooperation between the two countries.

Regarding *Argentine–Chilean relations,* the military regime of Pinochet in Chile could be considered sufficiently stable to turn to conflict resolution, given its inherent status quo approach towards the Beagle Channel dispute. In Argentina, however, the unsuccessful war waged by the military junta against the United Kingdom over the Falklands/Malvinas in early 1982 precipitated a return to democracy by late 1983 under the leadership of President Alfonsín. Between 1984 and 1989 the two countries improved their bilateral relations, although their cooperation was somewhat limited by the continuation of the military regime in Chile until 1989.

Mutual Satisfaction and Predictability of Behavior. Traditionally in the Southern Cone the perceptions of external threats have played a greater role in both authoritarian and democratic regimes than is usually recognized. Hence, the devaluation of the "hypotheses of conflict" was linked to the evolution of bilateral relations, as well as to the end of the Cold War, economic globalization, the need to reinsert South America in the global market, and the decay and obsolescence of geopolitical conceptions. In this context, a clear distinction should be drawn between the military rapprochement and economic cooperation between Argentina and Brazil, on the one hand, and the slower process of rapprochement between Argentina and Chile, on the other. Nowadays, the possibility of a war between Argentina and Brazil seems as ludicrous as a conflagration between the United States and Canada. In the Argentina–Chile dyad, however, the conclusions are not as evident.

Stable peace expectations and predictability of behavior have been linked to the evolution of the rapprochement between *Argentina and Brazil,* first in the nuclear realm and later in the economic area. The leadership in both nations came to appreciate the potential benefits of reducing tensions generated by their respective nuclear programs. Although military conflict was considered highly unlikely, a sustained military competition with a nuclear dimension could have been economically ruinous to their countries and could have threatened regional security by exacerbating traditional rivalries and fueling regional tensions. In fact, the two countries shared a history of cooperation in nuclear issues before stable peace—for instance, in their common defiant attitude towards the nonproliferation regime since 1968. This process built confidence and thereby facilitated the later expansion of cooperative practices. Increased mutual confidence followed from a far greater degree of transparency, leading to the establishment of a mutual safeguards regime in the 1990s.

As to *Argentine–Chilean relations,* it seems that Chile and Argentina have been satisfied with the 1984 peace treaty that resolved the Beagle Channel dispute. In the words of Argentine president Raúl Alfonsín, the treaty could be considered a broad step towards "peace, integration, and disarmament in Latin America"(quoted in Morris 1989, 98). Even if Chile did not constitute any longer a "conflict hypothesis" for the Argentine armed forces, this logic did not apply so easily the other way around. For instance, as late as in 1997, Chile's defense minister declared that the traditional conflict hypotheses in the region had not been overcome and that Argentina was an unreliable country with unpredictable behavior. Moreover, the Chilean armed forces have retained a great share of formal and informal power and resources in the current democratic regime. Furthermore, Chile has not entered any of the regional cooperative economic agreements. Although it has been an associated member of Mercosur since 1996, it has refused so far to become a full member (see Oelsner 1999, 5; *La Nación on Line*, May 6, 1997; May 12, 1997).

Open Communication Channels and Problem-Solving Mechanisms. These two conditions have been conducive to establishing stable peace in both of the cases in the ABC triangle. The institutionalization of relations at multiple levels (including transnational and transgovernmental), and the formalization of problem-solving mechanisms through bilateral agreements, including memoranda of understanding, CBMs, and arbitration procedures, have smoothed the way for the transition to stable peace in the region.

In the case of *Argentine–Brazilian relations*, the evolution of the nuclear rapprochement since 1979 has been linked not only to high-level, state-to-state communication channels but also to the underlying work of an incipient epistemic community in both countries. The efforts that paved the way for government action in the nuclear regime were marked by a number of discussions and consultations between Argentine and Brazilian scientists under the aegis of the societies of physicists of both countries. These exchanges helped to bring the subject to public attention through newspaper stories, and this increased attention facilitated the later actions of the two governments, especially after the return to democracy.

As to *Argentine–Chilean relations*, there has been a clear movement towards transnational contacts since 1984, especially on economic issues such as oil and gas pipelines and private investments. Following the historic presidential declaration of 1991 regarding the resolution of pending territorial disputes, the two countries have agreed on problem-solving mechanisms to establish and further their stable peace.

Conditions for the Consolidation of Stable Peace

Irrespective of the democratic character of the political regimes in the Southern Cone, the necessary conditions for the consolidation of stable peace are a continuing satisfaction with the status quo and a common normative framework that expresses a clear predilection for peaceful change and peaceful settlement of international disputes. In addition, spillover effects and nonmilitary public goods, embodied by economic factors such as enhanced economic interdependence, subregional cooperation and integration, and the quest for economic development and prosperity, have contributed to the maintenance and enhancement of stable peace, without being either necessary or sufficient. Moreover, the consolidation of stable peace is facilitated by the cognitive centrality of trust in the relations between the parties, the quality of their interaction, and the level of their cooperation.

Continuing Satisfaction with the Status Quo. Nowadays, there are no longer territorial claims involving the two salient dyads of the ABC triangle, with the possible exceptions of their frozen claims in Antarctica. This is more evident in the Argentine–Brazilian case than in the Chilean–Argentine one. Yet, even in the latter case, since 1991 the two countries have been ready to conclude their last two territorial disputes, over Laguna del Desierto (by arbitration, in 1996, this time in favor of Argentina), and over the Hielos Continentales (in June 1999). In this sense, it is obvious than Argentina, Brazil, and Chile continue to be satisfied with the territorial status quo in the region.

In the *Argentine–Brazilian case,* that satisfaction has been translated into a high level of transparency and institutionalization of their bilateral nuclear regime, a series of CBMs, and the redeployment of their armed forces away from their common border, while plans are being drawn up to increase their transportation and communication linkages. Cooperation has arisen in almost all areas of their bilateral relationship. Mutual conflict hypotheses have been completely dismantled; military spending, as well as arms imports and exports, declined steadily in the 1990s. At the same time, there have been only rather modest steps towards more "positive" or "activist" components of cooperative security, such as the construction of a collective security system with supranational elements.

In the *Argentine–Chilean case,* the satisfaction with the status quo has been expressed more at the high political level in the disposition of the leaders of both countries to resolve their last territorial disputes, rather than in military-strategic terms. The long common border has not been completely demilitarized, and procurement plans for the defense and projection of power have not been utterly abandoned by both countries. Following the resolution of the last territorial dispute in June 1999, there is a growing need for a cognitive shift, an ideological/cultural revision regarding the traditional territorial nationalism that has so far separated the two countries (see Romero 1999; Garretón 1999).

Common Normative Framework. There is some evidence that shared values and norms have played a significant role in consolidating stable peace and deepening the cooperation between Argentina and Brazil and, to a lesser extent, between Argentina and Chile. The most obvious have been democratic norms, although they were not the only ones that framed the normative consensus in the Southern Cone. Among the norms shared by the ABC countries are their Christian (Catholic) conception of life; liberal recognition of rights and liberties; mutual respect for sovereignty and nonintervention; belonging to the Western world and civilization; legal equality of states; prevention and repression of aggression; peaceful settlement of international disputes; and peaceful coexistence.

In the specific context of the *Argentine–Brazilian nuclear rapprochement*, it is crucial to refer to the common paradigms of technological autonomy and developmentalism (*desarrollismo*) as common norms and values that moved the two countries towards nuclear cooperation and economic integration. Only in the mid-1980s did democracy as a common principle become an explicit and necessary condition for economic and political integration (see Barletta, 1997, 2–3; Bocco 1989, 13–17). Conversely, in *Argentine–Chilean relations*, the norms of peaceful settlement of disputes and peaceful coexistence have been paramount, even before the return of democracy to Chile in 1989.

Spillover Effects and Nonmilitary Public Goods: Economic Cooperation, Prosperity, Interdependence, and Integration. The initial rapprochement in each dyad in the ABC triangle was motivated by security concerns and by the resolution of territorial disputes: Itaipú and nuclear cooperation in the Argentine–Brazilian case (1979–1980); and the de-escalation of a war crisis over the Beagle Channel, leading to the comprehensive Treaty of Peace and Friendship in the Argentine–Chilean case (1979–1984). However, while the trigger of the movement towards stable peace has been security linked, the democratization process has led to a dynamic expansion of the issues in the bilateral agenda, leading to spillover effects and the provision of nonmilitary public goods. Thus, the rapprochement and rapid improvement of bilateral relations has moved in the direction of a broader framework of economic, political, and even cultural integration. The provision of nonmilitary public goods has centered upon common issues of economic growth and development, resulting in an increasing web of economic interdependence that has helped to maintain peaceful relations over the long run. Recent state-led cooperation and the emergence of integrative frameworks in the mid-1980s and 1990s were designed to promote interdependence, not only to manage it. For political rather than economic reasons, such as the need to legitimize and enhance the new democratic regimes, the ABC states decided to create economic interdependence through the institutionalization of mutual cooperation, making interdependence the consequence, not the cause, of political cooperation and economic integration. Once economic interdependence grew, it affected the quality of regional peace. After the ABC countries became so interdependent at the bilateral level, a war between Argentina and Brazil, or even between Argentina and Chile, came to seem unprofitable, if not unthinkable.

This logic of economic consolidation of stable peace has worked effectively in the evolution of economic relations of the dyads. As the foreign policies of Argentina and Brazil diverged in the 1990s, common economic interests continued to grow as the ultimate guarantee of the continuation of their stable peace. A similar process of economic interdependence has taken place between Argentina and Chile in the last ten years, as epitomized by massive Chilean investments in Argentina and a series of binational transportation, mining, and communications projects.

The Centrality of Trust. If one were to analyze the conditions for the consolidation of stable peace only on a material basis (e.g., economic dimensions of interdependence), the relations between Argentina and Chile seem to be as consolidated as those between Argentina and Brazil, if not more so. However, there is a cognitive or intersubjective dimension to stable peace, related to the centrality of trust. To illustrate, one might compare the perceptions of interpersonal relations among members of the armed forces in the three countries. The conclusion is straightforward: there is more trust and more openness between Argentines and Brazilians than between Argentines and Chileans. The differences are not related to sheer numbers or considerations of material power (for instance, Brazil is vastly superior to Chile in relation to Argentina) but are, rather, linked to psychological, cultural, and political considerations and prejudices. For instance, the Argentines still suspect Chile's geopolitical intentions, as they still dislike Chile's national slogan ("by reason or by force"). Conversely, the Chileans are suspicious of Argentina's special status vis-à-vis NATO and its close relations with the United States (see Diamint 1998, 20–22).

Trust has been not only a condition for consolidating stable peace but also a consequence of its establishment (see Bengtsson, chapter 5; Väyrynen, chapter 6). This is particularly true in the Argentine–Brazilian case, more specifically in the building of a common nuclear policy and regime whose corollary was the two countries' ratification of the Tlatelolco treaty. Thus, Argentina and Brazil managed to build an original model of *contiguous mutual trust* in the area of nuclear security, working in sync with the more general regime of nuclear nonproliferation (see Brigagào and Valle Fonrouge 1996, 89–99). By contrast, in the stable peace between Argentina and Chile, mutual suspicions linger, and a serious element of trust is still missing from the equation (see *The Economist*, July 26, 1997; and *La Nación on Line*, May 12, 1997).

Quality of Interaction and Level of Cooperation between the Parties. The two remaining conditions that facilitate the consolidation of stable peace refer to the quality of interaction and the level of cooperation between (or among) the parties. Both relevant dyads in the ABC triangle get high scores in both areas, although the Argentine–Brazilian relationship seems to have developed further in the direction of a pluralistic security community, owing to a more benign history of conflict and cooperation between the parties.

In the *Argentine–Brazilian case*, their initial security relationship (in the 1980s) was increasingly embedded in a dense process of economic integration and transactions, organizations, and institutions in the 1990s. Hence, politics, economics, and security have been continually intertwined, reinforcing each other and creating a synergistic effect of a closer (security?) community. Conversely, in *Argentine–Chilean relations*, the political (and peaceful) resolution of territorial disputes triggered economic cooperation, leading to tentative steps of security cooperation in more recent times. Therefore, the quality of interaction and the level of cooperation have been more comprehensive between Argentina and Brazil than between Argentina and Chile.

Conclusion

The evolution of stable peace relations in the ABC triangle seems to be a story with a happy ending, although it is still a work in progress. Some tentative conclusions can be drawn about the movement towards a pluralistic security community in the Southern Cone, the importance of the regional approach, lessons from the nuclear rapprochement between Argentina and Brazil, and theoretical and policy implications for other regions.

Towards a Pluralistic Security Community in the Southern Cone of South America?

Has the Southern Cone of South America, and more specifically, its Argentine–Brazilian core, transformed itself into a pluralistic security community, in relation to which not only common threats but also shared perceptions and a common identity may be identified? In the economic sphere, Mercosur since 1991 has epitomized a serious effort of regionalization and institutionalization of economic cooperation, increasing interdependence, and economic integration. In the security domain, the level of cooperation regarding nuclear nonproliferation and banning chemical and biological weapons, as well as conventional arms control and CBMs, has been notable, especially between Argentina and Brazil, but also including to some extent Chile. Therefore, it seems that dependable expectations of peaceful change today characterize the relations among the Southern Cone countries. At the political level, however, it becomes more difficult to talk about Argentina and Brazil or the Southern Cone in general as a consolidated pluralistic security community. For instance, in the last decade we have seen a growing divergence in the foreign policies of Brazil and Argentina vis-à-vis the United States, showing an interesting reversal in their traditional roles.

Most of the necessary and helpful conditions for the development of a pluralistic security community have been in place, some even before the return to democracy in the 1980s. Yet, other favorable conditions, especially in the economic, social, and transnational realms, remain so far incipient. As a consequence, it is still premature to talk about a mature sense of community and shared identity ("we-feeling"), includ- ing mutual sympathy and loyalties. Argentina and Brazil, as well as the other members of Mercosur, still have a long way to go in terms of artic- ulating common foreign policies and coordinating their macroeconomic policies beyond the continuing development and growth of their nation- al economies. Needless to say, since the stable peace relations between Argentina and Chile (in contrast to those between Chile and Brazil, or even between Argentina and Brazil) have not yet been consolidated, Chile is even farther away from that security community.

The Importance of a Dyadic/Regional Approach

While this chapter has examined the overlapping dyads Argentina and Chile and Argentina and Brazil, it is important to note that the countries of the ABC triangle have related to each other from a regional point of view, both in terms of power considerations (before rapprochement) and of the establishment and consolidation of stable peace (after it). This approach appears to offer a promising model for other areas of conflict or tension in the world, since perceived threats are not as a rule global or sys- temic but emanate from the region itself. Consequently, the solutions to be found and negotiated are also regional, though they do not necessarily contradict global regimes. More specifically, the increasing nuclear coop- eration between Argentina and Brazil since 1979 and the confidence- building measures adopted by all three members of the ABC triangle can and should be studied as an encouraging model of regional solutions to regional conflicts. This model of cooperation overlaps (rather than con- tradicts) global regimes such as nuclear nonproliferation.

Theoretical and Policy Implications

What lessons can be drawn from the ABC experience with stable peace for other zones of peace and conflict? Is this rather encouraging story in a faraway region irrelevant to other hot spots, such as the Middle East or the Korean peninsula?

There is a clear distinction to be drawn between the Argentine–Brazil- ian and the Argentine–Chilean dyads. Unlike Argentina and Chile, which three times in their history confronted each other on the verge of war (the last time in December 1978), Brazil and Argentina had their last military crisis and confrontation in the mid-1870s. For a long century afterwards, they were suspicious competitors and rivals but not enemies. This distinguishes them from "true enemies" like Arabs and Israelis, Indians and Pakistanis, or North and South Koreans. At the same time, the Argentine–Brazilian nuclear rapprochement teaches us that cooperation between rivals on sensitive nuclear issues is possible and might be more effective than joining a global regime.

The Argentine–Brazilian experience, and to some extent the Argentine–Chilean relationship, also indicates the complex synergistic relationship between security and economic processes. What started as the resolution of a dispute between Argentina and Brazil over resources (Itaipú in 1979) and a narrow cooperation on nuclear issues (in the 1980s) became gradually embedded in a broader framework of economic and even political integration (in the 1990s). Similarly, in the case of Argentina and Chile, the de-escalation from an imminent war (in 1979) and the successful management and resolution of a long territorial dispute (in 1984) opened the way for economic cooperation and integration (in the 1990s), culminating in the final resolution of the last territorial dispute (in 1999). Hence, *pace* the neofunctionalists and neoliberals, the order of causality (or at least the chronology) in the movement towards stable peace has been from security cooperation to economic integration, rather than the other way around. It is also true, however, that once there is an embedded network of economic interdependence between the parties, it acts as an ultimate guarantee of the consolidation of stable peace.

The experience of the ABC triangle also shows us the importance of drawing distinctions among the different conditions for the two stages of stable peace in dyadic and regional terms. Furthermore, it is clear from this example that stable peace can be initiated before all the relevant dyads are democratic regimes (Argentina and Brazil in 1979 were authoritarian regimes; Chile in 1984 was still ruled by General Pinochet). In addition, although there is an overlap between stable peace and a security community, stable peace can be consolidated, as in the case of the Argentine–Brazilian relationship, without crossing the threshold to a well-established pluralistic security community.

Notes

I would like to acknowledge with gratitude the support of the Leonard Davis Institute for International Relations at the Hebrew University of Jerusalem and the research assistance of Lea Gedalia, as well as the comments and suggestions of Galia Press Bar-Natan, Yael Krispin, Rut Diamint, Gordon Mace, Kjell Goldmann, Patrick James, Magnus Jerneck, and Ole Elgström.

12

Israel–Egypt Peace: Stable Peace?

Yaacov Bar-Siman-Tov

The Israeli–Egyptian peace, the first case of conflict resolution in the Arab–Israeli conflict, is also the first test case of the shift from conflict resolution toward stable peace in this conflict. The experience until now has been very positive in terms of absence of war, threats of war, and crisis prevention, but not in terms of extensive political, economic, and cultural cooperation and transnational relations. The Israeli–Egyptian peace relations have never progressed beyond a "cold peace."

Since the signing of the peace agreement in 1979, and particularly since 1982, when the final stage of the Israeli withdrawal from the Sinai occurred, the Israeli–Egyptian peace has never been in danger of a collapse or serious deterioration that might precipitate a danger of war, a threat of force, or even a major crisis. Even during the war in Lebanon (1982) or throughout the *intifada* (1987–1993), the peace agreement was maintained. Nevertheless, Israeli–Egyptian relations have never transcended a minimal security and political cooperation that was required to maintain the peace. The shift towards a comprehensive peace in the Middle East that had started at the Madrid Conference in 1991 and reached its peak with the Israeli–Palestinian peace process (since 1993) and the Israeli–Jordanian peace agreement (1994) not only did not warm the peace relations between Egypt and Israel but made them even colder than before.[1]

This chapter aims to examine the following questions: (1) Is the Israeli–Egyptian peace stable? (2) How can one explain the fact that the peace relations between the two states have never deteriorated to a danger of war or a threat of war? (3) What are the explanations for the emergence of their cold peace? (4) What is the contribution of this peace to the stabilization of the Arab–Israeli conflict? (5) What are the paradoxes of comprehensive peace? and (6) What are the conditions and the prospects for stable peace between Israel and Egypt ?

Is It a Stable Peace?

This study argues that the peace between Israel and Egypt is not considered yet a stable peace as suggested by George (1992), Boulding (1978), Russett and Starr (1992), and Kacowicz (1998). Although the probability of war seems to be very small, both sides do not entirely exclude the use of military force, or even a threat of it, in a dispute between them. Their national security doctrine and their rearmament policy take into consideration the possibility of deterioration of the peace relations into a crisis or even war in case of a major war between Israel and Syria or between Israel and the Palestinians.[2] As long as war is still considered an option, even if its probability is very small, the Israeli–Egyptian peace cannot be regarded as a stable peace. Stabilization of the peace is nevertheless the "object of peace policy" and a "deliberate decision" for both sides (Boulding 1978, xi). Both parties are determined to maintain their peace and to avoid its deterioration into unstable strategic relations.

With the absence of a comprehensive peace in the Arab–Israeli regional system and a real reconciliation between the parties, as well as the lack of common characteristics such as political regimes, economic prosperity and development, and common norms and values, the Israeli–Egyptian peace after twenty years has not developed into a stable peace as in Western Europe. Therefore, I would define the Israel–Egyptian peace relations as still in the transitional stage towards stabilization rather than in the (consolidated) stable peace stage.

Stabilization, as we stated in chapter 1, is the process of establishing peace after the immediate resolution of a conflict and is a precondition to consolidated stable peace. Stabilization is limited to keeping peace in the short and middle term, when the parties are still confused about the change in their relationship and must adjust to the new reality. Immediately after the resolution of the conflict, the sides may prefer to limit their political and security cooperation only to a degree that is necessary for maintaining peace, without extending it to other domains.

Although it is difficult to say how long the stabilization stage should endure as a preparatory stage for stable peace, it seems that twenty years is probably already a "long peace." The fact that the Israeli–Egyptian peace is still in its stabilization stage indicates that one or both sides are not ripe yet for stable peace or are not interested in transforming their interaction and cooperation. The success of the stabilization phase does not encourage the sides to strengthen their cooperation and extend it into other domains. Thus, their limited political and security cooperation does not spill over to economic and cultural cooperation.

Why Is It Maintained?

The Israeli–Egyptian peace is maintained mainly because of realist rather than liberal arguments (Kacowicz 1998, 34–47).[3] I would like to suggest the following explanations:

- *Peace as a vital interest.* Both sides perceive peace as a great achievement of their foreign policy and crucial for their security. Maintenance of peace is a vital interest for both sides. Both parties realize that any deterioration of the peace into a violent conflict might be very risky and costly not only in security terms but also in political terms, since this will endanger their relations with the United States and the international community as a whole. This mutual consideration is probably the most important factor for maintaining their peace, as part of a rational cost–benefit analysis (Shaked and Dishon 1986, 380–81; Stein 1997, 307; Dessouki 1988, 97; Dowek 1998, 381–84).[4]

- *Stable political regimes.* Since 1979 both sides have enjoyed stable regimes. The Likud Party, which signed the peace agreement, remained the major ruling party in a governmental coalition or was an equal partner in a national unity government until 1992, and again in 1996–1999. Begin's successor, Yitzhak Shamir, who initially did not support the peace agreement, later realized its importance and became a strong supporter. The Labor Party, which supported the agreement from its beginning as an opposition party, has continued its support as the ruling elite (in 1992–1996 and since 1999). Hosni Mubarak's stable regime in Egypt was also a crucial factor in maintaining the peace. Mubarak, as President Anwar Sadat's deputy, felt personally responsible for maintaining peace with Israel.

- *Mutual satisfaction.* Both sides are indeed satisfied with the terms of their bilateral agreement and especially with the territorial arrangements. Even the Taba issue, which was left open in the peace treaty and created dissatisfaction in both parties, was settled by peaceful means (Rabinovich and Shaked 1988, 283–85). Yet, Egypt and Israel are not satisfied with the development of their relations, which has not lived up to initial expectations.

- *Stable peace expectations.* Although the two sides have different expectations about peace and there is a gap between their initial expectations and reality, both countries have learned that the most important expectation of peace that has been accomplished so far is the absence of war. However, the Israeli leaders and people are disappointed that warm peace, full normalization, and political and economic cooperation have not yet materialized. The coldness of peace and the very low degree of cooperation, the hostile attitude of the Egyptian political and nonpolitical elites and the media, and the very competitive style of the Egyptian leadership, especially since resuming the peace process in 1991, have created real disappointment. The Egyptian leaders and people, for their part, believe that Israel has exploited the peace with Egypt in order to strengthen its hand in its conflicts with other Arab actors, as in the destruction of the Iraqi nuclear reactor in 1981, the war in Lebanon in 1982, and the intifada in the late 1980s.

The movement towards comprehensive peace that began with the convening of the Madrid conference (1991) and the Washington talks, followed by the concluding of the Israeli–Palestinian interim agreement and the Israeli–Jordanian peace agreement, did not improve the balance between expectations and realities for both sides. Actually the gap between expectations and reality has widened. Egypt, because of its marginal role in the peace process, felt somehow isolated from the main developments and even threatened by the increased strategic and political importance of Israel. Israel was disappointed that even the movement towards comprehensive peace did not change Egypt's refusal to warm the peace relations. Both Egypt and Israel acknowledge the gap between expectations and reality and the contradiction between cold peace and stabilization of peace. Nonetheless, both accept that coldness and mutual disappointment should not undermine the maintenance of peace.

- *Predictability of behavior.* Israel and Egypt are mostly certain about each other's intentions and behavior as to the maintenance of peace. This certainty is based on the belief that each side perceives the maintenance of peace as a vital interest. Both parties also believe that violation or erosion of the peace treaty would entail tremendous costs not only to their bilateral relations but also to their relations with the United States and the international community as a whole.

- *Multiplicity of communication channels.* The high degree of information exchange and multiplicity of communication channels have proved to be very important for managing the relations between the states as mechanisms to avoid misunderstandings. In addition to direct contact via their embassies, meetings have been held at the highest level. Although Egyptian president Hosni Mubarak has refrained from visiting Israel, Israeli leaders have visited Egypt to sustain a dialogue. In addition, both sides have used the good offices of the United States to enhance their interaction (Dowek 1998, 156–95).[5]

- *Third party guarantees and involvement.* U.S. guarantees to both sides in the peacemaking stage were crucial for concluding the peace agreement. Since then, the U.S. contribution to the maintenance of peace has been limited to military and economic assistance to both sides and to participation in the international force in the Sinai. The United States plays in this regard a role of hegemonic power that both Egypt and Israel respect. This reality makes each side believe that the other is committed to the maintenance of peace. Nevertheless, the United States fails to warm the peace, although it contributes to its stabilization.

These conditions are indeed more limited than those required for stable peace and refer mainly to the parties' commitment to maintain the minimal requirements of peace. Both sides internalize the norm of managing their relations only by peaceful means and accept that force or threats of force are excluded as legitimate means. These conditions are necessary for creating mutual trust and confidence that the peace relations, with all their difficulties, will continue and its maintenance will promise mutual security. Nevertheless, the coldness of peace and its limitation mainly to security relations cannot promise any serious movement towards stable peace.

Different Perceptions of Stable Peace

It seems that since signing the peace agreement in 1979 Israel and Egypt differ as to the nature of the desired peace. While Israel urges a stable peace, Egypt prefers a durable but cold peace. Neither party uses the term "stable peace," referring instead to "normal relations" or "normalization." Although these concepts are far from clear or precise, Israel insisted on including the term "normal relationship" in the March 1979 peace treaty. The comprehensive nature of that normal relationship is spelled out in article 3 of the treaty: "The parties agree that the normal relationship established between them will include full recognition, diplomatic, economic, and cultural relations, termination of economic boycotts, and discriminatory barriers to the free movement of people and goods. The process by which they undertake to achieve such a relationship parallel to the implementation of other provisions of the treaty is set out in the annexed protocol."

Moreover, annex 3 of the treaty states: "Ambassadors will be exchanged upon completion of the interim withdrawal. All discriminatory barriers and economic boycotts will be lifted and, not later than six months after the completion of the interim withdrawal, negotiations for a trade and commerce agreement will begin. Free movement of each other's nationals and transport will be allowed and both sides agree to promote 'good neighborly relations.' . . . Road, rail, postal, telephone, wireless and other forms of communications will be opened between the two countries on completion of interim withdrawal" (quoted in Quandt 1986, 397–403).

The normalization of relations between the two sides is, therefore, a legal and binding obligation, and it is not made necessarily conditional on concluding peace agreements with other Arab actors. Absence of normal relations could be interpreted as a breach of the agreement. The comprehensive nature of normal relations as stated in the treaty implies that the sides agreed to establish stable peace, rather than just a cold peace. In this regard, indeed, as Aulas correctly remarks, "normalization as conceived in the Egyptian–Israeli agreements goes well beyond the classic boundaries of a peace agreement to lay down precise perspectives for the future" (Aulas 1983, 222). However, it seems that the two sides have different interpretations of the meaning and nature of a normal relationship and the conditions and the timing of its implementation.

Israel perceives normalization in broader terms than a formal peace, as warm peace based on extensive security, political, economic, and cultural interactions, as it indeed has been stated in the treaty. Israel believes that only normalization has the potential to maintain the peace because it is "an indication of the sincerity of Egyptians' readiness to turn over a new leaf in their relations with Israel, and an expression of commitment that would be harder to renege on" (Shamir 1988, 201). Normalization has a symbolic rather than a material importance. It signifies Egypt's readiness to legitimize Israel's existence in the area, accepting it and its integration into the Middle East as a regular member. Contrary to the Egyptian arguments that Israel insists on normalization as an attempt at economic imperialism or cultural invasion, Israel perceives it primarily as a litmus test of "real peace" rather than an attempt to gain material benefits from it (Shamir 1988, 201). The emphasis on normalization also reflects Israel's concern that while it made massive territorial concessions that involved security risks, it received in return only intangible and elusive commitments. Therefore, normalization reflects not only clear-cut Egyptian commitment to maintain the peace but also a fair and honest quid pro quo in the exchange of land for peace (Shamir 1988, 201; Dowek 1998, 138–45). Normalization also becomes the most important factor for the Israeli government in proving the benefits of the peace process and acquiring legitimacy for the concessions made. Only normalization would constitute clear-cut evidence that Israel's withdrawal from the Sinai was justified in terms of long-term Israeli interests (Bar-Siman-Tov 1994, 191–95).

Egypt perceives normalization as adherence to the letter of the peace treaty, implementation of its various protocols, and the maintenance of "correct" relations, though not particularly warm peace. Egypt rejects the idea that normalization means special relations with Israel or giving it a preferred status. Peace means the end of hostilities and the establishment and maintenance of proper relations, no more than that. Egypt also claims that normal relations are not unique and that actually its relations with all other states are normal. Nevertheless, it is difficult if not impossible to establish normal relations immediately after a bitter conflict, especially when the sides still differ over fundamental aspects of it. There is a need for adjustment to peace itself before warming it even more. Normalization of relations is primarily perceived as an obligation imposed upon Egypt against its will. Thus Egypt sees normalization "as a necessary evil, an obligation inscribed in the clauses of the treaty" (Aulas 1983, 223; Lesch 1986; Dowek 1998, 145–53).

The peace with Israel, and especially normalization, is also perceived as a threat to Egypt's national identity as an Arab state and to its status as a leader of the Arab world. Concerned by domestic and external Arab criticisms about the development of the Egyptian–Israeli peace into a separate peace while neglecting the Palestinian cause, Egypt sought to link the normalization process first to the autonomy talks and later to the development of a comprehensive peace (Aulas 1983, 223).

The fundamental imbalance between the Egyptian and Israeli perceptions of peace and normalization has prevented any serious progress towards stable peace. It seems that without common perceptions of stable or warm peace and a common willingness to shift in the direction of stable peace, the two sides will continue to remain at a stage inferior to that of stable peace.

Normalization, indeed, did not get very far from the beginning. It evolved gradually toward the completion of Israeli withdrawal from the Sinai because of Israel's pressure on Egypt, but it was frozen immediately after Israel invaded Lebanon in June 1982, and especially after the massacre of Sabra and Shatila in September 1982.

Why Cold Peace?

Since 1982, bilateral relations have assumed the form of what Boutros Boutros Ghali defined as cold peace: "a situation in which a stalemate prevails in the peace process and the level of normal interrelations is deliberately, but not always admittedly, restricted as a reaction to various Israeli policies and actions" (Shamir 1988, 204). This definition regards cold peace as a minimal level of peace relations, which is not necessarily "normal relations" in the terms stated in the peace treaty, and explains this development as an object of Egyptian policy resulting from Israeli behavior. Cold peace means, therefore, minimal normalization that is necessary for the maintenance of peace, limited to security issues, but without all other kinds of cooperation, such as economic, commercial, and cultural. Above all, it refers to the continuation of a hostile line in the media that goes beyond the criticism of Israel's policies to a total condemnation of Israel and even refers to it as an enemy (Lesch 1986, 10; Stein 1997, 308–10).

There are various explanations for why only a cold peace emerged in the Egyptian–Israeli relations. While Egypt blames Israel, we can also point out that the peace remains a separate one, since it did not develop into a comprehensive peace that includes the resolution of the Palestinian problem. In addition, the lack of a real reconciliation and internalization of the peace in Egypt may also explain the cold peace. The explanations include:

- *Israel's behavior.* Egyptian governmental circles tend to state that the freeze in the relations was a deliberate response to Israeli policies and actions that contradicted the Egyptian understanding of the peace treaty. Israeli actions against other Arab states and the Palestinians fueled Egyptian domestic opposition to the treaty and reinforced negative attitudes towards Israel. From this perspective, Israel exploited the peace treaty in order to act freely against other Arab actors, and by doing so, it embarrassed Egypt in the Arab world. Moreover, Israel's actions are perceived to be tests of Egypt's commitment to the peace treaty. The Egyptian list of complaints against Israel is long, and it includes the bombing of Iraq's nuclear reactor; the annexation of Jerusalem and the Golan Heights; the stalemate in autonomy talks; the invasion of Lebanon and the massacre of Sabra and Shatila in 1982; the retention of Taba; the continued growth and expansion of Jewish settlements in the occupied territories; the bombing of PLO headquarters in Tunis; the suppression of the intifada; the massacre of Palestinians in a Hebron mosque; the opening of a tunnel near the Western Wall in East Jerusalem; the delay in implementing the Hebron and Wye agreements; and support for the Ethiopians against the Copts over Deir al-Sultan in Jerusalem (Lesch, 1986, 10; and Stein 1997, 305–6).

- *A separate peace.* Some analysts point to the fact that the Israeli-Egyptian peace remains only a separate one. The lack of a comprehensive peace prevents Egypt from warming and deepening the relations; indeed, Egypt maintains that active normalization of its relations with Israel in the absence of overall resolution of the Arab–Israeli conflict would damage its relations with the Arab world. This explanation is based on the assumption that stable peace in the Middle East depends on reaching a comprehensive peace between and among all the participants in the Arab–Israeli conflict. Boutros Ghali said, "Relations between Egypt and Israel would not reach a stage of full normalization, quantitatively and qualitatively unless a comprehensive settlement of the Middle East crisis materializes" (Stein 1997, 307; Dessouki, 1988, 110). This means full Israeli withdrawal from the captured territories and an independent Palestinian state with East Jerusalem as its capital. The linkage between comprehensive peace and normalization is also necessary to justify Egypt's argument that its peace treaty with Israel is not a separate one and is only the first stage for reaching a just, comprehensive, and lasting peace in the Middle East.

- *The Palestinian problem.* Some claim that since the Palestinian–Israeli conflict politically and ideologically is the core of the Arab–Israeli conflict system, only its resolution will enable the warming of Egyptian–Israeli peace relations. This claim means that no Arab state will be satisfied with its own agreement with Israel until the Palestinian–Israeli conflict is resolved to the satisfaction of the Palestinians. Full normalization, economic interdependence, and reconciliation are conditional on resolving the Palestinian–Israeli conflict. This conditional linkage is especially crucial for Egypt in order to prove that it did not throw out the Palestinian problem when it entered into the peace agreement with Israel (Ibrahim 1988, 19).

- *Internalization of the peace.* Others maintain that Egypt is not domestically ripe for deepening its relations with Israel. The peace with Israel means its acceptance as a political entity in the Middle East and the termination of political and territorial conflict, although it does not mean ideological legitimation of, and reconciliation with, Israel. Israel is still perceived by Egypt's political and military elites and especially by its intellectuals, professional associations, and trade unions as a threat to Arab nationalism and culture as well as to Islam. The peace with Israel violated a basic idea of Arab solidarity and challenged one of the core values in Arab political culture. It created a severe identity crisis as a result of the break with the Arab world and the damage to Egypt's leadership. Moreover, normal relations cannot be "imposed" on Egypt by Israel but should develop only gradually, after the resolution of all other dyadic conflicts in the Arab–Israeli conflict, especially the Palestinian–Israeli one (Dessouki 1988, 102–4; Aulas, 1983, 220–23; Al-Mashat 1983; Gerges 1995, 69–78; Maddy-Weitzman 1997, 266).

These arguments indicate that Egypt is not ripe yet for warm peace while the peace is still a separate one. Comprehensive peace and resolution of the Palestinian problem become two necessary, although not sufficient, conditions, for normal and warm relations with Israel. It seems that Egypt is not ripe for warm peace also because peace has not yet been internalized by nonpolitical elites and by the public in general. Moreover, there are strong governmental limitations on private and nongovernmental cooperation with Israel. The emergence of stable peace depends also on Israel. Israel can contribute to that not only by refraining from actions that embarrass Egypt but also by reaching a comprehensive peace that includes the Palestinians and the Syrians.

Seen from Israel, the cold peace is perceived as a violation of the peace agreement. Egypt's demands for a comprehensive peace, including the resolution of the Palestinian issue as a precondition for normal relations, are not part of the peace treaty. As to the freezing of normal relations because of Israeli actions and behavior, it seems that many in Israel underestimated the intensity of the Egyptian grievance or doubted its validity. Many argue that Egypt never intended to normalize its relationship with Israel in the first place, so that it actually exploited Israel's actions against other Arab actors to freeze the normalization. Moreover, Egypt from the outset used normalization as a bargaining chip to extract more concessions from Israel in a way that fits Egyptian interests.

Some Israeli leaders still perceive normalization as the core of peace and believe that without normalization peace is not really valid. For example, Yitzhak Shamir, Israel's former prime minister, maintained in 1991 that "it is as if Israel and Egypt, were not living in peace but were two absolute alien and estranged countries" (quoted in Stein 1997, 39). Similarly, Israel and Egypt are only "in a stable cease fire," as was noted in 1992 by David Ivri, the director general of Israel's defense ministry (Ayalon 1995, 386). Nevertheless, it seems that others, such as Yitzhak Rabin, realized the dual nature of Egypt's peace policy. While normalization is very minimal, Egypt maintains the peace. The important thing is the fact that Egypt is outside the conflict, because this has minimized the danger of a new war initiated by the Arabs. There are also those who, while disappointed by the minimal level of normalization, realize that Egypt indeed has difficulties promoting normalization without a real advance in the comprehensive peace (Stein 1997, 312).

The Contribution of Israeli–Egyptian Peace to Regional Peace

The Israeli–Egyptian peace even as a separate peace has stabilized the Arab–Israeli conflict. The fact that Egypt is out of the Arab–Israeli conflict has in itself stabilized the conflict with other Arab states, since without Egypt, these states would be greatly handicapped in initiating a war against Israel. The absence of a major war in the Arab–Israeli conflict since 1973 is probably a direct outcome of these peace relations. Nevertheless, the dyadic peace failed to stabilize Israel's conflict with the Palestinians, and, indeed, it did not prevent military clashes between Israel and the Palestinians, which reached their peak in the war in Lebanon and in the intifada period. Moreover, the bilateral peace failed to prevent the Israel–Syria war in Lebanon (1982), Israel's attack on the Iraqi nuclear reactor (1981), and the Iraqi Scud attacks on Israel (1991). Nevertheless, the fact that most of these military clashes remained limited was probably due to the Egyptian–Israeli peace, which imposed limitations on the fighting rivals. While the Arab side realized its military weakness and was careful not to expand the war, Israel, too, restrained itself to avoid breaking the peace with Egypt.

Nonetheless, the Israeli–Egyptian peace failed for many years to encourage other Arab actors, especially Jordan, Syria, and the Palestinians, to follow Egypt. The assumption that other Arab actors would follow Egypt and join the peace process after a while proved to be wrong. The decision of Arab actors to participate in the Madrid conference in 1991 and in the Washington talks that followed was probably influenced by the existence of the Israeli–Egyptian peace relationship. However, it is not clear how important that impact was on the Palestinians and the Jordanians in concluding interim and peace agreements with Israel in 1993 and 1994.

The fact that Egypt resolved its conflict with Israel legitimized other peace processes for other Arab actors, especially for those who could not be first to conclude a peace agreement with Israel because of their military and political weaknesses. Nonetheless, it seems that the resolution of any dyadic conflict in the Arab–Israeli conflict system depends on its own ripeness and learning.

The Paradoxes of a Comprehensive Peace: From Cold Peace to Cold War?

The conclusion of an interim agreement between Israel and the Palestinians and the resolution of the Jordanian–Israeli conflict contribute to the possibility of stable peace in the Middle East, since they minimize the dangers of a regional war or even dyadic wars. Yet they fail to further stabilize and warm the Egyptian–Israeli peace relationship. Actually, it became even colder and developed sometimes into a cold war. It seems that neither Egypt nor Israel realized how the movement toward comprehensive peace and the possibility of restructuring of the Middle East would influence their roles in the area and their bilateral relations.

Egypt had mixed feelings about the new peace process. On the one hand, it welcomed the new peace agreements in the Middle East, because it perceived them as a great achievement of Egypt's foreign policy. After so many years of a separate peace, other Arab actors adopted the same policy and realized that Egypt was right in making peace with Israel. On the other hand, Egypt perceived these agreements as a political threat rather than a real achievement of its peace policy. The reasons for that perception are Egypt's marginal role in concluding the agreements, the improvement of Israel's political status in the area, and the character and composition of the new Middle East order following the resumption of the peace process.

Egypt's expectations that it would play a dominant role in the peace process because of its leadership of the Arab world, and because it was the first Arab actor to sign a peace treaty with Israel, proved to be wrong. The three new peace negotiations—between Israel and the Palestinians (Oslo A), between Israel and Jordan, and between Israel and Syria—have been managed without the participation of Egypt. Although Egypt played some role in reaching the Cairo agreement (May 1994) and the Oslo B agreement (September 1995) between Israel and the Palestinians, it was less important than the role played by the United States. The developments in the peace process proved that they could be carried out without Egypt's mediation. Egypt, which hoped to capitalize on the new peace process in order not only to regain its key position in the Arab world but also to endear itself to the United States, found itself outside the main developments. Its leading position was jeopardized by Israel's direct negotiations with Arab actors, including those in the Persian Gulf and the Maghreb areas (Gerges 1995, 69–71; Ayalon, 1995, 306–7; Ayalon and Maddy-Weitzman 1996, 275–80).

The fact that Arab states such as Morocco, Tunisia, Qatar, and Oman established some formal and informal economic and political relations with Israel, as well as the convening of international economic summits in Morocco and Jordan with Israel's participation with the aim of establishing a "new Middle East," created real concerns in Egypt that Israel was seeking a dominant regional role for itself at the expense of Egypt (Ayalon and Maddy-Weitzman 1996, 279).

The third Egyptian concern was Israel's talk of a new Middle East. Israeli foreign minister Shimon Peres's book and declarations in favor of constructing a new Middle East in which strong security, economic, and political ties between Israel and the Arab states would eliminate the danger of war in the area made Egypt's leaders very nervous and suspicious (Peres 1993; Gerges 1995, 69–70). Although Peres sincerely believed that a regional economic community like the European Common Market would improve the security, political, economic, and social situation for all actors in the Middle East, Egypt saw it as a plan to control the area and establish Israeli economic hegemony. Peres's calls for expanding the Arab League's membership to include Israel and other non-Arab Middle Eastern actors in a new regional order annoyed Egyptian leaders, who saw this vision as endangering Egypt's role in the area. The new Israeli–Turkish military and political alliance only increased these concerns, as it was taken as another indication that Israel was looking for regional influence, if not hegemony (Maddy-Weitzman 1997, 268; 1998, 276).

The movement towards comprehensive peace led, therefore, to heightened political competition and tension between Israel and Egypt instead of improving their cooperation. Since 1993, Egyptian and Israeli leaders have clashed publicly over a wide range of issues that have almost brought them to the brink of a cold war. The main points of contention have been the character and composition of the new Middle East and the roles of Egypt and Israel in it.

In this new competition Israel has three advantages over Egypt: military power, economic power, and a special relationship with the United States. Egypt's leadership felt that the new peace process as it was managed threatened Egypt and even further eroded its power in the area, because in the postpeace era there will be no need for Egypt's mediation. These perceptions led Egyptian leadership to act to minimize the perceived dangers by linking normalization with Israel and the future economic and political regional order to Israel's signing of the nonproliferation treaty (NPT) and to progress toward a comprehensive peace.

Although Egypt's concerns regarding Israel's nuclear option are not new, it seems that they have increased since the conclusion of agreements between Israel, the Palestinians, and Jordan and the prenegotiations between Israel and Syria. Egypt demonstrated its concerns by threatening not to sign the NPT when it came up for renewal in May 1995 unless Israel also signed and opened up its nuclear facilities to international inspections. Egypt hoped to resume its leadership by mobilizing Arab support for its stand and by showing Israel and the United States that Egypt would not accept any attempt made by Israel to dominate the area. Egypt, however, was constrained by the United States to sign the NPT and failed to convince Israel to do the same. This only aggravated Egypt's negative feelings towards Israel and the United States (Maddy-Weitzman, 1997, 267, 368–69).

Egypt also expressed its firm opposition to Israeli–Arab normalization before a comprehensive peace was reached. By linking again the normalization of economic relations between Arab actors and Israel to political progress, Egypt tried to control developments in the area. In this context, Egypt convened a mini–Arab summit in Alexandria in December 1994 with the participation of Saudi Arabia and Syria that aimed at coordinating a common Arab policy to slow cooperation with Israel. The decisions adopted called for postponing normalization of Arab relations with Israel until a comprehensive peace was concluded (Ayalon and Maddy-Weitzman, 1996, 279; Gerges 1995, 72). It is not surprising that the Egyptian leadership's stand for postponing normalization with Israel was widely accepted by nonpolitical sectors in Egypt that generally opposed normalization, if not peace, with Israel (Gerges 1995, 74).

For its part, Israel under the Rabin and Peres administrations (1992–1996) was upset and surprised by Egypt's competitive approach, its refusal to warm the peace, its campaign against Israeli attempts to normalize its relations with other Arab actors, its struggle against Israel's nuclear capability, and its overall public criticism. Israel, which concluded new peace agreements with other Arab actors and was acting to advance a comprehensive peace as demanded by Egypt since 1977, was dismayed by Egypt's negative and harmful reaction. It seems that Israel was not sensitive enough to Egyptian concerns over the new changes in the area that were perceived as threats rather than new opportunities.

Israel's leadership publicly expressed this frustration. Deputy Foreign Minister Yossi Beilin complained about Egypt's "mixed feelings" regarding the peace process and its normalization with Israel (Ayalon and Maddy-Weitzman, 1996, 279–80). Prime Minister Yitzhak Rabin accused Egypt of an extremist attitude on the nuclear issue and expressed doubts about the stability and viability of the Egyptian political system, implying that a hostile Islamic government might come to power in Egypt. He warned that Israel must prepare itself "to wage an all-out war [against the Arab states] in the medium or long term" (Gerges 1995, 73; Maddy-Weitzman 1997, 266). An interdepartmental working paper of the Israeli foreign ministry was leaked to the press; it recommended a "harsh response" to Egypt's negative position and spoke of "punishing" Egypt if it continued its negative policy. Among the punitive measures mentioned were intervention in Washington to reduce U.S. aid to Egypt and removal of the Israeli–Palestinian negotiations from Cairo (Gerges 1995, 73; Maddy-Weitzman 1997, 266). These Israeli reactions only intensified the tension. However, both sides acted immediately to defuse the situation via diplomatic exchange and clarifications. Both preferred not to strain the relationship and to resolve the problem immediately (Maddy-Weitzman 1997, 266).

The competition and tension in the Israeli–Egyptian relationship increased during Netanyahu's administration (1996–1999). The cold peace not only became colder but also developed into a verbal war, including implied threats, which may perhaps be defined as a cold war. The new problems in the Israeli–Egyptian relationship lay in the stalemate of the peace process with the Palestinians and with Syria, for which Egypt blamed Israel. According to the Egyptian view, "The true obstacle to peace is the belief of the new Israeli government in a different kind of peace" (Maddy-Weitzman 1998, 279). Egypt, which continued to see itself as the essential mediator in the peace process both on the Israeli–Palestinian track and on the Israeli–Syrian one, concluded that Israel was not interested in implementing the agreement with the Palestinians or in concluding a peace agreement with Syria.

The real concern perceived by Egypt was that the stalemate could lead to a severe deterioration in Israeli–Palestinian or Israeli–Syrian relations and also endanger Israeli–Egyptian peace relations. Egypt could not stand idle, as it had in the war in Lebanon or in the intifada, without endangering its leadership role in the Arab world. Indeed, the increased tension along the Syrian–Israeli border in the summer of 1996, which included some military movements, and the military confrontation between the Palestinians and Israel in September 1996 following Israel's opening of a tunnel in East Jerusalem prompted Mubarak to express his concern that "Netanyahu's policy is setting the Arab world on fire" (Maddy-Weitzman 1998, 52, 278).

Egypt again used the weapon of normalization against Israel by threatening it with reduced levels of normalization if it failed to implement the agreements with the Palestinians. Moreover, Egypt warned that if Israel did not fulfill its commitments to the Palestinians, it would be very difficult to convene an international economic summit at Cairo in November 1996. Israel, however, rejected Egypt's threats, believing that the conference was more important to Egypt than to Israel. It expressed its objection to deeper Egyptian involvement in the negotiations with the Palestinians, mainly because Egypt played a negative role by trying to sow discord between Israel and the Palestinians (Maddy-Weitzman 1998, 278–79, 379).

This exchange coincided with large-scale Egyptian military maneuvers in mid-September 1996 in the Sinai, in which the army simulated defense of the Suez Canal against an enemy located north of Egypt and which has nuclear and chemical weapons, a clear reference to Israel (Maddy-Weitzman 1998, 278; *Haaretz*, 13 April 1998). The Egyptian newspaper *al-Ahram* even described these military exercises as a message to Israel that the "end of war does not necessarily mean the achievement of peace, and vice versa." Israel viewed the maneuvers as a clear threat that "crossed all the lines" (Maddy-Weitzman 1998, 278). This exchange reflected not only a verbal conflict but also a severe crisis of confidence. It indicated that the two sides did not totally exclude the possibility of war from their strategic considerations.

With all these negative developments, at no point during this period did either side seriously consider an alternative option to their peace, which they continued to view as a vital interest that should be maintained. Both countries remained committed to the norm that problems in their relationship should be resolved only by peaceful means, especially by political dialogue. This included regular communications; periodic diplomatic exchanges, including official visits; and summit meetings between the leaders (Maddy-Weitzman 1998, 275). In addition, the United States continued to play a pivotal role in the Egyptian–Israeli relationship, advising both sides against worsening relations.

Conclusion

Stable peace as a situation that promises long and effective peace between and among nations is defined mainly in terms of the Western European experience. The required conditions combine the common characteristics of the actors, such as political regimes, and their unique interaction and cooperation. This kind of stable peace is closer to the definition of positive or warm peace, where stable peace is much more than the absence of war or threats of force.

The Israeli–Egyptian peace is enduring but cold. The peace itself was never in real jeopardy. On the formal level, it has been meticulously preserved by both sides, although the atmosphere of their dialogue remained cool. Beyond the existence of formal mechanisms of diplomatic relations and contacts necessary for maintaining the peace, the relationship has been uneasy, controversial, and often tense, characterized by intense and angry verbal exchanges over a variety of bilateral and regional issues. The relations have been dominated by mutual suspicion and disillusionment; expressions of estrangement have been far more common than cordial words.

The Egyptian refusal to warm the peace because of internal and external factors has limited the peace relations to minimal interactions and cooperation mainly in the security domain. This of course prevents extension of the peace relations to include economic cooperation and the shift from stabilization towards consolidated stable peace. In this case three conditions are necessary for stabilization: vital interest in maintaining the peace, stable regimes, and mutual satisfaction with peace relations. It seems that while the first two conditions in the Israeli–Egyptian peace relations are maintained, fluctuations in satisfaction create some problems that make the peace even colder, almost to the point of cold war.

The movement towards comprehensive peace, which is supposed to be an important step toward regional stable peace, fails to foster it. Against the common assumptions of comprehensive peace or regional stable peace, the shift from a dyadic separate peace agreement towards comprehensive peace does not necessarily secure regional stable peace. Indeed, it could be said to destabilize somehow the Israeli–Egyptian peace relations, since it has caused some political competition between Israel and Egypt.

What are the conditions and prospects for the establishment of a stable peace between Israel and Egypt? The lessons of the peace relations between 1979 and 1999 indicate that the Egyptian–Israeli peace as a dyadic one could not develop into a stable peace. It seems that the prospects for warming the Egyptian–Israeli peace depend on regional rather than bilateral conditions. However, reducing or even resolving other dyadic conflicts does not guarantee warming of the Egyptian–Israeli peace in the face of emerging Egyptian–Israeli competition for leadership in the Middle East. Warming the Egyptian–Israeli peace probably depends on three required conditions: a comprehensive peace, acceptance of restructuring of the Middle East, and true reconciliation and building of trust.

Although the movement towards comprehensive peace has so far failed to warm the Egyptian–Israeli peace, it seems that both sides agree that only a comprehensive peace can do so. After a painful learning process, Israel accepts Egypt's demand that only a comprehensive peace that includes the resolution of all dyadic conflicts in the Arab–Israeli conflict system has the potential to warm the Egyptian–Israeli peace relationship. The conclusion of the Oslo agreements with the Palestinians and the peace agreement with Jordan were important steps in that direction.

The coming to power of Netanyahu in 1996 weakened the movement towards a comprehensive peace; indeed, it cooled the cold peace even more. By contrast, the coming to power of Ehud Barak in 1999 has revived the idea of a comprehensive peace. Indeed, in his first speech in the Knesset, while presenting his new government, Barak maintained: "Comprehensive and stable peace can be established if it rests, simultaneously, on four pillars: Egypt, Jordan, Syria and Lebanon in some sense as a single bloc, and of course the Palestinians. As long as peace is not grounded on all these four pillars, it will remain incomplete and unstable" (*Haaretz*, 7 July 1999). Barak thus links comprehensive and stable peace. However, comprehensive peace is necessary, but not sufficient, for reaching stable peace.

Shimon Peres was the first to realize that a comprehensive peace is only the first step and "under no circumstances will it be the final one." In his view, maintenance of peace is dependent on conditions that are almost the same as those regarded by European-oriented scholars as necessary and sufficient for stable peace. In his own words, "Our ultimate goal is the creation of [a] regional community of nations, with the common market and elected centralized bodies, modeled on the European community" (Peres 1993, 62, 77).

Establishing a regional community in the Middle East requires restructuring the area. Peres's words and actions in this regard have destabilized the Israeli–Egyptian peace. The shift towards a comprehensive peace indicated that Egypt and Israel do not have common conceptions of a new structure for the region. While Egypt perceives it more as a threat, Israel views it as an opportunity. The differences regarding the two countries' roles in the new Middle East led to a political competition that has destabilizing effects on the peace relationship. Therefore, a common understanding of the new regional order and a joint effort to accomplish it in stages are needed.

Nevertheless, it seems that there is also a vital interest for both Israel and its Arab neighbors to bring other Middle Eastern actors into the new regional order. This means bringing Saudi Arabia, Iran, Iraq, Turkey, and the other actors in the Persian Gulf into a systemic regional peace. Without bringing in Iraq and Iran as well, it will be impossible to establish an effective regional arms control system or a regional security community. Accomplishing this is not simple and requires time. However, without an agreed concept of the new Middle East and the role of each actor in it, new conflicts may emerge that may endanger not only Egyptian–Israeli peace but also the regional peace as a whole.

Comprehensive peace and an accepted restructuring of the Middle East system are structural conditions, which are necessary but not sufficient for stable peace. Reconciliation is probably the most important condition for shifting the current peace towards stable peace. Only reconciliation can build mutual trust and provide mutual assurances for maintaining peace in the area. Reconciliation means mutual acceptance and recognition of each side's national identity, settlement of disagreements, satisfaction with the agreement, mutual forgiveness, and recognition that both sides have been victims of their conflict, while bringing the relations into a state of acquiescence and even harmony. In other words, both sides should agree that the former conflict between them would no longer play any role in their relations. Reconciliation is probably the most difficult condition because it asks for a deep cognitive change, a real change of beliefs, ideology, and emotions not only among the ruling elites but also among most if not all sectors of both societies.

Reconciliation requires an internalization of the peace not only as a necessary means to advance one's interests but also as a normative value in itself. This needs a long learning process and education for peace that may take a few generations. Is reconciliation possible given the lack of common characteristics among the actors, such as democratic regimes and common norms and values, in the midst of different cultures and mentalities and different levels of economic prosperity? The easy answer is no. However, since reconciliation is probably the most important factor for stable peace, both sides should internalize this idea and act together to accomplish it if they really want to maintain the peace in the long term.

Notes

1. The common assumption since the signing of the Israeli–Egyptian peace treaty has been that only the shift toward comprehensive peace can warm the peace.

2. On January 13, 1987, in a closed forum of officials, Egyptian deputy prime minister and defense minister Abu Ghazala reportedly described Israel as Egypt's "main and sole enemy, the peace agreement notwithstanding" and added that "if the Egyptian and Syrian military commands cooperate and coordinate their moves, they could together achieve a sweeping victory over Israel" (*Al-Ahram*, February 5, 1987, quoted in Rabinovich and Shaked 1989, 348; see also *Haaretz*, January 29, 1987; April 13, 1998). Israel for its part sees the modernization of Egypt's armed forces, especially its air force, as a threat to Israel's security, since Egypt has no significant external threats; in this regard, see Shamir 1988, 190; Dowek 1998, 286–92.

3. On the differentiation between realist and liberal explanations, see Kacowicz 1998, 34–47.

4. See, e.g., Mubarak's public expressions in this regard, *Al-Akhbar*, September 9, 1984, quoted in Shaked and Dishon 1986, 380–81; Stein 1997, 307; Dessouki 1988, 97; Dowek 1998, 381–84.

5. The only exception is Mubarak's refusal to meet Shamir when he was prime minister (1986–1992) because he did not believe that Shamir would like to advance the peace process. See Dowek 1998, 156–95.

13

Stable Peace in Europe

James Goodby

Peace has several definitions, and this book is dedicated to exploring one of them—a stable peace. Professor Alexander George of Stanford University conceived of the idea that peaceful relations between two states or groups of states can take at least three forms: a *precarious peace*, where war may be imminent; a *conditional peace*, where war may be unlikely but is not excluded as a policy option; and a *stable peace*, where war is simply not considered as a method of resolving disputes, and deterrence by military means is not part of the bilateral relationship. This chapter will discuss the proposition that North America, essentially all of Europe, and Russia eventually could live under a stable peace. This system of nations could be called the European or the North American–Eurasian system, and it is fair to say that a conditional peace has existed within this system as a whole for many years, certainly since the mid-1960s. In parts, as in Western Europe, a stable peace has been achieved, while in other parts, as in the Balkans, peace is still precarious.

The conditions that bring about a stable peace include a common value system—almost certainly democratic values. Other conditions probably are a similar sense of identity or self-image, transparency and some denationalizing of defense establishments, and a reasonably healthy economy. At some stage in the process of making a stable peace, a set of understandings, tacit or otherwise, about rules of international behavior will be developed. I think of a security community, as defined by Karl Deutsch and others, as very similar to a stable peace. Yet, I would argue that the political differentiation among states within a security community could be more pronounced than would be the case within a system of nations under a stable peace.[1] The process of getting to a stable peace or to a security community may be quite similar, however, and so in this chapter I have used the two ideas as long-term goals, more or less interchangeably. I also assume that a Europe that is "peaceful, undivided, and democratic," to use President Clinton's image, is a close approximation of a system of nations under stable peace. I believe that the general context of security relations also is important. A nation bent on political aggrandizement, which is possible in a democracy, almost certainly will not fit into a security community or promote the conditions for a stable peace. In contrast, a nation seeking a general equilibrium in its relations with others is likely to be an active participant in building a stable peace.

A Europe that truly is at stable peace may not be achievable. But treating the idea as a proposition meant to be taken seriously is a good starting point for considering how relations within a North American–Eurasian system of nations might change over the long term, given favorable conditions. And a hinge point in history, such as the present, certainly should be a time for strategic thinking. To understand why and how a peaceful, undivided, and democratic Europe might come to pass requires a major analytical effort, more than any government has given to the subject up to this point and more than this chapter can muster. Even to understand whose interests would be served by a Europe that could plausibly be described as having achieved a stable peace requires more delving into the specifics of the proposition. Hardly any analysis has appeared, so far, in the public domain.

Any analysis will have to take into account broad cultural, geopolitical, regional, demographic, economic, and technological developments, not just policies of governments. Governments can affect, probably in important ways, the prospects for a Europe that is whole and free. But such a Europe can one day become a reality only if it is in tune with fundamental movements in human affairs. These are difficult to gauge but not completely unpredictable. Clarity is also needed about what is meant by "Europe." I define it as extending well beyond the old, well-established Western democracies, including Russia as well. In addition, some reflection is required on how the European or the North American–Eurasian system of the future, even if it becomes solidly democratic from one end to the other, might be constituted. Would it be tightly integrated or simply a loose collection of friendly states that now and then cooperate for some important purpose? Will the European Union (EU) focus on Europe and define itself by its differences with Washington and Moscow, or will it be a union open to partnership in meeting global challenges? Judgments about these questions are needed in order to understand the advantages and disadvantages of a stable peace. And clearly an effort must be made to seek the people's views and to enlist public support, without which any long-term policy cannot be sustained. This chapter is intended to be a contribution to a public discussion of a vision held out by two U.S. presidents but which remains today, despite Kosovo, more a general aspiration than a considered policy.

U.S. Policy Declarations

For most of the past decade, the publicly declared foreign policy of the United States has asserted that with the Cold War ended, Europe could enter a new era, free of military confrontations and united by common values. Two post–Cold War U.S. presidents, Bush and Clinton, have held out a vision of a new Europe, a Europe vastly different from the divided, bipolar continent of the Cold War and different, too, from the historical Europe of power politics and arms races. Bush called his vision "Europe whole and free." Clinton spoke of a "peaceful, undivided, and democratic continent."[2] Both obviously were inspired by Wilsonian thinking, but neither elaborated his vision of this kind of Europe in any detail until Clinton found it necessary in 1999 to explain why the United States was bombing Yugoslavia. The closest approximation to public education prior to the war in Yugoslavia came in the context of the debate on NATO enlargement, and this, in the event, was focused more on a divided Europe than on a Europe whole and free.

On April 15, 1999, President Clinton spoke of "a Europe that is peaceful, undivided, and free" and of his vision of the Balkans as "a region of multiethnic democracies, a community that upholds common standards of human rights, a community in which borders are open to people and trade, where nations cooperate to make war unthinkable"(Clinton 1999a, A-23). Probably Clinton's vision, as he himself has suggested at least since 1996, applies not just to Western Europe or to geographic Europe but to a larger system of nations, including the United States and a democratic Russia. Until the NATO–Serbia conflict erupted, President Clinton did not explain how a peaceful, undivided, and free Europe might be achieved or what the United States had to do, if anything, to support this objective. He revealed more about his thinking when he explained to the American people in April 1999 and again in May 1999 that, since NATO was a community of common values, military intervention was one of the prices to be paid for supporting and extending those common values in Europe. To stand aside from Kosovo, he explained in April in San Francisco, would bring discredit on NATO "because its values and vision of Europe would be profoundly damaged" (Clinton 1999a, A-23). In an article in the *New York Times* in May, President Clinton wrote, "NATO itself would have been discredited for failing to defend the very values that give it meaning" (Clinton 1999b, 4-17).

Kosovo

Norms and rules are an inescapable part of the process of establishing a stable peace. In a book published in 1998 I wrote that "leaders must respond to ethnic or communal conflicts that threaten to vitiate the norms and rules that support international peace and security" (Goodby 1998). This would certainly apply to Kosovo. And indeed, Russian representatives participated actively and constructively in designing a political settlement for Kosovo in the spring of 1999. Washington and Moscow parted company over the means by which President Slobodan Milosevic was to be persuaded to accept the settlement and over the requirements to legitimize action against Yugoslavia. Factors driving Moscow's viewpoint must have included Russia's traditional interests in Serbia and her concern about precedents that someday might affect her. Moscow drew the line at the use of military force in a campaign of coercive diplomacy and insisted, to no avail, that the United Nations Security Council should be asked to authorize any actions against Yugoslavia. Public opinion in Russia, already more sympathetic to Serbia's problems in Kosovo than to the rights of Albanian Kosovars, then became inflamed as NATO aircraft began to bomb Yugoslavia in March 1999. Russians were convinced that the massive flow of ethnic Albanian Kosovar refugees toward Macedonia and Albania was mainly the result of NATO air attacks, not a deliberate policy of the Milosevic regime. Undoubtedly, many deep-rooted frustrations stemming from Russia's economic plight also fed the passions that were unleashed among the Russian people, including above all fear of an uncertain future.

Public opinion in the West, in the meantime, understood the situation quite differently. In Western Europe and North America, the public believed that President Milosevic had decided to expel ethnic Albanians from Kosovo. The brutal implementation of that decision fostered hostility toward the Milosevic regime and a public willingness to support military intervention. Russia's key role in bringing about a settlement was appreciated in the West, but the gratitude did not extend to offering Russia its own sector in policing Kosovo, and whatever good feelings existed were considerably diminished when Russian troops unexpectedly occupied the Pristina airport in Kosovo. Unless this breach between Russia and the West can be repaired, the idea of a stable peace will have to be shelved for quite a long time. There is no doubt that official Washington genuinely regretted the damage done to U.S.–Russian relations and has sought to repair it. The Clinton–Yeltsin meeting in Cologne in June 1999 and the Gore–Stepashin meeting in July 1999 were first steps in restoring the status quo ante. But on the Russian side, the wounds to the Russian psyche may take a long time to heal because they apparently penetrated so deeply into the public consciousness. Ironically, in view of strong British, French, and German support for the war, there are those Russians who evidently think that the gulf between Russia and Europe can be bridged but that the breach between Russia and the United States is permanent. I doubt that this is a correct reading, but the wars in the Balkans made it starkly clear: nearly a decade after the end of the Cold War, Europe is only conditionally at peace, and a major gulf still exists between Russia and the West.

The Causes of Peace

The explanations for how a stable peace develops between two or more states even if the overall environment is favorable are varied and certainly not universally agreed. I have mentioned above some factors that are likely to be involved. U.S. political leaders tend to accept, as a rule of thumb, the simple idea that democracies tend not to make war on one another. As Ronald Reagan put it, "the cause of democratic government is also the cause of peace." They have spent little time in arguing the finer points of a proposition that, to them, apparently is obvious. Extrapolating slightly from what Bush, Clinton, and Reagan have said seems to produce this thesis: A stable peace can exist within a system of nations that share common values and are run along democratic lines, for "aggression and war are rarely the work of a nation's people" (Reagan 1985).

Experience with cooperation within the European Union may show that democracies can achieve stable peace through a partial pooling of sovereignties. That is unlikely to happen, however, except in a community of shared values. The stable peace that now exists in Western Europe is one in which its members have excluded war against one another not just as a rational act of policy but as subrationally unthinkable. To arrive at this state of mind, it is almost certain that the members of this system of nations must be linked by a common set of democratic values. And this suggests that while NATO can be a vehicle for supporting the expansion of a security community or for helping to create some of the conditions for a stable peace, it is an insufficient basis for achieving this.

Peace by Other Means?

Fortunately, within some clusters of Western European nations—and between those nations and the United States—peace already has become stable. Extending that stable peace throughout Central and Eastern Europe, in essence, has been the Clinton administration's stated aim. NATO has added three new members for the purpose of expanding "the area in Europe in which wars simply do not happen."[3] But until the spring of 1999, wars between nation-states in most of Europe had become almost inconceivable. It seemed that war had been overtaken by economic integration, globalization, and the disappearance of ideological confrontation, and that old-style "great power, territorial politics" was out of date.[4] This vision of the future suggests that a stable peace could be achieved through a radical dilution or alteration of the role of nation-states in international relations. In this analysis, economic and technological factors have eroded the nation-state's authority from both the top and the bottom. Empowerment of regions or private citizens and enterprises and the sweep of globalization made possible by communications technologies have so altered the framework for human transactions that national governments find their major business is no longer the accretion of power. War would no longer be a thinkable policy because it would serve no useful purpose. One of the unintended consequences of the NATO–Yugoslav war is that this vision has been called into question.

The European system, or the North American–Eurasian system, includes the Balkans and some countries—Russia, the United States, and others—that affect Europe and are, in turn, affected by Europe because of powerful and inescapable reciprocal influences. In the event that anyone needs reminding today of the perils of complacency, it must be said that within this extended European family of nations, the possibility of war between nation-states remains firmly embedded in the thinking and planning of the major powers. The war in Yugoslavia has put that fact on public display. Thus, stable peace can only be achieved through interactions among national governments, not through the benign effects of globalization and technology.

Several years ago Harvard's Professor Stanley Hoffmann wrote about the shift from a world dominated by the strategic–diplomatic chessboard to a world dispersed into a variety of chessboards. This image is even more apt today in light of the new global agenda—trade and finance, the environment, ethnic conflicts, the terrorist threat, humanitarian and human rights issues, and the spread of democracy. But Hoffmann also pointed to the need for a synthesis in foreign policy between the hard realities of power politics and the demands of the other chessboards. Finding the right balance between policies that concern the direct interaction of the big powers and policies that deal with the newer global agenda is, I think, one of the profound conceptual challenges that the major nations now face. It is not being handled as well as it needs to be. For the United States, as indeed for most of the major powers, the situation in Kosovo was dramatically illustrative of the dilemmas inherent in finding the right balance. Stable peace is dependent on big-power relations, but the big powers cannot ignore internal events in third countries that undermine the common value system.

A Second Chance

Because fundamental factors like values and self-identity are involved, a long transition period will be required before a stable peace in all of the North American–Eurasian system could become a reality. During the transition, a high form of statecraft will be necessary even to entrench a benign form of conditional peace, a peace free of military confrontation. It should be possible to do this, despite the stresses generated by war in the Balkans. In fact, the solution to the Kosovo crisis may point to new ways of building a security community that embraces all the nations of Europe and North America. From this point of view, the participation of Russian military units in an international security force in Kosovo, and before that in Bosnia, is of fundamental importance because it may provide precedents for future cooperation. Norms, rules, and structures can be imprinted on an international system even before a stable peace has been achieved. This process will help in the creation of a shared value system. Indeed, this type of order-building diplomacy should be the first priority of a statecraft aimed at achieving a stable peace. This will require a consensus, however, on what constitutes a proper legitimizing authority. NATO, acting without UN authority, cannot be that legitimizing authority because it is seen, at least in Russia, as an instrument for Western expansion at Russia's expense. Conceivably, the NATO–Russia Permanent Joint Council could help with this problem, but it is not empowered to do so at this time.

Despite this difficulty, U.S. and Russian policymakers still have an opportunity to construct a post–Cold War set of norms, rules, and structures whose internal logic would guide Europe towards stable peace. In my 1998 book I argued that "leadership in the collective use of force is an essential element in creating and enforcing the rules of a peaceful international order." Regrettably, the West's effort to implement that principle damaged relations between Moscow and Washington just at a time when the need for U.S.–Russian cooperation in the interest of a stable peace was never more acute. Valuable time has been lost forever—and not only because of the Balkan wars, or because of NATO's actions. Moscow's politicians and the Russian media did little to inform the Russian people about what Milosevic was up to. Still, the optimist would say, Russia and the United States will have a second chance to build a new relationship when the NATO–Yugoslav war and its aftermath have become part of history. The pessimist would say that Moscow and Washington are irrevocably on different and probably conflicting courses. Whichever assessment proves ultimately to have been correct, and despite the undeniable setback to good U.S.–Russian relations, it would be disastrously premature to give up on the effort to secure a stable peace among the major powers of Europe and North America.

Few would now quarrel with the proposition that a Europe enjoying stable peace can be counted among the low-probability events of the world. And yet the unification of Germany also seemed to be a low-probability contingency, until it happened. A stable peace throughout Europe is not just a dream—it is a serious strategic objective within the realm of reality. It is worth considering and planning for, despite the long odds. Key to a stable peace, inevitably, is the relationship among the United States, Russia, and the European Union. Russia's commitment to democracy and the deep divide between Russia and the West over the Balkans and other issues are at the heart of the matter.

Democracy In Russia

The future of democracy in Russia remains uncertain. Pervasive gloom, the legacy of the Russian economic collapse of August 1998, tends to affect estimates. Russia has failed to incorporate constitutional liberalism within its political structure and practice. Although the practice of democracy and acceptance of the rule of law will be rootless and superficial until a democratic culture has been established, it is impressive to see how far Russia has traveled away from rigid authoritarianism:

- *Adherence to constitutional practices.* The fundamental rules of the present constitution have been observed in every political crisis since the disaster of October 1993.

- *Power sharing between the executive and the legislature.* The constitution gives enormous power to the president of the Russian Federation, but circumstances have permitted the legislature to redress the balance to a degree. The short-term results have not been constructive, on the whole, but the long-term results may be.

- *Devolution of authority.* Regions and localities have acquired authority from a weakened center. If democratic practices do not necessarily accompany this development, at least the decision-making process is spread among more actors.

- *Freedom of speech and freedom to travel.* These are relatively unfettered, with some notorious and tragic exceptions.

- *Transfer of power through elections.* The legislative elections of 1999 and the presidential elections of 2000 hardly will be the last word on this subject, but they will influence Russia's future for years to come.

Will Underlying Trends Support Stable Peace?

The objective of stable peace in Europe seems to be working with the grain of global economic developments, and yet culturally determined attitudes are likely to exercise an important limiting effect on the creation of a peaceful, undivided, and democratic Europe. A xenophobic strain of Russian nationalism may push her toward confrontation with the West. In the West, some insist that Russia is not a part of European culture. Changing demographics will affect these and other public attitudes, but no clear trend is yet visible throughout the Euro-Atlantic system. We are witnessing the passing from power and influence of the generation of West Europeans who built the European Union, the rise of a new generation of Russians that may be more attuned than their elders to Western concepts and practices, and the coming to power of a generation of Americans for whom issues beyond their borders have a low priority and for whom there is no unifying motif to capture their interest in foreign commitments. How these changes will affect public attitudes is not yet clear.

Conversely, the "invisible hand" of the global economy already has enjoyed some success in integrating the European Union and North America at the level of business concerns. The decision of the majority of European Union members to proceed with the euro stemmed in part from a desire to be more competitive in the global economy. Favorable economic factors traceable to the global economy have promoted subregional economic cooperation in Europe and elsewhere; for these subregions, the borderless world already is here.

Technology, too, has tended to promote a borderless world. The revolution in information systems has had an integrating effect across frontiers on societies that fully embrace it. But different rates of technological progress from country to country may also create divisions and raise barriers to cooperation. Again, the trend line is not so clear as some would see it (see Holm and Sørensen 1995).

Governmental decisions in each major nation of the European system may improve the outlook for a stable peace but may also create unintended adverse consequences that, like the butterfly's wings of chaos theory, greatly magnify the original input. One important indicator of the possible trajectory of government policies is public opinion. Recent polling data show that the public, both in Europe and in the United States, favors U.S.–European partnership. In fact, 80 percent of the Americans polled said that the relationship between the United States and the European Union should be one of equal partnership. The public on both sides of the Atlantic favors including Russia in NATO when it has shown that it can be stable and peaceful for a significant period. Public policies can be

fully successful only when they are perceived to be legitimate manifestations of national interests. Recent polls show that policies fostering closer
but more balanced transatlantic relations continue to meet this test. And
so do Western policies aimed at including Russia in a European security
community (based on Kull 1998).

The Influence of the Nuclear Genie

During the last half century a new technology has intruded itself into the
calculations of nations—the nuclear weapon. It has become an independent factor in determining whether stable peace can be achieved. The
notion that weapons are not the causes of tensions but, rather, tensions
generate a need for weapons precedes the nuclear era. It has long since
become a slogan for those who doubt the value of negotiating with adversaries about weapons. But it is a false dichotomy. Tensions do, of course,
give rise to arms races. It is also true that arms and arms races give rise to
tensions. On January 7, 1912, First Lord of the Admiralty Winston
Churchill wrote that "until Germany dropped the naval challenge her
policy here would be continually viewed with deepening suspicions and
apprehension" (quoted in Massie 1991, 820). World War I began two years
later. Similarly, Nikita Khrushchev, recalling his reasons for placing Soviet missiles in Cuba, said that the "missiles would have equalized what the
West likes to call 'the balance of power.' The Americans had surrounded
our country with military bases and threatened us with nuclear weapons,
and now they would learn just what it feels like to have enemy missiles
pointing at you."(Khrushchev 1970, 494). Commenting on the new elements that nuclear weapons had introduced into international relations,
Henry Kissinger wrote, "Arms buildups, historically, were more often a
reflection than a cause of political conflicts and distrust. But I substantially agreed that what marked our time as a period of revolutionary change
was the high state of readiness of strategic weapons and their destruc-
tiveness" (Kissinger 1979, 202).

The next few years are likely to be a watershed time in human history. Either we will move on to deeper reductions in nuclear weapons, or
the downward trend we have seen in recent years will be halted and perhaps reversed. There is even the possibility of a global nuclear arms race
if we take the wrong road in relations among the major powers. It is difficult for nations to be partners within a security community and, simultaneously, rivals in nuclear weaponry. Consequently, a safer strategic
environment with progressively less reliance on nuclear weapons would
contribute to stable peace. It would be a tragedy beyond words if the
major powers not only squandered this historical opportunity but also

missed the chance to thwart their common enemy, terrorism armed with weapons of indiscriminate destruction. Nuclear weapons remain an apocalyptic threat to civilization. It is a dangerous illusion to think that new international relationships following the end of the Cold War have somehow freed the world from that threat. All the ingredients for a catastrophe are still there.

Arms control has little relevance in a case where stable peace exists between two countries, since in such a situation there is no reason for an arms race. And it is true that arms control is next to impossible in a situation of precarious peace. The case of the Korean peninsula illustrates just how difficult it is. But under a conditional peace, such as that which has prevailed between the United States and the Soviet Union throughout most of the Cold War, and which still exists today between the United States and Russia and China, arms control can be a key element of the relationship. It can constrain an arms race and fulfill a broader preventive diplomacy role as well. A great lesson of the Cold War, not always heeded today, was that decision-making by one superpower that was truly autonomous generally miscalculated the interests of the other superpower and led to results that no one liked. Those critics who have dismissed the relevance of arms control today have failed to consider the various forms of peaceful relations, and they ignore the contributions that arms control negotiations can make to political relationships between two states.

Models of a Future Europe

Ambiguity and ambivalence concerning the nature of the cooperative security order that might be established within the North American–Eurasian system of states is commonplace even among those who think about it. So long as such fundamental uncertainties exist, stable peace will be difficult to attain. We have been spared the worst effects of these uncertainties because the major nations, without exception, have been preoccupied with their own internal affairs for the last few years. That is beginning to change, and as it does, the absence of clarity about basic common interests may generate tensions and instabilities. This is why it is so important to think now about long-term structural aspects of the relations among the major power centers.

President Clinton, in his speech of April 15, 1999, remarked that "we must look beyond [the current conflict] to what the whole continent of Europe should look like in 10 or 20 years" (Clinton 1999a, A-23). Taking up this presidential challenge is a useful exercise in showing how many structures could emerge, even under conditions that would encourage stable peace. The five models described below would look and act very differently from one another even though each assumes that all the major nations of the extended European system are democratic and have no military designs against one another. Needless to say, other, less desirable, outcomes can be imagined. For the sake of simplicity the models are constructed with the United States, Russia, and the European Union as the principal actors, but, of course, every other potential member of this system would have some part in determining how it is constituted. Each of these "models" is only a one-dimensional sketch, and they are not mutually exclusive; in the real world some other combination of the characteristics cited below could appear.

- A system with three loci of power—the United States, the European Union, and Russia. The United States remains engaged in Europe; Russia is a solid democracy and a functioning market economy; she takes an active and constructive interest in European matters; West European integration is successful, as is the enlargement to the East.

- A system in which the United States is first among equals owing to greater cohesion and economic strength. The European Union is powerful economically, but its foreign policy is fragmented; Russia has established a solid democracy and a functioning market economy but is lagging behind the European Union and the United States economically.

- A system in which the European Union is dominant, while the United States and Russia are only loosely engaged with Europe. Russia is democratic but remains weak economically and politically, less focused on external affairs than on internal problems and issues involving her southern flank. The United States devotes increasing attention and resources to Asia; Europe takes the lead in managing European matters, demonstrating consensus and strong, unified leadership.

- The West integrates while Russia becomes a peripheral player in European affairs. The United States and the European Union develop deeper trade relationships and closely coordinate their institutional arrangements. Russia is formally democratic in the constitutional sense but is experiencing internal difficulties, including inability of the central authorities to govern effectively throughout the Russian Federation. She looks for strategic partners to the south and east to support her quarrels with the West.

- The United States is dominant, but European coalitions, including Russia, are assembled to offset U.S. pressure. Europe is challenging

U.S. policies on key foreign policy issues globally, and trade competition is fierce. Russia makes common cause with the European Union as necessary to resist U.S. political and economic pressures.

Conflict Is Always with Us

These models are intended to show that a clear differentiation among major power centers and groups of states within a security community will exist even if substantial progress in all the factors that would promote a stable peace can be achieved. Fears of losing national identities in a featureless sea of Euro-Atlanticism are entirely misplaced. Differing sets of interests will continue to generate different solutions to international problems and, hence, give rise to disputes. The only remaining question is "How will they be settled, by resort to arms or otherwise?"

A system based on North America, Russia, and the European Union that had achieved stable peace is self-evidently preferable to the historical norm in which peace has been at best conditional, often precarious, and wars frequent. Some models of a system that might have come close to achieving stable peace might serve the interests of individual members better than others. For example, the above list is written in the descending order of preference from the standpoint of this U.S. citizen. But if a stable peace under any of the arrangements described above could be entrenched in Europe in the twenty-first century, it would be a clear improvement over the experience of most preceding centuries.

This might not be the end of small wars, for even after stable peace had been attained, pockets of authoritarianism might persist within the European system. The wars of the Yugoslavian succession may be unique in their scale of violence, but patches of ethnic or communal strife will be difficult to erase from the map. Small wars can destabilize relations among the major power centers, but they need not undermine a stable peace. Multilateral security arrangements, like those now evolving among the United Nations, NATO, the European Union, and the Organization for Security and Cooperation in Europe (OSCE) in the Balkans will be needed even in a system enjoying stable peace.

NATO already has become a hybrid defense system dealing with peacekeeping, as in Bosnia and Kosovo, as well as with collective defense. The air campaign against Yugoslavia fell in the latter category as a military operation. NATO may have reached its limits in peacekeeping with the Kosovo operation. When peacekeeping or peacemaking is the objective, participation of units from countries other than the major military powers is preferable. If this cannot be arranged because of politics or because military efficacy rules it out, the involvement of all the relevant military powers is the next best solution. And if that is not feasible, the U.S. profile in the operation should be kept to the lowest level compatible with effective operations. Such arrangements are difficult to manage under NATO supervision.

Moreover, there are political reasons for this set of rules. One of them is that, according to polling data, Americans generally like to have the United Nations take on these tasks, rather than NATO (Kull and Destler 1999, 78–80). There is much wisdom in this public attitude, since NATO's role in making a stable peace could be undermined if misperceptions arose about U.S. intentions. The most basic consideration is that the core function of U.S. military forces is to deter and, if necessary, to repulse armed state-on-state aggression in the Korean peninsula, in the Persian Gulf, and potentially at other points around Eurasia. In peacetime the presence of U.S. forces makes an essential contribution to stability and to cooperative relationships among the major military powers of Eurasia. U.S. defense operations and the defense budget should be oriented primarily toward that core function. The use of these forces in ways that would diminish their effectiveness in their core function should be minimized.

Reordering Foreign Policy Priorities

If a stable peace in Europe became a widely accepted strategic goal for the United States, like containment during the Cold War, effective transition strategies could be devised to help guide day-to-day decisions. The same is no doubt true for other nations as well, including Russia and members of the European Union. A reordering of foreign policy priorities in each of these nations would be required if Russia, the European Union, and the United States took the idea seriously.

First, the minimum requirement, in my view, would be a U.S. policy that encouraged a distinct center of power in Western and Central Europe—the European Union. On this foundation, other combinations could be established, whether a U.S.–EU or an EU–Russia partnership. Without it, little could be accomplished. Second, and related to this, is the requirement that U.S. economic policy should conform to its political objective of supporting the EU as a distinct center of power. This would entail U.S. acceptance of the euro as a major reserve currency in global financial markets and, as a consequence of that, closer U.S.–EU economic cooperation, possibly in the form of a transatlantic free trade area. Third, as regards Russia, the minimum requirement is constant U.S. (and EU) support for democracy in Russia, backed by economic support to underwrite what the Russians themselves are doing to strengthen their democracy. When Russia develops the economic strength necessary for her to become a third center of power within a North American–Eurasian system, U.S. (and EU) policy should encourage that. In the meantime, Russia's association with Euro-Atlantic and global institutions should be an option available to the Russian government. Fourth, the minimum requirement for U.S. policy as regards the geopolitical objectives of a nascent North American–Eurasian community is the sum of all the above—to create the conditions for a stable peace throughout the community. Beyond that, an equilibrium among the centers of power in Asia—Japan and China, above all—and the North American–Eurasian power centers will need to be established in a manner that encourages transparency, restraint, and mutual accommodation.

As Russia develops democratic traditions and the economic strength necessary to become an all-purpose center of power, Russian governments and the Russian people will likely be drawn toward the idea of cooperation within a peaceful, undivided, and free North American–Eurasian system, more so than at present. Accommodation will be required on all sides. Even now, greater accommodation to Russian views on the use of force, especially in Russia's neighborhood, and a growing sensitivity concerning the process of extending NATO's reach can be detected in the West. This should breed more responsiveness in Moscow to Western concerns for democratic norms, regional instabilities, and transnational security threats such as terrorism and proliferation of weapons of mass destruction.

A Two-Pronged Strategy

Summing up these policy recommendations suggests that if the United States, the European Union, and Russia wanted to make a stable peace in Europe, they would adopt some version of a two-pronged strategy designed to foster the conditions for the extension of the existing European security community. From a U.S. point of view, the first prong of the strategy would be to forge still closer links between the United States and the European Union, and the second would be to work for reconciliation between Russia and the West. Russia and the European Union would place a different emphasis on these connections, obviously, but the ultimate objective should be rather similar.

The most immediate need for a course correction arises from the fact that U.S.–Russian relations have degenerated into bickering over Iran, Iraq, the Balkans, and nonproliferation policies. Thus, the long-term strategic interests of the two countries are being defined by their differences rather than their common interests in a stable peace. A strategy aimed at making a stable peace in Europe must be aimed at creating something akin to a security community, that is, a single security space throughout Europe, including Russia. There is much that can be achieved along these lines, incrementally, while internal conditions in Russia are being sorted out. Institutional linkages, both with the federal government and the regions, joint peace operations as in Bosnia, and perhaps in Kosovo, and some forms of cooperative threat reduction can help. The United Nations, NATO, the European Union, and the OSCE all could contribute to the multiple linkages that will be required. The OSCE will be particularly useful for long-term conflict resolution efforts.

The complex set of relationships involved in making a stable peace cannot be expected to develop smoothly and probably not symmetrically. Differences over the Balkans have driven Russia and the West farther apart for a time. Those wounds will heal, but because of economic conditions in Russia, if for no other reason, a genuine and broad-based reconciliation with the West is likely to proceed slowly. A basic problem is that some Russians have great difficulties coming to terms with the idea that Russia is a member of a system of which the United States is a part, and this is especially so after the split over Kosovo. They see in this concept a threat of U.S. hegemony, and they seem to fear, in addition, that Russia might lose its special character and its standing as a great world power. Some Russians see a better fit with a European than with a Euro-Atlantic community.

Given this situation, it would appear that for the next few years a transatlantic commonwealth might have to serve as the engine of progress towards an undivided and democratic Europe and hence towards a stable peace in Europe. Would a deepening political relationship between the United States and Western Europe work to divide Europe rather than unite it? In the absence of a sustained determination, at least in the West, to bring Russia into Europe, it probably would. Paradoxically, however, it may be the case that without more North American–West European integration than is now being considered, an undivided and democratic Europe might not be achievable.

The potential for underlying factors—demography, geopolitical factors, economic developments, and others—to disrupt a march of events like those just sketched out is formidable. A protracted global economic recession, for example, could set nation against nation and destroy the impulse to cooperate. U.S. policies, therefore, need to be aimed at achieving some minimally satisfactory result if those outcomes that presume a peaceful, undivided, and democratic Europe are not achievable. The historical norm for Europe is one in which peace is conditional and could become precarious, but even in this situation, some outcomes are clearly better for almost any nation's interests than others. A revival of a Cold

War–type confrontation between Russia and the West must be avoided, even though the Western camp might be able to achieve unprecedented solidarity in many respects. A Europe that is fragmenting and resorting to maneuvering to maintain a power balance would be even worse, even if the United States was not directly engaged in the process. From the U.S. vantage point, the best of this bad lot would be the case of U.S. benign hegemony, accepted by all European states, including Russia, because they prefer it to other alternatives. But it is not likely to be a stable situation. Whenever Russia or a group of European states decided they had had enough of American tutelage, they would rise up to throw it off, perhaps with dangerous repercussions.

The Task Undone

After centuries of war in Europe, and with images of the latest one still fresh, historical experience does not encourage hopes for stable peace. But enough has changed in Europe to make the idea worthy of serious consideration, not least the fact that this kind of peace has materialized in places. Hardly any government within the European system has outlined a vision of a future Europe so compelling as those of the last few U.S. presidents, Reagan included. But if U.S. presidents have meant to hold out the possibility of a Europe peaceful, undivided, and democratic as something more than a slogan, much remains to be done. Now, at the beginning of a new millennium, it is time to reflect on how future U.S. administrations might pick up this task as one compatible with the most profound U.S. strategic interests.

The effort must begin with the recognition that the main axis of American strategic interests outside the Western Hemisphere runs through Eurasia and that a stable peace is dependent on relations among the United States, the European Union, Russia, China, and Japan. Second, the exigencies of our age demand that the United States act before a clear and present danger emerges; this, in turn, requires a fixed and predictable place in the international power structure for the United States and a national strategy that Americans support and others understand.

The strategic objectives of U.S. policy, like those of other countries, are not limited to securing a stable peace in Europe. Some Americans argue for a benign hegemony, while others urge a policy of devolution and equilibrium. Which of these policies is pursued, in practice if not in theory, is critically important to the question of whether a stable peace can be achieved in Europe. A quest for dominance, or benign hegemony, throughout the North American–Eurasian system of nations is not likely to foster the kind of environment that would be conducive to the achievement of stable peace. Limits on unilateralism and a bias toward accommodation to the strategic interests of each of the major power centers constitute a prickly and somehow unnatural process. It is unnatural because it seems like an unnecessary curb on America's ability to do good works or to defend her interests in whatever way her leaders see fit. The alternative is a world resentful of American unilateralism and eager to gang up on what would be perceived as a would-be hegemon. Working patiently and persistently with other nations within the North American–Eurasian system to create a community that is peaceful, undivided, and democratic will be the work of generations, as was containment, but this is the way to stable peace.

Notes

The author acknowledges with profound thanks the help he has received from Professor Alexander George of Stanford University. This chapter draws on the author's writings over the past few years on the subject of stable peace and on an as yet unpublished paper written with the generous support of the U.S. Institute of Peace. Among the published articles and books are Goodby 1998, 1999a, 1999b; and Goodby and Feiveson 1999.

1. Karl Deutsch and others described a security community as "one in which there is real assurance that the members of that community will not fight each other physically but will settle their disputes in some other way." Deutsch et al. also concluded that "military alliances [were] deemed to be relatively poor pathways . . . toward pluralistic integration. . . . To be effective, they had to be associated with nonmilitary steps" (Deutsch et al. 1957, 202). Emanuel Adler and Michael Barnett have added new dimensions to the security community idea by examining (1) phases in the development of a security community, (2) a set of indicators sensitive to these phases, and (3) disintegration of security communities. They believe that a "compatibility of core values and a collective identity are necessary for the development of security communities" (Adler and Barnett 1998b, 58). For different reasons, John Mueller believes war among major powers has become "subrationally unthinkable." He holds that war is rejected "not because it's a bad idea but because it remains subconscious and never comes up as a coherent possibility" (Mueller 1989, 240).

2. President Clinton's speech in Detroit, Michigan, October 22, 1996.

3. Secretary of State Madeleine Albright, Statement before the Senate Foreign Relations Committee, Washington, D.C., October 7, 1997, p. 3.

4. President Clinton, press conference, Madrid, Spain, July 9, 1997, the White House.

14

Stable Peace in *Mitteleuropa:*
The German–Polish Hinge

Adrian Hyde-Price

On September 1, 1939, the German warship *Schleswig-Holstein* opened fire on Polish fortifications at Westerplatte outside Danzig, signaling the start of the German blitzkrieg against Poland. Despite the often heroic resistance of the Polish army, within thirty-five days Poland had been overwhelmed by the Wehrmacht (see Zamoyski 1987, 357). Close behind the German army came the SS-Einsatzgruppen (Special Task Forces) that—often with the active participation of the Wehrmacht—systematically murdered teachers, doctors, officers, churchmen, landowners, civil servants, Jews, and aristocrats. By the end of the first week of the war, SS commanders were boasting of two hundred shootings a day. The aim was to destroy the Polish intelligentsia and produce a "leaderless labor force" that would serve Germany (see Deighton 1979, 92; Sydnor 1977, 37–63; Bartov 1992, 61–63). More than six million Poles were killed during the Second World War—a casualty rate of 18 percent. This compares with 0.2 percent in the United States, 1 percent in the United Kingdom, 7.4 percent in Germany, and 11.2 percent in the Soviet Union (Wandyzc 1992, 238). "No country in Europe," Misha Glenny notes, "witnessed such a sustained programme of barbarism during the war as Poland." Of the six million Poles killed by the Nazis, roughly half were Jewish, and it was on Polish territory that Hitler chose to erect the instruments for his "final solution of the Jewish question"—the extermination camps of Oscewiçim (Auschwitz), Majdanek, and Treblinka (Glenny 1990, 50; see also Browning 1992, 28–56).

Sixty years later, on September 1, 1999, President Johannes Rau of the Federal Republic of Germany and his Polish counterpart, President Alexsander Kwasniewski, traveled by motor launch together to the Polish war memorial at Westerplatte. There they held a joint service for the victims of the Second World War. This was not the first visit by a German head of state to this memorial to Polish war dead, but it was the first time that a German president had participated in the annual Polish commemorations at Westerplatte. For the Polish authorities, this was a clear signal that relations between the two countries had improved to such an extent that it was possible to jointly commemorate the past, and that even on Poland's Day of Remembrance the hand of friendship could be offered to their former enemies. On the same day, Polish television carried interviews with visitors to the controversial German exhibition on Wehrmacht war crimes. The overwhelming message was that young Germans had no intention of trying to forget or repress the horrors of the Nazi past but were concerned to understand the past in order to draw lessons for the future. This provided confirmation for former German president Gustav Heinemann's view that the only way other peoples would forget what Germany had done to them in the war was for Germans themselves never to forget their own past.

The transformation of relations between Germany and Poland since the end of the Second World War constitutes one of the most important—and encouraging—developments in contemporary Europe. Despite the legacy of the *Vernichtungskrieg* (war of extermination) and the *Shoa*, German–Polish relations now constitute the hinge of an emerging zone of stable peace in *Mitteleuropa* (Central Europe). The geostrategic vulnerability of *Zwischeneuropa* (as the lands between Germany and Russia have sometimes been called) has been one of the four main sources of conflict in modern Europe. The other three are Franco-German rivalry, Russia's place in European international society, and instability in the Balkans (Bildt in Agrell 1994, 46). With the integration of France and Germany in a pluralistic security community and the emergence of a close political and strategic partnership between Germany and Poland, prospects are good for establishing an extensive zone of stable peace stretching across much of Western, Central, and East-Central Europe. The dynamics of stable peace building in Mitteleuropa are, of course, highly complex. They involve intricate patterns of bilateral and multilateral relationships among a number of states and peoples. However, within this complex matrix of regional relationships, the German–Polish dyad is of primary importance, given the relative size and geopolitical weight of the two countries.

The aim of this chapter is to critically analyze contemporary developments in German–Polish relations, focusing on some of the key factors that have facilitated the gradual emergence of a stable peace relationship. Exploring this geopolitically important dyadic relationship, it is hoped, will not only shed light on the distinctive features of stable peace building in Mitteleuropa but also provide some valuable insights into the dynamics of stable peace building in general. In particular, it can help address the key question at the heart of the stable peace research agenda—namely, what are the necessary, sufficient, and favorable conditions for the emergence, maintenance, deepening, and consolidation of stable peace?

Dieter Senghaas has suggested that a stable peace involves a political order characterized by "permanent peaceful coexistence and reliable civilized conflict-resolution" in which a widely accepted process of peaceful conflict resolution routinely occurs (Senghaas 1995, 15; Senghaas 1997). Similarly, Hanns Maull has spoken of the "civilizationization" of international relations through a strengthening of normative prohibitions against violent forms of conflict resolution (Maull 1993, 115–31). A stable peace does not assume a total harmony of interests among the parties involved, only that they resolve their disputes through peaceful and nonmilitary means. This implies the absence of major territorial or ideological disputes, the existence of institutionalized forms of cooperation, and a high degree of societal interaction and economic interdependence. The key feature of a stable peace relationship, however—and what distinguishes it from a long period of precarious or conditional peace—is its cognitive dimension. It involves a shared perception that war is normatively and politically unthinkable as a means of resolving disputes. The emergence of a zone of stable peace thus involves changes in perceptions of self and others and the development of new intersubjectively constituted codes of international behavior based on trust and mutual understanding.

The central argument presented in this chapter is that the gradual emergence of a stable peace between Germany and Poland has been overdetermined by a number of developments. The most important of these are political democratization, deepening economic and societal interdependence, and the creation of institutionalized forms of bilateral and multilateral cooperation. The analysis presented here also draws attention to the importance of a visionary leadership. This involves the articulation of a conscious political strategy by elite groups designed to overcome the legacy of past conflicts and hatreds and facilitate political cooperation and deepening socioeconomic interdependence.

Finally, building a stable peace involves a complex dynamic between material and cognitive factors. With its emphasis on identity and the cognitive basis of international cooperation, stable peace theory shares much of the intellectual agenda of social constructivism (see, e.g., Adler 1997b, 319–64; Checkel 1998, 324–48). At the same time, it does not deny the mutually constitutive impact of material conditions. In the case of German–Polish relations, two material factors are of particular importance: the socioeconomic disparities between the two countries, and their asymmetrical power relationship. These material factors significantly complicate the process of stable peace building in the wider Mitteleuropa region. The conceptual framework presented here thus draws on the insights of social constructivism, liberal institutionalism, and classical realism. In doing so it seeks to identify with the "emerging synthesis" in the study of world politics that seeks "to link the international and the domestic, the societal and the transnational in a way that incorporates some of the elements of traditional Realism" (Bowker and Brown 1993, 2).

From *Vernichtungskrieg* to Willy Brandt's *Kniefall*

In the immediate postwar years, the search for rapprochement between Germany and Poland was severely complicated by the onset of the East–West conflict. The Peoples' Republic of Poland and the Federal Republic of Germany found themselves in two separate military and political alliance systems, each dominated—to a greater or lesser extent—by their respective superpower patrons. In addition to the still-open wounds of Vernichtungskrieg and the Holocaust and the deeper historical legacy of centuries of conflict between Teutons and Slavs, West German–Polish relations were made more difficult by postwar territorial arrangements. The new Polish state lost territory in the east to the Soviet Union, while gaining the German provinces of Silesia and Pomerania in the west. In effect, the country's borders were shifted about two hundred kilometers westwards. One consequence of this was to leave postwar Poland fearful of German revanchism and largely dependent on the Soviet Union for security guarantees (Zaborowski 1999, 158–73).

For much of the post–World War II period, therefore, relations between Poland and West Germany were characterized by a precarious peace. Bilateral relations were hampered by a number of outstanding problems. These included the Oder–Neisse line (the German–Polish border), compensation to the victims of Nazi aggression, and the status of ethnic Germans in Poland. These bilateral problems were reinforced by the systemic military and ideological conflict generated by East–West bipolarity. In the absence of any resolution of the underlying sources of conflict, therefore, a precarious peace emerged based on a military balance of power and nuclear deterrence.

The transition from a precarious peace to a conditional peace in West German–Polish relations only began in the mid-1960s. It is also interesting to note that the key actors that initiated the process of rapprochement were nongovernmental actors rather than states. These transnational actors were the German Evangelical Church and the Polish Catholic bishops.

In October 1965 the German Evangelical Church letter published a memorandum called "The Situation of the Expellees and the Relationship between the German People and their Neighbors to the East." In it, the church spoke of its desire for dialogue between Germans and Poles and suggested that a process of healing between Germans and Poles could not be left to politicians and governments but should involve the two societies. One month later, the Polish bishops responded with a letter to West German church leaders that contained a historic appeal to end the hereditary hostility between the two nations: "We extend our hand to you, granting you forgiveness and asking for forgiveness" (quoted in Davies 1981, 591–93).

These transnational and societal initiatives were subsequently complemented at the governmental level by the "new *Ostpolitik*" of Willy Brandt. The policy of *"Wandel durch Annäherung"* (change through rapprochement) introduced by the Social Democratic Party–Free Democratic Party coalition government signaled a major new attempt to forge rapprochement between Germans and their eastern neighbors. From the outset, Brandt and his colleagues knew that the most difficult aspect of this would be relations with the Poles. "The relationship to the Soviet Union constituted the most important part of *Ostpolitik*," Peter Bender has written, "the relationship to Poland the most difficult"(Bender 1996, 236). From its very inception, Ostpolitik was much more morally charged and inspired than is usually the case for foreign policy. Given the perceived impasse of Adenauer's *Politik der Stärke* (policy of strength), Brandt's coalition government embarked on a policy designed to open a formal process of reconciliation and rapprochement. This resulted in the *Ostverträge* (Eastern treaties) of the early 1970s but was most powerfully symbolized through the memorable *Kniefall* incident.

On his visit to the Warsaw ghetto on December 7, 1970, Brandt spontaneously knelt in expiation before the Memorial to the Victims of Nazi Oppression. The Kniefall, as it is known, demonstrates the power of symbolic gestures in politics and provides the most graphic illustration of the moral imperatives driving Brandt's Ostpolitik. The Kniefall was a spontaneous act made in recognition of the horrors of the Nazis' mechanized extermination of Polish Jews and was decisive in helping to shape a new image of Germany. In his memoirs, Brandt writes that, moved by the burden of German history and the legacy of millions murdered, "I did what people do when speech fails." He goes on to quote the words of a reporter who wrote: "Then he knelt, he who had no need so to do, for all those who should have knelt, but did not do so—either because they did not dare to or could not, or could not dare to" (Brandt 1989, 214).

With the famous Kniefall, Willy Brandt acknowledged that Germany had begun the war and that it was responsible for the systematic mass extermination and enslavement of Jews and Poles—a crime without parallel in modern European history. The picture of the Kniefall was widely circulated around the world and showed a side of Germany that was, for many people, new and astounding. "For a moment," Peter Bender has commented, "morality became a political force" (Bender 1996, 182).

Although controversial at the time, Ostpolitik became an established element of West German foreign policy and was continued by the Christian Democratic Union–Free Democratic Party coalition of Helmut Kohl. The political momentum generated by the Kniefall and the Ostverträge helped facilitate the transition from a precarious to a conditional peace in West German–Polish relations. However, the process of rapprochement was not able to develop beyond a conditional peace, given the overlay of the East–West conflict and remaining problems in Polish–German bilateral relations. These included the issues of compensation for German war crimes, the claims of the expellees, and the rights of ethnic Germans in Poland.

Nonetheless, Ostpolitik helped prepare the ground for the emergence of a stable peace in Mitteleuropa after the annus mirabilis of 1989. It did so by demonstrating that a democratic Germany was willing and able to begin a process of rapprochement with its eastern neighbors and to make amends for the past. In this way, Ostpolitik helped reduce fears in Central Europe about German power, thus making possible broad international agreement for the peaceful and democratic unification of Germany in 1990 (Bender 1996, 278).

The Close Connection between Domestic and International Developments

While Ostpolitik succeeded in creating some of the political preconditions for further rapprochement in German–Polish relations, the decisive catalyst for change was the collapse of communist authoritarianism and the associated demise of Cold War bipolarity. What the remarkable sequence of events in 1989–1991 demonstrates above all is the close connection between domestic and international developments in contemporary European politics.

Throughout the late 1980s, domestic and international events responded closely to each other. Gorbachev's reform policies were a response to severe domestic problems in the Communist bloc. His external policies sought to create an international environment conducive to perestroika (see Leebaert and Dickinson 1992). However, the relaxing of Soviet control associated with the "new thinking" in Soviet foreign policy in turn stimulated an accelerating process of domestic political change in Eastern Europe. The events of 1989 thus came about through an interaction of two processes, each with its own logic and dynamic, although each was closely bound up with the other. The first was external: the end of the Brezhnev doctrine and its replacement with the "Sinatra doctrine." The second was internal: the peaceful revolutions of 1989, which culminated in the collapse of communism across Central and Eastern Europe (see Pravda 1992; Dawisha 1988).

The case of Central Europe therefore suggests that the emergence of a stable peace involves both domestic political and societal change, as well as change in the external environment. It also suggests that—contrary to realist assumptions—change in the international system is bound up with change at the domestic level. The interrelationship between domestic and international politics has increased significantly in the age of globalization and deepening interdependence. This has been particularly the case in Poland and the countries of East Central Europe. "A constant theme in the politics of East Central Europe in the twentieth century," Judy Batt has written, "has been the close linkage between domestic developments and the external environment. This arises from what is often referred to as the region's 'geopolitical predicament,' which is one of vulnerability to external pressures and endemic challenges to the internal integrity of the state" (Batt 1994, 30). This blurring of the boundaries between domestic and international politics has clear implications for the future direction of research on the conditions favoring the emergence, consolidation, and deepening of stable peace orders.

Political Leadership: The Importance of the "Vision Thing"

A central issue of debate in international relations is the agent–structure problem. Not surprisingly, therefore, the agent–structure issue figures prominently in stable peace theory. While the forging of a stable peace order inevitably requires certain structural preconditions—in particular, democratic political processes and institutionalized mechanisms for the peaceful resolution of disputes—leadership is also a vital factor. Leaders with a clear sense of vision are necessary in order to seize opportunities, shape the policy agenda, and take the risks that forging a stable peace requires. Structural conditions may make a stable peace possible, but leadership is required if opportunities are to be translated into reality. This is clearly evident from the case of Mitteleuropa.

We have already noted the example of Willy Brandt, "probably the most visionary chancellor in the history of the Federal Republic" (Paterson 1998, 22–23). His charisma and sense of strategic direction, coupled with his formidable leadership qualities and political skills, made Ostpolitik both successful and domestically popular. Brandt was willing to confront his domestic political opponents and to take the risks necessary to begin a process of reconciliation with countries in Central and Eastern Europe that had suffered so greatly at the hands of Nazi Germany.

Hans-Dieter Genscher, Germany's longest-serving foreign minister since Bismarck, demonstrated similar qualities of visionary leadership. Not only did he strive to conserve a modicum of détente through the "Second Cold War" of the early 1980s, he also saw the need to match the Bundesrepublik's postwar rapprochement with France with a similar process of post–Cold War rapprochement with Poland. In his memoirs, he outlined his vision of Franco-German-Polish cooperation, situating the Weimar Triangle (as this form of trilateral cooperation became known) in the context of a new Europe characterized by cooperation and peaceful relations. "Germany's relations with France and Poland," he argued, "are a decisive determinant of the future of the whole continent." When Germans, French, and Poles work together as Europeans and stop any manifestation of nationalism, the prospects for building trust and peaceful cooperation in Europe as a whole will be greatly improved. "This commonality for Europe can and must lead to new attitude and culture of living together in Europe" (Genscher 1995, 895).

Genscher's pan-European vision was complemented by that of Helmut Kohl. On taking power in 1982, Kohl was seen as a master tactician and skilled political operator, rather than as a politician with a clear strategic vision. But as his long chancellorship developed, Kohl demonstrated vision in terms of both *Europapolitik* and German unification. Following unification, Kohl's vision was of a united Germany anchored in an integrated Europe. He frequently stressed that European integration was a question of "war and peace." Of particular note was the importance he attached to the development of a strategic partnership with Poland. His vision of Europe, it has been noted, was "notably larger than Adenauer's" and accorded "a privileged role to Poland, to which he often assigns a role comparable to postwar France in his speeches" (Paterson 1998, 28).

In the case of communist Poland, official attitudes were more reserved. The Polish communist leaders viewed the Federal Republic with considerable suspicion and mistrust, and their responses to Brandt's Ostpolitik were ambivalent. The Warsaw leadership tended to oscillate from concern about German "revisionism," on the one hand, to a fear of German indifference, on the other. The tendency to try to derive political capital from deep-seated public fears about Germany, coupled with an awareness of the close attention paid to West German–Polish relations in Moscow and East Berlin, often made it difficult to distinguish between conviction and tactics in Polish policy towards Germany. It was also noticeable that while Germans were often too quick to speak about "reconciliation" (*Aussöhnung*), Poles tended to speak about a more gradual process leading from "normalization" to "understanding" and finally—perhaps—to reconciliation (Bender 1996, 236).

With the negotiated transfer of power from the PZPR (the Polish United Workers Party) to the first Solidarity government of Prime Minister

Mazowiecki in September 1989, a new foreign policy line emerged that enjoyed broad support among both the postcommunist elite and the Polish public. The policy consisted of three key elements: developing and broadening cooperation with the country's neighbors, east and west; integrating Poland in Western economic, political, and security systems (particularly NATO and the EU); and building wider regional and pan-European frameworks for institutionalized multilateral cooperation. Despite a series of changes in government, Poland's foreign and security policy has demonstrated remarkable consistency. Indeed, it often appears to be the sole element of stability in an otherwise turbulent domestic political scene (Hyde-Price 1996, 16).

The guiding philosophy behind both foreign and domestic policy reforms has been the idea of a "return to Europe." This is a vision that has united nearly all strands of Poland's postcommunist domestic political scene. The notion of a return to Europe remains somewhat vague and poorly defined, but it has had important consequences for the shaping of a stable peace order in Mitteleuropa. First of all, it implies joining existing European and transatlantic multilateral institutions—above all, NATO and the EU (Stefanowicz 1995, 55–64). Second, the Poles have realized that their way back to "Europe" lies through Germany and that forging good relations with their western neighbor must be a foreign policy priority (Freudenstein 1998, 41–54). Third, they recognize that to be accepted as Europeans, they must live up to European standards and principles. This means respecting human rights (including those of their ethnic minorities); promoting values of democracy, liberalism, and tolerance; and peacefully settling differences with their neighbors (Cziomer 1997, 26).

With the change of regime and the coming to power of the first noncommunist government in over four decades, the political conditions in Poland were created to begin a gradual transition from conditional to stable peace. Both German and Polish political elites developed foreign policy strategies based on the notion of a "community of interests" (Eberwein and Reiter 1999). This phrase, which was coined by Poland's first noncommunist foreign minister, Krzysztof Skubiszewski, stressed Germany and Poland's shared interest in deepening cooperation in Mitteleuropa and beyond. For Poland, this involved the notion of returning to Europe. For Germany, it involved a commitment to build a new strategic partnership with Poland to complement its existing partnership with France, along with a clear rejection of traditional power politics. The experience of the German–Polish dyad thus underlines the importance of ideas for foreign policy behavior (see Goldstein and Keohane 1993). It also suggests that visionary leadership is an essential element in developing a stable peace order.

The Conflict Resolution Process

Before a stable peace order can begin to develop, major conflicts and disputes need to be settled. The nature of the conflict resolution process is of
considerable importance for the subsequent quality of the peace-building
process. If disputes are not adequately addressed, the durability of the
emerging peace order will be limited. Stable peace theory thus attaches
considerable importance to analyzing how conflicts are resolved and
whether the terms of the agreement satisfy all parties concerned.

In the case of Polish–German relations, a series of outstanding issues
needed to be addressed as a consequence of the end of communism and
German unification. The first and most important was the status of the
Oder–Neisse line, which delineated the postwar German–Polish border.
The second was the rights of ethnic Germans in Poland. The third was the
issue of compensation for war crimes and forced labor. Underlying all of
these questions was a fourth, more profound, issue: how to come to terms
with the past and find ways to overcome painful and traumatic memories
(what the Germans call *Vergangenheitsbewältigung*).

Of the four, the border issue was the most controversial. Despite the
December 1970 West German–Polish treaty—one of the key *Ostverträge* of
Brandt's Ostpolitik—along with the East German–Polish treaties of July
1950 and May 1989, the Oder–Neisse line remained the only post–World
War II border whose legal status remained provisional. During late 1989
and early 1990, Chancellor Kohl argued that only a unified Germany
could sign a legally binding treaty settling the border question once and
for all. His reason for doing so was domestic political problems with his
own right wing in the CDU/CSU, which feared the rise of the far-right
Republikaner. Whatever his reasoning, his handling of the issue generated
considerable suspicion about the character of the new Germany and seriously complicated the prospects of forging a stable peace between Germany and Poland. Few believed that the German government would risk
international opprobrium by seeking to redraw the border. Nonetheless,
Kohl's behavior at this time conjured up ghosts from the past and
prompted serious concerns about German assertiveness and insensitivity.
At the very least, Kohl's willingness to place domestic political considerations (based on his concern about the rise of extremist right-wing nationalists) above relations with an important eastern neighbor was disquiet-
ing for many inside and outside Germany. Whatever his domestic
political calculations, Kohl's government paid a heavy political price
internationally (Stent 1999, 118–19).

In the end, the issue was settled in the framework of the Two-plus-Four
negotiations (Zelikow and Rice 1995, 217–22, 295, 343). At France's insistence, Poland was brought into the relevant session dealing with the bor-

der question on July 17, 1990. A final treaty recognizing the existing border was signed on November 14, 1990. With the border question settled, the most important obstacle facing the transition away from precarious and conditional peace was removed, and the foundations were laid for a new strategic partnership to emerge between Germany and Poland.

The foundations for this new relationship were laid by the Treaty of Good Neighborliness and Friendly Cooperation signed on June 17, 1991. The 1991 treaty contained thirty-eight articles covering a comprehensive range of issues. The preamble dealt with the past. It expressed a common determination to close the painful chapters of the past but also noted that relations between their two peoples had often been characterized by cooperation over previous centuries. Article 5 committed both parties to the peaceful resolution of disputes and pledged their mutual support for cooperative security structures. The treaty itself stressed the importance of peace, territorial integrity, and national sovereignty. It called for broad cooperation across a range of issues and institutionalized regular consultations at all levels. It also included a commitment by Germany to support Poland's entry into the EU. Consciously drawing on the experience of Franco-German rapprochement, the treaty called for the establishment of a wide range of contacts and exchanges between civic groups and associations, including political parties, trade unions, churches, party foundations, sports organizations, parliamentarians, youth groups, teachers, and students. Additional agreements were also signed at the same time as the Treaty on Good Neighborliness and Friendly Cooperation. These covered cross-border cooperation and established both the German–Polish Youth Project (DPJP) and a joint environmental council.

The second outstanding problem in German–Polish relations, minority rights, was also addressed in the 1991 treaty. Article 2 defined minorities in positive terms as a bridge between the two peoples, and article 20 outlined an extensive list of minorities' rights. It is important to note that the issue of minority rights, along with the associated question of the rights of the expellees, is much less controversial in the German–Polish case than that of Germany and the Czech Republic. Nonetheless, it remains a sensitive issue, as the ill-tempered exchange between the Bundestag and the Sejm in 1998 concerning the question of the right of resettlement of German expellees illustrates (see Lichtenstein 1998, 907–10).

The final issue, compensation, was first addressed in August 1975, during the Brandt era. The German government provided Poland with $500 million (although this was not officially described as reparations) and $400 million in trade credits in exchange for Poland's allowing 120,000 ethnic Germans to emigrate. In October 1991 the German government provided another $500 million for a reconciliation (*Aussöhnung*) foundation for the victims of Nazism. Although it no longer constitutes a fundamental problem in German–Polish relations, the question of compensation for victims of Nazi forced labor remains a disputed issue.

To sum up: after some initial German wavering on the issue of the Oder–Neisse border, both sides worked hard to resolve their outstanding differences and lay the foundations for long-term cooperation. Not all issues were fully resolved. It is also clear that some questions (such as the right of expellees to buy property in Poland) will take on a completely different complexion in the context of Poland's future entry into the EU. Nonetheless, developments in 1990–1991 demonstrated willingness on the part of both sides to find mutually acceptable solutions to their outstanding disputes and to build a peaceful, cooperative relationship. This involved a high level of institutionalization of their bilateral relations, consciously drawing on the Franco-German model. The plethora of institutions and bilateral mechanisms for consultation created at this time were designed to facilitate a process of mutual interest formation and to generate shared role conceptions and compatible identities. The highly institutionalized character of Franco-German relations has helped to generate a shared understanding of common interests and concerns. It is hoped that by embedding German–Polish relations in an analogous institutional matrix, a growing sense of trust and "we-ness" will emerge over time. This will provide a key pillar for the development of a stable peace in the wider Mitteleuropa region.

The Multilateral Context

One of the key dimensions of stable peace building in Western Europe and the wider transatlantic area has been the development of institutionalized forms of multilateral cooperation. Franco-German enmity, which resulted in three major wars and which lay at the heart of the "German question," has been effectively solved through the integration of both states into a regional pluralistic security community. Multilateral integration facilitates the emergence of a stable peace relationship by encouraging habits of mutually beneficial cooperation based on deepening trust and common interests.

One particularly significant consequence of multilateral integration is that the process of institutionalized cooperation helps transform the way states perceive their interests. In this manner, it gives states a new sense of their identity as European nations and creates the normative and ideational basis for deepening cooperation. The European integration process has thus made a major contribution to the creation of a zone of stable peace in the transatlantic area in which war, or the threat of war, no longer plays a role. In this way, multilateral integration has contributed to the emergence of a *foedus pacificum* (pacific union) of democratic republics, as advocated by Kant in his classic work *Perpetual Peace* (1795).

The lesson that Germany—along with most other Western European states—has drawn from the experience of multilateral cooperation is that integration provides an important means of building more peaceful relations in the wider Europe. Germany has been a particularly strong advocate of the opening up of Euro-Atlantic organizations to the new democracies of East Central Europe. This reflects Germany's "reflexive multilateralism," which has become encoded in its national identity, and its belief that its relations with its eastern neighbors need to be embedded in multilateral structures (Katzenstein 1997). As we saw above, Germany's commitment to EU enlargement provides an ideal complement to the Poles' desire to return to Europe and was formally cemented in the 1991 Treaty on Good Neighborliness and Friendly Cooperation.

Germany's relations with Poland and the countries of East Central Europe will increasingly be mediated through a dense network of multilateral institutions and forms of transnational governance. The key organizations are NATO and the EU. In addition, other European and regional organizations reinforce patterns of multilateral cooperation. These include the Council of Europe, the Organization for Security and Cooperation in Europe, and the Council of Baltic Sea States. German–Polish relations have also been anchored within two trilateral frameworks: the Weimar Triangle, and trilateral military cooperation with Denmark in the framework of NATO (Feldmann and Gareis 1998, 992). Thus, not only are German–Polish bilateral relations becoming highly institutionalized, but also they have been placed within a multilateral and trilateral international context.

This multilateral context has a number of important ramifications for the wider development of the European security system and for Germany's multilateral *Einbindung* (integration). First, the integration process will involve not just Poland but also the other East Central European democracies that are striving to return to Europe. The implications of this integration for the wider European security system are enormous. Traditionally, the small and medium-sized states of Central and Eastern Europe have served as buffer states among the regional great powers. As Henry Kissinger has observed, "The principal cause of European conflicts in the past 150 years has been the experience of a no-man's land between the German and Russian peoples" (quoted by Nastase 1992, 27). The dual enlargement process implies that the resolution of this geostrategic security dilemma will be through multilateral integration into Euro-Atlantic structures, rather than through traditional balance of power politics. Relative power capabilities, self-help strategies, and the struggle for survival in an anarchic system—all these traditional realist preoccupations fail to capture the richness and complexity of late-twentieth-century European security relations. Instead, security in contemporary Europe is inextricably linked to a process of integration involving not just institutional integration but also growing economic interdependence alongside thickening webs of transnational social and cultural interaction. As EU commissioner Hans van den Broek has commented, "Enlargement to the east is in the very first place a political issue relating to security and stability on our continent " (*The Guardian*, November 5, 1994).

While most commentators regard the enlargement of the EU and NATO to the east as very positive, some concern has been expressed about its implications for German Einbindung. These concerns arise from a worry that bringing the Visegrad countries into Euro-Atlantic structures may alter the way Germany perceives and acts on its interests in the wider European states system. For example, it may weaken Germany's postwar *Westbindung* (its "western integration"). As the Federal Republic of Germany develops ever closer relations with its eastern neighbors, some fear that it may attach less importance to its relations with its traditional postwar Western partners, particularly Paris and Washington. Others have invoked the realist logic of geopolitics to argue that Germany will find itself in a *neue Mittellage* (a "new middle position") between a stable West and an unstable East and will have to develop a new foreign policy accordingly. At the same time, the Federal Republic may find it increasingly difficult to manage the growing dilemmas of its Ostpolitik. Closer relations with Poland and the East Central Europeans may be unwelcome to Moscow, with whom Bonn has also sought to cultivate a special relationship. Many Russians are concerned that Germany's endeavor to develop closer relations with its eastern neighbors will be at their expense. Concomitantly, many in East Central Europe fear that Germany will attach more importance to good relations with the regional great power, Russia, than to their concerns. These worries have been crystallized by the debate over NATO's eastern enlargement—one of the most divisive issues on the European security agenda in the 1990s and beyond.

Germany's evolving relationship with Poland and the countries of Mitteleuropa thus has significant consequences for the wider constitution of the European order. Embedding German–Polish relations within a wider multilateral context is widely perceived as reassuring by Germany's neighbors and partners in both east and west. Nonetheless, there are some concerns that the enlargement of Euro-Atlantic structures will weaken Germany's multilateral Einbindung and lead to changes in its foreign policy behavior. Given the country's central geographical location, its economic weight, and its political influence, the evolution of German foreign policy is of major importance for the wider Europe. The competing demands of its Westbindung and its Ostpolitik mean that, "as usual, Germany has to juggle more balls than most" (Joffe 1994, 38). Within Germany, however, there is broad agreement that "the key challenge for Germany is to come to better terms with its eastern neighbors while staying on good terms with its neighbors to the west" (Hellmann 1996, 23).

Shared Norms and Values

The shaping of a durable and stable peace between Germany and Poland reflects not simply the existence of common or compatible interests but, rather, shared normative values and cognitive frameworks. Rather than being driven by common interests per se (such as mutually advantageous economic relations or shared security concerns), cooperation between Germany and Poland in Central Europe arises from *perceptions* of common interests. These perceptions are determined by normative conceptions, identities, and underlying cognitive frameworks.

Understanding the dynamics of stable peace building in Mitteleuropa thus entails analyzing the impact of cognitive frameworks, political identity, and normative values on states' behavior. This means that rationalist approaches to international politics, which assign explanatory primacy to material factors, are of limited value for analyzing the emergence of a zone of stable peace. Rationalist approaches, whether of realist, liberal-institutionalist, or Marxist paradigms, treat states' interests as materially derived and exogenously given. Cognitivist or knowledge-based approaches, by contrast, argue that processes that produce identities of particular states are "shaped by normative and causal beliefs that decision-makers hold and that, consequently, changes in belief systems can trigger changes in policy" (Hasenclever et al. 1997, 136).

Rationalist approaches have traditionally held a dominant position in international relations. For realists, for example, the texture of international politics can only be understood by objectively determined interests, defined in terms of power. This assumption of the objectivity of interests is shared by many Marxists, who emphasize the centrality of economically determined class interests, and by most neoliberal institutionalists, who "continue to treat actor identities and interests themselves as preexisting and fixed" (Kowert and Legro 1996, 458).

However, the assumption of the objectivity of interests—and of their central role in determining a state's foreign policy—is of limited help when it comes to assessing the changing nature of international politics in Mitteleuropa. Neorealism is particularly unhelpful when it comes to understanding post–Cold War German foreign policy. The neorealist assumptions of Waltz, for example, lead him to predict that Germany's improved security environment and its enhanced relative power since unification will lead it to pursue a policy of "autonomy maximization" (Waltz 1993, 62–70). There is, however, little substantial evidence that Germany is shedding its multilateral and integrationist orientation.

Thus, while an analysis of Germany's material resources and geopolitical location can yield some obvious insights, it provides only a partial and one-dimensional picture of its foreign policy preferences and policies. Physical and material factors are clearly important in shaping and constraining the range of options available to states, but these factors do not determine how states will behave towards others. Germany's relations with the Visegrad states, for example, is inevitably strongly influenced by two inescapable material factors: first, the asymmetry in their size, and, second, their economic relations and trading patterns (see Markovits, Reich, and Westermann 1996). Yet while these material and physical factors have remained fairly constant over the last hundred years or so, German policy towards its neighbors in Mitteleuropa has demonstrated considerable variation—from the bestialities of National Socialism to Willy Brandt's Kniefall. Thus, although geopolitical and economic interests constrain the range of options available to each state, they do not determine state behavior.

The preferences and policies of states are explicable only by reference to *perceptions* of material structures (see Walt 1987; Barnett 1996). Interests are not objectively and exogenously determined, either by the domestic socioeconomic structures or by the distribution of relative power resources in the international system. Rather, actors define their interests according to their own identity, values, and foreign policy role conceptions. Consequently interests and identities are mutually constitutive—neither can be defined in the absence of the other. This has important implications for stable peace building.

German Identity and Stable Peace Building

The concept of identity, however fuzzy and imprecise it might seem, is essential for understanding the dynamics of Germany's relations with the countries of East Central Europe. In the last 150 years, it is not so much Germany's physical and material interests in Central Europe that have changed as its *identity*. Germany has long been the regional great power in Mitteleuropa—economically, militarily, and politically. Its relative power capabilities and material resources have not changed drastically since the time of Bismarck. What has changed, however, is Germany's perception of its interests—in other words, its identity, its prescriptive values, and its foreign policy role conceptions.

In the interwar years, for example, German identity was deeply colored by the dominant conservative-nationalist political discourse. This was reflected in widely held consensus on the nature of war and international politics that by the 1930s dominated the foreign policy role conceptions of Weimar Germany's political, military, and economic elites. The strongly militarist component of German political culture, which so marked German identity in the first half of the twentieth century, was epitomized by the cult that grew up around Langemark. The "battle" of Langemark in 1914 was a military fiasco but became one of the central myths around which German interwar militarism was reconstructed. The futile charges of hastily trained volunteers against the machine guns of the British Expeditionary Force became a model of selfless heroism that the Nazis were subsequently to exploit (see von Krochow 1997, 19–23; Herwig 1997, 116). More generally, German political and intellectual culture in the interwar years was characterized by a strong sense of illiberalism, anti-Semitism, and eschatological aspirations. Writing about the mood of this fateful time, Thomas Mann spoke of a Saint Vitus "dance of fanaticism" from which "Reason hides her face."

The epistemological break in Germany's political culture and self-identity came about as a result of the crushing of the Nazi regime and the revelations of the Holocaust. The postwar identity of the Bundesrepublik Deutschland (BDR) was subsequently constructed anew around four key discourses and institutions. First, it was defined in opposition to the Third Reich. For the BRD, Nazi Germany and the dark soul of Germany's authoritarian and militarist past provided the "other" against which postwar West German identity was forged. Second, postwar West German identity was defined in consciously European and Western terms. The emphasis sometimes varied between a (West) European identity and a transatlantic one, but the identity was clearly and unambiguously Western and was given institutional expression through multilateral organizations such as the Council of Europe, NATO, and the EEC/EU. This Europeanized identity also led to an unwillingness to define Germany's national interests.

Third, it was closely linked to a number of domestic institutions—namely, the constitution, the currency, and the social market economy. This produced both a *Verfassungspatriotismus* (constitutional patriotism) and the development of a German national identity closely linked to the deutsche mark. Finally, West German identity was linked to a specific foreign policy role conception. This new approach to foreign policy was articulated by, among others, Hans-Dietrich Genscher. He argued that Germany would be able to influence international developments in the future only if it eschewed *Machtpolitik* (power politics) in preference to its postwar commitment to *Verantwortungspolitik* (policy of responsibility)

(Genscher 1995, 1016). The "grand strategy" of the Bonn republic has thus been built around a decisive rejection of traditional power politics and a commitment to a policy of peaceful relations with neighbors and reconciliation with former foes.

German unification and the emergence of the Berlin republic have stimulated a lively debate on German identity. Many of the central planks of the Bonn republic's identity have been questioned and critically appraised. However, this has not resulted in a significant reorientation of German foreign policy. There has certainly been a lively debate about whether Germany is primarily a Western or a Central European power (Garton Ash 1994, 381). There has also been a growing interest in defining some specifically German national interests, along with an intense debate over whether Germany should now be seen as a "normal" country. Despite these debates, however, there is a powerful element of continuity linking the identity of the Bonn and Berlin republics. This is particularly evident from the continuing commitment to a Europeanized national identity and a strong sense of Germany's moral responsibilities (Duffield 1998, 225).

This sense of moral responsibility has had important consequences for its relations with Poland and the other Visegrad states. Most important, the strong normative component in German policy towards its eastern neighbors has altered the dynamics of power relations in Mitteleuropa. The German government's commitment to building a stable peace order in the region has strengthened the negotiating hand of Poland and the other East Central European democracies vis-à-vis its hegemonic Western neighbor (Hampton 1998, 85). This changed power relationship was evident in the treaties of friendship Germany signed with its eastern neighbors in 1991.

Conclusion

This chapter has traced the transition from a precarious to a conditional peace in German–Polish relations that was made possible by the annus mirabilis of 1989. It has also suggested that the 1990s witnessed the steady evolution of this conditional peace into a stable peace relationship. It has highlighted the importance of normative and ideational factors for this process, thereby underlining the utility of constructivist approaches to international cooperation. It has also drawn attention to the importance of a number of key factors and developments. These include the role of Ostpolitik in preparing the ground for the transition from precarious to conditional peace; the interaction of domestic and foreign developments; the importance of political leadership and the "vision thing"; the nature of the conflict resolution process; and the impact of identity and political culture on foreign policy behavior.

"Without any doubt," it has been argued, "internal and international conditions for a permanent Polish–German reconciliation are now better than at any time in recent history" (Rachwald 1993, 247). As we have seen in this chapter, both governments are committed to cementing a close strategic partnership as the hinge of a wider stable peace in Mitteleuropa and beyond. Considerable progress has been made in this regard. Two issues, however, might make the transition from a stable peace to a security community in Central Europe problematic. The first concerns the substantial economic asymmetries in Central Europe. The second derives from the unequal power resources of Germany and its eastern neighbors.

Dieter Senghaas has suggested that a durable peace order is difficult to achieve in the absence of a degree of perceived economic fairness and social justice. The existence of substantial social and economic inequalities, he argues, impedes the emergence of trust and social capital that is a vital ingredient in any durable peace order. It also complicates constructive conflict resolution (Senghaas 1997, 15). This suggests that consolidating stable peace and developing a security community will be problematic between states with marked socioeconomic asymmetries. In postwar Western Europe a process of informal societal integration was made easier by the absence of such asymmetries between countries such as France, Germany, and the Benelux states. This greatly facilitated the transition from a stable peace order to a pluralistic security community based on a sense of community or "we-ness."

In Central Europe, by contrast, there are sharp disparities in living standards and economic prospects between EU countries and their postcommunist neighbors. These are particularly marked along the German–Polish border. While these asymmetries have not yet threatened the stability of the post-1989 peace order in Mitteleuropa, they will make the emergence of a security community much more difficult. First, perceived economic disparities will make it more difficult to define common interests. This is already evident given the fear of some in Germany that they will not be able to compete with relatively cheap Polish labor. Second, it will make the emergence of shared identities and a sense of we-ness more difficult, particularly as socioeconomic asymmetries may serve to reinforce existing cultural differences and historical animosities between "Slavs" and "Teutons." One open question is what impact EU membership will have on this economic asymmetry. It is not yet clear whether Poland's accession to the EU will help diminish the inequality of living standards between Germany and its eastern neighbors or exacerbate them. It may be that cross-border cooperation will help stimulate economic activity on both sides of the Oder–Neisse line. In this case, however, it might well deepen political and social tensions within countries, particularly between the western and eastern parts of Poland.

Linked to the issue of economic asymmetries is the more controversial problem of Germany's "hegemony" (see Markovits and Reich 1991). The power capabilities of Germany and Poland are clearly unequal, and even the moral dimension of German foreign policy referred to above cannot compensate for this unequal power relationship. But does this asymmetry mean that Germany acts as a hegemon in Mitteleuropa? Can an asymmetrical relationship be nonhegemonic? This is a difficult and controversial question that is beyond the scope of this chapter to address. Nonetheless, it is one that should figure prominently on the research agenda of stable peace theory. If Germany does act as a hegemon in the region, then rather than speaking of a stable peace it would be more accurate to speak of the existence of a Pax Germanicus—in other words, a region in which conflicts and disputes are resolved peacefully, not because of shared values and beliefs in the value of peace per se, but because the German hegemon has been able to impose its interests and concerns on the region. Such a Pax Germanicus would be peaceful, but it would be a long way from the foedus pacificum Kant outlined in *Perpetual Peace*.

Notes

The research for this chapter was made possible by a grant from the Nuffield Foundation (reference number SGS/LB/0800).

15

Stable Peace: Conclusions and Extrapolations

Ole Elgström and Magnus Jerneck

This book has introduced a multifaceted and dynamic dimension to the study of peace relations. Peace as a concept has been problematized. Peace is not, we argue, an unproblematic, unidimensional phenomenon but should be seen as comprising a number of stages, from precarious peace, where only immediate deterrence prevents the outbreak of war, to stable peace, where war is considered unthinkable.

As evidenced by several chapters in this book, stable peace is not a utopian dream. In terms of conflict, stable peace rarely (or never) requires a total harmony of interests among the involved parties. The main point is rather that political and other conflicts that arise between states are consistently solved by other than military means. This does not entail the abolition of all coercive behavior among states, as long as war is outside the realm of expected behavior.

Our cases demonstrate that both historical contingencies and the organization of political space are important factors in creating or sustaining stable peace. Political space may be defined in geographical terms, stressing the importance of physical location, or in functional terms, downplaying physical proximity and underlining the importance of a political, economic, or mental propinquity across territorial distances. In either case, boundaries and interests are still crucial. International power structures, political configurations, and normative standards are usually time bound, and thus historically specific. Even if ideas do matter, they vary in importance and scope.

The quality of peace may thus change with the passage of time. Even though history does not follow a linear pattern, it seems to us that the notion of stable peace has gained a broad acceptance and has become more legitimate as a political objective. In ontological terms one could therefore argue that ideas and norms have become more powerful in relation to other factors determining the future development of international relations. In that respect, we regard ourselves to be modest constructivists in our outlook.

The chapters in this book have, to various degrees, dealt with conceptual and theoretical issues as well as with empirical illustrations and cases. Starting from the theoretical framework delineated by Arie M. Kacowicz and Yaacov Bar-Siman-Tov in chapter 1, the contributors have emphasized different aspects of stable peace theory. Some have focused on the processes leading from highly unstable peace relations to more stable ones (processes of stabilization), others have delved into the processes that deepen stable peace relations and make them durable (processes of consolidation).

In some parts of the world, notably the Organization for Economic Cooperation and Development (OECD) community of states, we find security communities, or zones of consolidated stable peace. Some of these have reached a very high level of sophistication, as in the European Union (EU) or the U.S.–Canadian relationship. Some regions, however, are still experiencing war or unstable peace, whereas others are characterized by a situation that just approximates stable peace. Therefore, it seems important to us to try to draw lessons from successful and unsuccessful experiences of peace processes. This is one of the tasks of this concluding chapter.

We start with a conceptual review, in which we underline a number of important distinctions stemming from the collective research endeavor of this book. Then we turn to factors of stabilization and assess what we have learned about how fragile peace conditions are transformed into stable peace. Next, considerable attention is paid to processes of peace reproduction, that is, factors and conditions that lead to the consolidation of stable peace. In the final section we discuss policy implications and relate our findings to the ongoing debate on the nature of the future world system.

Facets of Peace: A Dynamic Perspective

Peace is not a homogeneous phenomenon. The quality of peace relations varies and is subject to change. This is, indeed, one of the major lessons of this volume. In this book, we have utilized a scale depicting a series of conflictual and cooperative relations of varying severity. At one end of the scale we find precarious peace, characterized by immediate deterrence and threats of military confrontation. A less tense state of affairs is conditional peace, where the parties consciously try to avoid war by relying on appeasement and diffuse deterrence. The highest form of peace is stable peace, defined as a situation where war or threats of war are unthinkable as instruments for resolving conflicts between states.

By introducing a typology of peace relations, we point to the importance of trying to explain why and how states progress from one point on the scale to another. The dynamics of peace transformations becomes a major area of research. Stable peace is often preceded by precarious and conditional peace. Hence, it is not common for states to jump from warlike or otherwise tense relations to stable peace without passing so-called intermediate stages of peace. A related question has to do with the extent to which processes of reconciliation and changes of self-images such as going from a conquering warring state to a cooperative trading state, in any way represent historical turning points in previously hostile relations.

The dynamics of peace transformations may point to the fact that some processes are difficult and lengthy, whereas others run more smoothly, as instances of "easy" stable peace. Some of these are analytically less important because they exhibit very few (or even no) elements of interaction between the parties. In such cases, stable peace is mainly an abstraction, existing only in a formal sense. Typical examples are those in which states are geographically distant or politically far apart— for instance, Iceland and Uruguay. Our emphasis on change means that we are not interested in such uncomplicated cases of easy stable peace.

As witnessed by the cases in this study, stable peace may occur in dyadic as well as multilateral relations. Nation-state A may entertain stable peace relations with B but experience other types of peace with C and D. When stable peace exists between all dyads in a certain area over a longer period of time, we may talk about a zone of stable peace or about regional stable peace. A security community is such an area of peace, but is, according to most of the scholars in the book, also characterized by shared norms and values and an identifiable common identity. Thus, we could say that a process of consolidation might result in a security community.

Some contributors have noted the variety of situations that may be subsumed under the umbrella of conditional peace. This category includes situations of cold war as well as fairly stabilized peace relations, where the actors have resolved most of the conflictual issues among them but are still not fully confident that military instruments could not be used should circumstances change. For instance, Benny Miller in chapter 4 introduces the concept of normal peace to denote such a resilient peace but points to the risk that a change of regime or the rise of a revisionist party might demolish the hope for stable peace. Rikard Bengtsson in chapter 5 favors the concept of integrative peace to characterize a situation where trust exists between the actors, but not confidence; hence, stable peace is not taken for granted. Magnus Ericson points out that even though two small states may be convinced that neither of them has any thought of using military force in their relationship, a mental preparedness may remain. That is, changing great power configurations might force them into different camps in a future great power conflict. He labels such a situation "approximate stable peace" (Ericson 2000; see also chapter 7). Whatever term is used, there seem to be good reasons for differentiating between peace relations where stabilization processes have diminished distrust and created a momentum for stable peace and situations of more fragile conditional peace.

The cognitively oriented definition of stable peace used here does not in itself say anything about the temporal dimension of the relation, that is, its durability. It does, however, put the focus on time-related phenomena like confidence-building, learning, and institutionalization. Yet, stable peace is hardly an unalterable state, even if it possesses a certain measure of resilience. Stable peace relations may exhibit varying degrees of permanence and robustness. For example, recent liberal arguments have associated the existence and viability of stable peace in Western Europe with democracy and economic integration (Russett and Starr 1992). The endurance of these potentially peace-producing factors is itself a matter of some controversy, however. Consequently, long peace is not necessarily the same as stable peace, and stable peace is not irreversible.

Having established the conceptual parameters, we will next address the dynamics of peace transformation. What answers do the contributions in the book give to two major questions raised in chapter 1: (1) Why and how do stable peace relations emerge? and (2) What are the conditions for maintaining and consolidating stable peace over time?

Stabilizing Peace

Several explanations exist as to the question of how the initial peace-making mechanisms work. There is the question whether an observed period of peace has been caused by conscious peace strategies or whether it has been the result of chance or of favorable or less favorable external conditions. A state may strive for war and nevertheless get peace. The force of intentionality should not be underestimated, though. The Swedish case (Elgström and Jerneck, chapter 10) demonstrates how even small states may, if only marginally, act as peace promoters. The creation of stable peace in the OECD can partly be said to be the result of a deliberate choice. The partners in the OECD sphere have gradually tried to design an international subsystem characterized less by competition and antagonistic power struggle and more by cooperation and negotiation. Entering into a stable peace relationship may be seen as an instrument of binding oneself to the mast (like Ulysses), hoping to gain the adversary's respect or international recognition and legitimacy. The fragile and still not very stable peace process in the Middle East is a good illustration of such a behavior.

A successful promotion or defense of stable peace relations seems to a large extent to be actor driven. Thus, the importance of leadership should not be underestimated. As our cases illustrate, however, one should make a distinction between political motivation and skill and various social, cultural, and economic preconditions.

As suggested by Kacowicz and Bar-Siman-Tov, the terms of a peace agreement, constituting the transformation from a context of war to a context of peace, seem to exert considerable influence on ensuing developments. Obviously, the passage from one stage of peace to another does not necessarily involve any peace agreement at all. For example, Swedish relations with Russia have involved both precarious and conditional peace and, today, even integrative peace (see Bengtsson, chapter 5), without any war for more than two hundred years. Nevertheless, as Kjell-Åke Nordquist amply demonstrates in chapter 9, the quality of peace agreements, when they exist, is a solid predictor of future relations. Mutual satisfaction with the territorial status quo prevents ideas of revision and supports the forces that are against adventurism. The establishment of problem-solving mechanisms may facilitate nonviolent solutions to remaining issues of contention.

Domestic stability and policy predictability are other variables that seem to be associated with international stabilization. The case of the ABC triangle of South America (Kacowicz , chapter 11) shows that stable political regimes in the region were linked to the return of democracy, with a positive effect on the prospects for stable peace. Although the movement towards stable peace was initiated by military regimes, the stability caused by the spread of democracy throughout the Southern Cone of Latin America constituted a sufficient condition for establishing stable peace. Furthermore, peace expectations and predictability were closely associated with the evolution of rapprochement between regional actors in the nuclear and economic areas. This process built confidence and facilitated cooperative practices later on. Likewise, Yaacov Bar-Siman-Tov stresses in chapter 12 that the certainty, based on the belief that each side sees the maintenance of peace as a vital interest, among Israeli and Egyptian leaders about each other´s intentions and behavior has contributed to the gradual stabilization of peace between the two countries.

Joe Hagan in chapter 2 establishes a link between peace stabilization and two domestic political factors: the orientation of a state´s ruling elite and the intensity of domestic opposition. His basic assertion is that systemic stability is enhanced when key powers have rulers who have restrained and flexible orientations toward foreign affairs and who are willing to insulate diplomacy from severe domestic political pressures. Hagan reminds us of the importance of domestic factors and leadership in supporting stabilization. Similarly, Adrian Hyde-Price, in his account of German-Polish relations in chapter 14, highlights the interaction of domestic and foreign developments and the vital role of political leadership and vision. These are factors that were perhaps not sufficiently emphasized in our initial theoretical framework.

Explanations that have their origin in "internationalism" (Goldmann 1994) emphasize spillover effects and the impact of communication, organization, and international law. In fact, increasing economic prosperity, which is sometimes associated with peace, is in many chapters mentioned as a driving force behind stabilization of peace and the consolidation of stable peace (Bar-Siman-Tov, Elgström and Jerneck, and Miller in this volume). Alfred Tovias in chapter 8 argues that symmetric, mutual economic dependence ("irrevocable interdependence") is of utmost importance. Former enemies become reluctant to resume conflicting behavior because of the enormous costs involved in breaking up economic relations. When the benefits of bilateral cooperation are substantial and the realization of these benefits is dependent upon continued transactions between the former enemies (when there is a "balance of prosperity"), a strong incentive exists for stabilization of peace relations. Vested interests in peace prevent the resumption of hostile activities.

Still, external forces and third parties—not least great power configurations—seem to be rather vital for the initiation of peace processes, even among like-minded countries. Stable peace may, as a matter of fact, in some instances be the result of conquest or domination. Situations of stable peace characterized by political dominance, in which political subordination goes hand-in-hand with violation of sovereignty, typically occur between small countries and great powers. In other cases, stable peace relations between smaller powers may be the result of great power pressures. Benny Miller underlines in chapter 3 how great power intervention may take a regional conflict from war to peace, or from precarious to conditional peace, but he claims that it can never by itself create stable peace. To this may be added the relevance of systemic qualities. A system with hungry, revisionist states that are dissatisfied with the status quo is not very likely to lead to stable peace. In contrast, a system of satisfied actors increases the likelihood of stabilization.

Normative structures may be essential preconditions for the creation of stable peace (Boulding 1978, 12; see also Väyrynen, chapter 6). According to Boulding, in periods when the support for "war norms" dwindles and the "peace norm" gathers strength and becomes dominant, we may expect the emergence of stable peace. The evolution of norms against war is actually a fundamental trend that is claimed to characterize today's world (see Price 1998). Sometimes it is argued that this trend constitutes a qualitative leap compared with earlier periods of history and makes global stable peace a distinct possibility. Such norm consolidation may be the effect of evolutionary learning (Modelski 1990) on a grander scale, integrating both causal and normative ideas into a new mental frame that dominates international discourse at the time.

Regardless of the strength and prevalence of such global norms, however, they might arguably not be able to serve as triggering causes of peace, turning adversarial, hostile relations in a concrete relationship into friendlier ones. In concrete regional or bilateral situations, however, normative conceptions and common perceived identities may actually produce a transformation of peace relations. The crucial point is that the way the actors "perceive each other is a major determinant of how they interact" (Buzan 1999, 2). According to Adrian Hyde-Price (chapter 14), "the shaping of a durable and stable peace between Germany and Poland reflects not simply the existence of common or compatible interests but, rather, shared normative values and cognitive frameworks." Peace processes are thus often driven by the perception of shared norms rather than by common interests per se.

Consolidating Stable Peace

Even stable peace relations exhibit varying degrees of permanence and robustness. In the conceptual framework presented by Kacowicz and Bar-Siman-Tov, it is postulated that two conditions seem necessary to ensure the consolidation and maintenance of stable peace: a general and continuous satisfaction with the status quo; and a common normative framework often, but not necessarily, linked to well-developed democratic regimes. Economic prosperity and interdependence are claimed to also facilitate the deepening of regional peace.

The liberal logic, which relates stable peace consolidation to the simultaneous consolidation of democracy and the gains created by free trade and other economic transactions, is referred to, and supported by, several contributors. Democracy is certainly a dominant factor as both a causal and a sustaining mechanism of stable peace. According to Benny Miller, the cornerstone of the liberal approach is democratization, and all other elements—free market economies, regional institutions, and transnational interactions—help to strengthen stable peace only when the regional actors are liberal democracies. Magnus Ericson in chapter 7 makes two interesting observations: First, while there is no necessary linkage between stable peace theory and democratic peace theory, significant elements of democratic peace discourse purport to account for stable peace. Second, these elements are historically contingent in their logic. Ericson problematizes the relationship between stable peace and liberal peace beyond their common challenge to neorealist assumptions of an inescapable security dilemma and the irrelevance of the internal life of states. Specifically, he argues that to the extent that the democratic peace is a stable peace, this ought not to be understood as the automatic result of democratic norms and institutions but as a historically specific development. The employment of stable peace theory demonstrates, for example, that the democratic peace proposition is weaker prior to World War II than afterwards. In other words, what it means to be democratic is a human construct that has to be understood in terms of its wider social and political context. Ericson makes a forceful claim that development and refinement of democratic peace theory may benefit substantially from introducing a qualified definition of peace, including stable peace. The propensity for democracy to engender stable peace may, for example, be contingent on considerations of realpolitik.

James Goodby in chapter 13 also argues for a close association between democratic values and stable peace. He introduces the proposition that a similar sense of identity is another crucial factor. Arguing in the same vein, John Owen in chapter 4 strongly maintains that the relationship between stable peace and common identity is a necessary one; a common identity should be seen either as part of the definition of stable peace (a move that we do not advocate) or as a necessary cause thereof. Owen also argues that a common political identity requires a common enemy and that therefore the development of a robust peace among one group of states is likely to generate a group of enemy states. This *problématique* is empirically mirrored in the debate on whether the demarcation of the European Union creates, deliberately or unwittingly, strong patterns of inclusion and exclusion, where a "we-feeling" is contrasted with a sense of estrangement towards outsiders.

In the OECD community, the interplay between democracy and trade has relaxed and gradually eroded the military dimension of the external security dilemma, defined in the literature as a situation in which mutual suspicion and necessary self-help lead to armament measures that create insecurity for other groups of actors. The resultant peace dividend of this growing amity and trust has paved the way for a strengthening of the economic performance and further integration in the political field. Territorial integrity and political autonomy ("surviving") as the core values of high politics have, within the OECD community, partly been replaced by economic prosperity ("thriving") (see Sperling and Kirchner 1997).

One could argue that a well-defined and stable international democratic peace community in the long run promotes the consolidation of internal democracy within the states in question, and vice versa. In the Western sphere, the internal aspect of the double security dilemma has narrowed down. We have a situation where the agents of the state are constrained to reproduce and preserve it within the frames of a liberal, democratic system, and only that. Conversely, a consolidated internal democracy has functioned as an important normative factor for creating peaceful relations among the members of the group (Risse-Kappen 1994). Hence, there has been interplay between the internal and external qualities of a stable peace in the OECD community.

The arguments above have primarily concerned the systemic conditions for peace. Turning to the consolidation process, the time factor (the durability of peace), in combination with a benign type of path dependency, seems to be important. Drawing a parallel to the strengthening of democracy, it is a matter of consolidating one's gains (Huntington 1996a). A consolidated stable peace is a relation where the use of nonmilitary instruments to solve conflicts is the only game in town (Linz and Stepan 1996). One could argue that a consolidated stable peace refers to a relation that has survived a series of political crises unscathed. Consolidation may be perceived as a reproduction process in which the essential elements are continuously reconstructed and strengthened. Trust is in this process transformed into confidence, and peaceful relations come to be taken for granted (see Bengtsson, chapter 5). Following the reasoning of democratization theory and stressing the importance of values and norms, people "are habituated to the fact that . . . violations of these norms are likely to be both ineffective and costly" (Linz and Stepan 1996, 16).

Analogous to democratization, stable peace "becomes routinized and deeply internalized in social, institutional, and even psychological life, as well as in political calculations" (Linz and Stepan 1996, 16). Consolidation is, in this light, closely connected to learning. Peaceful expectations are produced through positive experiences of interaction.

Political craftsmanship often identifies both causal and principled ideas as core elements in mutual—and sophisticated—learning processes creating or furthering stable peace. Visions and ideas are sometimes seen as important movers in politics. They function as road maps in the sense that they diagnose different lines of action and also by their capacity to guide interests, thus facilitating the choice between different political paths. Both causal and normative ideas might favor some options over others. Quite often, ideas have certain consolidating qualities; once they become institutionalized, their inertia may constrain specific policies (Goldstein and Keohane 1993). Hence, although causal ideas and norms (peace norms) do not necessarily create peace initially, they might function as very important long-term legitimizers of peace. One possible learning pattern links consolidation of stable peace to the democratic peace hypothesis: democratic structures produce behavior that in turn allows states to trust one another to have benign intentions (Ericson 2000).

Using as a point of reference the consolidation of a zone of stable peace in the European Union, the deepening of stable peace seems to imply the gradual emergence of an integrative, problem-solving mode of negotiation to replace threats, manipulation, and other types of distributive bargaining behavior (see Elgström and Jönsson 1999). In the European Union, negotiations are continuously ongoing. Indeed, the EU has been characterized as a "permanent negotiation institute" (Bal 1995, 1) and as a "multilateral inter-bureaucratic negotiation marathon" (Kohler-Koch 1996, 367). In such an environment, "the shadow of the future" is almost infinite, and therefore peaceful cooperation becomes easily institutionalized. Member-states are no longer victims of specific reciprocity; as they are secure in their expectations of a future mutually beneficial exchange, they do not need to demand prompt and equal concessions at any particular round of negotiations. Instead, EU negotiations are characterized by diffuse reciprocity, that is, the willingness of member-states to permit unilateral concessions at one point in time because of their conviction that they will get this concession back in future negotiations.

Negotiations in the European Union are permeated by a rich consensus culture. It is an institutionalized reflex to seek solutions that all actors can agree to. At all levels, member-states hesitate to ride roughshod over minority governments and instead use a problem-solving approach to find creative ways of saving the face of a government that is unhappy with a particular solution (Elgström and Jönsson 1999). Even when majority voting is a possibility, actors refrain as long as they can from using this option.

Highly consolidated—and sophisticated—zones of stable peace, we claim, are thus closely associated with the emergence of an integrative negotiation environment. Conflicts are resolved through negotiations without any reflection on alternatives. In general, this gradual transformation takes place through cooperation. Actors learn to trust each other. They find that peaceful problem-solving is beneficial to all parties and that this creates "virtuous circles" involving peace and prosperity. Institutionalized norms of mutual peaceful behavior are developed and solidify already existing propensities.

Extrapolations and Policy Implications

At the start of a new millennium, completely contrasting predictions compete with respect to the future of the world system, not least on the prevalence of peace and war. Francis Fukuyama (1992) announced the "end of history," celebrating the victory of democracy worldwide and therefore also the beginning of global peaceful relations. Samuel Huntington (1996b) expressed his vision of a "clash of civilizations," implying a much more violent future.

In a widely quoted article, James Goldgeier and Michael McFaul (1992) discussed the emergence of the "two worlds," one, mainly the Western part of the world, a zone of peace, characterized by peaceful conflict resolution; the other, mainly the Third World, still an anarchy, where distrust and constant preparedness for military violence are still the rule.

This book on stable peace presents both pessimistic and optimistic scenarios. On the one hand, the emphasis on shared values, democracy, and common identities as preconditions for stable peace indicates that global peace cannot be expected to emerge, at least for the short to mid-term. The third wave of democratization (Huntington 1991) was not as successful as many observers, including Fukuyama, first believed it to be. In many countries, democratic processes were reversed; in others chaos, rather than stability, has been the order of the day. The prevalence of weak states in probably a majority of the Third World countries does not bode well for the future of democracy (Miller, chapter 3), and building stronger states is a long-term process.

The increasing incidence of internal conflicts, often ethnically based, is another worrisome sign. In a study by Kalevi Holsti (1996), 66 percent of all conflicts between 1945 and 1993 were identified as internal. Other studies (such as Rasmussen 1997, 27–28) demonstrate that domestic conflicts have become even more predominant in the post–Cold War era. Stable peace theory is primarily concerned with the abolishment of international conflicts. It is not entirely clear whether the mechanisms that create and consolidate international zones of peace also counteract the growing prevalence of internal, often intractable conflicts. Obviously, internal and international conflicts are often closely associated, and processes leading to increased interaction and democracy may well produce both internal and external stability. Still, we may envisage a future with few international wars but with internal unrest in many countries.

Furthermore, as Owen points out, the future of stable peace is not ensured even once such a status has been reached (Owen, chapter 4). The development of a robust peace among one group of states, Owen claims, is likely to generate a group of enemy states. A community with common values that bind them together needs an "other," a common enemy with competing values. Therefore, the elimination of violent conflict among certain actors may introduce the possibility of such conflict with other actors.

On the other hand, this study also demonstrates the important role of agency. Many contributions present evidence that individual leadership can produce substantial change in peace relations if conditions are ripe (Hagan, Kacowicz, Elgström and Jerneck, Hyde-Price, and Goodby in this volume). We would therefore like to emphasize the role of political vision, political will, and craftsmanship. The general context of security relations and participating states' satisfaction with the status quo are, however, of utmost importance in this regard. As Goodby points out, nations bent on political aggrandizement will certainly not promote conditions for a stable peace. States in a zone of peace have to seek a general equilibrium in their relation with others. Actively satisfied states not only accept the status quo but also work to defend and cement it.

The argument illustrates that political visions have to be combined with measures creating long-term commitments. Choices between different normative pathways are very important in this respect. Following the reasoning of path dependency, one can argue that ideational road maps offer alternative ways to reach a destination. Once an alternative is chosen, others are in general not available ex post, since one cannot easily return to the original point of departure. Consequently, a chosen path normally excludes other alternatives: it is a situation of lock-in. These lock-in positions can be produced not only accidentally but also deliberately, either by an individual state ("binding oneself") or by imposition. However, if the lock-in position is to last, a strong element of consent is probably required on the part of the state entering into such a position. That is why the system of states not only contains preventive elements but also has to leave room for permissive attitudes in relation to the aspirations of the individual states.

Another structural factor working in favor of peace is the spread and consolidation of peace norms. The notion that war serves to invigorate the national spirit and bring forward positive values like heroism and self-lessness, common in the nineteenth century and also in twentieth-century autocracies, is being increasingly replaced by much more negative images that emphasize the destructive forces of war and the resulting suffering of civilians and soldiers alike. Peace as an overarching value has been enshrined in the UN Charter and is constantly reiterated and propagated by myriad norm entrepreneurs, individuals, nongovernmental organizations, and international agencies. Bans on chemical weapons and land mines are just easily observed indications of this more general trend. Today, international peace norms are supported by a strong transnational community. Nevertheless, this development is probably reversible, and war norms are still going strong in several parts of the world. Hence, constant vigilance and undiminished, relentless efforts to consolidate ideas of disarmament and peaceful relations are needed.

Thus, we argue, one has to create a system in which, in the Buzan's words, "sentience makes a difference," as compared to the raw logic of realism (Buzan 1999, 6). An intellectual point of departure is the interesting distinction between two forms of international society, the pluralist and the solidarist. Whereas both are rationalistic in the sense that they put the establishment of shared norms and rules at the center of political activity, they represent different approaches to such an endeavor. While pluralism is instrumental, practical, and somewhat conservative in its effort to limit the disorder produced by international anarchy, solidarism has more far-reaching aims. Its views on the creation of an international society are progressive, or even revolutionary, when it comes to the development of a certain international civicness, for instance, by means of mutual codes of conduct. Whereas a pluralist version of international society is "thin," the solidarist one is "thick" (Buzan 1999). For the long-term prospects for stable peace, the solidarist way seems to be the most promising path to follow. To move from a relationship or system of pluralism to an enabling system of solidarism, elements of voluntary compliance and lock-in behavior might be necessary, but not sufficient. A so-called directional leadership, based not only on problem-solving but also on consensus-seeking strategies and the ambition to further collective goals rather than myopic self-interests (Malnes 1995), seems to be quite crucial.

Once again, the experience of the EU and the OECD might be relevant. The stable peace of these political entities is not merely a system in which military confrontation as a means of statecraft is ruled out. It is also a system in which states place a fairly low emphasis on reproducing their autonomy as compared to their effort to create an international society built upon a set of common norms (Bull 1977). As regional "societies," the EU and the OECD have been preserved and propagated by acts of mutual recognition and common practices (Buzan, Jones, and Little 1993, 165–68). The important thing, however, is that some of the major powers do not use the system just for their own purpose, forcing minor or subordinate states to adopt a cooperative strategy, while they themselves pursue a competitive one (Buzan, Jones, and Little 1993, 167). Both major and subordinate states share cooperative norms and common values, thus propagating and consolidating a stable peace among nations.

References

Acharya, Amitav. 1998. "Collective Identity and Management in Southeast Asia." Pp. 198–227 in *Security Communities*, edited by Emanuel Adler and Michael Barnett. Cambridge: Cambridge University Press.

Acton, Edward. 1995. *Russia: The Tsarist and Soviet Legacy.* New York: Longman.

Acuña, Carlos H., and William C. Smith. 1995. "The Politics of 'Military Economics' in the Southern Cone: Comparative Perspectives on Democracy and Arms Production in Argentina, Brazil, and Chile." *Political Power and Social Theory* 9: 121–57.

Adler, Emanuel. 1997a. "Imagined (Security) Communities: Cognitive Regions in International Relations." *Millennium: Journal of International Studies* 26, no. 2 (Summer): 249–77.

———. 1997b. "Seizing the Middle Ground: Constructivism in World Politics." *European Journal of International Relations* 3, no. 3 (September): 319–64.

Adler, Emanuel, and Michael Barnett. 1996. "Governing Anarchy: A Research Agenda for the Study of Security Communities." *Ethics and International Affairs* 10: 63–98.

———, eds. 1998a. *Security Communities.* Cambridge: Cambridge University Press.

———. 1998b. "A Framework for the Study of Security Communities." Pp. 29–65 in *Security Communities*, edited by Emanuel Adler and Michael Barnett. Cambridge: Cambridge University Press.

Agrell, W. 1994. *Alliansfri—tills Vidare: Ett Svenskt Säkerhetsdilemma.* Stockholm: Bokförlaget Natur och Kultur.

Arad, Ruth, Seev Hirsch, and Alfred Tovias. 1983. *The Economics of Peace-Making: Focus on the Egyptian–Israeli Situation.* London: Macmillan (for the Trade Policy Research Center).

Aulas, Marie Christine. 1983. "The Normalization of Egyptian–Israeli Relations." *Arab Studies Quarterly* 5: 220–36.

Ayalon, Ami, ed. 1995. *Middle East Contemporary Survey.* Vols. 16, 17. Boulder, Colo.: Westview Press.

Ayalon, Ami, and Bruce Maddy-Weitzman, eds. 1996. *Middle East Contemporary Survey.* Vol. 18. Boulder, Colo.: Westview Press.

Ayoob, Mohammed. 1993. "Unravelling the Concept: 'National Security' in the Third World." Pp. 31–55 in *The Many Faces of National Security in the Arab World*, edited by Vahgat Korany, Paul Noble, and Rex Brynen. London: Macmillan.

———. 1995. *The Third World Security Predicament.* Boulder, Colo.: Lynne Rienner.

———. 1997. "Defining Security: A Subaltern Realist Perspective." Pp. 121–46 in *Critical Security Studies*, edited by Keith Krause and Michael C. William. Minneapolis: University of Minnesota Press.

Baier, Annette. 1986. "Trust and Antitrust." *Ethics* 96: 231–60.

Baker, Pauline H. 1996. "Conflict Resolution versus Democratic Governance: Divergent

Paths to Peace?" Pp. 563–71 in *Managing Global Chaos: Sources of and Responses to International Conflict*, edited by Chester A. Crocker and Fen O. Hampson. Washington, D.C.: United States Institute of Peace Press.

Bal, Leendert Jan. 1995. *Decision-Making and Negotiations in the European Union*. Leicester: University of Leicester, Centre for the Study of Diplomacy, Discussion Paper 7.

Barber, Bernard. 1983. *The Logic and Limits of Trust*. New Brunswick, N.J.: Rutgers University Press.

Barletta, Michael. 1997. "The Legitimate Imposition of Transparency: Emergence of an Argentine–Brazilian Nuclear Regime." Paper presented at the International Studies Association Annual Meeting, Toronto, Canada, March 20.

Barnett, Michael. 1992. *Confronting the Costs of War: Military Power, State, and Society in Egypt and Israel*. Princeton, N.J.: Princeton University Press.

———. 1996. "Identity and Alliances in the Middle East." Pp. 400–450 in *The Culture of National Security*, edited by Peter J. Katzenstein. New York: Columbia University Press.

Barnett, Michael, and Emanuel Adler. 1998. "Studying Security Communities in Theory, Comparison, and History." Pp. 413–41 in *Security Communities*, edited by Emanuel Adler and Michael Barnett. Cambridge: Cambridge University Press.

Bar-Siman-Tov, Yaacov. 1983. *Linkage Politics in the Middle East: Syria between Domestic and External Conflict, 1961–1970*. Boulder, Colo.: Westview Press.

———. 1994. *Israel and the Peace Process, 1977–1982*. Albany: State University of New York Press.

———. 1995. "Security Regimes: Mediating between War and Peace in the Arab–Israeli Conflict." Pp. 33–55 in *Regional Security Regimes: Israel and Its Neighbors*, edited by Efraim Inbar. Albany: State University of New York Press.

Bartlett, C. J. 1996. *Peace, War, and the European Powers, 1814–1914*. New York: St. Martin's Press.

Bartov, Omer. 1992. *Hitler's Army: Soldiers, Nazis, and War in the Third Reich*. Oxford: Oxford University Press.

Batt, Judy. 1994. "The Political Transformation of East Central Europe." Pp. 30–47 in *Redefining Europe: New Patterns of Conflict and Cooperation*. London: Pinter.

Bender, Peter. 1996. *Die "Neue Ospolitik" und ihre Folgen: Vom Mauerbau bis zur Vereinigung*. 4th ed. Munich: Deutscher Taschenbuch Verlag.

Bendersky, Joseph W. 1983. *Carl Schmitt: Theorist for the Reich*. Princeton, N.J.: Princeton University Press.

Bengtsson, Rikard. 1996. "Trust and the Middle East." Paper presented at the Workshop on Stable Peace, Hebrew University of Jerusalem, Jerusalem, June 14–16.

———. 1998. "Stable Peace in the Baltic: Prospects and Problems." Paper presented at the Third Pan-European International Relations Conference, Vienna, September 17.

Benson, Michelle, and Jack Kugler. 1998. "Power Parity, Democracy, and the Severity of Internal Violence." *Journal of Conflict Resolution* 42, no. 2 (April): 196–209.

Berenger, Jean. 1997. *A History of the Habsburg Empire, 1700–1918*. New York: Longman.

Binder, Leonard. 1958. "The Middle East as a Subordinate International System." *World Politics* 10, no. 3 (April): 408–29.

Bjereld, Ulf. 1995. "Critic or Mediator? Sweden in World Politics, 1945–90." *Journal of Peace Research* 32, no. 1 (February): 23–36.

Blackbourn, David. 1997. *The Long Nineteenth Century: A History of Germany, 1780–1918*. New York: Oxford University Press.

Bocco, Hector Eduardo. 1989. "La cooperación nuclear Argentina–Brasil: Notas para una educación política." FLACSO—*Serie de Documentos e Informes de Investigación.* No. 82, October.

Boulding, Kenneth E. 1978. *Stable Peace.* Austin: University of Texas Press.

———. 1990. "Peace Theory." Pp. 3–8 in *A Reader in Peace Studies,* edited by Paul Smoker, Ruth Davies, and Barbara Munske. Oxford: Pergamon Press.

———. 1991. "Stable Peace among Nations: A Learning Process." Pp. 108–14 in *Peace, Culture, and Society: Transnational Research and Dialogue,* edited by Elise Boulding, Clovis Brigagao, and Kevin Clements. Boulder, Colo.: Westview Press.

Bowker, Mike, and R. Brown, eds. 1993. *From Cold War to Collapse: Theory and World Politics in the 1980s.* Cambridge: Cambridge University Press.

Brandt, Willy. 1989. *Erinnerungen.* Frankfurt am Main: Propyläen Verlag.

Brecher, Michael. 1963. "International Relations and Asian Studies: The Subordinate State System of Southern Asia." *World Politics* 15, no. 2 (January): 213–35.

Bremer, Stuart A. 1993. "Democracy and Militarized Interstate Conflict, 1816–1965." *International Interactions* 18, no. 3 (February): 231–49.

Bridge, Francis Roy, and Roger Bullen. 1980. *The Great Powers and the European States System.* New York: Longman.

Brigagao, Clovis, and Marcelo F. Valle Fonrouge. 1996. "Argentina y Brasil: Modelo Regional de Confianza Mutua para la Seguridad Nuclear." Pp. 87–101 in *Integración solidaria: America latina en la era de la globalización,* edited by Ana Carrillo G. Caracas.

Briggs, Asa. 1959. *The Age of Improvement.* New York: Longman.

Brown, Michael, Sean M. Lynn-Jones, and Steven E. Miller, eds. 1996. *Debating the Democratic Peace.* Cambridge: MIT Press.

Browning, Christopher. 1992. *The Path to Genocide.* Cambridge: Cambridge University Press.

Bueno de Mesquita, Bruce J., and David Lalman. 1992. *War and Reason.* New Haven, Conn.: Yale University Press.

Bull, Hedley. 1977. *The Anarchical Society: A Study of Order in World Politics.* New York: Columbia University Press.

Bury, John Patrick T. 1949. *France, 1814–1940.* London: Methuen.

Buzan, Barry. 1984. "Peace, Power, and Security: Contending Concepts in the Study of International Relations." *Journal of Peace Research* 21, no. 2 (May): 109–25.

———. 1991. *People, States, and Fear: An Agenda for International Security Studies in the Post–Cold War Era.* Boulder, Colo.: Lynne Rienner.

———. 1999. "The English School as a Research Program: An Overview, and a Proposal for Reconvening." Paper presented at the British International Studies Association Conference, Manchester, England, December.

Buzan, Barry, Charles Jones, and Richard Little. 1993. *The Logic of Anarchy: Neorealism to Structural Realism.* New York: Columbia University Press.

Buzan, Barry, and Richard Little. 1996. "Reconceptualizing Anarchy: Structural Realism Meets World History." *European Journal of International Relations* 2, no. 4 (December): 403–38.

Buzan, Barry, Ole Wæver, and Japp de Wilde. 1998. *Security: A New Framework for Analysis.* Boulder, Colo.: Lynne Rienner.

Caballero-Anthony, Mely. 1998. "Mechanisms of Dispute Settlement: The ASEAN Experience." *Contemporary Southeast Asia* 20, no. 1 (April): 38–66.

Calmfors, Lars, Harry Flam, Janne Haaland Matlary, Magnus Jerneck, Rutger Lindahl,

Christina Nordh Berntsson, Ewa Rabinowicz, and Anders Vredin. 1997. *EMU: A Swedish Perspective*. Boston: Kluwer Academic Publishers.

Carasales, Julio C. 1996. "A Surprising About-Face: Argentina and the NPT." *Security Dialogue* 27, no. 3 (September): 325–35.

CARI (Consejo Argentino de Relaciones Internacionales). 1993. *El rol de las fuerzas armadas en el Mercosur*. Buenos Aires: CARI.

———. 1995. *Las relaciones Argentino-Chilenas: Política económica, exterior, y de defensa*. Buenos Aires: CARI.

Carr, Edward H. 1964. *The Twenty Years' Crisis*. New York: Harper & Row.

Carr, William. 1991. *A History of Germany, 1815–1990*. London: Arnold.

Checkel, Jeffrey T. 1997. "International Norms and Domestic Politics: Bridging the Rationalist–Constructivist Divide." *European Journal of International Relations* 3, no. 4 (December): 473–95.

———. 1998. "The Constructivist Turn in International Relations." *World Politics* 50, no. 2 (January): 324–48.

Child, Jack. 1985. *Geopolitics and Conflict within South America: Quarrels among Neighbors*. New York: Praeger.

Chipman, John. 1993. "Managing the Politics of Parochialism." Pp. 237–63 in *Ethnic Conflict and International Security*, edited by Michael E. Brown. Princeton, N.J.: Princeton University Press.

Chongkittavorn , Kavi. 1999. "ASEAN Splits over East Timor Crisis." *Nikkei Weekly*, October 4, p. 14.

Clark, Ian. 1989. *The Hierarchy of States: Reform and Resistance in the International Order*. Cambridge: Cambridge University Press.

Clinton, William Jefferson. 1999a. "Speech by President Clinton to the American Society of Newspaper Editors, San Francisco, CA, April 15, 1999." As reported in the *Washington Post*, April 16, p. A-23.

———. 1999b. "A Just and Necessary War." *New York Times*, May 23, pp. 4, 17.

Cohen, Raymond. 1994. "Needed: A Disaggregate Approach to the Democratic Peace Theory." *Review of International Studies* 20, no. 3 (July): 324–25.

Coleman, James S. 1990. *Foundations of Social Theory*. Cambridge: Harvard University Press, Belknap Press.

Collins, Alan. 1999. "Mitigating the Security Dilemma the ASEAN Way." *Pacifica Review* 11, no. 2: 95–114.

Copeland, Dale C. 1995. "Economic Interdependence and War: A Theory of Trade Expectations." *International Security* 20, no. 4 (Spring): 5–41.

Craig, Gordon A. 1961. *Europe since 1815*. New York: Holt, Rinehart & Winston.

———. 1978. *Germany: 1866–1945*. New York: Oxford University Press.

Craig, Gordon A., and Alexander L. George. 1990. *Force and Statecraft: Diplomatic Problems of Our Time*. New York: Oxford University Press.

Crawford, Neta C. 1994. "Cooperation among Iroquois Nations." *International Organization* 48, no. 3 (Summer): 345–85.

Cziomer, Erhard. 1997. "Polen auf dem Wege zur EU-Mitgliedschaft." *Zeitschrift für Politikwissenschaft* 7, no. 1: 21–32.

Dahl, Ann-Sofie. 1999. *Svenskarna och NATO*. Stockholm: Timbro.

David, Steven R. 1991. "Explaining Third World Alignments." *World Politics* 43, no. 2 (January): 233–56.

Davies, Norman. 1981. *God's Playground: A History of Poland. Vol. 2: 1795 to the Present.* Oxford: Clarendon Press.

Dawisha, Karen. 1988. *Eastern Europe, Gorbachev, and Reform.* Cambridge: Cambridge University Press.

Deighton, Len. 1979. *Blitzkrieg: From the Rise of Hitler to the Fall of Dunkirk.* London: Book Club Associates.

De Nevers, Renée. 1993. "Democratization and Ethnic Conflict." Pp. 61–78 in *Ethnic Conflict and International Security*, edited by Michael E. Brown. Princeton, N.J.: Princeton University Press.

Dessouki, Ali E. Hillal. 1988. "Egyptian Foreign Policy since Camp David." Pp. 94–110 in *The Middle East: Ten Years after Camp David*, edited by William B. Quandt. Washington, D.C.: Brookings Institution.

Deutsch, Karl W., et al. 1957. *Political Community and the North Atlantic Area: International Organization in the Light of Historical Experience.* Princeton, N.J.: Princeton University Press.

Diamint, Rut. 1998. "Política de seguridad argentina, estabilidad democrática, y regímenes internacionales." Paper presented at the 1998 meeting of the Latin American Studies Association, Chicago, September 14–26.

Diamond, Larry, and Marc F. Plattner, eds. 1994. *Nationalism, Ethnic Conflict, and Democracy.* Baltimore, Md.: Johns Hopkins University Press.

Dixon, William. 1994. "Democracy and the Peaceful Settlement of International Conflict." *American Political Science Review* 88, no. 1 (March): 14–32.

———. 1996. "Third-Party Techniques for Preventing Conflict Escalation and Promoting Peaceful Settlement." *International Organization* 50, no. 4 (Autumn): 653–82.

Doran, Charles F. 1992. "The Globalist–Regionalist Debate." In *Intervention in the 1990s*, edited by R. J. Schrader. Boulder, Colo.: Lynne Rienner.

Dowek, Ephraim. 1998. *In Spite of All Peace* (in Hebrew). Tel Aviv: Yediot Ahronot.

Doyle, Michael W. 1983a. "Kant, Liberal Legacies, and Foreign Affairs, Part 1." *Philosophy and Public Affairs* 12, no. 3 (Fall): 205–35.

———. 1983b. "Kant, Liberal Legacies, and Foreign Affairs, Part 2." *Philosophy and Public Affairs* 12, no. 4 (Winter): 323–53.

———. 1986. "Liberalism and World Politics." *American Political Science Review* 80, no. 4 (December): 1151–69.

———. 1997. *Ways of War and Peace: Realism, Liberalism, Socialism.* New York: Norton.

Droz, Jacques. 1967. *Europe between Revolutions, 1815–1848.* New York: Harper & Row.

Duffield, John. 1998. *World Power Forsaken: Political Culture, International Institutions, and German Security Policy after Unification.* Stanford, Calif.: Stanford University Press.

Dunn, John. 1988. "Trust and Political Agency." In *Trust: Making and Breaking Cooperative Relations*, edited by Diego Gambetta. Oxford: Basil Blackwell.

Eberwein, Wolf-Dieter, and Janusz Reiter. 1999. *Die Deutsch–Polnischen Beziehungen: Eine Interessen- und Wertegemeinschaft? Zur ersten Deutsch–Polnischen Elitestudie.* Berlin: Wissenschaftszentrum Berlin für Sozialforschung.

Elgström, Ole. 1982. *Aktiv Utrikespolitik.* Lund: Studentlitteratur.

———. 1996. "Stable Peace, Images, and Trust: Lessons for the Middle East." Paper presented at the Workshop on Stable Peace, Hebrew University of Jerusalem, Jerusalem, June 14–16.

————. Forthcoming. *Images and Strategies for Autonomy: Explaining Swedish Security Policy Strategies in the Nineteenth Century.* Boston: Kluwer Academic Publishers.

Elgström, Ole, and Magnus Jerneck. 1997. "Activism and Adaptation: Swedish Security Strategies, 1848–85." *Diplomacy and Statecraft* 8, no. 3 (Fall): 210–36.

Elgström, Ole, and Christer Jönsson. 1999. "Negotiations in the European Union: Bargaining or Problem-Solving?" Paper presented at the colloquium "The European Union as a Negotiated Order," Loughborough University.

Elman, Miriam Fendius. 1997a. "Testing the Democratic Peace Theory." Pp. 473–506 in *Paths to Peace: Is Democracy the Answer?* edited by Miriam Fendius Elman. Cambridge: MIT Press.

————, ed. 1997b. *Paths to Peace: Is Democracy the Answer?* Cambridge: MIT Press.

Ember, Carol R., Melvin Ember, and Bruce Russett. 1992. "Peace between Participatory Polities: A Cross-Cultural Test of the 'Democracies Rarely Fight Each Other' Hypothesis." *World Politics* 44, no. 4 (July): 573–99.

Ericson, Magnus. 1996. "A Liberal Peace?" Paper presented at the Workshop on Stable Peace, Hebrew University of Jerusalem, Jerusalem, June 14–16.

————. 1997. "The Liberal Peace Meets History: The Scandinavian Experience." Paper presented at the Annual Meeting of the International Studies Association, Toronto, Canada, March.

————. 1998. Review of *On Liberal Peace: Democracy, War, and the International Order,* by John MacMillan. *Millennium* 27, no. 3 (Winter): 732–34.

————. 2000. "Constructing a Realist Stable Peace: Power, Threat, and the Development of a Shared Norwegian–Swedish Democratic Security Identity, 1905–1940." Ph.D. diss., Department of Political Science, Lund University.

Evans, Eric J. 1996. *The Forging of the Modern State: Early Industrial Britain, 1783–1870.* New York: Longman.

Farber, Henry S., and Joanne Gowa. 1995. "Polities and Peace." *International Security* 20, no. 2 (Fall): 123–46.

Feldmann, Eva, and Sven B. Gareis. 1998. "Polens Rolle in der NATO: Zur Bedeutung externer Hilfen bei der Stabilisierung Osteuropas." *Zeitschrift für Politikwissenschaft* 8, no. 3: 983–1003.

Finnemore, Martha. 1996. *National Interests in International Society.* Ithaca, N.Y.: Cornell University Press.

Franck, Thomas M. 1990. *The Power of Legitimacy among Nations.* Oxford: Oxford University Press.

————. 1995. *Fairness in International Law and Institutions.* Oxford: Clarendon Press.

Freudenstein, Roland. 1998. "Poland, Germany, and the EU." *International Affairs* 74, no. 1 (Summer): 41–54.

Fukuyama, Francis. 1992. *The End of History and the Last Man.* New York: Free Press.

Fulbrook, Mary. 1990. *A Concise History of Germany.* Cambridge: Cambridge University Press.

Furet, François. 1992. *Revolutionary France, 1770–1880.* Oxford: Basil Blackwell.

Gaddis, John Lewis. 1982. *Strategies of Containment: A Critical Appraisal of Postwar American National Security Policy.* New York: Oxford University Press.

————. 1986. "The Long Peace: Elements of Stability in the Postwar International System." *International Security* 11, no. 4 (Spring): 99–142.

————. 1991. "Great Illusions, the Long Peace, and the Future of the International System." Pp. 25–55 in *The Long Postwar Peace*, edited by Charles W. Kegley. New York: HarperCollins.

Gallie, W. B. 1978. *Philosophers of Peace and War*. Cambridge: Cambridge University Press.

Gambetta, Diego. 1988. "Can We Trust Trust?" In *Trust: Making and Breaking Cooperative Relations*, edited by Diego Gambetta. Oxford: Basil Blackwell.

Garretón, Manuel Antonio. 1999. "Hora de construir espacios regionales." *Clarín Digital*, May 31. <www.clarin.com.ar>.

Garton Ash, Timothy. 1994. "Germany's Choice." *Foreign Affairs* 73, no. 4 (July/August): 65–81.

Genscher, Hans-Dietrich. 1995. *Erinnerungen*. Berlin: Siedler Verlag.

George, Alexander L. 1980. "Domestic Constraints on Regime Change in U.S. Foreign Policy: The Need for Policy Legitimacy." Pp. 232–62 in *Change in the International System*, edited by Ole R. Holsti, Randolph M. Siverson, and Alexander L. George. Boulder, Colo.: Westview Press.

———. 1992. "From Conflict to Peace: Stages along the Road." *United States Institute of Peace Journal* 5, no. 6 (December): 7–9.

———. 1998. Preface to *Europe Undivided*, by James Goodby. Washington, D.C.: United States Institute of Peace Press.

George, Alexander L., and Andrew Bennett. 1997. "The Role of Case-Studies in the 'Democratic Peace' Research." Manuscript.

George, Alexander L., Philip Farley, and Alexander Dallin, eds. 1988. *U.S.–Soviet Security Cooperation: Achievements, Failures, Lessons*. New York: Oxford University Press.

Gerges, A. Fawaz. 1995. "Egyptian–Israeli Relations Turn Sour." *Foreign Affairs* 74, no. 3 (May–June): 69–78.

Geyer, Dietrich. 1987. *Russian Imperialism: The Interaction of Domestic and Foreign Policy, 1860–1914*. New Haven, Conn.: Yale University Press.

Gilbert, Felix, Eugene F. Rice, Richard S. Dunn, Leonard Krieger, Charles Breunig, and Norman Rich. 1971. *The Norton History of Modern Europe*. New York: Norton.

Gildea, Robert. 1987. *Barricades and Borders: Europe, 1800–1914*. New York: Oxford University Press.

Gleditsch, Nils P. 1993. "Geography, Democracy, and Peace." Paper presented at the International Studies Association Annual Meeting, Acapulco, Mexico, March.

Glenny, Misha. 1990. *The Rebirth of History: Eastern Europe in the Age of Democracy*. London: Penguin.

Goldemberg, José, and Harold A. Feiveson. 1994. "Denuclearization in Argentina and Brazil." *Arms Control Today* 24, no. 2 (March): 10–14.

Goldgeier, James, and Michael McFaul. 1992. "A Tale of Two Worlds: Core and Periphery in the Post–Cold War Era." *International Organization* 42, no. 2 (Spring): 467–91.

Goldmann, Kjell. 1978. *Det internationella systemet: En teori och dess begränsningar*. Stockholm: Aldus.

———. 1988. *Change and Stability in Foreign Policy*. Princeton, N.J.: Princeton University Press.

———. 1994. *The Logic of Internationalism: Coercion and Accommodation*. London: Routledge.

Goldstein, Judith, and Robert O. Keohane, eds. 1993. *Ideas and Foreign Policy: Beliefs, Institutions, and Political Change*. Ithaca, N.Y.: Cornell University Press.

Gonzalez, Guadalupe, and Stephan Haggard. 1998. "The United States and Mexico: A

Pluralistic Security Community?" Pp. 295–332 in *Security Communities*, edited by Emanuel Adler and Michael Barnett. Cambridge: Cambridge University Press.

Goodby, James. 1998. *Europe Undivided*. Washington, D.C.: United States Institute of Peace Press.

———. 1999a. "A Stable Peace in Europe." *Brookings Review* (Summer).

———. 1999b. "The Role of Nuclear Weapons." A Report by a U.S.–Japan Working Group Co-Chaired by Professor Tomohisa Sakanaka, President, Research Institute for Peace and Security, Tokyo, and James E. Goodby, Atlantic Council, Washington, D.C. (available from the Atlantic Council).

Goodby, James, and Harold Feiveson. 1999. "Preventive Diplomacy through Negotiation." In *Ending the Threat of Nuclear Attack*, edited by William Zartman. Stanford, Calif. : Institute for International Studies, Stanford University.

Gowa, Joanne. 1995. "Democratic States and International Disputes." *International Organization* 49, no. 3 (Summer): 511–22.

Gralnick, Alexander. 1988. "Trust, Deterrence, Realism, and Nuclear Omnicide." *Political Psychology* 9, no. 1 (March): 175–88.

Grenville, J. A. S. 1976. *Europe Reshaped, 1848–1878*. Ithaca, N.Y.: Cornell University Press.

Guglialmelli, Juan E. 1979. *Geopolítica del Cono Sur*. Buenos Aires: El Cid Editor.

Gurr, Ted Robert. 1988. "War, Revolution, and the Growth of the Coercive State." *Comparative Political Studies* 21, no. 1 (April): 45–65.

Gustavsson, Jacob. 1998. *The Politics of Foreign Policy Change*. Lund: Lund University Press.

Hagan, Joe D. 1993. *Political Opposition and Foreign Policy in Comparative Perspective*. Boulder, Colo.: Lynne Rienner.

———. 1999. "Domestic Political Sources of International Stability: Leaders, Oppositions, and the Varieties of Great Power Peace since 1815." Paper presented at the 1999 Comparative Interdisciplinary Studies Section/International Studies Association Conference, Paris, August 9–10.

Hagan, Joe D., Margaret G. Hermann, and Charles F. Hermann, eds. Forthcoming. *Leaders, Groups, and Coalitions: How Decision Units Shape Foreign Policy.*

Hall, Martin. 1999. "Constructing Historical Realism. International Relations as Comparative History." Ph.D. diss., Department of Political Science, Lund University.

Hampton, Mary. 1998. "Poland, Germany, and NATO Enlargement Policy." *German Comments* 49: 85–94.

Harvey, Donald J. 1968. *France since the Revolution*. New York: Free Press.

Hasenclever, Andreas, Peter Mayer, and Voker Rittberger. 1997. *Theories of International Regimes*. Cambridge: Cambridge University Press.

Hegel, G. W. F. [1821] 1991. *Elements of the Philosophy of Right*, edited by Allen Wood, translated by H. B. Nisbet. Reprint, New York: Cambridge University Press.

Hellmann, Günther. 1996. "Goodbye Bismarck? The Foreign Policy of Contemporary Germany." *Mershon International Studies Review* 40, no. 1 (Spring): 1–39.

Henderson, Jeannie. 1999. "Reassessing ASEAN." Adelphi Paper 328. London: International Institute of Strategic Studies.

Herwig, Holger. 1997. *The First World War: Germany and Austria–Hungary, 1914–1918*. London: Arnold.

Hirst, Mónica. 1999. "Mercosur's Complex Political Agenda." Pp. 35–47 in *Mercosur:*

Regional Integration, World Markets, edited by Riordan Roett. Boulder, Colo.: Lynne Rienner.

Hirst, Mónica, and Hector E. Bocco. 1992. "Nuclear Cooperation in the Context of the Programme for Argentine–Brazilian Integration and Cooperation." Pp. 214–29 in *Averting a Latin American Nuclear Arms Race,* edited by Paul Leventhal and Sharon Tanzer. London: Macmillan.

Hoffmann, Stanley. 1980. *Primacy or World Order?* New York: McGraw-Hill.

Holborn, Hajo. 1969. *A History of Modern Germany, 1840–1945.* Princeton, N.J.: Princeton University Press.

Holm, Hans-Henrik, and Georg Sørensen, eds. 1995. *Whose World Order? Uneven Globalization and the End of the Cold War.* Boulder, Colo.: Westview Press.

Holsti, Kalevi J. 1991. *Peace and War: Armed Conflicts and International Order, 1648–1989.* Cambridge: Cambridge University Press.

———. 1996. *The State, War, and the State of War.* Cambridge: Cambridge University Press.

Holsti, Ole R. 1976. "Foreign Policy Decision Makers Viewed Psychologically: 'Cognitive Process' Approaches." In *In Search of Global Patterns,* edited by James N. Rosenau. New York: Free Press.

Holsti, Ole R., and James N. Rosenau. 1984. *American Leadership in World Affairs: Vietnam and the Breakdown of Consensus.* Boston: George Allen & Unwin.

Huldt, Bo. 1997. Introduction to *Baltic Security: Looking towards the Twenty-first Century,* edited by Gunnar Artéus and Atis Lejins. Riga and Stockholm: Latvian Institute of International Affairs and the National Defense College of Sweden.

Huntington, Samuel P. 1991. *The Third Wave: Democratization in the Late Twentieth Century.* Norman: University of Oklahoma Press.

———. 1996a. "Democracy for the Long Haul." *Journal of Democracy* 7, no. 2: 3–13.

———. 1996b. *The Clash of Civilizations and the Remaking of World Order.* New York: Simon & Schuster.

Hurrell, Andrew. 1995a. "Regionalism in Theoretical Perspective." Pp. 37–73 in *Regionalism in World Politics: Regional Organizations and International Order,* edited by Louise Fawcett and Andrew Hurrell. Oxford: Oxford University Press.

———. 1995b. "Regionalism in the Americas." Pp. 250–82 in *Regionalism in World Politics: Regional Organization and International Order,* edited by Louise Fawcett and Andrew Hurrell. Oxford: Oxford University Press.

———. 1998. "An Emerging Security Community in South America?" Pp. 228–64 in *Security Communities,* edited by Emanuel Adler and Michael Barnett. Cambridge: Cambridge University Press.

Hyde-Price, Adrian. 1996. *The International Politics of East Central Europe.* Manchester: Manchester University Press.

Ibrahim, Saad Eddin. 1988. "Domestic Developments in Egypt." Pp. 19–62 in *The Middle East: Ten Years after Camp David,* edited by William B. Quandt. Washington, D.C.: Brookings Institution.

Ikenberry, John G., and Charles A. Kupchan. 1990. "The Legitimation of Hegemonic Power." Pp. 49–70 in *World Leadership and Hegemony,* edited by David Rapkin. Boulder, Colo.: Lynne Rienner.

Jackson, Robert H. 1990. *Quasi-States: Sovereignty, International Relations, and the Third World.* Cambridge: Cambridge University Press.

Jardin, André, and André-Jean Tudesq. 1973. *Restoration and Reaction, 1815–1848.* Cambridge: Cambridge University Press.

Jelavich, Barbara. 1987. *Modern Austria: Empire and Republic, 1815–1986.* Cambridge: Cambridge University Press.

Jepperson, Ronald L., Alexander Wendt, and Peter J. Katzenstein. 1996. "Norms, Identity, and Culture in National Security." Pp. 33–75 in *The Culture of National Security,* edited by Peter J. Katzenstein. New York: Columbia University Press.

Jerneck, Magnus. 1983. *Kritik som Utrikespolitiskt Medel.* Lund: Dialogos.

————. 1990. "Olof Palme: En internationell propagandist." In *Socialdemokratin och svensk utrikespolitik: Från Branting till Palme,* edited by Bo Huldt and Klaus Misgeld. Stockholm: Utrikespolitiska Institutet.

————. 1996. "Stable Peace: A Conceptual Inventory." Paper presented at the Workshop on Stable Peace, Hebrew University of Jerusalem, Jerusalem, June 14–16.

Jerneck, Magnus, and Ole Elgström. 1996. "Stable Peace: The Case of Sweden." Manuscript, Department of Political Science, University of Lund.

Jervis, Robert. 1976. *Perception and Misperception in International Politics.* Princeton, N.J.: Princeton University Press.

————. 1983. "Security Regimes." Pp. 173–94 in *International Regimes,* edited by Stephen Krasner. Ithaca, N.Y.: Cornell University Press.

————. 1986. "From Balance of Power to Concert: A Study of International Security Cooperation." Pp. 58–79 in *Cooperation under Anarchy,* ed. Kenneth Oye. Princeton, N.J.: Princeton University Press.

Job, Brian, ed. 1992. *The Insecurity Dilemma: National Security of Third World States.* Boulder, Colo.: Lynne Rienner.

Joffe, J. 1994. "After Bipolarity: Germany and European Security." In *European Security after the Cold War,* Part 2. Adelphi Paper no. 235. London: Brasseys.

Johnson, Branden B., and Paul Slovic. 1995. "Presenting Uncertainty in Health Risk Assessment: Initial Studies of Its Effects on Risk Perception and Trust." *Risk Analysis* 15, no. 4: 485–94.

Jones, Dorothy V. 1991. *Code of Peace: Ethics and Security in the World of the Warlord States.* Chicago: University of Chicago Press.

Juergensmeyer, Mark. 1993. *The New Cold War? Religious Nationalism Confronts the Secular State.* Berkeley and Los Angeles: University of California Press.

Kacowicz, Arie M. 1994. "Pluralistic Security Communities and 'Negative' Peace in the Third World." Working Paper Series on Regional Security, no. 2. Global Studies Research Program. University of Wisconsin, Madison, June.

————. 1995. "Explaining Zones of Peace: Democracies as Satisfied Powers?" *Journal of Peace Research* 32, no. 3 (August): 265–76.

————. 1997. "Negative International Peace and Domestic Wars: The West African Case, 1957–1996." Paper presented at the Annual Meeting of the International Studies Association, Toronto, Canada, March.

————. 1998. *Zones of Peace in the Third World: South America and West Africa in Comparative Perspective.* Albany: State University of New York Press.

Kagan, Korina. 1997–98. "The Myth of the European Concert: The Realist–Institutionalist Debate and Great Power Behavior in the Eastern Question, 1821–41." *Security Studies* 7, no. 2 (Winter): 1–57.

Kann, Robert A. 1974. *A History of the Habsburg Empire, 1526–1918.* Berkeley and Los Angeles: University of California Press.

Kant, Immanuel. 1991. *Political Writings*. Edited by Hans Reiss. 2d ed. Cambridge: Cambridge University Press.

———. [1797] 1996. *The Metaphysics of Morals*. Edited and translated by Mary Gregor. Reprint, New York: Cambridge University Press.

Kaplan, Morton. 1964. "Intervention in Internal War: Some Systemic Sources." Pp. 92–121 in *International Aspects of Civil Strife*, edited by James N. Rosenau. Princeton, N.J.: Princeton University Press.

Katzenstein, Peter J. 1976. *Disjoined Partners: Austria and Germany since 1815*. Berkeley and Los Angeles: University of California Press.

———. 1996. "Regionalism in Comparative Perspective." *Cooperation and Conflict* 31, no. 2 (June): 123–59.

———, ed. 1997. *Tamed Power: Germany in Europe*. Ithaca, N.Y.: Cornell University Press.

Kegley, Charles W., Jr., ed. 1995. *Controversies in International Relations Theory: Realism and the Neoliberal Challenge*. New York: St. Martin's Press.

Kegley, Charles W., Jr., and Gregory A. Raymond. 1990. *When Trust Breaks Down: Alliance Norms and World Politics*. Columbia: University of South Carolina Press.

Kelstrup, Morten. 1993. "Small States and European Political Integration." In *The Nordic Countries and the EC*, edited by Teija Tilikainen and Ib Damgaard Pedersen. Copenhagen: Copenhagen Political Studies Press.

Keohane, Robert O. 1984. *After Hegemony: Cooperation and Discord in the World Political Economy*. Princeton, N.J.: Princeton University Press.

———. 1986. "Reciprocity in International Relations." *International Organization* 40, no. 1 (Winter): 1–27.

Keohane, Robert O., and Joseph Nye, eds. 1972. *Transnational Relations and World Politics*. Cambridge: Harvard University Press.

———. 1977. *Power and Interdependence: World Politics in Transition*. Boston: Little, Brown.

Khong, Yuen Foong. 1997. "ASEAN and the Southeast Asian Security Complex." Pp. 318–39 in *Regional Orders: Building Security in a New World*, edited by David A. Lake and Patrick M. Morgan. University Park: Pennsylvania State University Press.

Khrushchev, Nikita. 1970. *Khrushchev Remembers*. Boston: Little, Brown.

Kiser, Edgar, Kriss Drass, and William Brustein. 1995. "Ruler Autonomy and War in Early Modern Western Europe." *International Studies Quarterly* 39, no. 1 (Spring): 109–38.

Kissinger, Henry. 1964. *A World Restored*. New York: Universal Library.

———. 1979. *White House Years*. Boston: Little, Brown.

Klaar, Toivo. 1997. "Estonia's Security Policy Priorities." In *Baltic Security: Looking Towards the Twenty-first Century*, edited by Gunnar Artéus and Atis Lejins. Riga and Stockholm: Latvian Institute of International Affairs and the National Defense College of Sweden.

Klein, Robert A. 1974. *Sovereign Equality among States: The History of an Idea*. Toronto: University of Toronto Press.

Knudsen, Olav F. 1999. "Security on the Great Power Fringe: Dilemmas Old and New." Pp. 3–19 in *Stability and Security in the Baltic Sea Region*, edited by Olev F. Knudsen. London: Frank Cass.

Koch, H. W. 1978. *A History of Prussia*. New York: Longman.

Kohler-Koch, Beate. 1996. "Catching Up with Change: The Transformation of Governance in the EU." *Journal of European Public Policy* 3, no. 3: 359–80.

Kowert, Paul, and Jeffrey Legro. 1996. "Norms, Identity, and Their Limits." Pp. 451–97 in *The Culture of National Security*, edited by Peter J. Katzenstein. New York: Columbia University Press.

Krasner, Stephen D. 1978. *Defending the National Interest: Raw Materials Investments and U.S. Foreign Policy*. Princeton, N.J.: Princeton University Press.

Krochow, Christian Graf von. 1997. *Von Deutschen Mythen*. Munich: Deutscher Taschenbuch Verlag.

Kull, Steven. 1998. *Seeking a New Balance*. Program on International Policy Attitudes, School of Public Affairs, University of Maryland, College Park, June.

Kull, Steven, and I. M. Destler. 1999. *Misreading the Public*. Washington, D.C.: Brookings Institution.

Kupchan, Charles A. 1994. *The Vulnerability of Empire*. Ithaca, N.Y.: Cornell University Press.

Kupchan, Charles A., and Clifford Kupchan. 1991. "Concerts, Collective Security, and the Future of Europe." *International Security* 16, no. 1 (Summer): 114–61.

Lake, David A. 1997. "Regional Security Complexes: A Systems Approach." Pp. 45–67 in *Regional Orders: Building Security in a New World*, edited by David A. Lake and Patrick M. Morgan. University Park: Pennsylvania State University Press.

———. 1999. *Entangling Relations: American Foreign Policy in Its Century*. Princeton, N.J.: Princeton University Press.

Lake, David A., and Robert Powell. 1999. "International Relations: A Strategic Choice Approach." Pp. 3–38 in *Strategic Choice and International Relations*, edited by David A. Lake and Robert Powell. Princeton, N.J.: Princeton University Press.

Larson, Deborah Welch. 1997. *Anatomy of Mistrust: U.S.–Soviet Relations during the Cold War*. Ithaca, N.Y.: Cornell University Press.

Latham, Robert. 1997. *The Liberal Moment: Modernity, Security, and the Making of Postwar International Order*. New York: Columbia University Press.

Layne, Christopher. 1993. "The Unipolar Illusion: Why New Great Powers Will Rise." *International Security* 17, no. 4 (Spring): 5–51.

———. 1994. "Kant or Cant: The Myth of the Democratic Peace." *International Security* 19, no. 2 (Fall): 5–49.

Lebow, Richard Ned. 1981. *Between Peace and War: The Nature of International Crisis*. Baltimore, Md.: Johns Hopkins University Press.

Lee, Stephen J. 1997. *Aspects of British Political History, 1815–1914*. London: Routledge.

Leebaert, Derek, and Timothy Dickinson. 1992. *Soviet Strategy and New Military Thinking*. Cambridge: Cambridge University Press.

Leffler, Melvin P. 1992. *A Preponderance of Power: National Security, the Truman Administration, and the Cold War*. Stanford, Calif.: Stanford University Press.

Leifer, Michael. 1996. "The ASEAN Regional Forum: Extending ASEAN's Model of Regional Security." Adelphi Paper 302. London: International Institute of Strategic Studies.

Lejins, Atis, and Zaneta Ozolina. 1997. "Latvia: The Middle Baltic State." In *Baltic Security: Looking towards the Twenty-first Century*, edited by Gunnar Artéus and Atis Lejins. Riga and Stockholm: Latvian Institute of International Affairs and the National Defense College of Sweden.

Lesch, Ann Mosely. 1986. "Egyptian–Israeli Relations: Normalization or Special Ties?" UFSI Reports 35.

Leventhal, Paul, and Sharon Tanzer. 1992. Introduction to *Averting a Latin American Nuclear Arms Race*, edited by Paul Leventhal and Sharon Tanzer. London: Macmillan.

Levy, Jack S. 1983. "Misperception and the Causes of War: Theoretical Linkages and Analytical Problems." *World Politics* 36, no. 1 (October): 76–99.

———. 1988. "Domestic Politics and War." Pp. 79–99 in *The Origin and Prevention of Major Wars*, edited by Robert I. Rothberg and Theodore K. Rabb. New York: Cambridge University Press.

———. 1989. "The Diversionary Theory of War: A Critique." Pp. 259–88 in *Handbook of War Studies*, edited by Manus I. Midlarsky. Boston: Unwin Hyman.

———. 1991. "Long Cycles, Hegemonic Transitions, and the Long Peace." Pp. 147–76 in *The Long Postwar Peace*, edited by Charles W. Kegley Jr. New York: HarperCollins.

———. 1994. "The Theoretical Foundations of Paul W. Schroeder's International System." *International History Review* 16, no. 4 (November): 661–80.

Lichtenstein, Heiner. 1998. "Warnsignal aus Warschau." *Blätter für Deutsche und Internationale Politik* 2: 907–10.

Lincoln, W. Bruce. 1978. *Nicholas I: Emperor and Autocrat of All the Russias*. DeKalb: Northern Illinois University Press.

Lindgren, Raymond E. 1959. *Norway–Sweden: Union, Disunion, and Scandinavian Integration*. Princeton, N.J.: Princeton University Press.

Linz, Juan, and Alfred Stepan. 1996. "Toward Consolidated Democracies." *Journal of Democracy* 7, no. 2: 14–33.

Lödén, Hans. 1999. *"För säerhets skull": Ideologi och säkerhet i svensk aktiv utrikespolitik*. Stockholm: Nerenius and Santérus Förlag.

Luhmann, Niklas. 1988. "Familiarity, Confidence, Trust: Problems and Alternatives." In *Trust: Making and Breaking Cooperative Relations*, edited by Diego Gambetta. Oxford: Basil Blackwell.

Macartney, C. A. 1968. *The Habsburg Empire, 1790–1918*. New York: Macmillan.

MacMillan, John. 1998. *On Liberal Peace: Democracy, War, and the International Order*. London: I. B. Tauris.

Maddy-Weitzman, Bruce, ed. 1997. *Middle East Contemporary Survey*. Vol. 19. Boulder, Colo.: Westview Press.

———. 1998. *Middle East Contemporary Survey*. Vol. 20. Boulder, Colo.: Westview Press.

Magraw, Roger. 1986. *France, 1815–1914*. New York: Oxford University Press.

Malnes, Raino. 1995. "'Leader' and 'Entrepeneur' in International Negotiations: A Conceptual Analysis." *European Journal of International Relations* 1, no. 1 (March): 87–112.

Mandel, Robert. 1994. *The Changing Face of National Security: A Conceptual Analysis*. Westport, Conn.: Greenwood Press.

Mann, Michael. 2000. "The Downside of Democracy: The Modern Tradition of Ethnic and Political Cleansing." In *Democracy, Liberalism, and War: Rethinking the Foundations of the Democratic Peace Debate*, edited by Tarak Barkawi and Mark Laffey. Boulder, Colo.: Lynne Rienner.

Mansfield, Edward D., and Jack Snyder. 1996. "Democratization and the Danger of War." Pp. 301–36 in *Debating the Democratic Peace*, edited by Michael Brown et al. Cambridge: MIT Press.

Maoz, Zeev. 1997. "The Controversy over the Democratic Peace: Rearguard Action or Cracks in the Wall?" *International Security* 22, no. 1 (Summer): 162–98.

Maoz, Zeev, and Bruce Russett. 1992. "Alliance, Contiguity, Wealth, and Political Stability: Is the Lack of Conflict among Democracies a Statistical Artifact?" *International Interactions* 17, no. 3: 245–68.

Markovits, Andrei, and Simon Reich. 1991. "Should Europe Fear the Germans?" *German Politics and Society* 23 (Summer): 1–20.

Markovits, Andrei, Simon Reich, and Frank Westermann. 1996. "Germany: Hegemonic Power and Economic Giant?" *Review of International Political Economy* 3, no. 4 (Winter): 698–727.

Marzo, Marco A., Alfredo L. Biaggio, and Ana C. Raffo. 1994. "Nuclear Cooperation in South America: The Brazilian–Argentine Common System of Safeguards." *IAEA Bulletin* 36, no. 3: 30–35.

al-Mashat, Abdul Monem. 1983. "Egyptian Attitudes toward the Peace Process: An Alert Elite." *Middle East Journal* 37, no. 3 (Summer): 394–411.

Massie, Robert K. 1991. *Dreadnought: Britain, Germany, and the Coming of the Great War.* New York: Random House.

Maull, Hanns. 1993. "Civilian Power: The Concept and Its Relevance for Security Studies." Pp. 115–31 in *Mapping the Unknown: Towards a New World Order,* edited by Lidija Babic and Bo Huldt. Stockholm: Swedish Institute of International Affairs.

May, Arthur J. 1951. *The Habsburg Monarchy, 1867–1914.* Cambridge: Harvard University Press.

McCord, Norman. 1991. *British History, 1815–1906.* New York: Oxford University Press.

Mead, George Herbert. 1982. *The Individual and the Social Self: Unpublished Work of George Herbert Mead,* edited by David L. Miller. Chicago: University of Chicago Press.

Mearsheimer, John J. 1990. "Back to the Future: Instability in Europe after the Cold War." *International Security* 15, no. 1 (Summer): 5–56.

———. 1994/1995. "The False Promise of International Institutions." *International Security* 19, no. 3 (Winter): 5–49.

Melko, Matthew. 1973. *Fifty-two Peaceful Societies.* Toronto: Canadian Peace Research Institute Press.

Mercer, Jonathan. 1995. "Anarchy and Identity." *International Organization* 49, no. 2 (Spring): 229–52.

———. 1996. *Reputation and International Politics.* Ithaca, N.Y.: Cornell University Press.

Migdal, Joel S. 1988. *Strong Societies and Weak States: State–Society Relations and State Capabilities in the Third World.* Princeton, N.J.: Princeton University Press.

Miller, Benjamin. 1992. "A New 'World Order': From Balancing to Hegemony, Concert or Collective Security?" *International Interactions* 18, no. 1: 1–33.

———. 1994. "Explaining the Emergence of Great Power Concerts." *Review of International Studies* 20, no. 4 (October): 327–48.

———. 1995. *When Opponents Cooperate: Great Power Conflicts and Collaboration in World Politics.* Ann Arbor: University of Michigan Press.

———. 1996. "Competing Realist Perspectives on Great Power Crisis Behavior." *Security Studies* 5, no. 3 (Spring): 309–57.

———. 1997. "Blowing Hot and Cold: Explaining Regional War and Peace." Paper presented at the Annual Meeting of the International Studies Association, Toronto, Canada, March.

———. 1998. "How to Advance Regional Peace? Competing Strategies for Peacemaking." Paper presented at the Third Pan-European International Relations Conference, Vienna, September 17.

———. 1999a. "Explaining Regional War-Propensity: The Middle East in a Comparative Perspective." Paper presented at the Annual Meeting of the International Studies Association, Washington, D.C., February.

———. 1999b. "The Sources of Regional War and Peace: Integrating the Effects of Nationalism, Liberalism, and the International System." Paper presented at the Annual Meeting of the American Political Science Association, Atlanta, Georgia, September.

———. 1999c. "Between War and Peace: Systemic Effects on the Transition of the Middle East and the Balkans from the Cold War to the Post–Cold War Era." Paper presented at the Annual Meeting of the American Political Science Association, Atlanta, Ga., September.

———. 1999d. "The Global Sources of Regional Transitions from War to Peace: The Case of the Middle East." Davis Occasional Papers, Hebrew University of Jerusalem, Leonard Davis Institute for International Relations.

———. Forthcoming. "Hot War, Cold Peace: International–Regional Synthesis." In *War in a Changing World*, edited by Zeev Maoz and Azar Gat. Ann Arbor: University of Michigan Press.

Miller, Benjamin, and Korina Kagan. 1997. "The Great Powers and Regional Conflicts: Eastern Europe and the Balkans from the Post-Napoleonic Era to the Post–Cold War Era." *International Studies Quarterly* 41, no. 1 (March): 51–85.

Milner, Helen. 1993. "The Assumption of Anarchy in International Relations Theory: A Critique." Pp. 143–69 in *Neorealism and Neoliberalism: The Contemporary Debate*, edited by David A. Baldwin. New York: Columbia University Press.

Misztal, Barbara A. 1996. *Trust in Modern Societies: The Search for the Bases of Social Order.* Cambridge, England: Polity Press.

Modelski, George. 1990. "Is World Politics Evolutionary Learning?" *International Organization* 44, no. 1 (Winter): 1–24.

Möller, Yngve. 1990. "Östen undéns utrikespolitik." In *Socialdemokratin och svensk utrikespolitik. Från Branting till Palme*, edited by Bo Huldt and Klaus Misgeld. Stockholm: Utrikespolitiska Institutet.

Monnet, Jean. 1955. *Les Etats Unis d'Europe ont commencé.* Paris: Robert Laffont.

Morris, Michael A. 1989. *The Strait of Magellan.* Dordrecht: Martinus Nijhoff.

Morrow, James D. 1997. "A Rational Choice Approach to International Conflict." In *Decisionmaking on War and Peace: The Cognitive–Rational Debate*, edited by Nehemia Geva and Alex Mintz. Boulder, Colo.: Lynne Rienner.

Möttölä, Kari. 1998. "Security around the Baltic Rim: Concepts, Actors, and Processes." Pp. 363–404 in *The NEBI Yearbook 1998: North European and Baltic Sea Integration*, edited by Lars Hedegaard and Bjarne Lindström. Berlin: Springer Verlag.

Mouritzen, Hans. 1988. *Finlandization: Towards a General Theory of Adaptive Politics.* Aldershot, England: Avebury.

———. 1993. "The Two Musterknaben and the Naughty Boy: Sweden, Finland, and Denmark in the Process of European Integration." *Cooperation and Conflict* 28, no. 4 (Winter): 373–402.

———. 1994. "Testing Weak-Power Theory. Three Nordic Reactions to the Soviet

Coup." In *European Foreign Policy. The EC and Changing Perspectives in Europe*, edited by Walter Carlsnaes and Steve Smith. London: Sage.

———. 1996. "Polarity and Constellations." In *European Integration and National Adaptations*, edited by Hans Mouritzen, Ole Wæver, and Håkan Wiberg. Commack, N.Y.: Nova Science.

Mueller, John. 1989. *Retreat from Doomsday*. New York: Basic Books.

Munõz, Heraldo. 1986. *Las relaciones exteriores del gobierno militar chileno*. Santiago de Chile: Editorial Ormitorronco.

Narine, Shaun. 1998. "ASEAN and the Management of Regional Security." *Pacific Affairs* 71, no. 2 (Summer): 195–214.

Nastase, Mr. 1992. "A New Security Order in Europe." In *Symposium of the Assembly of the Western European Union*, Berlin, 31 March–2 April 1992, official record. Paris: Assembly of the WEU.

Neumann, Iver B. 1994. "A Region-Building Approach to Northern Europe." *Review of International Studies* 20, no. 1 (January): 53–74.

———. 1996. "Self and Other in International Relations." *European Journal of International Relations* 2, no. 2 (June): 139–74.

Nilsson, Ann-Sofie. 1991. *Den moraliska stormakten*. Stockholm: Timbro.

Nordquist, Kjell-Åke. 1992. "Peace after War: On Conditions for Durable Boundary Agreements." Doctoral diss., Department for Peace and Conflict Research, Uppsala University.

———. 1998. "Issues and Stable Agreements as Conditions for Stable Peace." Paper presented at the Third Pan-European International Relations Conference, Vienna, September 17.

Noreen, Erik. 1983. "The Nordic Balance: A Security Policy Concept in Theory and Practice." *Cooperation and Conflict* 18, no. 1 (Spring): 43–56.

Norman, Torbjörn. 1990. "Hjalmar Branting, nationernas förbund och naturrätten." In *Socialdemokratin och svensk utrikespolitik:. Från Branting till Palme*, edited by Bo Huldt and Klaus Misgeld. Stockholm: Utrikespolitiska Institutet.

Nye, Joseph. 1990. *Bound to Lead: The Changing Nature of American Power*. New York: Basic Books.

Oelsner, Andrea. 1998. "Argentine–Brazilian Rapprochment: A New Pluralistic Security Community." MScs thesis, London School of Economics.

———. 1999. "Security in the Southern Cone of South America." Ph.D. proposal (draft), London School of Economics.

Olmos, Mario Eduardo. 1986. *La cooperación Argentina–Brasil: Nucleo impulsor de la integración latinoamericana*. Buenos Aires: Instituto de Publicaciones Navales.

Osgood, Charles E. 1962. *An Alternative to War or Surrender*. Urbana: University of Illinois Press.

Owen, John M., IV. 1994. "How Liberalism Produces Democratic Peace." *International Security* 19, no. 2 (Fall): 87–125.

———. 1997. *Liberal Peace, Liberal War: American Politics and International Security*. Ithaca, N.Y.: Cornell University Press.

———. 1998/99. "The Canon and the Cannon: A Review Essay." *International Security* 23, no. 3 (Winter): 147–78.

———. 1999. "If Regime Type Doesn't Matter, Why Do States Export Regimes?" Paper presented at the Annual Meeting of the International Studies Association, Washington, D.C., February.

Oye, Kenneth, ed. 1986. *Cooperation under Anarchy.* Princeton, N.J.: Princeton University Press.

Palomar, Jorge. 1996. "Chile: Una invasión pacifica." *La Nación OnLine,* 13 October. <www.lanacion.com.ar>

Pande, Savita. 1993. "Argentina–Brazil Nuclear Accord: Competition to Cooperation." *Strategic Analysis* 16, no. 4 (July): 425–37.

Paterson, William E. 1998. "Helmut Kohl, 'The Vision Thing,' and Escaping the Semi-Sovereign Trap." Pp. 64–85. In *The Kohl Chancellorship,* edited by Clay Clemens and Willie Paterson. London: Frank Cass.

Penã, Felix. 1995. "New Approaches to Economic Integration in the Southern Cone." *Washington Quarterly* 18, no 3 (Summer): 113–22.

Peres, Shimon. 1993. *The New Middle East.* New York: Holt.

Pervin, David J. 1997. "Building Order in Arab–Israeli Relations: From Balance to Concert?" Pp. 271–95 in *Regional Orders: Building Security in a New World,* edited by David A. Lake and Patrick M. Morgan. University Park: Pennsylvania State University Press.

Petersen, Nikolaj. 1989. "Mod en general teori om adaptiv politik." *Politica* 21, no. 2 (Spring).

Posen, Barry. 1993. "The Security Dilemma and Ethnic Conflict." *Survival* 35, no. 1 (Spring): 27–47.

Pravda, Alex. 1992. *The End of the Outer Empire: Soviet–East European Relations in Transition.* London: Sage.

Price, Richard. 1998. "Reversing the Gun Sights: Transnational Civil Society Targets Land Mines." *International Organization* 52, no. 3 (Summer): 613–44.

Price, Roger. 1993. *A Concise History of France.* Cambridge: Cambridge University Press.

Puchala, Donald. 1970. "Integration and Disintegration in Franco–German Relations, 1954–65." *International Organization* 24, no. 2 (Spring): 183–208.

Quandt, B. William. 1986. *Camp David: Peace Making and Politics.* Washington, D.C.: Brookings Institution.

Rabinovich, Itamar, and Haim Shaked, eds. 1988. *Middle East Contemporary Survey.* Vol. 10. Boulder, Colo.: Westview Press.

———. 1989. *Middle East Contemporary Survey.* Vol. 11. Boulder, Colo.: Westview Press.

Rachwald, Arthur. 1993. "Poland and Germany: From Foes to Friends?" Pp. 231–50 in *The Germans and Their Neighbors,* edited by Dirk Verheyen and Christian Soe. Boulder, Colo.: Westview Press.

Ramm, Agatha. 1967. *Germany, 1789–1919: A Political History.* London: Methuen.

Rasmussen, J. Lewis. 1997. "Peacemaking in the Twenty-first Century: New Rules, New Roles, New Actors." In *Peacemaking in International Conflict: Methods and Techniques,* edited by I. William Zartman and J. L. Rasmussen. Washington, D.C.: United States Institute of Peace Press.

Ray, James Lee. 1995. *Democracy and International Conflict: An Evolution of the Democratic Peace Proposition.* Columbia: University of South Carolina Press.

Reagan, Ronald. 1985. "Address before the Assembly of the Republic of Portugal in Lisbon, May 9, 1985." *Public Papers of the Presidents.* Washington, D.C.

Redick, John R. 1995. "Iniciativas de no proliferación nuclear de Argentina y Brasil." *Revista Occidental* 12, no. 3: 341–59.

Redick, John R., Julio C. Carasales, and Paulo S. Wiebel. 1995. "Nuclear Rapprochement: Argentina, Brazil, and the Nonproliferation Regime." *Washington Quarterly* 18, no. 1 (Winter): 107–23.

Rengger, Nicholas. 1997. "The Ethics of Trust in World Politics." *International Affairs* 73, no. 3 (Winter): 469–87.

Resende-Santos, João. 1998. "From Enduring Rivalry to Cooperation in South America." Paper presented at the Annual Meeting of the Latin American Studies Association, Chicago, September 24–26.

Riasanovkty, Nicholas V. 1984. *A History of Russia.* New York: Oxford University Press.

Risse-Kappen, Thomas. 1994. "The Long-Term Future of European Security: Perpetual Anarchy or Community of Democracies?" In *European Foreign Policy, the EC, and Changing Perspectives in Europe,* edited by Walter Carlsnaes and Steve Smith. London: Sage.

————. 1995a. "Democratic Peace—Warlike Democracies? A Social Constructivist Interpretation of the Liberal Argument." *European Journal of International Relations* 1, no. 4 (December): 491–517.

————. 1995b. *Cooperation among Democracies.* Princeton, N.J.: Princeton University Press.

————. 1996. "Collective Identity in a Democratic Community: The Case of NATO." Pp. 357–99. In *The Culture of National Security,* edited by Peter J. Katzenstein. New York: Columbia University Press.

Rock, Stephen. 1989. *Why Peace Breaks Out.* Chapel Hill: University of North Carolina Press.

————. 2000. *Appeasement in International Politics.* Lexington: University Press of Kentucky.

Roe, Paul. 1999. "The Intrastate Security Dilemma: Ethnic Conflict as a 'Tragedy.'" *Journal of Peace Research* 36, no. 2 (May): 183–202.

Rogger, Hans. 1983. *Russia in the Age of Modernization and Revolution, 1881–1917.* New York: Longman.

Romero, Luis Alberto. 1999. "Repensar nuestro pobre nacionalismo." *Clarín Digital,* May 31. <www.clarin.com.ar>

Rosecrance, Richard. 1986. *The Rise of the Trading State: Commerce and Conquest in the Modern World.* New York: Basic Books.

Rosenau, James N. 1969. *Linkage Politics: Essays on the Convergence of National and International Systems.* New York: Free Press.

Rothstein, Robert L. 1992. "Weak Democracy and the Prospect for Peace and Prosperity in the Third World." Pp. 15–50 in *Resolving Third World Conflicts: Challenges for a New Era.* Washington, D.C.: United States Institute of Peace.

————. ed. 1999. *After the Peace: Resistance and Reconciliation.* Boulder, Colo.: Lynne Rienner.

Rousseau, Jean-Jacques. 1991. "The State of War." In *Rousseau on International Relations,* edited by Stanley Hoffmann and David P. Fidler. Oxford: Clarendon Press.

Rummel, R. J. 1983. "Libertarianism and Interstate Violence." *Journal of Conflict Resolution* 27, no.1 (March): 27–71.

Russett, Bruce M. 1963. *Community and Contention: Britain and America in the Twentieth Century.* Westport, Conn.: Greenwood Press.

————. 1967. *International Regions and the International System.* Chicago: Rand McNally.

————. 1993. *Grasping the Democratic Peace: Principles for a Post–Cold War World*. Princeton, N.J.: Princeton University Press.

Russett, Bruce M., Christopher Layne, David A. Spiro, and Michael Doyle. 1995. "Corresponding : The Democratic Peace." *International Security* 19, no. 4 (Spring): 164–84.

Russett, Bruce M., and Harvey Starr. 1992. *World Politics: The Menu for Choice*. 4th ed. New York: W. H. Freeman.

Saudargas, Algirdas. 1998. "Baltic Security Is European Security." *NATO Review*, no. 4 (Winter): 5–7.

Saunders, David. 1992. *Russia in the Age of Reaction and Reform, 1801–1881*. New York: Longman.

Schmitt, Carl. [1932] 1996. *The Concept of the Political*, translated by George Schwab. Chicago: University of Chicago Press.

Schroeder, Paul W. 1994a. "The Nineteenth Century System: Balance of Power or Political Equilibrium." *Review of International Studies* 15, no.1 (January): 135–53.

————. 1994b. "Historical Reality vs. Neo-realist Theory." *International Security* 19, no. 1 (Summer): 108–48.

Schweller, Randall. 1992. "Domestic Structure and Preventive War: Are Democracies More Pacific?" *World Politics* 44, no. 2 (January): 235–69.

————. 1994. "Bandwagoning for Profit: Bringing the Revisionist State Back In." *International Security* 19, no. 1 (Summer): 72–107.

Segre, Magdalena. 1990. "La cuestión Itaipú–Corpus: El punto de inflexión en las relaciones argentino-brasileñas." *FLACSO—Serie Documentos e Informes de Investigación*, no. 97 (September): 1–39.

Selcher, Wayne. 1985. "Recent Strategic Developments in South America's Southern Cone." Pp. 87–120 in *Latin American Nations in World Politics*, edited by Heraldo Muñoz and Joseph S. Tulchin. Boulder, Colo.: Westview Press.

Senghaas, Dieter, ed. 1995. *Den frieden Denken*. Frankfurt am Main: Suhrkamp Verlag.

————, ed. 1997. *Frieden machen*. Frankfurt am Main: Suhrkamp Verlag.

Sergounin, Alexander A. 1998. "Russia's Security Policies in the Baltic Sea Area." In *The NEBI Yearbook 1998: North European and Baltic Sea Integration*, edited by Lars Hedegaard and Bjarne Lindström. Berlin: Springer Verlag.

Seton-Watson, Hugh. 1967. *The Russian Empire, 1801–1917*. New York: Oxford University Press, 1967.

Shaked, Haim, and Daniel Dishon, eds. 1986. *Middle East Contemporary Survey*. Boulder, Colo.: Westview Press.

Shamir, Shimon. 1988. "Israel's Views of Egypt and the Peace Process: The Duality of Vision." Pp. 187–216 in *The Middle East: Ten Years after Camp David*, edited by William B. Quandt. Washington, D.C.: Brookings Institution.

————. 1992. "From Conflict to Peace: Stages along the Road." *United States Institute of Peace Journal* 5, no. 6 (December): 7–9.

Sheehan, James J. 1989. *German History, 1770–1866*. New York: Oxford University Press.

Shore, Sean M. 1998. "No Fences Make Good Neighbors: The Development of the U.S.–Canadian Security Community, 1871–1940." Pp. 333–67 in *Security Communities*, edited by Emanuel Adler and Michael Barnett. Cambridge: Cambridge University Press.

Singer, Max, and Aaron Wildavsky. 1993. *The Real World Order: Zones of Peace and Zones of Turmoil*. Chatham, N.J.: Chatham House, 1993.

Sked, Alan. 1989. *The Decline and Fall of the Habsburg Empire, 1815–1918.* New York: Longman.

Skidmore, David. 1997. *Contested Social Orders and International Politics.* Nashville, Tenn.: Vanderbilt University Press.

Snyder, Glenn H., and Paul Diesing. 1977. *Conflict among Nations: Bargaining, Decision Making, and System Structure in International Crises.* Princeton, N.J.: Princeton University Press.

Snyder, Jack. 1991. *Myths of Empire: Domestic Politics and International Ambition.* Ithaca, N.Y.: Cornell University Press.

Snyder, Jack, and Robert Jervis. 1999. "Civil War and the Security Dilemma." Pp. 15–37 in *Civil Wars, Insecurity, and Intervention,* edited by Barbara F. Walter and Jack Snyder. New York: Columbia University Press.

Solingen, Etel. 1998. *Regional Orders at Century's Dawn: Global and Domestic Influences on Grand Strategy.* Princeton, N.J.: Princeton University Press.

Speck, W. A. 1993. *A Concise History of Britain, 1707–1975.* Cambridge: Cambridge University Press.

Sperling, James, and Emil Kirchner. 1997. *Recasting the European Order: Security Architecture and Economic Cooperation.* Manchester: Manchester University Press.

Stanley, Ruth. 1992. "Co-operation and Control: The New Approach to Nuclear Non-Proliferation in Argentina and Brazil." *Arms Control* 13, no. 2 (September): 191–213.

Starr, Harvey. 1991. "Democratic Dominoes: Diffusion Approaches to the Spread of Democracy in the International System." *Journal of Conflict Resolution* 35, no. 2 (June): 356–81.

Stefanowicz, Janusz. 1995. "Central Europe between Germany and Russia: A View from Poland." *Security Dialogue* 26, no. 1 (March): 55–64.

Stein, Janice G. 1991. "Deterrence and Reassurance." Pp.8–72 in *Behavior, Society, and Nuclear War,* vol. 2, edited by Philip E. Tetlock, Jo L. Husbands, Robert Jervis, Paul C. Stern, and Charles Tilly. New York: Oxford University Press.

———. 1994. "Political Learning by Doing: Gorbachev as Uncommitted Thinker and Motivated Learner." *International Organization* 48, no. 2 (Spring): 155–83.

Stein, W. Kenneth. 1997. "Continuity and Change in Egyptian–Israeli Relations, 1973–97." Pp. 296–320 in *From Rabin to Netanyahu,* edited by Efraim Krash. London: Frank Cass.

Stenelo, Lars-Göran. 1972. *Mediation in International Negotiation.* Lund: Studentlitteratur.

Stent, Angela. 1999. *Russia and Germany Reborn: Unification, the Soviet Collapse, and the New Europe.* Princeton, N.J.: Princeton University Press.

Strömvik, Maria. 1999. "Sverige och EU:s utrikes- och säkerhetspolitik: Ett intensivt men hemligt förhållande?" In *Sverige I EU,* edited by Karl Magnus Johansson. Stockholm: SNS Förlag.

Sundelius, Bengt. 1995. "Sverige bortom småstatsbindningen: Litet men smart i ett internationaliserat Europa." In *Utvidgning och Samspel, SOU.*

Sydnor, Charles. 1977. *Soldiers of Destruction: The SS Death's Head Division, 1933–1945.* Princeton, N.J.: Princeton University Press.

Taylor, Charles. 1975. *Hegel.* New York: Cambridge University Press.

Thompson, William R. 1996. "Democracy and Peace." *International Organization* 50, no. 1 (Winter): 141–74.

Thomson, David. 1950. *England in the Nineteenth Century, 1815–1914*. Baltimore, Md.: Penguin.

Tombs, Robert. 1996. *France, 1814–1914*. New York: Longman.

Vasquez, John. 1993. *The War Puzzle*. Cambridge: Cambridge University Press.

———. 1999. *The Power of Power Politics: From Classical Realism to Neotraditionalism*. Cambridge: Cambridge University Press.

Väyrynen, Raimo. 1984. "Regional Conflict Formations: An Intractable Problem of International Relations?" *Journal of Peace Research* 21, no. 4 (November): 337–59.

———. 1986. "East–West Rivalry and Regional Conflicts in the Third World." Pp. 85–120 in *Fragmentation and Integration: Aspects of International System Change*, edited by Harto Hakovirta. Helsinki: Finnish Political Science Association.

———. 1988. "Domestic Stability, State Terrorism, and Regional Integration in the ASEAN and the GCC." Pp. 167–202 in *Terrible beyond Endurance? The Foreign Policy of State Terrorism*, edited by Michael Stohl and George A. Lopez. New York: Greenwood.

———. 1998. "Towards a Pluralistic Security Community in the Baltic Sea Region?" Pp. 149–74 in *And Now What? International Politics after the Cold War: Essays in Honor of Nikolaj Ptersen*, edited by Georg Sörensen and Hans-Henrik Holm. Aarhus: Politica.

———. 1999. "The Security of the Baltic Countries: Cooperation and Defection." pp. 204–22. In *Stability and Security in the Baltic Sea Region*, edited by Olev F. Knudsen. London: Frank Cass.

Viner, Jacob. 1950. *The Customs Union Issue*. New York: Carnegie Endowment for International Peace.

Vitkus, Gediminas. 1997. "At the Cross-Road of Alternatives: Lithuanian Security Policies in 1995–1997." In *Baltic Security: Looking towards the Twenty-first Century*, edited by Gunnar Artéus and Atis Lejins. Riga and Stockholm: Latvian Institute of International Affairs and the National Defense College of Sweden.

Wæver, Ole. 1995a. "Securitization and Desecuritization." Pp. 46–86, in *On Security*, edited by Ronnie Lipscuttz. New York: Columbia University Press.

———. 1995b. "Power, Principles, and Perspectivism: Understanding Peaceful Change in Post–Cold War Europe." Pp. 208–82 in *Peaceful Changes in World Politics*, edited by Heikki Patomki. Tampere, Finland: Tampere Peace Research Institute.

———. 1998. "Insecurity, Security, and Asecurity in the West European Non-War Community." Pp. 69–118 in *Security Communities*, edited by Emanuel Adler and Michael Barnett. Cambridge: Cambridge University Press.

Wahlbäck, Krister. 1990. "Rickard Sandlers nordiska politik." In *Socialdemokratin och svensk utrikespolitik:. Från Branting till Plame*, edited by Bo Huldt and Klaus Misgeld. Stockholm: Utrikespolitiska Institutet.

Wallensteen, Peter. 1991. "Is There a Role for Third Parties in the Prevention of Nuclear War?" In *Behavior, Society, and Nuclear War*, edited by Philip E. Tetlock, Jo L. Husbands, Robert Jervis, Paul C. Stern, and Charles Tilly. New York: Oxford University Press.

Wallensteen, Peter, and Margareta Sollenberg. 1998. "Armed Conflict and Regional Conflict Complexes, 1989–97." *Journal of Peace Research* 35, no. 5 (September): 621–34.

Walt, Stephen M. 1985. "Alliance Formation and the Balance of World Powers." *International Security* 9, no. 4 (Spring): 208–48.

———. 1987. *The Origins of Alliances*. Ithaca, N.Y.: Cornell University Press.

Waltz, Kenneth. 1959. *Man, State, and War*. New York: Columbia University Press.

———. 1979. *Theory of International Politics*. Reading, Mass: Addison-Wesley.

———. 1993. "The Emerging Structure of International Politics." *International Security* 18, no. 2 (Fall): 44–79.

Wandyzc, Piotr. 1992. *The Price of Freedom*. London: Routledge.

Weber, Max. 1978. *Economy and Society: An Outline of Interpretive Sociology*. Berkeley and Los Angeles: University of California Press.

Wendt, Alexander. 1994. "Collective Identity Formation and the International State." *American Political Science Review* 88, no. 2 (June): 384–96.

———. 1995. "Constructing International Politics." *International Security* 20, no. 1 (Summer): 71–81.

Westwood, J. N. 1993. *Endurance and Endeavor: Russian History, 1812–1992*. New York: Oxford University Press.

Williams, Glynn, and John Ramsden. 1990. *Ruling Britannia: A Political History of Britain, 1688–1988*. New York: Longman.

Williams, Michael C. 1997. "The Institutions of Security: Elements of a Theory of Security Organizations." *Cooperation and Conflict* 32, no. 3 (September): 287–307.

———. 1998. "Identity and the Politics of Security." *European Journal of International Relations* 4, no. 2 (June): 204–25.

Willis, F. Roy. 1965. *France, Germany, and the New Europe, 1945–1963*. Stanford, Calif.: Stanford University Press.

Wolfers, Arnold. 1962. *Discord and Collaboration*. Baltimore, Md.: Johns Hopkins University Press.

Wright, Gordon. 1995. *France in Modern Times*. 5th ed. New York: Norton.

Wright, Quincy. 1942. *A Study of War*. Chicago: University of Chicago Press.

Wriggins, Howard, ed. 1992. *Dynamics of Regional Politics*. New York: Columbia University Press.

Yergin, Daniel. 1977. *Shattered Peace: The Origins of the Cold War and the National Security State*. Boston: Houghton, Mifflin.

Yesson, Erik. 1995. "Sovereignty, Domestic Politics, and Stable Peace." Revised version of a paper presented at the APSA Annual Meeting, Chicago, September.

Young, Oran. 1968. "Political Discontinuities in the International System." *World Politics* 20, no. 3 (April): 369–92.

Zaborowski, Marcin. 1999. "Polens Westgrenze: Zwischen Rationaler Politik und historischer Erinnerung." *Welt Trends* 23 (Summer): 158–73.

Zacher, Mark W., and Richard A. Mathew. 1995. "Liberal International Theory: Common Threads, Divergent Strands." Pp. 107–50 in *Controversies in International Relations Theory: Realism and the Neoliberal Challenge*, edited by Charles W. Kegley Jr. New York: St. Martin's Press.

Zamoyski, Adam. 1987. *The Polish Way: A Thousand-Year History of the Poles and Their Culture*. London: John Murray.

Zelikow, Philip, and Condoleezza Rice. 1995. *Germany Unified and Europe Transformed: A Study in Statecraft*. Cambridge: Harvard University Press.

Index

ABC Triangle: consolidation, 205–7, 213–15; democratization, 210–12; economic interdependence, 215–16; 216–217, 219; predictability, 212–13; problem-solving, 213; security, 104, 110–11, 112, 206–10, 219; trust, 216; two-stage model, 7. *See also* Argentina; Brazil; Chile
accommodation, 42
activism, Swedish, 181–82, 187–88, 189–91, 194
adaptation: in boundary agreements, 169–70; Swedish, 182–83, 184, 186, 192–93, 194
Adler, Emanuel: on confidence, 97–98; and democratic peace, 140; on identity, 116, 118, 119; on liberalism, 118, 121; on organizations, 100; on power, 98; on security communities, 16, 256n1; on transactions, 99, 100; on trust, 93, 96, 115
adversarial peace. *See* precarious peace
Africa, xiv, 117, 118, 172
agreements, 25, 165, 167–75, 281. *See also* Egypt–Israel relations; German–Polish relations
al-Ahram, 234
Alexander I, 45
Alexander II, 45, 53
Algeria, 172
alliances, 81–82, 256n1
Amsterdam Treaty, 192
anarchy, 93
antiliberalism, 87–89
appeasement, xv
Arab–Israeli relations, 20, 219, 227, 230–35. *See also* Egypt–Israel relations
Arad, Ruth, 152, 155
Argentina: and Brazil, xiv, 23, 202–7, 213, 214, 216, 217, 218–19; and Chile, 173, 208, 209, 212, 213, 214, 216, 217, 218–19. *See also* ABC Triangle
arms control, 249

ASEAN (Association of Southeast Asian Nations), 34, 87, 121–24, 126
Austria, 45–47, 52
authoritarian states, 219
authority structures, 41
autonomy, 284, 289
avoidance, 42
Ayoob, Mohammed, 113

Baier, Annette, 96
balance of power: and Cold War, 82; and consolidation, 30; constructivist view, 110; and offense–defense balance, 108; post–Crimean War, 185–87; and realism, 65; regional, 61; and security community, 116; and stable peace, 39
balance of power theory, 82
balance of prosperity, 152, 154, 163, 282
Baltic region, 98–99, 100–102, 104–5, 124–25
Barak, Ehud, 236
Barber, Bernard, 97
bargaining, 42
Barnett, Michael: on confidence, 97–98; on liberalism, 118; on organizations, 100; on power, 98; on security communities, 16, 256n1; on transactions, 99, 100; on trust, 93, 96, 115
Bar-Siman-Tov, Yaacov: on agreements, 281; on consolidation, 283; on Egypt–Israel relations, 7–8, 220–38; on two-stage model, 5, 11–34
Batt, Judy, 263
Beagle Channel dispute, 173, 204, 207
Beilin, Yossi, 233
Bender, Peter, 261
Bengtsson, Rikard: on cognitive dimension, 6, 18, 92–107; consolidation conditions, 31; on integrative peace, 279
bilateral relationships. *See* dyadic relationships
biological weapons, 210
Bismarck, Otto von, 48

About the Contributors

YAACOV BAR-SIMAN-TOV is Giancarlo Elia Valori Professor of International Relations at the Hebrew University of Jerusalem and director of the Leonard Davis Institute for International Relations. He is the author of *The Israeli–Egyptian War of Attrition, 1969–1970: A Case-Study of Limited Local War* (1980), *Linkage Politics in the Middle East: Syria between Domestic and External Conflict, 1961–1970* (1983), *Israel, the Superpowers and the War in the Middle East* (1987), and *Israel and the Peace Process, 1977–1982: In Search of Legitimacy for Peace* (1994).

RIKARD BENGTSSON is a research fellow in the Department of Political Science, Lund University, Sweden. He recently finished his Ph.D. disseration, "Trust, Threat, and Stable Peace: A Study of Swedish Great Power Perceptions, 1905–1939." His main research interests concern European security affairs. He is currently involved with a comparative research project on the Swedish European Union (EU) council presidency, and his work now focuses on EU enlargement and EU–Russian relations.

MAGNUS ERICSON is a research fellow in the Department of Political Science, Lund University. His main research interests are the changing nature of security politics and international relations theory. His recent Ph.D. dissertation is entitled "A Realist Stable Peace: Power, Threat, and the Development of Shared Norwegian–Swedish Democratic Security Identity, 1905–1940."

OLE ELGSTRÖM is associate professor of political science at Lund University. His research interests are small-state foreign policy and international negotiation. He has recently finished a book on images guiding Swedish foreign-policy makers in their choice of strategies during the nineteenth century. He has published articles in *Negotiation Journal; International Negotiation; Cooperation and Conflict;* and *Diplomacy and Statecraft.*

ALEXANDER L. GEORGE is Graham H. Stuart Professor of International Relations emeritus at Stanford University. His first book, *Woodrow Wilson and Colonel House* (1956), written with his wife, Juliette L. George, is widely regarded as a classic study of the role of personality in politics. He is also the author or coauthor of several books, including *Deterrence in Foreign Policy* (with Richard Smoke, 1974), which won the 1975 Bancroft Prize; *Presidential Decisionmaking in Foreign Policy* (1980); *Force and Statecraft* (with Gordon A. Craig, 1983); *Managing U.S.–Soviet Rivalry* (1988); *Avoiding War: Problems of Crisis Management* (1991); and *Bridging the Gap* (1993).

JAMES GOODBY is senior research fellow, Massachusetts Institute of Technology; senior fellow (nonresident), the Brookings Institution; and Distinguished Service Professor Emeritus, Carnegie Mellon University. He has taught at Stanford University and Georgetown University. He is the author of *Europe Undivided* (1998) and the author or coauthor of four other books and many articles on security issues. He entered the U.S. Foreign Service in 1952, rising to the rank of career minister and serving in many capacities during his forty-year diplomatic career.

JOE D. HAGAN is professor of political science and director of the international studies program at West Virginia University. His research interests include domestic political systems and international relations, particularly how leaders and oppositions shape foreign policy with regard to war and change. His articles on these issues have appeared in journals such as *Foreign Policy; Mershon International Studies Review; Cooperation and Conflict;* and *International Organization.* His current research, from which his chapter in this book draws, will provide the basis for a book tentatively titled "Rulers, Oppositions, and the Great Powers, 1815–1980s."

ADRIAN HYDE-PRICE is a senior lecturer in the international politics of East Central Europe at the University of Birmingham. He has lectured at the Universities of Kent, Manchester, and Southampton and was formerly a researcher at the Royal Institute of International Affairs, London. His main publications include *European Security beyond the Cold War: Four Scenarios for the Year 2010* (1991), *The International Politics of East Central Europe* (1996), and *Germany and European Order: Enlarging NATO and the European Union.*

MAGNUS JERNECK is associate professor of political science at Lund University. His major fields are international politics, European affairs, regionalization, and internationalization of the nation-state. He is the coauthor of *The Bargaining Democracy* (with Lars Göran Stenelo, 1996) and coeditor of *EMU: A Swedish Perspective* (1997). He is director of the Centre for European Studies at Lund University.

ARIE M. KACOWICZ is senior lecturer in international relations at the Hebrew University of Jerusalem. He is the author of *Peaceful Territorial Change* (1994) and *Zones of Peace in the Third World: South America and West Africa in Comparative Perspective* (1998). His research interests include the normative dimension of international politics and Latin American international relations. He is currently completing a book on the impact of international norms in the Latin American international society.

BENJAMIN MILLER is senior lecturer in international relations at the Hebrew University of Jerusalem. He is the author of *When Opponents Cooperate: Great Power Conflict and Collaboration in World Politics* (1995). He has published numerous articles on international relations theory and international security. He has been a research fellow at Harvard University, Massachusetts Institute of Technology, and Princeton University. His current work focuses on constructing a theory of regional war and peace and applying it to the Balkans, South America, Western Europe, and the Middle East in the nineteenth and twentieth centuries.

KJELL-ÅKE NORDQUIST is associate professor and head of department in the Department of Peace and Conflict Research, Uppsala University, Sweden. His major research interest is the peaceful resolution of conflicts with a territorial dimension, including boundary conflicts, autonomies, and state formation processes. He is the author of several articles on those issues, including "Autonomy as a Conflict-Solving Mechanism," in *Autonomy, Applications, and Implications* (1997), edited by Markku Suski.

JOHN M. OWEN IV is assistant professor of government and foreign affairs at the University of Virginia. He is the author of *Liberal Peace, Liberal War: American Politics and International Security* (1997), and has also contributed to *International Security* and several edited volumes. He has been a postdoctoral fellow at Harvard and Stanford Universities and has also taught at Bowdoin College.

ALFRED TOVIAS is an associate professor in the Department of International Relations at the Hebrew University of Jerusalem and deputy director of the Helmut Kohl Institute for European Studies of the Hebrew University. He has been a consultant to the UN Conference on Trade and Development and the World Bank. He is the author of *Tariff Preferences in Mediterranean Diplomacy* (1997) and *Foreign Economic Relations of the European Community: The Impact of Spain and Portugal* (1990) and coauthor of *The Economics of Peace-Making: Focus on the Egyptian-Israeli Situation* (1983).

RAIMO VÄYRYNEN is professor of government and international studies at the University of Notre Dame, where he is also a senior faculty member of the Joan B. Kroc Institute for International Peace Studies. He served as director of the institute from 1993 to 1998. He has also taught at the University of Helsinki. His most recent publications are *Globalization and Global Governance* (1999), which he edited, and *Breaking the Cycles of Violence: The Prevention of Intra-State Conflicts* (1999), which he coauthored.